Haydn

A CREATIVE LIFE IN MUSIC

BY KARL GEIRINGER

W · W · NORTON & COMPANY · INC · New York

First Edition

Book Design by John Woodlock

TO

ELIZABETH SPRAGUE COOLIDGE

whose courageous promotion of contemporary

chamber music would have greatly pleased

the Father

of the

String Quartet

CONTENTS

Contents

ILLUSTRATIONS

·PREFACE

A GREAT musicologist contended that the lives of eminent composers ought to be rewritten at least once in every generation. If this is so, it alone would give sufficient justification for a new book on Joseph Haydn. The existing biographies of the composer in English were written some forty years ago and they in turn were based on the first two volumes of Haydn's biography by Carl Ferdinand Pohl, published in 1875 and 1882 respectively. New editions of some of these works, while having a few alterations, have left them fundamentally unchanged. On the other hand the research about Haydn has developed greatly during the last forty years. Various critical investigations have been undertaken, particularly in central Europe, and since the two hundredth anniversary of Haydn's birthday in 1932 valuable studies on special problems have been published.

This book is, accordingly, in a position to give in its biographical section, especially with regard to the family and the youth of the master, facts unknown to the English reader. It aims not only at introducing novel material but at arranging it in such a way as to produce a picture of the unconventional and eternally young personality of the man who is most deceptively known as "Papa Haydn."

In the second part of this biography the author has investigated Haydn's creative output, discussing and analyzing a great number of works (especially compositions written before 1790) which have hardly been mentioned in any English life of Haydn. As the majority of the compositions are not available in modern editions, extensive studies in the great Haydn libraries of Vienna, Budapest, Paris, Brussels, and London had to be made. For eight years the author was curator of the Society of Friends of Music in Vienna. Their archives which for more than fifty years have been a center for research on Haydn have proved invaluable for his work.

It seems hardly necessary to say that this book can only reflect conditions before the Second World War. There is as yet no possibility of ascertaining in each individual case whether old buildings or manuscripts referred to have been partially or completely destroyed during the war. And it may be that some of the autographs are not to be found in their former place any more.

The author owes a deep debt of gratitude to Mary Caroline Hardy, who gave most generously of her time, her sympathy, and her unerring linguistic feeling to revise the English text of the book.

He wishes gratefully to remember the unfailing spirit of cooperation and encouragement of the late W. W. Norton.

He has to thank Mr. W. F. H. Blandford, Mr. Paul H. Lang, and Mr. Leonard Burkat for their constructive criticism and valuable advice; Mr. Richard S. Hill, Reference Librarian of the Library of Congress, Washington, D.C., Dr. Dorothy Slepian, and Mr. Robbins Landon for useful suggestions; Mr. Henry S. Drinker for excellent translations of German originals; the *Musical Quarterly* (G. Schirmer, Inc.) and *Musical America* for permission to quote from the author's articles published in these journals. Last but not least, he extends his sincere thanks for their patience, understanding, and helpfulness to the staff of W. W. Norton & Company.

The writer hopes he will not be censured for ending this preface with a more personal word. It seems to be a well-established tradition that members of an author's family contribute silently to his work. In the present case this co-operation has extended much further than is usual. Dr. Irene Steckel Geiringer (Mrs. Karl Geiringer) has been the untiring helper and friend of this biography. Not only has she revised but also advised; not only typed but written important sections of this book. If it were not for her determined protests, her name would appear on the title page.

KARL GEIRINGER

Part One

LIFE

Introduction

THE HAYDNS AND THE KOLLERS

THE QUESTION of Joseph Haydn's origin has been much disputed. No less than four different theories have been put forward; all are interesting and merit examination, although they fail to furnish a complete solution of the problem. The families of both of Haydn's parents had their homes in the eastern part of Lower Austria, north of the large Neusiedler lake, a district of many different races. Ever since 1533, besides the predominant German element, a large number of Croats have settled in this district, and from the adjacent Hungarian border there has come, through the centuries, a steady stream of Hungarian immigrants. The Slav ethnologist, Dr. Franz Kuhač,[1] has contended that Haydn's family was by race Croatian, that the names of Haydn and Koller (the family name of the composer's mother) were both Croatian, and that many of Haydn's melodies bear a close resemblance to Croatian folk songs. Undue publicity was given to this theory by Sir Henry Hadow who declared both in the *Oxford History of Music* and in Grove's *Dictionary of Music and Musicians* [2] that Haydn was a typical Croatian composer. His theory has been generally adopted in the English-speaking countries. On the other hand, the Hungarian historian, Elemér Schwartz, has attempted to prove Haydn's Hungarian descent.[3] He bases his theory on the fact that the village of

[1] This champion of the importance of Croatian art had, incidentally, the purely German name of Koch, which he changed later into the Slav form of Kuhač.

[2] Hadow's statements are to be found in the "Haydn" articles of the second and third editions of Sir George Grove's *Dictionary of Music and Musicians.* In the fourth edition the writer of this book refuted the Kuhač-Hadow theory. *See also* Hadow's little biography of Haydn, *A Croatian Composer* (London: 1897).

[3] In the daily publication, *Magyarság* (Budapest: April 20, 1932).

15

Tadten (Hungarian: Tétény) where Haydn's great-grandfather lived
before he moved to Hainburg, was in the seventeenth century predominantly Hungarian. In 1659 the Bishop of Raab wrote about
Tadten: "All the members of the parish are Hungarian Lutherans
with the exception of a few German houses." [4] There has even been
an attempt by the Slav philologist Dedaelus to claim a gypsy origin
for Haydn. This induced Ernst Fritz Schmid to make elaborate genea-
logical researches, tracing the family names in German districts back
to the Middle Ages and studying the lists of inhabitants in the respective villages. His final conclusions confirm what had been maintained
before by French and German authors: [5] that there can be no doubt
that the Haydn and Koller families were of German origin.

But blood and race alone do not determine one's nationality. By
race Haydn was a German, by nationality an Austrian. He lived in
a melting pot of races, a country in which cultural elements from both
central and eastern Europe were fused together. It was quite natural
that he should be familiar with the way of life of the Croats and the
Hungarians. He heard their music from his childhood and attended
their festivities; he admired their artistic craftsmanship and the color
of their holiday garb. With the instinct of genius he absorbed all these
impressions and brought them to life in his music. The inner enrichment that he owed to his acquaintance with the different cultures of
Austria and Hungary was more than a minor factor in making him
the great artist he was.

Great composers usually have someone of artistic or intellectual
leanings among their ancestors. Joseph Haydn, one of the most independent spirits of musical history, was exceptional also in this
respect. Going back to his great-grandfathers on both sides, we fail
to find among them a single musician or even one man who pursued
any kind of intellectual occupation. They all toiled with their hands,
as vinegrowers, farmers, wheelwrights, or millers. They were hard-
working, honest men whose infinite diligence, patience, and perti-
nacity succeeded in raising them from extreme poverty to well-
ordered circumstances and esteemed positions in the community.
This they achieved under the most difficult conditions, for war raged
almost continuously in that part of central Europe during the seven-

---

[4] *"parociani omnes sont lutherani hungari praeter aliquot domos Germanos."*
[5] For instance, cf. Michel Brenet, *Joseph Haydn* (Paris: 1909) and Karl Geiringer,
Joseph Haydn (Potsdam: 1932).

teenth and eighteenth centuries. The little section of eastern Austria where the Haydn family lived lies close to the Hungarian border. It was feebly fortified and thus fell easily to any nation that chose to make war on Austria. Haydn's great-grandfather, Caspar Haydn, and his wife lost their lives when the town of Hainburg was captured by the Turks in 1683. Of the house and possessions acquired with heart-breaking toil only ruins were left to their one surviving son, Thomas. But less than four years later Thomas had already built himself a new house and had been nominated a "citizen" of Hainburg. This meant definite progress, for his father had started his career at Hainburg as a modest *Burgknecht,* a day laborer with a permanent domicile.

On the other side, Haydn's maternal grandfather, the farmer Lorenz Koller, after witnessing as a boy of eight the ravages wrought by the Turkish invasion, lost all his possessions in 1704 when the *Kuruczes,* the peasant army of the anti-Habsburg Hungarian party, plundered the border village of Rohrau. One year later he rebuilt his house, only to see it go up in flames a second time when, in 1706, the Hungarians returned. But Lorenz Koller was not a man to give up. Again and again he started from the beginning and so good was his progress that in 1713 he was offered the office of *Marktrichter* (a magistrate supervising peace and propriety of the market), a position in which his son-in-law, the father of Joseph Haydn, was to succeed him.

As to Haydn's parents, the information supplied by documents is supplemented by stories based on the master's own accounts. Haydn's mother, Maria Koller, was born on November 10, 1707 to the sound of cannons firing against the *Kuruczes* attempting another assault on the village of Rohrau. Her father died when she was eleven years old. She became a cook for the lords of Rohrau, the Counts of Harrach, and in their castle she saw something of the way of life of the Austrian nobility. The kitchen staff comprised nine persons, for whom a yearly salary of a thousand florins was budgeted. Menus preserved in the archives of the castle show that the Harrachs exacted a high culinary skill from their cooks. Maria had to handle such delicacies as turtles and crayfish and had an abundance of material at her disposal. We are told for example, that something like eight thousand eggs, two hundred capons, and three hundred chickens were delivered annually to the castle by the inhabitants of Rohrau as part of their duties to their patron. It must have been quite a change for Maria Koller when, in 1728 at the age of twenty-one, she left the castle to marry the wagonmaker, Mathias Haydn. Although she brought her husband a dowry of one hundred and twenty florins and an "honest outfit" (according to the marriage contract), every penny had to be accounted for in the little house, especially with so large a family to rear. Maria bore her husband twelve children but six of them died in infancy. Her famous son often testified to Maria's excellent housewifely qualities. She was scrupulously clean and neat, an indefatigable worker; and these were the points that she stressed in bringing up her children. She was deeply religious, this being a characteristic trait of the family. We know that her father bequeathed in his will eighty-eight florins to the church, a considerable sum for the modest people of Rohrau. It was Maria Haydn's great dream to see Joseph's talents devoted to the Catholic Church and she never overcame her disappointment at his preference for the irresponsible life of a musician to that of the sacred profession of a priest. Haydn often lamented that his dear mother did not live to see him succeed; before he got his first post, Maria Haydn, worn out by a life of ceaseless toil, had died in 1755 at the age of forty-eight.

Haydn's father, Mathias Haydn, was born on January 31, 1699 in the town of Hainburg, a son of the wheelwright Thomas Haydn. Only two years after the infant's birth, Thomas died, leaving a widow of thirty with six sons, the eldest being only barely twelve. In those troubled times, with war and plague threatening the population, the widow Katharina Haydn naturally sought male support and four months after her husband's death she married Mathias Seefranz, also a wheelwright. She bore him four children, among them Juliane Rosine whom we shall meet again as the wife of the schoolmaster Franck. Seefranz, who later became a member of the Hainburg council, was a rather difficult and quarrelsome person and life with him may not have been too easy for his young stepsons, who were all learning the family trade under his instructions. In 1717 Mathias Haydn finished his apprenticeship and set out on the traditional travels of the journeyman, which brought him as far as Frankfort on the Main. When he came home he brought with him a harp, which someone had taught him to play. Although he could not read a note it was his great delight to accompany himself on the harp when he sang his favorite folk tunes in a pleasant tenor voice. In 1727 Mathias decided to settle down in the near-by town of Rohrau, remaining at the same time a member of the Hainburg guild of wheelwrights. Why his choice fell on this rather uninviting, little market town is not known but it is not unlikely that the person of his future bride attracted him to it. In 1728 Mathias Haydn and Maria Koller were married and for twenty-seven years they lived happily together. But Haydn's father was certainly no sentimentalist. When his good wife died, the man of fifty-six did not hesitate to marry his servant girl of nineteen.

Mathias lived in Rohrau in a cottage built by himself and from the outset was fairly prosperous. It has been the custom of Haydn's biographers to stress the extreme poverty of his father and judging from the appearance of the house in which the Haydns lived throughout their whole life, this attitude seems to be justified. The little, low-roofed, thatch-covered cottage is bound to fill us with pity and we all feel like Beethoven, who on his deathbed, when shown a picture of the Haydn house, exclaimed, "Strange that so great a man should have been born in so poor a home!" For all that, Mathias Haydn was by no means a poor man, and he could probably have built himself a much better house if he had felt his cottage to be inadequate. Several of the bills that he made out have been preserved; and it is known that he was given plenty of work and was not paid badly by the Counts of Harrach for making wheels, repairing wagons, and even undertaking house-painting jobs. From the taxes he paid we see that he had his own wine cellar, his own farmland, and some cattle. The high esteem which he rated is proved by his nomination to succeed his father-in-law in the office of *Marktrichter* which he held from 1741 to 1762. The list of his duties is imposing but only a few can be mentioned here. He was responsible for the good conduct of the population and kept a sharp outlook for adultery or excessive gambling. He had to see that people went to church and did not break the Sunday rest. It was his job to allot among the inhabitants of Rohrau the labor enforced by the patron, Count Harrach, and he was responsible for keeping the local roads in good repair. On Sundays at six in the morning he had to report on all such matters to the count's steward.[6] Every two years an open-air meeting of the whole community took place at which the *Marktrichter* rendered a detailed account of the work done during the past period. To be at the same

[6] These early hours were kept during the period from April to September. In the other months the *Marktrichter* did not have to report until 8:00 A.M. every fortnight.

time a wagonmaker, farmer, vinegrower and wine producer, and an important official and to carry out all these duties well, was no small matter. Mathias Haydn must have been as efficient as he was diligent.

No personal documents of Haydn's parents or any of his forbears have been preserved. No portraits, letters, or diaries have come down to us. Nevertheless we know that it was not a mean heritage that they passed on to their great offspring. A deep religious sense, a stubborn tenacity of purpose, and a passionate desire to rise in the world are qualities which we find in all his ancestors. Combined with them were a great pride in good craftsmanship, a warm love of the soil, and a healthy streak of sensuality. Indeed, it might be said that this heritage gave Joseph Haydn the very qualities necessary for the life he was to lead.

Chapter 1

ROHRAU AND HAINBURG

1732 — 1740

ROHRAU, Haydn's home town, is by no means an attractive place. The surrounding country is flat and marshy (as may be inferred by the name, which means a reedy meadow) and the houses in the little township are mainly low, thatched cottages built of clay. Life is not easy there, for the Leitha river, which at Rohrau forms the border between Austria and Hungary, has an unpleasant tendency to flood the countryside; and in the hot dry summers fires frequently play havoc with the thatched houses. The Haydn house, for instance, was burned in 1813, 1833, and 1899 but was always carefully restored to its original form.

Franz Joseph [1] Haydn, the second child of Mathias and Maria, was born on March 31, 1732 and baptized on April 1.[2] His earliest childhood would have been spent like that of any Austrian peasant boy but for one important difference. His musical talent began to show itself at a very early age and many anecdotes are extant about it. In the evenings, when work was done, his father and mother used to sit by the fireplace and sing their favorite folk tunes to the accompaniment of the harp proudly handled by Mathias. Little Sepperl, as the boy was called in the Austrian fashion, joined in with perfect intonation and a beautiful voice, which attracted the attention of all the neigh-

---

[1] It was a family custom to call the children by their second name. Cf. Johann Michael Haydn, known as Michael Haydn.

[2] There is some difference of opinion about the date of Haydn's birth, as both March 31st and April 1st were mentioned by members of the family. Haydn himself always maintained that it was March 31st and the unpublished diary of the master's friend, J. C. Rosenbaum (preserved in the Vienna National Library), states that the birth took place at 4:00 P.M.

bors. Before long the boy's ambition went further. He wanted to play an instrument as his father did, and having seen the schoolmaster perform on a violin, he took two sticks and pretended they were a violin and a bow. Thus he accompanied the songs, keeping time with amazing accuracy. People began to comment on Sepperl's strange behavior, and in the hearts of the parents there stirred a hope that one day their son might rise to a position far above theirs. Perhaps he would work with his brains instead of his hands; perhaps he would become a schoolmaster, or even, as his mother fervently hoped and prayed, a priest. The auspices seemed good, for Sepperl showed a deep religious faith which throughout his life was never to desert him.

Both parents must have felt dimly that the poor little village could not offer sufficient opportunities for the education of their eldest son. Then one day, as chance would have it, a cousin, Johann Mathias Franck, the husband of Mathias Haydn's stepsister, Juliane Rosine Seefranz, came from Hainburg to pay the Haydns a visit. He was the school principal as well as the precentor of the Church of St. Philip and St. James in Mathias' native town and, in the eyes of the wheelwright and the former cook, a person of indisputable authority. Franck soon noticed Sepperl's musical talent and suggested taking the boy to Hainburg where he could get a proper education, mainly in music. This offer was not wholly objective however, for any payment Franck might receive for Sepperl's board and tuition would be a most welcome addition to his meager budget.[3] At first Maria Haydn objected, for she wanted Sepperl to be trained for the priesthood, whereupon Franck argued that if the boy should later decide to take holy orders, his musical education would be most helpful. Still the mother hesitated, for Sepperl was not yet six years old and she knew that if he left home her chances of seeing him, if any, would be few and far between, for traveling in those days was practically impossible for a woman as busy as she. But finally the parents decided to accept Franck's offer, feeling that they were unable to give the boy a fitting education in Rohrau. It was certainly the best thing they could have done for Joseph. The child's intellect was craving nourishment that his native village could not provide. To satisfy it seemed imperative, much more imperative than that the child should be given loving

[3] Just what the sum paid by Haydn's parents was, is not known; Schmid mentions that as late as 1760 Mathias owed Franck thirty florins.

care and understanding. So Sepperl, at the age of five-and-a-half [4] was sent away, never to return to Rohrau except for rare and short visits. All close contact with his father and mother ceased, and gradually the thoughts of the narrow life he had shared with them at home became, when mellowed by distance and nostalgia, most tender memories. When Haydn, as an old man, told his biographers about his youth he described his mother who had surrendered her child while he was still an infant as "having always given the most tender care to his welfare." And when in 1795 the then world-famous composer visited Rohrau to see the monument erected in his honor by Count Harrach, he knelt down and kissed the threshold of the humble cottage he had shared with his parents for less than six years.

Rohrau once left behind, it was a very different air that Sepperl breathed, a new and different landscape that he saw. Gone was the dreary monotony of the marshes and the boy's eyes could hardly take in all the new sights that he saw on his way. There were many relics of times past to admire, for in this part of Austria the Romans had once built important cities. In the middle of the plain stands a gigantic triumphal arch, now called the "Heathen Gate" and not far from it are the remains of the city of Carnuntum, which once witnessed the coronation of Septimius Severus as Roman Emperor. Even if Sepperl did not understand the historical meaning of such monuments, he could not help being thrilled by the lovely surroundings of the city he was approaching.

At Hainburg the mountains slope down steeply to the imposing Danube river and, covered with rocks or dense woods among which appear the ruins of the castle that gave the city its name, they make a picturesque background to the little town. Even today the visitor to Hainburg feels that he is back in the Middle Ages. The ancient and enormous gates through which the city is entered still stand, and next to one of them, the Vienna Gate, lived Haydn's grandmother. Imposing walls and towers testify to the part that Hainburg once played as a fortress against foes from the East, and within the gates are beautiful baroque façades and the interesting Church of St. Philip and St. James. Truly it was a new world into which Sepperl had entered.

Here his artistic and intellectual curiosity found full satisfaction.

[4] Haydn's exact age when he left Rohrau is a matter of conjecture. It seems likely that the departure occurred some time between his fifth and sixth birthday.

It was fortunate for him that according to an old Hainburg custom Franck's duties were much more numerous than those which a school-teacher of the present time would be willing to undertake. He had, with the aid of two assistants paid by him, to instruct some eighty children in reading, writing, arithmetic, singing, and prayers; he was in charge of the church music, playing the organ himself and direct-ing the singers and instrumentalists who according to south-German tradition took part in every service. In addition Franck had to keep the church register, look after the church clock, and ring the bells both for the services and for special occasions such as thunderstorms or fires. To many of these activities little Sepperl was introduced with-out delay. The daily schedule of the six-year-old boy became very crowded indeed. School began at seven in the morning and lasted for three hours, after which all the children went to Mass, some participating as altar boys. At eleven they went home for their noon-day meal, and from twelve to three there was school again. For the rest of the day there was the study of homework, and what was most important of all, very extensive musical instruction. We do not know exactly which instruments Haydn studied with Franck, but he him-self wrote in his autobiographical sketch: [5] "Our Almighty Father had endowed me with so much facility in music that even in my sixth year I stood up like a man and sang Masses in the church choir and I could play a little on the clavier and violin." Furthermore, Georg August Griesinger in his Haydn biography based on direct informa-tion from the master states that he studied the "kettledrum as well as other instruments." How he learned to play the drum at the age of six has been told by another contemporary biographer, the painter Albert Christoph Dies, and is quoted here as evidence of the child's peculiar gift for self-instruction. Dies relates:

> It was in the Week of the Cross [May 11–18], when many proces-sions take place, that Franck was in great distress because of the death of his drummer. He thought of Joseph; the boy should learn to play the instrument at once. He showed Joseph how to make the strokes and left him alone. Joseph took a little basket, such as peasants use for baking bread, covered it with a cloth, placed his contrivance on an upholstered chair, and drummed with such enthusiasm that he did not notice the flour pouring out of the basket and ruining the chair. He was scolded, but his teacher was easily appeased when he

[5] Published in 1778 in *Das gelehrte Oesterreich. Ein Versuch.*

saw to his amazement that Joseph had already become a perfect drummer.[6]

So the boy proudly marched in the procession. The instrument was strapped upon a hunchback to make it possible for the little fellow to play it. What a comical sight this pair must have been—the hunchback in front with the kettledrum on his back, little Haydn following, beating his drum and probably not always aiming quite straight. Fifty years later, when Haydn showed an English orchestral musician how to play the timpani, he may have remembered with amusement his own first efforts with these instruments. As regards other instruments mentioned by Griesinger, although Haydn probably did not learn to play them properly, he certainly had ample opportunity to become acquainted with them. The standards of the music directed by Franck were not too low. The inventory of the church comprised, for example, as many as eight trumpets and eight violins. Although on ordinary Sundays the music was confined to a four-part chorus, two violins and organ (the ensemble still used in Haydn's first mass), on festive occasions the violoncello, double bass, trumpets, horns and timpani were added. Franck had a rather extensive collection of manuscript music, which he even lent to the churches of larger cities. It is not unlikely that he made his gifted little pupil copy music for him and in this way Haydn became familiar at an early age with the sacred music of the period.

Apart from the ordinary routine, in itself interesting enough for the lad, there were special occasions when even a small town like Hainburg displayed the baroque splendor so dear to the Austrian heart. In 1738 the Catholic Church arranged a *jubileum universale*. During two weeks prayers were said for a victory over the Turks, to the accompaniment of an abundance of music that must have kept young Sepperl tremendously busy. Another great event was the solemn entry of the imperial Commissary Cetto a Cronstorff into Hainburg on May 2, 1739. He came to witness the election of the city councilors and little Hainburg wanted to pay every possible honor to the guest from Vienna. He was received at the Vienna Gate by the city judges

[6] A friend of the writer, an expert in the field of musical instruments, justly remarks about this anecdote: "This is a good story but most improbable. In the absence of a drum, or a pair of drums, practicing must be done on a properly resilient surface, and the idea of using a basket covered with a cloth seems absurd. Also that the handling of timpani can be learned with so short a study as the story implies would be rejected by any experienced drummer. *Se non è vero, è ben trovato!*"

and councilors and conducted in state to the church. In front of the portal stood trumpeters and drummers in their red cloaks and the civil guard resplendent in their uniforms. To the sound of fanfares the commissary entered the church, where Franck directed a motet *Veni Sancte Spiritus* before the Mass and a *Te Deum* after it. On the following day the elections took place, and were followed by another solemn church service. To the sound of impressive fanfares the names of the new councilors were announced from the high altar, among them, to Joseph's pride, that of Mathias Seefranz, the second husband of his grandmother, and father-in-law of Franck. Two months later Hainburg celebrated with all the splendor it could afford the peace concluded between Austria and France. Besides such outstanding events, there were the many great feast days of the Catholic Church, and the processions then held followed age-old tradition, when the Almighty was entreated to protect the people and their holdings from thunderstorms, hail, frost, and other disasters. In all these little Sepperl took an active part and they must have made a deep impression on his fertile brain. What he particularly loved was Corpus Christi day, the feast day of the various guilds, among them that of the wheelwrights. Masters were admitted and journeymen discharged, all with the same solemn ritual that Haydn's grandfather, father, and uncles had witnessed in this very place. To Sepperl's joy, in 1738, his own father attended a meeting in order to bind a new apprentice. Such occasional contacts with his parents meant much to the little boy who, in spite of a life filled to the brim with new discoveries, must often have felt homesick.

It is necessary now to reveal another side to the Hainburg picture and one that was much less pleasant. The Francks were very poor. On his modest salary, consisting mainly of allowances in kind, the school rector had to support a steadily growing family. Juliane Franck seems to have lacked the housewifely qualities of Haydn's mother. Her home was never kept in good order and she was already so busy with her two infant daughters, who were joined by a son in November, 1739, that she saw in her nephew of six, not a child needing love and care, but a useful helper with the housework. Sepperl did not resent doing the tasks she set him, but he did suffer from the neglect of his person. He, who had been trained by his mother in unimpeachable cleanliness and order, lost his neat appearance. The few clothes he possessed were not washed and mended very often. Dies relates that Haydn, as an old man, when talking of Hainburg said: "I could not help perceiving, much to my distress, that I was gradually getting very dirty, and though I thought rather highly of my little person, I was not always able to avoid stains on my clothes, of which I was dreadfully ashamed—in fact, I was a regular little ragamuffin." At that time Haydn also began to wear a wig "for the sake of cleanliness." His meals were insufficient and he admitted in later years that he got from his strict teacher "more floggings than food." Regarding the flogging, we should not blame Franck too much; it was at that time the customary method of education. For instance Schmid tells us of an "Instruction for the Schoolmaster" in which the Hainburg Council admonishes the rector to refrain from pulling out the hair of his pupils, but to keep them strictly in order with the cane.

Still, if we balance the two sides of Haydn's life at Hainburg the final result is certainly favorable. Haydn got what he most needed, extensive musical instruction. Furthermore, he was endowed by nature with a rare combination of gifts, a wiry resilience and a contented disposition. Hardships never made him bitter and never broke him. In spite of being hungry and dirty, in spite of the rough treatment occasionally meted out to him, Sepperl was happy. Throughout his life, whenever Franck's name was mentioned, Haydn had words of praise for his first teacher. "I shall be grateful to that man as long as I live, for keeping me so hard at work," he said to Griesinger. In his house Haydn piously kept a portrait of Franck which he left in his last will, together with one hundred florins, to his teacher's daughter, Anna R. Schimpel.[7]

Little Sepperl progressed fast, but in the nature of things after a time Hainburg had given him all it had to offer. To stay longer within its medieval walls would have meant a retarding of his artistic and intellectual growth. Fortunately there appears to be some natural law that directs the artistic destiny of a genius and leads him to the path best suited for his art, even though it may not contribute to his personal happiness.

Karl Georg Reutter the younger, court composer and newly appointed choirmaster at the famous Cathedral of St. Stephen in Vienna, went on a tour in search of good choristers, in the course of which he came to Hainburg and stayed at the house of the pastor, Anton Johann

---

[7] See Johann R. von Lucam, "Haydn und die beiden Originalportraits seiner Eltern," *Wiener Allgemeine Zeitung* (1852).

Palmb. On hearing of Reutter's quest, Palmb recommended young Haydn whose "weak but sweet voice" he had noticed. The rest of the story is best told in the words of the contemporary biographer Giuseppe Carpani:

> Reutter gave him a tune to sing at sight. The precision, the purity of tone, the spirit with which the boy executed it surprised him; but he was more especially charmed with the beauty of the young voice. He remarked that the lad did not shake (trill), and smilingly asked him the reason. The boy replied promptly: "How can you expect me to shake when my cousin does not know how to himself?" "Come here," said Reutter, "I will teach you." He took him between his knees, showed him how he should produce the notes in rapid succession, control his breath, and agitate the palate. The boy immediately made a good shake. Reutter, enchanted with the success of his pupil, took a plate of fine cherries and emptied them into the boy's pockets. [According to Dies, he also gave Sepperl a piece of money.] His delight may be readily conceived. Haydn often mentioned this anecdote to me, and added, laughing, that whenever he happened to shake he still thought he saw those beautiful cherries.

Reutter offered to take Sepperl to Vienna as a chorister at St. Stephen's and to give him a thorough musical education, providing his parents consented to it. A meeting was quickly arranged and Sepperl's father and mother were overjoyed with Reutter's promise that he would henceforth look after their boy. It was agreed that Sepperl should go to the imperial capital when he reached his eighth year. Reutter urged him to practice singing scales and solfeggios in the meantime so as to develop his voice. As Franck was unable to teach Sepperl anything of the kind, the boy himself found a practical method and with his characteristic diligence and ambition worked so hard that he made good progress.

The last few months were filled with joyous anticipation and passed quickly. Haydn was all impatience; he could hardly wait to see with his own eyes the wonders of the Austrian capital and to begin the musical training that Vienna's great cathedral had to offer.

Chapter 2

AT ST. STEPHEN'S

1740 — 1749

THERE is one building in Vienna that never fails to fill even the least sensitive inhabitant of the Austrian capital with awe and amazement: the Cathedral of St. Stephen. This church is so full of power, so imbued with the mystery of life in all its aspects, whether lofty or humorous, that it would be impossible ever to know it completely or to plumb its profundities. The outside of the Gothic cathedral displays a bewildering variety of high slender buttresses, beautiful stained-glass windows, gargoyles in the form of dragons, and countless statues of the great of the Church and of the House of Austria. The big south tower of St. Stephen's is the distinctive feature of Vienna. From its top, more than four hundred feet high, one may look east far into the Hungarian plain, north toward the Danube and the fertile fields of Moravia, west and south toward the green Vienna woods and the foothills of the Alps. Although the outside of the church is entirely medieval, inside there are many baroque decorations and altars. In the typical Austrian manner purity of style is completely lacking, but the daring mixture of old and new is always in good taste and works of the fourteenth to the eighteenth centuries succeed in being beautifully harmonious. In this imposing cathedral the imagination is never at rest. Every step brings new surprises and wonders and the whole building is filled with a sense of great mystery, always eluding one, always leading one further. This Gothic architecture seems to lift one from earth into higher and more spiritual spheres, filling the soul of even the most matter-of-fact person with awe. How great must have been the effect of St. Stephen's upon the highly imaginative child whose constant resort it was for nine years!

While the surroundings in which the boy Haydn dwelt in Vienna were all that could be expected, and even more, closer acquaintance with the man in whose hands his fate lay proved sadly disappointing. Georg Reutter [1] lived with the six choirboys, a subcantor, and two preceptors in the *Cantorei* house next to the cathedral. He was entirely responsible for the pupils' education and musical training, as well as for their food and clothes, for which he received a yearly sum of 1,200 florins from the city of Vienna. Unfortunately the man who so generously filled Sepperl's pockets with cherries at Hainburg had turned into a stern principal who provided the boys with even less and poorer food than Sepperl had received from his impecunious relatives in Hainburg. Dies relates: "Joseph's stomach had to get accustomed to continuous fasting. He tried to make up for it with the musical academies [concerts that the choir gave in the houses of the Viennese nobility], where refreshments were offered to the choristers. As soon as Joseph made this discovery, so important for his stomach, he was seized with an incredible love for academies. He endeavored to sing as beautifully as possible so as to be known and invited as a skilled performer, and thus to find occasions to appease his ravenous hunger." But the insufficient food was not the worst, for "it seemed as if they wanted to starve the mind as well as the body." To Reutter the boys were merely choristers. He saw that they became expert singers and sight readers; he also made them learn to play the clavier and the violin, but he was not interested in their general education and they received no instruction in musical theory. Sepperl lacked any encouragement or help whatever in his groping attempts at composition. Once Reutter found him writing a *Salve Regina* in twelve parts, for at that time the boy thought that to write good music he had only to fill a page with plenty of notes. The Capellmeister merely laughed mockingly and exclaimed: "Oh, you silly child, aren't two parts enough for you?" But he made no attempt to show Sepperl how to work out these two parts, contenting himself by advising the boy to modify and arrange the motets he sang in church. The diligent and ambitious lad must certainly have followed his

[1] There were two Viennese composers of this name. Georg Reutter, the father (1656–1738) was choir director of St. Stephen's and court organist. His son, J. A. Karl Georg (1708–72) was Haydn's teacher. It is not always easy to distinguish between the compositions of the father and the son. *See* Norbert Hofer, "Die beiden Reutter als Kirchenkomponisten," a thesis manuscript (Vienna: 1915).

teacher's advice, but it is doubtful whether Reutter ever deigned to correct his efforts. Anyway, Haydn said later that he had had no more than two lessons from the Capellmeister during the many years he stayed with Reutter, who could have taught him so much.

The younger Reutter was, in fact, a very fertile and experienced composer. His music was distinguished by brilliance, harmonic richness, and excellent instrumentation. Burney, it is true, characterized his work by the terse comment, "great noise and little meaning," but even if this opinion (which was by no means shared by the Viennese public) were correct, Reutter's good workmanship could have been of immense help to young Haydn. The fact that the Capellmeister did not choose to give any such assistance was not due to any animosity toward Haydn; it was simply that he was too busy. Ambition and a continual lack of money turned him into that unpleasant type of man who accumulates appointments as a confirmed pluralist. In 1731 he became court composer, seven years later conductor at St. Stephen's and thus head of the choir school. These two positions should have been sufficient, but Reutter, who was knighted in 1740 by the Emperor Charles VI, succeeded in 1746 in also being appointed second court conductor. A fourth job was added in 1756. St. Stephen's, in addition to the main ensemble of vocalists and instrumentalists, had a special band and choir that performed in a smaller chapel which was adorned with a miraculous painting of the Virgin said to shed real tears. Reutter was not satisfied until he became leader of this ensemble as well. Thereafter he managed, by intrigue and clever handling of the persons responsible, still further to consolidate his position at court until he was appointed first court conductor in 1769. It was of course, impossible for one man to fill so many offices well and as he was naturally more interested in his duties at court, he neglected St. Stephen's. C. F. Pohl quotes a reprimand of the city council that "the church music was becoming worse and worse, thus leading to inattention and even disgust instead of gracious Christian edification." Reutter's income from various sources must have been considerable and to it was added the unusually high salary of 3,500 florins paid to his wife, the excellent court singer Therese Holzhauser. But even so he kept the boy choristers on the shortest possible rations.

Lack of a thorough musical education, however, did not mean lack of work for the boys and herein lay Haydn's salvation. The choristers' duties were very heavy; they had to take part every day in two full choral services (High Mass and Vespers) besides innumerable extra appearances on feast days, especially during Holy Week, and at festivities, private academies, funerals, processions, and even in Latin shows given by the Jesuits.[2] Reutter's double duties brought, as a great advantage, repeated invitations to court, where the singers of St. Stephen's and the court chapel joined forces. The practical musical knowledge which the impressionable boy derived from these various performances was enormous. He became thoroughly acquainted with the sacred music of such contemporary composers as Caldara, Fux, Reutter, Tuma, Ziani, Palotta, and he also heard many secular works. According to Johann Friedrich Rochlitz Haydn once said: "Proper teachers I have never had. I always started right away with the practical side, first in singing and in playing instruments, later in composition. I listened more than I studied but I heard the finest music in all forms that was to be heard in my time, and of this there was much in Vienna. Oh, so much! I listened attentively and tried to turn to good account what most impressed me. Thus little by little my knowledge and my ability were developed."

In addition to these rich musical impressions baroque Vienna offered many thrilling sights. Young Haydn would certainly not have shared the opinion of Lady Mary Wortley Montagu who in 1716 wrote from Vienna: "The processions I see very often are a pageantry as offensive, and apparently contradictory to all common sense, as the pagodas of China."[3] He was too much of an Austrian and a Catholic to be anything but elated by the lavish display of color and sound at festive occasions. One unforgettable experience for instance, was the jubilee of Vienna's cardinal archbishop Sigismund von Kollonicz in 1749 to celebrate the fiftieth year of his priesthood, when an enormous procession of clergy and dignitaries marched solemnly into the cathedral lit by myriads of candles. Archbishops, bishops, and prelates assisted at High Mass, all dressed in the most ornate robes and carrying gorgeous wreaths on their arms. Cardinal Kollonicz' wreath was of pure gold, a present from the Empress Maria Theresa, and the

[2] The *Wiener Diarium* mentions a performance in the Jesuits' Theater on December 16, 1743, when a Latin drama on the Emperor Constantine with music by Reutter was performed by a cast of two hundred, including the pupils of the Jesuit College, St. Stephen's, and various other institutions. The show was attended by the Empress Maria Theresa and the highest nobility and clergy.
[3] *See* the letters of Lady Mary Wortley Montagu in Everyman's Library (1906).

Joseph Haydn. Oil painting by Thomas Hardy, London, 1792

Haydn's birthplace in Rohrau

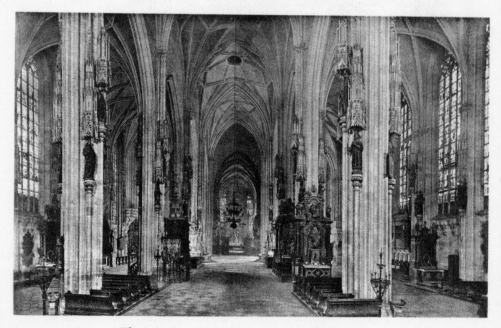

The interior of St. Stephen's Cathedral, Vienna

chalice he used was adorned by a magnificent wreath wrought in silver, a gift from the queen of Portugal. The imperial family was carried to the building in golden sedan chairs and accompanied by the Knights of the Golden Fleece, the ambassadors, and the high nobility, all resplendent in robes of gold and silver encrusted with precious stones.[4] Surely such magnificence must have made any pageant that Sepperl had seen in Hainburg seem mean in comparison.

In connection with such processions the boys from St. Stephen's frequently took part in outdoor performances. Thus, in honor of St. John music was performed on brilliantly illuminated boats lying in the Danube Canal opposite the saint's statue, while on St. Nepomuk's Day an evening performance of a Reutter oratorio was given on the beautifully decorated Vienna "High Bridge" in the presence of a distinguished audience.

Outings of any kind were greatly enjoyed by young Haydn, for in spite of the beauty of St. Stephen's, its atmosphere could at times be oppressive. Sepperl had the natural craving of any healthy boy for exercise and fun and even the very rigid discipline of the *Cantorei* did not prevent him from occasionally breaking loose. Once the choir was ordered to sing before the Empress Maria Theresa at her newly erected castle of Schönbrunn. The scaffolding had not yet been removed, and what was more natural than for the boys to climb on it with shouts of delight and laughter? Angrily the empress appeared at a window and commanded the noisy group to get down immediately, threatening a good thrashing to anyone seen there again. Nevertheless next day Joseph could not resist the temptation. Alone he climbed to the top and was duly observed by the empress, who instantly ordered the Capellmeister to give this "fair-haired blockhead" the promised punishment.

Not often, however, did Joseph displease her Majesty. Usually she was well satisfied with his execution of important solos, which she was qualified to judge, being herself, like most of the Habsburgs, a well-trained musician. (It is reported that her beautiful singing made the famous male soprano Senesino burst into tears.) Altogether, young Haydn, during his first years at St. Stephen's, was very successful, although he never created a sensation, and again, as at Hainburg, he was too busy and too interested in everything to be unhappy. But from 1745 on things seemed to grow steadily worse.

[4] *See Wiener Diarium* (1749).

Slowly the voice of the boy approaching puberty began to deteriorate. This became all the more noticeable as a new voice had joined St. Stephen's choir school, a fine soprano with the remarkable compass of three octaves. This voice belonged to Joseph's brother, Michael,[5] who had joined the *Cantorei* in 1745 at the age of eight. At first Joseph was delighted to have a member of his family with him and he felt very proud when he was ordered to instruct his younger brother in various subjects. Michael showed outstanding gifts and seemed even more brilliant than Joseph. He learned rapidly and before long he played the organ so well that for the payment of a few pennies he acted as deputy for the cathedral's organist. He also showed initiative by organizing among his schoolmates a club for the detection of plagiarism in their own compositions. We do not know what Joseph's feelings were for he was not the man to dilate on such personal matters to his biographers. It seems highly unlikely however that his "pleasure" in Michael's presence, mentioned by the contemporary writers, could have persisted when his young brother snatched all the laurels from him. Joseph was given no more solos after the empress had complained about his "crowing like a cock"; instead they were entrusted to Michael. In point of fact, Michael earned from the imperial couple applause such as had never been given to Joseph. It was customary for the empress to celebrate annually the Festival of St. Leopold, the patron saint of Lower Austria, in the magnificent near-by monastery of Klosterneuburg. In 1748 when the imperial chapel, enlarged by St. Stephen's choir, had the task of executing the music for this festive occasion, Michael sang a *Salve Regina* so admirably that the emperor and empress received the boy in a special audience, complimented him, and gave him twenty-four golden ducats. Asked by Reutter what he would do with such a fortune, Michael answered: "Half of it I'll send my father who has just lost a cow, the other half please keep for me until my voice breaks too." Reutter agreed but he never bothered to give the money back.

According to Haydn's pupil, Ignaz Pleyel, Reutter, noticing Joseph's distress about his breaking voice, hinted that there was a means of preserving the fine quality of his singing. There were still quite a few *castrati* in Vienna who had good positions in the imperial chapel and Joseph could imitate their example. Fortunately, Mathias Haydn,

[5] Johann Michael Haydn, a gifted composer in his own right, was born on September 14, 1737 at Rohrau.

hearing about this plan, rushed to Vienna to put a stop to any such project.

More and more Joseph Haydn became useless to St. Stephen's as a singer. Reutter might of course have employed him as a violinist until his voice had regained its strength, had he bestowed any thought on the welfare of the boy who for nine years had given him such valuable service. But Reutter was no sentimentalist and did not have too good a memory of promises given long ago to anxious parents. On the other hand, Joseph himself made no suggestions. Was it shyness or lack of initiative that kept him waiting dumbly for the inescapable catastrophe? Or was it the instinct of genius that prompted him to give up the familiar routine of life at the *Cantorei* and try for something entirely new? The latter seems more likely, though the boy himself may not have been conscious of such tendencies. He spent his days in great unhappiness and it must have been a relief when at last the blow fell. A pretext was provided by none other than the victim himself. Joseph, always keen on playing practical jokes, could not resist testing a new pair of scissors by cutting off the pigtail of a fellow chorister. When Reutter heard about it, he exclaimed: "You will be caned on the hand." Joseph, seventeen years old, thought such punishment unbearable and rashly cried: "I would rather leave the *Cantorei* than be caned." This was the opportunity for which Reutter had been waiting. "Of course you will be expelled," he answered, "after you have been caned." And so it happened. On a cold November day in 1749 Haydn, with three ragged shirts and a worn coat as his sole possessions, without any money, without any recommendation, was turned out on the street to fight for his very existence.

Chapter 3

MAKING SOMETHING OUT OF NOTHING

1750 — 1759

THE WRITERS of the eighteenth century are full of praise of Vienna as a musical center. Dr. Burney, after visiting it in 1772 wrote: "Vienna is so rich in composers, and incloses within its walls such a number of musicians of superior merit, that it is but just to allow it to be, among German cities, the imperial seat of music, as well as of power." And the Prussian court conductor, J. F. Reichardt, declared: "The court made music with passion and the Austrian nobility was perhaps the most musical that ever existed." The Empress Maria Theresa, following a firmly established tradition in the Habsburg family, was enormously interested in music and the stage. Although not a composer herself, as were many of her ancestors,[1] and in her struggle for the very existence of her empire unable to spend money for music as lavishly as her predecessors did, she saw to it that artists of the very first rank were invited to Vienna and engaged for academies and festive occasions at court. The high nobility of the country followed the example of the imperial dynasty. They vied with each other in establishing their own excellent orchestras. The academies, such as those that Prince Joseph Friedrich von Hildburghausen arranged with his own band in the exquisite palace built by the great architect Johann Fischer von Erlach, were of the very highest standard.

From 1750 onwards the middle class also began to become more interested in music. Public concerts were inaugurated, following the

---

[1] Ferdinand III, Leopold I, Joseph I, and Karl VI all composed sacred music, while Maria Theresa once jokingly called herself the oldest virtuoso in Europe because her father had made her sing on the stage when she was but five years old. *See* Burney, *The Present State of Music in Germany,* I, 206 *et seq.*

model of the Paris Concerts Spirituels and before long they enjoyed great popularity. The love of the Viennese for spectacle found satisfaction in its two theaters, the Theater nächst der Burg in which mainly opera was played and the Theater nächst dem Kärntnerthor which concentrated on German and French plays. Under the Habsburgs Vienna became a center of the reigning Italian opera of Naples and on the other hand, the city was also the first to witness, in 1762, the birth of Gluck's musical drama. Great attention was also given to the art of the ballet which was to achieve in this century a summit of perfection under the great ballet master Noverre. Many native composers like Fux, Wagenseil, Dittersdorf, Reutter, Starzer, and Eberl added a specifically Austrian touch to the colorful picture of Vienna's music culture during the reign of Maria Theresa.

Bearing all this in mind, one might be inclined to regard as fortunate any young and gifted musician who was ambitious of making his way in the Vienna of 1749. Surely, one would think, some one of the aristocratic music lovers who spent such enormous sums on the cultivation of this passion must have discovered young Haydn's talent and given him the opportunity of developing it. In reality nothing of the kind happened. Haydn, as he bitterly complained in his autobiographical sketch, "had to wander around sorrowfully" for many miserable years before his luck began to change. The reasons for this predicament are clear enough. When he left St. Stephen's he did not play any instrument more than moderately well (even on the violin, his favorite, he was, as he said, not "a conjuror"), his voice for the time being was nonexistent, and his compositions were nothing but groping attempts lacking any theoretical foundation. He was miserably dressed, unattractive in appearance, and on account of his secluded life in the *Cantorei*, unused to the great world and therefore shy and uncouth. What could such a destitute young musician do? Scholarships did not exist in the eighteenth century. Help from his family was neither given nor expected.[2] His parents might have considered assisting him if Joseph had followed his mother's ardent desire and taken holy orders. The young man, however, for all his innate faith and the strong ties that bound him to the Catholic Church, never seriously considered this possibility. With the tenacity that had made

[2] Just at the most critical time, Haydn's parents had to use all their resources to provide a dowry for their eldest daughter, Franziska, who married the baker J. Vieltzwiser on February 8, 1750.

his grandfather Lorenz Koller rebuild his house again and again after each devastation, young Haydn clung to his intention. He wanted to be a musician; not merely a mediocre performer but a real composer. Therefore the position of a musical valet, which was very common in the eighteenth century when a footman had to be able to play in his master's chamber music,[3] made no appeal to and was not sought by him. It would take up too much of his time and not bring about the artistic development for which he craved. On the other hand, Haydn fully realized how sadly unprepared he was for the career he had chosen. He needed a good teacher of theory, or at least sufficient time for self-instruction. There seemed only one way open to him: to support himself by odd musical jobs and to spend all the time and energy he had left on the improvement of his musical knowledge. It was a long and tortuous way, a way filled with privations, but it led Haydn to his ultimate goal.

When the young musician left St. Stephen's in November, 1749, he did not even know where to spend the night. At this critical point he was first helped, characteristically enough, by one who himself was not much better off than poor Joseph. As he wandered desperately through the chilly streets, Haydn chanced upon a man he knew slightly, Johann Michael Spangler, a singer in the Church of St. Michael and a private teacher. When Spangler heard of Joseph's misfortune he invited him to share the poor garret where he lived with his wife and a baby boy nine months old. With what relief did the homeless lad accept this generous offer! A roof was found and now he had only to earn his food (for here the impecunious singer was unable to help). Slowly Joseph began to make connections. He played at dances, he made arrangements of compositions for various instruments, he took pupils for miserably small fees. Most of all, he went "gassatim," which means that he took part in serenades. Like Italy, old Austria had a great fondness for open-air music at night and many musicians were needed to fill the continuous demand. An eighteenth-century Viennese almanac gives a lively description of this custom:

> On fine summer nights you may come upon serenades in the streets at all hours. They are not, as in Italy, a mere matter of a singer and

[3] A typical advertisement in the *Wiener Zeitung* (1789) states: "Wanted by nobleman a servant who plays the violin well and is able to accompany [on his instrument] difficult piano sonatas."

a guitar. Here serenades are not meant for declarations of love, for which the Viennese have better opportunities. Such night music may be given by a trio or a quartet or wind instruments, and works of some extent may be played. The evening before the name day of some fair lady will produce a lot of this kind of entertainment; and however late a serenade is given, all windows are soon filled and in a few minutes the musicians are surrounded by an applauding crowd.

Haydn made the best use of this fashion. He earned a little money this way and drew from the rich well of Viennese folk music which has been a source of inspiration to Mozart, Beethoven, Schubert, Brahms, and many others.

In this way he somehow got through the first difficult months, but he was aware that this state of affairs could not and must not last. In the Spanglers' crowded garret it was impossible for him to undertake the serious studying upon which he was determined. On the other hand, Frau Spangler was expecting another baby and after its arrival there simply would be no room for him.[4] In the spring of 1750, as a temporary escape from his problems, he joined a party of pilgrims to the miraculous shrine of the Virgin at Mariazell, a beautifully situated village in Styria which was, and still is, frequented by crowds of worshipers. By this time, apparently, his voice had resumed its normal state, for he introduced himself to the choirmaster, Father Florian Wrastil, as a former chorister of St. Stephen's and asked to be admitted to the choir. His shabby appearance did not inspire confidence and apparently Father Wrastil had had unfortunate experiences with other traveling musicians so he rudely sent him away. Thereupon Haydn stole into the church choir, snatched the vocal part out of the singer's hand, and sang the solo with such perfection that "all the choir held their breath to listen." The choirmaster repented; young Haydn was invited to stay with him for a week. During this time he was able to enjoy the exquisite, and for him unfamiliar, sensation of getting all the food he wanted. He returned to Vienna well rested, full of confidence in his ultimate success, and even with a little cash collected from the musicians of Mariazell. Before long this confidence bore fruit. A tradesman and *Marktrichter* in Vienna (a sort of colleague of Mathias Haydn), by the name of Anton Buchholz, de-

[4] The child was Maria Magdalena, born September 4, 1750. In 1768 Haydn engaged her as a singer for Prince Eszterházy. She performed the soprano solo in the first performance of Haydn's *Il Ritorno di Tobia* in 1775. Her husband was Haydn's good friend, the tenor Karl Friberth.

cided to help the young musician to pursue his studies and lent him
unconditionally one hundred and fifty florins, a sum which must at
that time have seemed enormous to Haydn. In 1801 the composer
wrote in his will: "To Fräulein Anna Buchholz, one hundred florins,
inasmuch as in my youth her grandfather lent me one hundred and
fifty florins when I greatly needed them, which, however, I repaid
fifty years ago." If the date mentioned is correct, Haydn must have
repaid the loan as early as 1751, a year after he had received it; a
really remarkable achievement in his circumstances.

Now Haydn was in a position to leave the good Spanglers and
settle down in a room of his own. He chose, of course, the cheapest
place available. It was a garret, partitioned off from a larger room, in
the old Michaelerhaus near Vienna's ancient Romanesque Church of
St. Michael. His neighbors in the attic were a cook, a journeyman
printer, a footman, and a house-stoker, who tended the fires in the
house of some wealthy man. To all outward appearances the new
lodgings were anything but pleasant. Indeed, the contemporary biographers have done their utmost to stress the hardships Haydn en-
dured there. Carl Bertuch writes: "He lived on the sixth story, and
his room in the garret had neither stove nor window; in winter his
breath froze on his coverlet, and the water that he fetched himself
from the spring in the morning for washing was frequently changed
into lumps of ice before his arrival in these elevated regions." [5] Such
drawbacks were, however, of no great consequence to a youth like
Haydn. Here he was, as he said, "too happy to envy the lot of kings,"
for he had at last the privacy he craved for his studies and he was the
proud owner of an "old, worm-eaten clavier." His first mass, written
at the beginning of the seventeen-fifties, reflects this state of mind,
but also his artistic immaturity. Haydn now set about to fill the big
gaps in his theoretical knowledge. He devoured Johann Joseph Fux's
famous *Gradus ad Parnassum,* Johann Mattheson's *Der vollkommene
Capellmeister,* and David Kellner's *Unterricht im Generalbass.* The
copies he used have been preserved and their numerous annotations
reveal the passion with which young Haydn threw himself into the
study of these subjects.

Perhaps even more important than these manuals was his discovery
of the first six piano sonatas by Philipp Emanuel Bach, which opened
a new world to him. "I did not leave the clavier," he said to Dies, "until

[5] See *Journal des Luxus und der Moden* (Weimar: 1805).

I had mastered them all. Innumerable times I played them for my own delight, especially when I felt oppressed and discouraged by worries and always I left the instrument gay and in high spirits." [6]

One of the reasons for Haydn's reactions was the strong emotional appeal emanating from the works of the "Hamburg Bach." [7] So free an expression of feeling was revolutionary at that time and it was in accord with Philipp Emanuel's famous axiom "A musician cannot move others unless he himself is moved." Haydn, who incidentally shared his admiration of Johann Sebastian's second son with Mozart and Beethoven, used to emphasize in later years how much he owed to this man. As a matter of fact, no other composer, with the exception of Mozart, influenced him to such an extent as the north-German master.

But while the works of Philipp Emanuel Bach opened new vistas to the young musician, it was only natural for Haydn to maintain connection with Austrian folk music, and in 1752 this resulted in his first dramatic attempt. The story is best told in the words of Bombet [8] based on the report of Haydn's friend, Giuseppe Carpani:

> Haydn composed for his amusement, a serenata for three instruments, which he performed with two of his friends, in different parts of Vienna. The Kärntnerthortheater was at that time directed by Kurz-Bernardon, a celebrated harlequin who amused the public with his puns and drew crowds to the theater by his originality. He had, moreover, a handsome wife; and this was an additional reason for our nocturnal adventurers to perform their serenade under the harlequin's window. Bernardon was so struck with the originality of the music that he came down into the street to ask who had composed it. "I did," replied Haydn boldly. "Come upstairs." Haydn followed the comedian, was introduced to the handsome wife, and redescended with the libretto of an opera, entitled *The Limping Devil* [*Der krumme Teufel*]. The music, composed in a few days, had a brilliant success. But a nobleman, who probably was not handsome, suspected that he was being ridiculed under the name of the "Limp-

[6] See Rochlitz, *Für Freunde der Tonkunst* (1832), IV, 274. Rochlitz was in personal contact with Haydn.

[7] Philipp Emanuel Bach.

[8] In 1814 the French writer Marie Henri Beyle (writing mostly under the pseudonym of Stendhal) published his *Lettres écrites de Vienne en Autriche, sur le célèbre compositeur J. Haydn par L. A. C. Bombet*. This is only a translation with very slight adaptations of Carpani's *Le Haydine* (1812). Beyle's book was translated into English in 1817 and an American edition appeared in 1839.

ing Devil" and caused the piece to be prohibited. Haydn often said that he had had more trouble in devising a mode of representing the motion of the waves in a tempest shown in this opera than he afterwards had in writing fugues with a double subject. Bernardon, who had spirit and taste, was difficult to please and there was also another obstacle. Neither of the two authors had ever seen either sea or storm. How can a man describe what he knows nothing about? Bernardon, all agitation, paced up and down, while the composer was seated at the harpsichord. "Imagine," said he, "a mountain rising and then a valley sinking, and then another mountain and another valley; the mountains and the valleys follow rapidly one after the other." This fine description was of no avail and in vain did the actor add thunder and lightning. At last, young Haydn, out of all patience, extended his hands to the two ends of the harpsichord, and bringing them in a glissando rapidly together, he exclaimed: "The devil take the tempest!" "That's it, that's it," cried the harlequin, springing upon his neck and almost stifling him. Many years later when Haydn crossed the Straits of Dover in bad weather, he laughed during the whole of the passage, remembering the storm in *The Limping Devil*.

While most of the lessons Haydn gave were for him just "a miserable mode of earning daily bread," one played an important part in his career. As luck would have it, there lived on the third floor of the old Michaelerhaus the great Italian writer, Pietro Metastasio, poet laureate of the Habsburgs since 1730 and author of numerous operatic librettos which were set to music by a greater number of eminent composers than those of any other librettist. According to Dr. Burney, who was Metastasio's first biographer, the Italian poet's writings "contributed more to the refinement of vocal melody, and consequently of music in general, than the joint efforts of all the great composers in Europe." The great man shared his apartment with the family of a Spanish friend, Nicolás de Martinez, and was greatly interested in the education of his two daughters. In particular the elder one, Marianne (born on May 4, 1744), was the apple of his eye and he bestowed the greatest care on the development of her outstanding musical talent. Somehow Metastasio must have noticed Haydn. Perhaps in quiet nights the sounds of the clavier, on which the young man was improvising, penetrated from the miserable garret down to Metastasio's elegant apartment. He decided to engage the unknown youth as piano teacher for Marianne, then ten years old. For three years Haydn worked daily with the girl, receiving free board in ex-

change for his labors, and there is no doubt that he learned a great
deal himself while studying with so unusual a pupil, whose subsequent achievements as pianist, singer, and composer were praised by
all Viennese musicians. (Even Mozart loved to play piano duets with
her.) Besides, Haydn was naturally brought into contact with the
gentle Metastasio, whose "simplicity and decorum" (Burney) exercised a good influence on the young teacher's demeanor. The lessons
with Marianne had, moreover, another result of still greater importance. She received singing instruction from the famous Italian composer and singing teacher, Niccolò Porpora, who lived in Vienna from
1753 to 1757. Haydn acted as accompanist in these lessons, and thus
had the good fortune to meet the "patriarch of melody." Porpora was
then seventy years old and had probably forgotten his own early
struggles, about which Carpani tells the following amusing story:

> In the time of Charles VI [father of Maria Theresa], the celebrated
> Porpora lived at Vienna, poor and unemployed. His music did not
> please the imperial connoisseur, being too full of trills and mordents.
> Hasse wrote an oratorio for the emperor, who asked him for a second.
> He entreated his Majesty to permit Porpora to execute it. The em-
> peror at first refused saying that he did not like that capering style;
> but, touched by Hasse's generosity, he at length complied with his
> request. Porpora, having received a hint from his friend, did not in-
> troduce a single trill into the whole oratorio. The emperor, surprised,
> continually repeated, during the rehearsal: " 'Tis quite a different
> man; here are no trills!" But when they came to the fugue, which
> concluded the sacred composition, he observed that the theme com-
> menced with four trilled notes. Now you know that in fugues, the
> subject passes from one part to another, but does not change. When
> the emperor, who was said never to laugh, heard in the full height
> of the fugue this deluge of trills, which seemed like the music of
> some enraged paralytic, he could no longer maintain his gravity,
> and laughed, perhaps for the first time in his life. It was the com-
> mencement of Porpora's fortune.

Those days were passed and now Porpora was "sour beyond all
that can be imagined" (Carpani). This did not deter Haydn. Here
was an excellent teacher within his grasp and he did not mean to let
the opportunity slip. He asked for permission to become Porpora's
accompanist in order to study his method and in exchange he offered
menial service. Porpora accepted and took Haydn to the fashionable

baths of Mannersdorf, where they were both to stay in the house of the Venetian Ambassador Pietro Correr, whose mistress was Porpora's devoted pupil. In this favorite summer resort Haydn met various prominent composers like Gluck, Wagenseil and Bonno, and he attended the academies of the Prince of Hildburghausen. He was, however, much more interested in the "old bear," whom he served diligently, "cleaning his shoes, beating his coat, and arranging his antique periwig." The treatment he received was not too good, for the choleric Italian was quite fluent with his tongue and active with his hand, but Haydn did not really resent being called a "blockhead" or a "beast" or receiving sundry cuffs, so long as Porpora was willing to correct his valet's compositions. After three months when he left the maestro, he had improved enormously in singing and in Italian, which he could write in later years nearly as well as German, and had learned, as he said, "the genuine fundamentals of composition."

While Joseph was thus acting as a valet to Porpora, his brother Michael was treading the path toward a successful career. Just as he had outshone Joseph at St. Stephen's, so now he seemed to show more ability than his elder brother. After leaving the Vienna cathedral he went to Hungary, being only too well aware of the difficulties that the imperial capital presented to an unknown musician. A full-length mass by Michael which bears the inscription *Temesvár, 1754* has been preserved and shows a surprising familiarity with the laws of counterpoint for a lad of seventeen. What else he did in Hungary is unknown, except that he was engaged, at the age of twenty, as conductor to the bishop Count Firmian at Grosswardein. Joseph must have felt deeply impressed and somewhat shaken when he got the news, for he remembered only too well in what utter poverty he had lived when he was twenty. Even now, five years later, he had nothing to show his father—his mother had died in 1754—that could match Michael's success. Considerations of this kind, however, did not really discourage him. They only strengthened his determination to persevere; and although he could not as yet display visible proofs of success, he felt that he was steadily climbing upwards, that he was, in his own words, "making something out of nothing." [9] Slowly he began to gain admission to the only circle which in eighteenth-century

[9] According to Dies, Haydn said once: "Young people can learn from my example that something can come out of nothing. What I am, is all the result of the direst need."

Vienna could assure a composer's fortune, that of the nobility. The charming Countess Thun, after coming across one of Haydn's sonatas, wanted to meet the composer. When he stood before her, she was at first shocked by his appearance. Could this undersized, dark-complexioned youth with a face pitted by smallpox, a large aquiline nose, and legs too short for his body, really be the creator of such lovely and graceful tunes? But a closer inspection revealed a noble forehead and dark grey eyes sparkling with humor and kindness, which somehow made the countess forget the young man's general ugliness, his awkward manners, and shabby clothes. So, when she had made sure that she was not being tricked by an impostor, Countess Thun began to study the clavier and singing with Haydn, and apparently with much success. Dr. Burney, who met this "most agreeable and accomplished lady" in 1772, has placed on record that she possessed as great skill in music as any person of distinction he ever knew. The family of the countess, who incidentally was on very friendly terms with Gluck, Mozart, and later Beethoven, was able to do much for Haydn. Perhaps it was due to their recommendation that he established another important contact. He was invited by the ardent music lover, Karl Joseph von Fürnberg, to his country home, Weinzierl, in order to take part in chamber music performances. Haydn spent a delightful time in the hospitable little castle, charmingly situated in a hilly country and offering a splendid view of mountains six thousand feet high. There three other musicians joined him: his host's steward, the local pastor, and the violoncellist Albrechtsberger (not identical with the famous teacher of Beethoven). For this group Haydn wrote his first string quartets which were received with so much praise in Fürnberg's circle that he was encouraged to continue on this line.

From this time on, Haydn's situation improved continually. The number of his pupils grew, his fees were raised, and various other engagements filled his time. Haydn worked from sixteen to eighteen hours a day. "At daybreak he took the part of first violin at the Church of the Fathers of the Order of Mercy; [10] from thence he repaired to the chapel of Count Haugwitz where he played the organ; at a later hour he sang the tenor part at St. Stephen's; and lastly, after having been on foot the whole day, he passed a part of the night at the harpsichord." (Carpani.) And so it went on from day to day.

[10] According to Griesinger, he received for this work a yearly salary of sixty florins.

At last he was able to harvest the fruits of such utter concentration. In 1759 Fürnberg recommended him to the Bohemian, Count Ferdinand Maximilian von Morzin, and Haydn was engaged as music director and *Kammercompositor*. Not only socially, but also financially this was a great step forward for Haydn was now paid two hundred florins a year, besides receiving free board and lodging. Both the count and his wife, the beautiful Countess Wilhelmine, were great lovers of music. They had their own orchestra of about sixteen musicians which played in the winter in Vienna, and in the summer at Lukavec, the Morzin's country house in Bohemia. The new responsibilities paved the way for Haydn to a great artistic development. It was at Lukavec that his first symphony was composed and in its performance he earned great applause. Haydn, conducting it in the traditional way from the harpsichord, had no idea that at this moment his fate was being decided for the following thirty years. Among the audience there sat a man who thought it might be worth while to make note of the name of this young composer. It was the Prince Paul Anton Eszterházy.[11]

[11] There is a discrepancy in the spelling of Esterházy, the family name, and Eszterháza, its ancestral home in western Hungary. The letter "y" in Esterházy, the family name, is a preposition, being the Hungarian equivalent of "de" or "von," pasted at the end of the name, Hungarian being an agglutinative language. The other form, Eszterháza, is a place name, the "a" at the end being the genitive suffix, i.e., the house of Esther. The explanation of the different spelling rests in the fact that while the old family name retained its original spelling, the geographical name adopted, toward the end of the fifteenth century, the more modern Hungarian spelling of the consonant "s" which, when spelled without an additional "z" is pronounced "sh." However, because of the confusion that the two different spellings might cause the reader, the author feels it would be better to use the same spelling for both the family name and the family home; therefore, the "z" will be used in the spelling of both the name and the home.

Chapter 4

THE HONORABLE OFFICIAL OF
A PRINCELY HOUSE

1760 — 1766

HARDLY anything is known about Haydn's life with Count Morzin. There is, however, one little episode mentioned by Griesinger that is not without significance. The countess was a good singer and it was Haydn's duty to accompany her on the piano. Once, while she was leaning over him to look more closely into the music, her neckerchief became unfolded, whereupon Haydn stopped playing as if struck by thunder. Reprimanded by the fair countess, he exclaimed naïvely, "But, your Highness, who would not lose his head over this?" There cannot be any doubt that the composer's interest in the fair sex began to develop much more strongly now that he had outgrown the phase of artistic apprenticeship and had gained a modest foothold on the social ladder. He felt that the time had come to consider marriage seriously. The events leading to this fateful step are unfortunately rather obscure and the various contemporary statements contradict each other. The only fact established beyond doubt is that Haydn did not marry the girl of his choice. Among his pupils in Vienna were the daughters of a hairdresser, Johann Peter Keller. Haydn fell in love with one of these girls, but his feelings were apparently not reciprocated and Therese, whose family was deeply religious, entered a convent under the name of Sister Josepha. Pohl places the event in the year 1760, shortly before Haydn's marriage. However, Haydn himself told Breitkopf & Härtel (book and music publishing company in Leipzig that began publishing around 1542) that he had written

47

his Organ Concerto in C (of 1756) for the ceremony at which Therese Keller took her vows as a nun. This information was given when Haydn was old and his memory was not wholly reliable, and it seems possible that he may have confused this work with some other sacred composition which he really wrote for his first love. The organ concerto certainly reveals nothing of the passion or melancholy with which other composers have imbued works written for a lost love (*See* Mozart's aria, "Alcandro lo confesso," K.294, composed for Aloysia Weber, and Brahms's second string sextet, composed under the spell of Agathe v. Siebold). Be that as it may, Haydn did not stop visiting the Keller family and when he entered the service of Count Morzin and his financial position was much improved, the hairdresser naturally tried to secure the promising young artist for another member of the family. There was an elder daughter, thirty-one years old and so much less attractive than Therese that there seemed little prospect of her entering the state of holy matrimony. We do not know what pressure the Kellers brought to bear on Haydn, but unfortunately they succeeded, and the composer took a wife who was probably the most unsuitable life partner that he could have chosen. It is hard to understand his utter blindness and passivity, for it is known that Haydn, as a rule, was a keen judge of human nature and there are many recorded facts to prove his skill and shrewdness in dealing with other people. It seems most likely that he was prompted by reasons similar to those which Mozart expressed in a letter to his father before he married. Mozart had suffered a fate not very different from that of Haydn. After falling passionately in love with the singer, Aloysia Weber, and being jilted by this "false coquette," Mozart let himself be cajoled into marrying her sister, Constanze. Here is the explanation he gave to his father:

> The voice of nature speaks as loud in me as in others, louder perhaps, than in many a big strong lout of a fellow. I cannot possibly live as do most young men in these days. In the first place, I have too much religion; in the second place, I have too great a love for my neighbor, and am too honorably minded to seduce an innocent maiden; while in the third place, I have too much care for my health . . . I can think of nothing more necessary to my disposition than a wife, inclined as I am to quiet domesticity more than to revelry. A bachelor, in my opinion, is only half alive.[1]

[1] Letter of December 15, 1781.

Haydn, too, felt that he needed marriage, and the partner herself did not seem of such great importance to him now that the one who really mattered was inaccessible. So, although Maria Anna Aloysia Apollonia was three years his senior, not good-looking, not pleasant, and not interested in music, he married her on November 26, 1760. In so doing he made a disastrous mistake, perhaps the only great mistake of his life. Haydn expected marriage to provide him with a comfortable, peaceful home and with children, for whom he felt a great fondness. Neither of these hopes was fulfilled. Maria Anna was quarrelsome, jealous, bigoted, and not even a good housekeeper and Haydn reproached her particularly for being very wasteful. As to progeny, Haydn once remarked to Griesinger: "My wife was unable to bear children and for this reason I was less indifferent toward the attractions of other women." What irritated him most, however, was his wife's utter lack of appreciation of his work. "She doesn't care a straw whether her husband is an artist or a cobbler," he exclaimed indignantly. Members of Haydn's orchestra even said that Frau Haydn, out of pure mischief, liked to use the master's manuscript scores as linings for her pastry or for curl papers. Haydn must have felt a diabolical pleasure when he came across the following poem by Lessing for which he composed a canon:

> If in the whole wide world
> But one mean wife there is,
> How sad that each of us
> Should think this one is his!

It would not be quite fair to put all the blame for the couple's domestic misery on Frau Haydn, whose position, indeed, was not an easy one. That she was unable to grasp the importance of her husband's creative work was, after all, not her fault. She was not made that way, and if Haydn had tried to know her better before their marriage he would have found that music meant nothing to her. In her own peculiar way, Maria Anna may have been fond of her husband. It is known, for instance, that she cared so much for a certain portrait of Haydn by Ludwig Guttenbrunn, that she brought it with her when taking the cure at Baden and did not want to part with it even when it was required for copying. Haydn, it must be admitted, interpreted her behavior in a less flattering way, declaring that the reason his wife liked the picture so much was because Guttenbrunn had once been her lover. But unless she was quite indifferent toward her husband, Frau Haydn must have suffered agonies of jealousy throughout her married life. She could not forget that Haydn had cared deeply for her younger and prettier sister and that she was right in this respect is proved by the fact that as late as 1801 the master remembered his first love in his will.[2] Quite apart from that, the sight of her husband, whose inflammable nature she knew, working constantly with the attractive singers of his ensemble was not easy for this plain woman to bear. The difference of age further aggravated the situation. Haydn, who had developed with extreme slowness, was unusually young for his age, while Frau Haydn, according to the views of the time, felt and behaved like an elderly matron while still in her middle thirties. The way each of them spent money proved to be yet another source of irritation. Frau Haydn was as much annoyed at her husband's supporting scores of his poor relatives as he himself was at his wife's liberality toward the clergy. There is no doubt that in this unhappy union both partners suffered deeply. Frau Haydn found consolation in her church to which she gave freely of her love and devotion. Haydn, deprived of the comforts of a cheerful home, put all the forces of his being into the service of his art.

It was fortunate that soon after the marriage, at the very time when Haydn became aware of his fatal error, all his energies were required to cope with a new situation that had arisen. Count Morzin found himself in financial difficulties and decided to give up his expensive orchestra. Thus Haydn was left without a position, although not for long. Prince Paul Anton Eszterházy, hearing of Morzin's troubles, remembered Haydn's charming symphony, and realized that now he must secure this musician for his court at Eisenstadt (Hungarian, Kismarton). As he already had a conductor, old Gregorius Joseph Werner, who had served the princely house since 1728, Prince Eszterházy offered the young composer the post of assistant conductor and Haydn accepted with enthusiasm.

Here was a patron of infinitely greater importance than Count Morzin. The Eszterházys stood at the very top of the powerful Hungarian nobility. They were the oldest and wealthiest magnates of the country and had the longest record of zeal in the promotion of music and the fine arts. The first member of the family of barons to be raised

---

[2] Haydn mentions her as *exnonn,* former nun, which would indicate that she had not stayed in the convent.

to the rank of prince of the Holy Roman Empire was Paul (1635–1713) who, a staunch supporter of the House of Habsburg, was largely instrumental in promulgating the law that made the Austrian monarch hereditary king of Hungary. Paul was a great Maecenas. He acquired a magnificent picture gallery for his castle of Forchtenstein, and established in his residence at Eisenstadt his own band of music. He was also a composer and in 1711 published a series of his church hymns with orchestra, written for all the holidays of the ecclesiastical year. The grand scale on which he liked to organize his enterprises is clearly illustrated by the account of a pilgrimage which he had his subjects make to the shrine at Mariazell in 1692. It consisted of no less than 11,200 persons who walked for six days, among them members of the high nobility, clergy in ornate robes, girls with golden crowns on their heads, musicians, banner bearers. Under Prince Paul's reign the splendid castle of Eisenstadt was erected. In this magnificent baroque building with its proud towers at the four corners there were no less than two hundred rooms for guests and a beautiful reception hall adorned with frescoes. The building also contained a chapel, a library, and a picture gallery. Great care was given to the planning of the immense park surrounding the castle and it abounded in artificial waterfalls, ponds, grottoes, and beautiful trees.[3]

Prince Paul's successors continued in the tradition established by this Maecenas, at the same time consolidating their enormous wealth. (At the beginning of this century the Eszterházy estate comprised twenty-nine lordships, with twenty-one castles, sixty market towns, and four hundred and fourteen villages in Hungary alone, besides several lordships in Lower Austria and a county in Bavaria.) Prince Paul Anton (1710–1762) began his reign in 1734. He had a genuine love of music and played the violin and violoncello himself. During his travels through Italy and Germany he collected a great number of manuscript scores and had a detailed catalogue of them made in 1759 by the violinist Champée. His various duties at first made it impossible for the prince to plan for the improvement of the Eszterházy orchestra, functioning, since 1728, under the leadership of Gregorius Joseph Werner. For some years Paul Anton was ambassador

[3] The park built on the slopes of the Leitha hills was changed several times according to the fashion of the period. In 1754 it was arranged in the style of the gardens at Versailles, while in the nineties of the century, it was reorganized in the English fashion.

at the Court of Naples, besides taking a very active part in the wars that Austria fought in the reign of Maria Theresa. Twice he supplied his royal mistress with a complete and well-equipped regiment of hussars and as a reward was given the rank of a field marshal. When at last, at the end of the seventeen-fifties, the prince was able to settle down at Eisenstadt, he showed that he had a perfect understanding of what was needed for his orchestra. New musicians were engaged, among them, in 1759, the excellent tenor, Karl Friberth, who was destined to become one of Haydn's great friends and one year later, the soprano singer, Anna Maria Scheffstos. The prince's most important act, however, which has awarded him a permanent place in the history of music, was the engagement of Joseph Haydn. The contract was concluded on May 1, 1761 and the interesting document which has been preserved in the Eszterházy archives is reproduced here in full:

This day (according to the date hereto appended) Joseph Heyden, native of Rohrau in Austria, is accepted and appointed Vice-Capellmeister in the service of his Serene Highness Paul Anton, Prince of the Holy Roman Empire, of Eszterháza and Galantha, etc., subject to conditions here following:

1. Whereas the Capellmeister at Eisenstadt, namely Gregorious Werner, having devoted many years of true and faithful service to the princely house, is now, on account of his great age and infirmities, unfit to perform the duties incumbent on him, it is hereby declared that the said Gregorious Werner, in consideration of his long services, shall retain the post of Capellmeister, and the said Joseph Heyden as Vice-Capellmeister shall, so far as regards the music of the choir, be subordinate to the Capellmeister and receive his instructions. But in everything else relating to musical performances, and in all that concerns the orchestra, the Vice-Capellmeister shall have the sole direction.

2. The said Joseph Heyden shall be considered and treated as a member of the household. Therefore his Serene Highness is graciously pleased to place confidence in his conducting himself as becomes an honorable official of a princely house. He must be temperate, not showing himself overbearing toward his musicians, but mild and lenient, straightforward and composed. It is especially to be observed that when the orchestra shall be summoned to perform before company, the Vice-Capellmeister and all the musicians shall appear in uniform, and the said Joseph Heyden shall take care that

he and all the members of his orchestra follow the instructions given, and appear in white stockings, white linen, powdered, and with either a queue or a tiewig.

3. Whereas the other musicians are referred for directions to the said Vice-Capellmeister, he shall therefore take the more care to conduct himself in an exemplary manner, abstaining from undue familiarity and from vulgarity in eating, drinking, and conversation, not dispensing with the respect due to him, but acting uprightly and influencing his subordinates to preserve such harmony as is becoming in them, remembering how displeasing the consequences of any discord or dispute would be to his Serene Highness.

4. The said Vice-Capellmeister shall be under obligation to compose such music as his Serene Highness may command, and neither to communicate such compositions to any other person, nor to allow them to be copied, but he shall retain them for the absolute use of his Highness, and not compose for any other person without the knowledge and permission of his Highness.

5. The said Joseph Heyden shall appear daily in the antechamber before and after midday, and inquire whether his Highness is pleased to order a performance of the orchestra. On receipt of his orders he shall communicate them to the other musicians, and take care to be punctual at the appointed time, and to ensure punctuality in his subordinates, making a note of those who arrive late or absent themselves altogether.

6. Should any quarrel or cause of complaint arise, the Vice-Capellmeister shall endeavor to arrange it in order that his Serene Highness may not be incommoded with trifling disputes; but should any more serious difficulty occur, which the said Joseph Heyden is unable to set right, his Serene Highness must then be respectfully called upon to decide the matter.

7. The said Vice-Capellmeister shall take careful charge of all music and musical instruments, and be responsible for any injury that may occur to them from carelessness or neglect.

8. The said Joseph Heyden shall be obliged to instruct the female vocalists, in order that they may not forget in the country what they have been taught with much trouble and expense in Vienna, and, as the said Vice-Capellmeister is proficient on various instruments, he shall take care himself to practice on all that he is acquainted with.

9. A copy of this agreement and instructions shall be given to the said Vice-Capellmeister and his subordinates, in order that he may be able to hold them to their obligations therein laid down.

10. It is considered unnecessary to detail the services required of the said Joseph Heyden, more particularly since his Serene Highness is pleased to hope that he will of his own free will strictly observe not only these regulations, but all others that may from time to time be made by his Highness, and that he will place the orchestra on such a footing, and in such good order, that he may bring honor upon himself and deserve the further favor of the prince his master, who thus confides in his zeal and discretion.

11. A yearly salary of four hundred florins to be received in quarterly payments is hereby bestowed by his Serene Highness upon the said Vice-Capellmeister.

12. In addition, the said Joseph Heyden shall board at the officers' table, or receive a half-gulden per day in lieu thereof.

13. Finally, this agreement shall hold good for at least three years from May 1, 1761, with the further condition that if at the conclusion of this term the said Joseph Heyden shall desire to leave the service, he shall give his Highness six months' previous notice of his intention.

14. His Serene Highness undertakes to keep Joseph Heyden in his service during this time, and should he be satisfied with him, he may look forward to being appointed Capellmeister. This, however, must not be understood to deprive his Serene Highness of the right to dismiss the said Joseph Heyden at the expiration of the term, should he see fit to do so.

Duplicate copies of this document shall be executed and exchanged. Given at Vienna this first day of May, 1761.

Ad mandatum Celsissimi Principis,

JOHANN STIFFTELL, *Secretary*

The number and variety of the duties expected from Haydn are staggering. There is no great conductor today who has to do one-half of what was required of Haydn. Three different spheres of activity were entrusted to him. He was conductor, which meant daily practice with orchestra and singers and very frequent performances; he had to compose a great part of the enormous amount of music performed; finally, he was an important officer of administration, uniting in his person the positions of librarian, supervisor of instruments, and chief of the musical personnel. All this Haydn did, and he performed his duties extremely well. That he succeeded far beyond Prince Eszterházy's fondest hopes as a composer, need not be emphasized here. As a conductor, playing the violin or the harpsichord, he was outstanding too. There is a humorous report that his face while conducting was so expressive that society snobs who wanted to demonstrate their understanding of music, just "dexterously placed themselves in a situation where they could see Haydn and regulate by his smile the ecstatic applause by which they testified to their neighbors the extent of their own rapture." While great achievements in the field of music are to be expected only of a Haydn, it proves an amazing versatility that he handled the rest of his duties with equal skill. Here, then, is the rare case of a genius who was a great realist. We know that Johann Sebastian Bach was often in opposition to his chiefs, that Handel's life was a continual fight with the members of his opera company. Haydn did not fight, he was apparently never in opposition; nevertheless, he succeeded in having things done exactly the way he wanted. His musicians respected and loved "Papa Haydn," as they came to call him soon after he became the assistant conductor. The nickname must not, however, lead to the misconception that Haydn was in any way easygoing. In musical matters he was adamant. The instructions he wrote down for the execution of his *Applausus* at the Monastery of Göttweig, where he could not attend rehearsals show very vividly to what extent he insisted on the clearness and accuracy of every detail, and how well he knew what mistakes the musicians were likely to make. If one of his "children" failed, however, in matters other than artistic, he did his utmost to intercede on behalf of the culprit with the prince, and he seemed always to know the best approach, were it a humorous remark, a promise expressed submissively or, perhaps most successful of all, a new composition which he knew would particularly please his patron. He also performed the more menial duties with the conscientiousness typical of the grandson and son of diligent wheelwrights. According to Griesinger, he even tuned his pianoforte. As bills in the Eszterházy archives reveal, the conductor also saw to it that old instruments were repaired at the lowest possible cost. In many cases this amazing man even found time to copy his newly composed works with his own hand. But sometimes the load of work was too heavy even for him. Once, when composing a horn concerto for a new horn player, Thaddäus Steinmüller, Haydn mixed up the staves for oboe and violin, and remarked in the score as an excuse "written while asleep." [4]

[4] The original manuscript of this concerto is preserved in the library of the Society of Friends of Music in Vienna. *See* p. 212.

The contract between Prince Eszterházy and Haydn is also interesting from another point of view. Modern readers may be shocked to see a genius treated not much better than a servant. Imagine a composer in the throes of inspiration having to wait twice a day, at certain hours, in the prince's antechamber, to receive the master's orders; or having to compose whatever the prince wished; and who, even in his appearance, had to conform absolutely to the instructions of his Serene Highness. It would, however, be wrong to view such regulations from the vantage point of the twentieth century. Haydn himself, at least at that time, considered them as matters of course. Composing to order was the usual practice of every musician of his time; it is only since Beethoven that musicians have begun to compose independently of special orders or occasions. To await the commands of so exalted a personage as Prince Eszterházy, who used to say, and prove by action, that what the emperor did he too could do, was not humiliating for a man who had only recently risen from the depths of poverty. As regards Haydn's clothes, Griesinger remarks: "Mathias Haydn still lived to experience the joy of seeing his son in the princely blue uniform braided with gold." [5] Haydn himself probably felt much the same way. The only point in the contract that the composer must have considered unfair was the stipulation that all his compositions were to belong to Prince Eszterházy and that he was not to compose for anyone else. Haydn, however, soon succeeded in modifying this condition. Although we do not know of any document canceling this stipulation, there can be no doubt that, shortly after his appointment, Haydn's works began to be distributed outside the court of Eisenstadt and that he later derived quite a substantial and steadily growing income from the sale of his compositions to publishers.

When Haydn arrived in Eisenstadt the Eszterházy orchestra was still rather small, but in the same year various new musicians joined the band, among them, as its most important member, the outstanding violinist, Luigi Tomasini (born 1741), who in 1757 was brought by Prince Paul Anton from Italy to Eisenstadt as a valet. Haydn seems to have discovered the unusual musical talent of the young man and made him join the orchestra. The new Vice-Capellmeister was also responsible for the engagement of the eminent violoncellist, Joseph Weigl. These two artists, neither more than twenty years old, together

[5] Mathias Haydn died on September 12, 1765.

with the new conductor, brought indeed a breath of fresh air into Eisenstadt's musical life, and it was not easy for the head conductor, Gregorius Werner, to adapt himself to the altered conditions. Old Werner was a most conservative musician who excelled in sacred compositions in the polyphonic style.[6] His works required outstanding musicianship from his performers, without giving them grateful tasks. (It was the kind of music characterized in Vienna by the comment "noble but dull.") A composer so deeply rooted in the past considered everything new a symptom of decline. For Haydn's music Werner had nothing but derision and he called the newcomer a "mere fop" or "a scribbler of songs." Still, he could not help noticing the great esteem enjoyed by the Vice-Capellmeister whose salary, raised one year after his appointment to six hundred florins, exceeded considerably his own four hundred and twenty-eight. Naturally enough, the old man grew more and more embittered, retired as much as possible from court, and devoted himself to composing sacred music. In the five years until his death in 1766, Werner wrote no less than sixteen masses, five *Salve Reginas,* and nine other sacred works. Haydn, on his side, treated the head conductor with the great respect that he really felt for him. Many years after Werner's death when the "scribbler of songs" stood at the summit of his fame, he arranged six of Werner's fugues for string quartet and had them published by Artaria "out of sincere esteem for this celebrated master." Nevertheless, in spite of his esteem the young Vice-Capellmeister managed to take complete charge of the whole musical organization and to increase its size whenever there was a chance to do so. By July 1, 1762 the establishment comprised: five violins, one violoncello, one double bass, one flute, two oboes, two bassoons, and two horns. For singers he had two sopranos, two tenors, a contralto, and a bass. For the choir various servants of the prince were employed.

This year of 1762 marked a turning point in the history of the orchestra. A new prince succeeded Paul Anton, who had died on March 18, 1762, and the new sovereign far surpassed his predecessor in his passion for music and in his Medicean dream of creating a center of culture at his court. Haydn's new patron was Prince Nicholas, the Magnificent, as he was called because of his love for splendor

[6] The old composer had long since lost his sense of humor shown in such burlesque compositions of his younger years as "The Old Clothes Market of Vienna," "The Election of a Village Justice," "A New and Very Curious Musical Instrumental Calendar," all published in 1748.

and display. For nearly thirty years these two men were destined to live together in a unique sort of companionship. Outwardly the prince was the personification of wealth; his coat covered with diamonds was a sensation in many capitals of Europe. The man who wore it was certainly worth knowing. Goethe, who saw the prince in 1764, professed a "particular sympathy for him" and described him as "not tall but well built, vivacious and distinguished, and at the same time without haughtiness and coldness." Judging from the various petitions and documents preserved in the family archives, Prince Nicholas must have been extremely generous and kindhearted, and as these qualities were combined with a true feeling for music, he was in many respects the ideal patron of a composer, especially if the latter were fortunate enough to be able to put up with his patron's autocratic manner.

On May 17, 1762 Nicholas made his solemn entry into Eisenstadt with the splendor that was to characterize the numerous festivities of the years to come. Haydn had the task of composing five Italian operettas for the occasion, most of which have been lost. A special stage was erected for these performances in a glasshouse, and a painter, Le Bon, was engaged for the decorations. By July 1st, Le Bon was given permanent employment, on condition that his wife and daughter should sing in the choir. Even more splendid was the pompous celebration of the marriage of Prince Nicholas' son to Countess Erdödy in 1763, when Eisenstadt, as the *Wiener Diarium* stated, saw "greater festivities and more exalted personages than ever before." Haydn wrote for the wedding his pastorale *Acide* and appeared at the performance in the new Eszterházy uniform of crimson and gold. In the next year the prince had to attend the coronation of Archduke Joseph as Holy Roman Emperor at Frankfort. Here, Nicholas, the Magnificent in the true sense of the word outshone every other ambassador by arranging a "fairylike" (Goethe) illumination of a main street in celebration of the great event. Before going to Frankfort, Prince Nicholas had been in Paris. The beauty and splendor of Versailles made a deep impression on him and when he returned home he decided to create a Versailles of his own in Hungary.

Chapter 5

AT ESZTERHÁZA

1766 — 1779

THE CASTLE of Eszterháza which Prince Nicholas built after his return
from France was a typical product of the eighteenth century. It reflected that attitude toward life adopted by the high aristocracy
when neither trouble nor money was spared to satisfy a whim. Prince
Nicholas, the Magnificent, having seen the Palace of Versailles, decided to rival the king of France. In choosing a site for his country-
seat, he went out of his way to find the very place that would present
the greatest obstacles to his plan. The Eszterházy family owned a little
hunting lodge near the large lake known as Neusiedler See. The lake
had overflowed the surrounding country producing a huge swamp
covering no less than sixteen square miles. It was a desolate place,
filled with mud as far as the eye could see. Every sort of insect
abounded there and fever was a permanent guest. Here Prince Nicholas decided to erect his Versailles. The abundance of wild fowl in
the marshes may have attracted him, but still more perhaps, the
thought that he, the Magnificent, would triumph over nature at its
worst. So the swamps were cleared, canals were dug, a magnificent
dam was built, and after tremendous difficulties and the expenditure
of something like eleven million florins (more than five million dollars!), the castle of Eszterháza came into existence in 1766. A large
and richly illustrated book was devoted solely to the description of
its wonders.[1] A few selections from it may help to give an idea of
the place where Haydn was to spend so much of his time during the
following twenty-five years:

[1] *Beschreibung des hochfürstlichen Schlosses Esterhásy im Königreiche Ungarn*
(Pressburg: 1784). Its author was probably Prince Nicholas himself.

The castle is in Italian style, without visible roof, surrounded by a beautifully proportioned stone gallery. Most valuable are two rooms used by the prince. One of them contains ten Japanese panels in black lacquer adorned with golden flowers and landscapes, each of which cost more than a thousand florins. The chairs and divans are covered with golden fabric. There are also some extremely valuable cabinets and a bronze clock which plays the flute. In the second room, richly adorned with golden ornaments, is another gilded clock with a canary on top that moves and whistles pleasant tunes when the clock strikes, as well as an armchair that plays a flute solo when you sit on it. The chandeliers are made from artistically wrought rock crystal. In the library there are 7500 books, all exquisite editions, to which novelties are being added daily. It also contains numerous manuscripts and many excellent old and new engravings by the best masters. The picture gallery is liberally supplied with first-class original paintings by famous Italian and Dutch masters, which fill the eye of the connoisseur with delight and admiration.

In an alley of wild chestnut trees stands the magnificent opera house. The boxes at the sides open into charming rooms, furnished most luxuriously with fireplaces, divans, mirrors, and clocks. The theater easily holds four hundred people. Every day, at 6:00 P.M., there is a performance of an Italian *opera seria* or *buffa,* or of German comedy which is always attended by the prince. Words cannot describe how both eye and ear are here delighted. When the music begins, its touching delicacy, the strength and force of the instruments penetrate the soul, since the great composer, Herr Haydn, is himself conducting. But the audience is also overwhelmed by the admirable lighting and the deceptively perfect stage settings. At first we see the clouds on which the gods are seated sink slowly to earth. Then the gods rise upwards and instantly vanish, and then again everything is transformed into a delightful garden, an enchanted wood or, it may be, a glorious hall.

Opposite the opera house is the marionette theater, built like a grotto. All the walls, niches, and apertures are covered with variegated stones, shells, and snails that afford a very curious and striking sight when they are illuminated. The theater is rather large and the decorations are extremely artistic. The puppets are beautifully formed and magnificently dressed; they play not only farces and comedies, but also *opera seria.* The performances in both theaters are open to everyone.

Behind the castle is the park. Everyone entering it stands still in amazement and admiration at the majestic sight, for it fills the soul with rapture. The park was built after the prince's own designs, and is without doubt the most gorgeous example of its kind in the whole kingdom. Art and nature are here combined in an extremely noble and magnificent way. In every corner there is something to attract the eye—statues, temples, grottoes, water works; everywhere are the glory of majesty, gentle smiles of nature, joy, and delight!

At the gates stand the princely guard consisting of one hundred and fifty grenadiers, very handsome and finely trained men, mostly six feet tall. Their uniform is a dark blue coat with red flaps and lapels, white tie, white vest and trousers, and a black bearskin cap with yellow visor.

Only a few of the splendors are described here. There were also marvelous hothouses and orangeries, and immense game preserves in the park, while the castle boasted one hundred and twenty-six richly gilded and paneled guest rooms and two exquisite halls for entertainments, the parade hall, decorated entirely in white, and the *sala terrena* tiled with white marble and overflowing with art treasures. This latter hall was used on festive occasions for music. Truly Nicholas, the Magnificent had achieved something worthy of his name. It must have given him real satisfaction when he read in the *Letters of a traveling Frenchman* by Risbeck: "There is no place perhaps, except Versailles, that equals this castle in splendor."

Eszterháza proved to be for the prince much more than a passing whim. The more he improved it the more attached he became to this, his own, creation. Planned first as a summer resort, Eszterháza became the prince's residence for the greater part of the year. Eisenstadt, although much healthier and richer in natural beauties, was completely eclipsed by the new castle. The prince returned to the old residence for a short sojourn during the winter, while his visits to Vienna grew more and more rare. When he was obliged to travel to the capital in the course of his official duties, he had, to the despair of his employees, a disconcerting way of suddenly striking his tents and rushing back to Eszterháza. The unpleasantly damp climate, not greatly changed even by all the canals he built, did not appear to affect Prince Nicholas, nor did he suffer from the "vexatious, penetrating north wind" which caused Haydn much discomfort. As long as he could be at Eszterháza, busily engaged in some new scheme and enjoying the excellent music offered to him, he was the best of patrons and the most charming host to a continual stream of visitors.

A great staff had to be engaged to fulfill the prince's dream of a cultural center. There were two painters, Johann Basilius Grundmann and Pietro Travaglia,[2] who painted the portraits of the family, adorned the castle with frescoes, and most of all, designed the stage scenery. There were also a librarian, a director of the picture gallery, landscape gardeners for the constantly growing park, and a great number of employees connected with the two theaters. The marionette theater was entrusted to P. G. Bader and J. K. v. Pauersbach who supplied the librettos, and to the pantomime master Bienfait. The dialogue for the puppets was usually recited by actors from one of the well-known strolling troupes, whom the prince used to hire for several months at a time. After Werner's death Haydn had become Capellmeister in 1766, and for the opera he engaged excellent singers, mostly from Italy or, at least trained by Italian masters. Among the male singers Friberth, Dichtler, Specht, Gherardi, Lambertini, Jermoli, Griessler, Bianchi, Totti, Ungricht; among the women Weigl, Dichtler, Spangler, Cellini, Prandtner, Jermoli, Poschwa, Puttler, Ripamonti, and Zannini deserve mention, since they appeared in Haydn's own operas of this period. The ballet was for some years in the hands of Ludovico Rossi. The orchestra comprised from sixteen to twenty-two players, whose artistic qualities more than compensated for the smallness of their number. Haydn saw to it that only highly promising musicians were engaged and it can be imagined how they developed under the continual training of so able a conductor. At the first desk throughout Haydn's stay at Eszterháza sat Luigi Tomasini, a great favorite of the prince, and also of the Capellmeister, who used to remark that no one (himself excluded) could play his string quartets like his "brother Luigi." Of the violoncellists, Haydn's friend, Joseph Weigl [3] stayed from 1761 to 1769 when he joined the Vienna court orchestra; his colleagues, Franz Xaver Marteau and Anton Kraft, maintained the same high standard. The prince could afford always to choose the best as the salaries he paid were even higher than those offered by the imperial court at Vienna.

This costly staff of musicians and artists was kept constantly busy by the prince. The normal routine included the performance of two operas and two concert academies a week, and it should not be for-

---

[2] Travaglia also painted parts of the decorations for the performance of Mozart's *La Clemenza di Tito* at Prague.

[3] Haydn stood godfather to his son, Joseph, who became famous as the composer of German Singspiele, like *Die Schweizerfamilie*. See also p. 122.

gotten that concert programs in the eighteenth century were much longer than they are today. In addition there was chamber music in his Serene Highness' private apartments, with Nicholas often taking part himself. The prince was a passionate lover of the baryton, a very complicated instrument related to the viola da gamba, which has become obsolete. The baryton is a most uncommon instrument and is extremely hard to play. This may be the reason the ambitious prince preferred it to the violin or violoncello. He became quite an adept player and Haydn could hardly keep pace with his patron's demands for new baryton compositions. To give the prince a pleasant surprise, Haydn began to practice playing the baryton secretly and when he had acquired some skill, he offered to show his art to the prince, but to his disappointment his attempt was received with icy indifference, and he realized that his patron wanted him only to compose for the baryton, not to play it. Likewise, when the cellist Kraft played baryton duets with the prince, all the solos had to be planned so that there were no great technical difficulties, for they were to be executed by the prince and not by Kraft. As Nicholas remarked: "It is no credit to you to play better than I do; it is your duty."

Frequently the ordinary routine was interrupted by the visit of some distinguished guest and preparations for the occasion had to be made a long time ahead. An outstanding event was the visit of the Empress Maria Theresa herself in 1773. The *Wiener Diarium* and a special booklet afford detailed accounts of the festivities, a résumé of which is given here as an example of the entertainments provided amid the marshes and swamps of Hungary:

On her arrival the empress and her retinue were escorted in fifteen of the prince's magnificent carriages through the park, the wonders of which Maria Theresa could not sufficiently admire, although she was used to a beautiful park in the French style at her own residence of Schönbrunn. In the evening Haydn's burletta *L'infedeltà delusa* was performed, which so impressed the imperial guest that she was overheard to say: "If I want to enjoy a good opera, I go to Eszterháza" (a remark that before long was repeated all over Vienna). The performance was followed by a masked ball in the luxurious halls of the castle. Then the empress was taken to the Chinese pavilion, whose mirror-covered walls reflected countless lampions and chandeliers flooding the room with light. On a platform sat the princely orchestra in gala uniform and played under

Haydn's direction his new symphony Maria Theresa (No. 48 of the Collected Edition) together with other music. The empress then retired to her magnificent suite, while her retinue continued to enjoy the masked ball until dawn. The next day a great banquet took place in the *sala terrena,* during which the virtuosos of the orchestra demonstrated their skill. In the afternoon the empress attended a performance of Haydn's opera *Philemon and Baucis* in the marionette theater and she was so fascinated by it that four years later she had the complete outfit sent to Vienna for some special festivities. After the "souper" the imperial guests watched huge fireworks planned by the pyrotechnist Rabel, their variety and brilliance surpassing all expectations. Afterwards the prince took the monarch to an immense open space, which was hung with multicolored lights forming artistic designs. Suddenly, about a thousand peasants appeared in their beautiful Hungarian or Croatian costumes and performed national dances to the entrancing tunes of their own folk music. The next morning the empress left, after distributing costly presents. Haydn received a valuable golden snuffbox filled with ducats. He was proud to have impressed her Majesty not merely as a musician, for during her stay he succeeded in killing with one shot three grouse which were graciously accepted for the empress's table.

Entertainment of this kind took place once a year or even more frequently, and most of Haydn's operas were written for such occasions. For visitors who would enjoy a more robust form of entertainment than appealed to the empress, the prince took care not to neglect the comic element in arranging his plans. In 1775, for example, when an Austrian archduke and archduchess visited Eszterháza, a whole country fair was set up in the park with quack doctors, mountebanks, cheap-Jacks, and stalls and booths. Here the guests had all the fun they desired and the merry mood was heightened still further by an entrancing parody of Gluck's *Alceste* in the marionette theater. No less than fourteen hundred guests attended the masked balls arranged in honor of the exalted visitors.

Time never hung heavy on the hands of Prince Eszterházy's retainers. But in spite of the interesting work under the leadership of their beloved "Papa," in spite of the good salaries they received, the musicians were often much discouraged by their stay at Eszterháza dragging on and on far into the autumn. The prince, who never hesitated to adorn the park with a new and expensive monument, and

Haydn in court uniform. Oil painting by Grundmann (ca. 1768)

Prince Nicholas Eszterházy, "The Magnificent"

who spent about six thousand florins on the production of the marionette opera *Dido*, saw no necessity for providing living quarters ample enough to house his musicians and their families. All the instrumentalists and singers, all the actors, painters, copyists, as well as some of the servants, had to live in a single moderate-sized building. In 1772 the prince, therefore, gave strict orders that no musician was to bring his wife or children to Eszterháza. Only Haydn, Friberth, Dichtler, and Tomasini were exempted from this rule. Three rooms were reserved for the Capellmeister, whereas two musicians generally had to share a single chamber. By paying the married members an extra fifty florins for the expenses incurred through the double household, the prince felt that he had settled the matter generously enough, and it did not trouble him that these husbands had to live for the greater part of the year away from their families. The musicians felt differently. According to Griesinger: "The affectionate husbands appealed to Haydn to help them. Haydn decided to write a symphony [No. 45 of the Collected Edition, known under the name of Farewell Symphony] in which one instrument after the other ceases to play. The work was executed as soon as an occasion presented itself, and each player was instructed to put out his candle when his part was ended, seize his music and leave with his instrument tucked under his arm. The prince instantly understood the meaning of this pantomime and the next day he gave the order to leave Eszterháza."

The biographer fails to tell us what happened in the following years. Surely, Haydn was not always able to invent something new to humor the prince. The musicians actually had to give in or accept a position elsewhere, which quite a few did. The Capellmeister himself was tied to Eszterháza just as closely as his subordinates. "I never can obtain leave, even to go to Vienna for four-and-twenty hours," he complained once in a letter.[4] "It is scarcely credible, and yet the refusal is always couched in such polite terms as to render it utterly impossible for me to urge my request." This does not mean that Haydn never visited Vienna, but most of his trips were made officially in the retinue of the prince. In 1768 the Eszterházy ensemble performed Haydn's opera *Lo speziale* in the house of a Viennese nobleman, Freiherr von Sumerau. In 1775 Haydn conducted in the capital

---

[4] Letter to Marianne von Genzinger, May 30, 1790. This and the following letters to Marianne von Genzinger are quoted from Ludwig Nohl, *Musikerbriefe* (Leipzig: 1867). The English version is based partly on the translation by Lady G. M. Wallace (London: 1867).

the first performance of his oratorio, *Il ritorno di Tobia,* for the Tonkünstlersocietät, a charitable institution for assisting destitute musicians and their families. The performance had an Eszterházy standard, as Haydn brought with him three singers as well as Tomasini and Marteau. This was the first occasion when Haydn sought the approval of a large audience in a capital city. Its success was notable. The public was enchanted, and after the deduction of all expenses, there remained some two thousand florins for the charitable purposes. Some of the critics were very enthusiastic. The "k.k.priv.Realzeitung der Wissenschaften" declared: "Nature and art were so delicately interwoven in this work that the audience had to love the one and to admire the other. The choruses especially displayed a fire to be found previously only in Handel's compositions." [5]

The great success of *Il ritorno di Tobia* may have been responsible for the request sent to Haydn in 1776 to write an autobiographical sketch for Lucca's publication *Das gelehrte Oesterreich,* a sort of Austrian *Who's Who.*[6]

In spite of Haydn's steadily growing fame, which was spreading beyond his native country, praise of his music was by no means unanimous in Vienna. There was a strong movement against him led by people who either envied him his excellent position or did not understand his peculiar style. Dr. Burney's quotation from a letter which a friend from Hamburg wrote him about Haydn in 1772, reveals exactly the attitude of many Viennese musicians. "His mixture of serious and comic is disliked, particularly as there is more of the latter than the former in his work and, as for rules, he knows but little of them." That was the way Maria Theresa's son and successor to the throne, Joseph II, felt. For him Haydn's music was just "tricks and nonsense" and this dictum did not make the Capellmeister from Eszterháza overpopular at the Viennese court. It is not surprising therefore, that when Haydn tried to penetrate further into these circles he was roughly rebuffed. In 1776, after the Archduke Ferdinand had returned from Eszterháza with a glowing account of what he had heard and seen there, Haydn was commissioned to compose the opera *La Vera Costanza* for Vienna. He did so, but when he came to the capital to rehearse with the singers, such a flood of intrigues was let loose

[5] (April 6, 1775), p. 218.
[6] Parts of this article have been quoted in the earlier chapters of this book.

against him that he withdrew his work in disgust, leaving the field to Pasquale Anfossi, who had composed music to the same libretto. Two years later Haydn's opera was performed at Eszterháza.

Even when dealing with the Tonkünstlersocietät, which was so greatly indebted to him for his *Il ritorno di Tobia,* Haydn had good reason for anger. To obtain a kind of insurance for himself and his wife, Haydn applied to the society for admission in 1778, depositing the amount of three hundred florins requested from him as a non-resident. The society, however, was not satisfied and asked him to sign an agreement pledging himself to supply compositions of importance whenever required. Haydn, highly indignant, declined this offer as being incompatible with his duties toward Prince Eszterházy, whereupon the Societät calmly refused to have him enrolled on their register of members.

Incidents of this kind made Haydn appreciate more and more the advantages of his life at Eszterháza. As he once remarked to Griesinger: "My prince was always satisfied with my works. Not only did I have the encouragement of constant approval, but as conductor of an orchestra I could make experiments, observe what produced an effect and what weakened it, and was thus in a position to improve, to alter, make additions or omissions, and be as bold as I pleased. I was cut off from the world; there was no one to confuse or torment me, and I was forced to become original."

No one was more aware of Joseph Haydn's good fortune than his brother Michael. The positions of the two brothers had now changed. Michael had been appointed director and concertmaster to the archbishop of Salzburg (the patron of Leopold Mozart and his son, Wolfgang) in 1762, a position in which he remained until 1800. The archbishop was not so devoted to music or in any way so generous as Prince Eszterházy. Michael's annual salary was only three hundred florins and although it was doubled eventually when he had reached the summit of his career, these six hundred florins were no more than Joseph had received after a single year of service with the Eszterházys. As a composer also, Michael was more and more eclipsed by Joseph. He felt, however, that he had just as great a talent as his elder brother and once exclaimed: "Give me an encouraging hand, like that lent to my brother, and I will not fall behind him."

Although this is far from the truth—Michael's talent could never have competed with Joseph's genius—it cannot be denied that Haydn's life in the service of Prince Nicholas gave him just the opportunities he needed for his artistic growth. The very monotony of the daily routine, the lack of diversions of any kind, which probably would have been unbearable to an artist like Mozart, helped him to find himself. The "originality" attained in Eszterháza did not mean, however, that Haydn was unaffected by the great spiritual and artistic movements of the time. Indeed, this period offered a very interesting proof of Haydn's sensitiveness to contemporary trends.

The eighteenth century was the age of rationalism. Religion, culture, and art—everything was governed by the intellect. But before long a reaction followed. In all countries Jean Jacques Rousseau, with his motto of "Return to Nature," called forth a storm of opposition to things purely intellectual. The result was a new attitude toward the arts, the first traces of which can be found in England. Edward Young showed in 1759 in his *Conjectures on Original Composition* that the man of genius creates not by means of his intellect, but with the aid of divine inspiration. A scintilla of this inspiration can be seen in the folk song. When in 1765 Bishop Thomas Percy published his collection of old English and Scotch ballads under the title *The Reliques of Ancient English Poetry,* everybody began to be deeply interested in folk songs. Laurence Sterne wrote his humorous works, one of which, *Sentimental Journey through France and Italy* (1768) revealed the poesy of the human heart and made the word "sentimental" the great fashion of the time. In Germany in particular similar collections were initiated. This movement, which in Germany was called *Sturm und Drang* (Storm and Stress) was not limited to literature. We find it in the music of that time, in compositions by Dittersdorf and Mozart, and especially in Haydn's works. He was seized by the Storm and Stress movement in about 1770 and the "romantic crisis," after reaching a climax in 1772, can be observed in his works through most of the seventies. The passion and melancholy breaking forth in many compositions of this period were not due to external occurrences or even to a possible unhappy love affair. If anything in Haydn's personal life were responsible for these unrestrained outbursts, it was not the excess, but rather the starvation of his emotional life. Here lay the danger in his existence at Eszterháza. His wife meant nothing to him; friends like Tomasini, Weigl, Friberth, while very pleasant comrades, were receivers rather than givers in their relation to the master. So all the emotional forces of which this artist was capable inundated his music, sometimes even to the extent of marring its artistic quality. What Haydn needed for full mastery in his art was the inner enrichment of vital human contacts.

Chapter 6

LOVE AND FRIENDSHIP

1780 — 1790

In 1779, Prince Eszterházy engaged an Italian violinist, Antonio Polzelli, and his wife, Luigia, a mezzo-soprano. Neither proved very
satisfactory. The violinist suffered from very poor health and often
could not fulfill his duties, while his wife, with the help of much
coaching from Capellmeister Haydn, was able to master only roles of
secondary importance. Although their salaries were comparatively
small—each received four hundred and sixty-five florins a year,
whereas another singer, Matilda Bologna, had a salary of one thousand florins—the prince felt that their performances did not justify
even this expenditure. Their contract was due to expire at the end of
1780, but even before that date they were told that their services
would no longer be required. In spite of this, the Polzellis stayed on,
receiving their former salaries, even though the consumptive Antonio
in time disappeared from the orchestra and was not even mentioned
in the list of its members. For once the prince did not insist on his
wishes being carried out, since it became clear to him that if he wanted
a contented Capellmeister, he must put up with the presence of
Luigia Polzelli.

The singer was only nineteen, thus twenty-eight years younger than
Haydn. She was a typical Italian brunette, with dark vivacious eyes,
an oval face, an olive complexion, and a graceful figure. Her marriage
with the aged and infirm Antonio was most unhappy. Haydn understood her plight only too well. The helplessness of the young singer
roused all his protective instincts, and before long his sympathy grew
into a deep passion. He seemed to feel that the miseries which for
years he had suffered in his union with Maria Anna absolved him

70

from any obligation to his marriage vows. Indeed, he was so over-whelmed by his love for Luigia that he made no attempt to hide it. Everybody at Eszterháza knew what was going on. Frau Haydn was just as aware of it as Signor Polzelli, and both were helpless against the elemental force that was drawing Joseph and Luigia together.

We know practically nothing about Luigia. No portrait of her is in existence and we have to imagine what picture we can of her from the dry description in a passport issued many years later. Her character remains equally obscure; in fact, the only thing we know is that, in later years, after her husband's death, the widow continually asked for and received Haydn's pecuniary assistance. This shows her, of course, in not too pleasant a light, but it does not prove—as many biographers seem to assume—that ten years before, Luigia had submitted to Haydn's love for mercenary motives. It is known that women were often attracted by Haydn. The composer himself admitted it, sarcastically adding that it could not have been his good looks which were responsible for it. There is no reason why Luigia should not have succumbed to the strong personality and abounding vitality of her musical mentor, and why she should not have loved him genuinely.

As for Haydn, again there is in existence no document that shows his feelings for Luigia in those first years. So long as they lived in the same place, they wrote no letters. A correspondence in Italian (which Haydn mastered perfectly) began only in 1791 after they had been separated. This was twelve years after their first meeting and at a time when Haydn was being overwhelmed by new experiences. Even then he wrote to her: "I love you as on the first day, and I am always sad when I cannot do more for you. But be patient, perhaps the day will arrive when I can show you how much I love you." [1] "Oh, my dearest, you will always live in my heart. Never, never, shall I forget you, my beloved." [2]

Haydn here was referring to a possible marriage when they should both be free. After Antonio Polzelli's death he even wrote: "Perhaps the time will come, for which we have so often wished, when two pairs of eyes will be closed. One pair is shut already. But what of the other? Well, be it as God wills." [3]

[1] Letter of October 13, 1791. Cf. Botstiber-Pohl, *Joseph Haydn* (Leipzig: 1927).
[2] Letter of January 14, 1792.
[3] Letter of August 4, 1791.

Whatever his real feelings were when he was writing to her (and it is not unlikely that he expressed himself more ardently than he felt at the time), there is no doubt that in the first years after he met Luigia she made him very happy. He had at last found the object on which he could lavish his passion. Uncertainty, bliss, anxiety, disappointment—all the imponderables of contact with a beloved person upset the smoothly running routine, making Haydn's life more exciting and immeasurably richer. Today we cannot ascertain whether Luigia was worthy of the love of a man like Joseph Haydn. Probably she was not, just as Aloysia Weber was not worthy of that of Wolfgang Amadeus Mozart. Nevertheless, at the time when Haydn was deeply in love, Luigia gave him what he needed and by awakening his emotional life played an important part in his development. It seems doubtful whether Haydn could ever have achieved the artistic maturity that his works of the seventeen-eighties reveal so splendidly, had his passion for the Italian singer not opened to him new vistas of life.

There is still another side to their relationship that should not be overlooked. Haydn, as has been mentioned before, suffered deeply from his wife's childlessness. He loved children and was beloved by them. Luigia had two sons,[4] Pietro, born in 1777 in Bologna, and Aloysius Anton Nicolaus, born in 1783 at Eszterháza. Rumor persisted that the younger boy was Haydn's son. Although this will probably never be clearly proved, the imputation can certainly not be definitely rejected. Haydn took a loving interest in both boys and did not differentiate between the two. If anything, he rather preferred the elder. He taught them both music, watching with pleasure the unfolding of their talents, gave them much financial assistance, and helped them to obtain their first appointments.[5] After their mother ceased to mean much to Haydn, the two Polzelli boys were still sure of the master's unfailing sympathy. He certainly had the feelings of a father for both and he made this so clear that even Frau Haydn, in spite of her hatred for Luigia, was resigned to accept this state of

[4] A daughter, Antonia, born in 1786 at Eszterháza, died two years later.

[5] Pietro Polzelli, known as Pietrucchio, after working as second violinist in a Vienna orchestra, died at the age of nineteen from tuberculosis. Anton Polzelli entered the Eszterházy orchestra in 1803 and became its music director in 1813. Later he turned to agriculture, working as an estate agent for various Hungarian magnates. In 1826 he was knighted in Rome. Through different speculations and lawsuits he lost his fortune and returned to music, dying as a music teacher in Budapest in 1855. Various compositions show him as a talented disciple of Haydn.

affairs and received Pietro Polzelli for a prolonged stay in her home "very kindly." [6]

Pietro and Anton Polzelli were not the only young people Haydn worked with during the later years of his stay at Eszterháza. For five years another musician studied with him there. This was Ignaz J. Pleyel, who had shown such great promise that an aristocratic patron, Count Ladislas Erdödy, entrusted him to the master's care. Pleyel proved an excellent pupil, and after leaving Haydn he became Count Erdödy's music director and gained a reputation as a capable composer. Later the master and his disciple were to meet again in very peculiar circumstances. Haydn's pupils also included the brothers, Fritz and Edmund von Weber, and both showed some promising talent but in later years were entirely eclipsed by their young half brother, Carl Maria von Weber. Fritz taught him music and once made this statement: "A musician you will never be!"

Absorbed though Haydn was in his personal affairs, through his love for Luigia, and his interest in the young people whom he taught, these years brought him yet another experience of equal, or perhaps even greater, importance. He met Wolfgang Amadeus Mozart, who had moved from Salzburg to Vienna in 1781. Naturally, they had known of each other before this; now, however, a very close personal friendship was established between them which grew stronger from year to year.

It is difficult to conceive of two personalities fundamentally more different than these two great men. Mozart developed with amazing rapidity, while Haydn's progress was incredibly slow. Indeed, at the age of thirty-six (Mozart died at this age) Haydn had written hardly any important compositions. In person Mozart was the typical artist, his moods undergoing rapid changes from buoyant gaiety to deep melancholy, from fits of temper to an almost feminine gentleness. Haydn was of a rather even temperament, mostly calm and gay, and with a great sense of humor. Mozart was a born dramatic composer and a brilliant virtuoso on both the piano and violin; thus he gained tremendous success as a performer. Haydn's gifts as a composer for the stage were limited; he preferred to conduct his own works inconspicuously from the harpsichord and was free from any ambition to gain laurels as a soloist. There was little sense of order

[6] Postscript by Haydn to one of Pietro's letters to his mother dated October 22, 1792.

and regularity in Mozart's life, no understanding of the value of money. Haydn's existence throughout the greater part of his life had something of an automatic precision; neatness and regularity were indispensable to him; in financial matters he was a match for his publishers and he left considerable property at his death, while Mozart died a pauper.

Perhaps it was the very differences between these two men of genius that drew them to each other. Had they constantly lived together they might have got on each other's nerves, but as they did not visit each other too frequently, every meeting became an event. Haydn was fascinated by Mozart's quicksilver personality, while Mozart enjoyed the sense of security that Haydn's steadfastness and warmth of feeling gave him.

But for both their artistic relations far transcended in importance their personal contacts. At that time Mozart was twenty-five, Haydn forty-nine, but the older composer who had developed so slowly and the younger master who had grown so rapidly had much to impart to each other. Whenever Haydn came to Vienna he had the joy of playing chamber music with Mozart. In 1785, when Mozart's father visited his son, Wolfgang's new string quartets were performed for him by Haydn, the two Barons Tindi, and the composer. Then Haydn took Leopold Mozart aside and said to him: "I tell you before God as an honest man that your son is the greatest composer known to me either in person or by reputation. He has taste and, what is more, the most profound knowledge of composition." [7] Mozart would not accept this praise for himself but insisted that it was solely from Haydn that he had learned how to write string quartets (which, to some extent, was true). To acknowledge this to the musical world, he published in 1785 six quartets dedicated to his "beloved friend Haydn" expressing his deep gratitude in touching words. But he went much further than that, for he allowed no one to say anything against Haydn in his presence. Typical indeed, was his repartee to Leopold Koželuch, teacher of the pianoforte at the court of Vienna. This composer, on hearing a daring passage in one of Haydn's quartets, remarked somewhat contemptuously: "I would never have written that." Whereupon Mozart (who was quick on the uptake) replied: "Nor would I! And do you know why? Because neither you nor I would have had so excellent an idea." And on another occasion he

[7] Letter from Leopold Mozart to his daughter Nannerl, dated February 14, 1785.

exclaimed to Koželuch: "Sir, even if they melted us both together, there would still not be stuff enough to make a Haydn." This attitude was reciprocated by Haydn. After the Vienna premiere of *Don Giovanni* sundry passages were criticized in his presence and he immediately exclaimed: "I cannot settle this dispute but this I know: Mozart is the greatest composer that the world possesses now." And when someone expressed surprise at a daring disregard of the rules of harmony in Mozart's quartet in C major, he replied sharply: "If Mozart wrote it so he must have had a good reason for it." It was Mozart's art that made Haydn aware of the limits of his own talent. Two letters illustrate this. In 1781 Haydn wrote to his Vienna publisher, Artaria:

> Monsieur le Gros, director of the Concerts Spirituels, wrote me a great many nice things about my *Stabat Mater* which had been given there [at Paris] four times with great applause; so this gentleman asked permission to have it engraved. They made me an offer to engrave all my future works, on very advantageous terms, and are much surprised that my compositions for the voice are so singularly pleasing. I, however, am not in the least surprised, for as yet they have heard nothing. If they could only hear my operetta *L'Isola disabitata* and my last Shrovetide opera *La Fedeltà premiata,* I do assure you that no such work has hitherto been heard in Paris, or perhaps in Vienna either. My great misfortune is that I live in the country.[8]

This letter, besides revealing Haydn as an efficient salesman, shows how highly he thought of his own dramatic works. But in the following years Mozart composed his great masterpieces, *Le Nozze di Figaro, Così fan tutte, Don Giovanni,* and Haydn began to see his own dramatic attempts in a new light. In December, 1787 a great admirer of his from Prague, by the name of Roth, asked him to write an opera for Prague (as Mozart had done) and Haydn now answered:

> You wish me to write an *opera buffa* for you. Most willingly if you are desirous of having a vocal composition of mine for yourself alone; but if it is with the idea of producing it on the stage at Prague I cannot comply with your wish, all my operas being too closely connected with our personal circle [Prince Eszterházy's, in Hungary] so that they could never produce the proper effect, which I have calculated in accordance with the locality. It would be very different

[8] Cf. note 4 of preceding chapter regarding this and the following letters.

if I had the invaluable privilege of composing a new opera for your theater. But even then I should be taking a big risk, for scarcely any man could stand comparison with the great Mozart.

Oh, if only I could explain to every musical friend, and to the leading men in particular, the inimitable art of Mozart, its depth, the greatness of its emotion, and its unique musical conception, as I myself feel and understand it, nations would then vie with each other to possess so great a jewel within their frontiers. Prague ought to strive not merely to retain this precious man, but also to remunerate him; for without this support the history of any great genius is sad indeed, and gives very little encouragement to others to adopt a musical career, and for lack of this support many promising talents are lost to the world. It enrages me to think that the unparalleled Mozart has not yet been engaged by some imperial or royal court. Do forgive this outburst—but I love that man too much.[9]

Such an "outburst" was indeed a rarity with Haydn. It proves how much Mozart's welfare meant to him, that he was willing to disparage his own achievements, if by so doing he could put the genius of his colleague in the right light.

Mozart, it must be pointed out, exercised much more than a passive influence on Haydn, for that master did not hesitate to learn from his young friend. Therefore, when discussing Haydn's works of the seventeen-eighties and nineties, the name of Mozart must be mentioned again and again. This is a striking proof of Haydn's broadmindedness. Even as a man of fifty he was by no means set in his ways. Fundamentally, there was an amazingly small difference between the youth, who twenty-five years previously had devoured manuals on music while nearly starving in his Vienna garret, and the master who by now had achieved world fame.

World fame it was indeed that came to Haydn while he worked in the solitude of Eszterháza. His name traveled far beyond the borders of his own country, and in the whole of Europe there was hardly a music lover who did not know of, and admire, the works of Joseph Haydn.

The first indications of the composer's widespread reputation came from Spain. As early as 1779, the poet Yriarte wrote glowing praise of his music in the poem *La Música*. Two years later King Charles III of Spain sent Haydn a golden snuffbox set with diamonds. What pleased

[9] The letter was first published by Franz Xaver Niemetschek in his *Lebensbeschreibung des K. K. Kapellmeisters Wolfgang Amadeus Mozart* (Prague: 1798).

the recipient perhaps even more than the gift itself was the manner
in which it was presented. The secretary of the Spanish Legation
came to Eszterháza for the sole purpose of handing over the royal
gift and expressing his monarch's great esteem for Haydn's music—
a ceremony which must have afforded keen satisfaction to both the
composer and his patron, who was probably much more ambitious
for his conductor than was Haydn himself. What the Spanish court
thought of Haydn is also reflected in the attitude of the composer,
Luigi Boccherini, who was staying at that time in Madrid under the
patronage of the king's younger brother. Boccherini adopted Haydn's
style to such an extent that the Neapolitan violinist, Giuseppe Puppo,
nicknamed him "Haydn's wife." Spain was also responsible for the
composition of a work to which Haydn himself attached the greatest
importance: *The Seven Last Words of Our Saviour on the Cross*.[10]
In his preface to the score of the work published by Breitkopf &
Härtel in 1801 Haydn wrote:

> About fifteen years ago I was requested by a canon of Cádiz to
> compose instrumental music on *The Seven Last Words of Our Saviour
> on the Cross*. It was customary at the Cathedral of Cádiz to produce
> an oratorio every year during Lent, the effect of the performance
> being not a little enhanced by the following circumstances. The
> walls, windows, and pillars of the church were hung with black cloth,
> and only one large lamp hanging from the center of the roof broke
> the solemn obscurity. At midday the doors were closed and the cere-
> mony began. After a short service the bishop ascended the pulpit,
> pronounced the first of the seven words (or sentences) and delivered
> a discourse thereon. This ended, he left the pulpit and prostrated
> himself before the altar. The pause was filled by music. The bishop
> then in like manner pronounced the second word, then the third, and
> so on, the orchestra following on the conclusion of each discourse.
> My composition was subject to these conditions, and it was no easy
> matter to compose seven adagios to last ten minutes each, and suc-
> ceed one another without fatiguing the listeners; indeed, I found it
> quite impossible to confine myself within the appointed limits.

In spite of these difficulties the work Haydn wrote made a tremendous impression and was before long played and printed in other
countries. Thus, as early as 1793 the first performance took place in

[10] In a letter to W. Forster (April 8, 1787) he said: "Its subject was expressed
by instrumental music in such a way as to make the deepest impression on even the
least cultivated mind."

the United States.[11] The Spanish canon, incidentally, used an original way to present the honorarium. Haydn received a little box from Cádiz and upon opening it, he saw to his surprise a chocolate cake. Angrily he cut into it, only to find it filled with gold pieces.

Spain's neighbor, France, adopted the same attitude toward Haydn. The flattering letter from Monsieur le Gros has already been mentioned. In 1784 another society, the Concerts de la Loge Olympique invited Haydn to write six symphonies specially for them, an invitation to which we owe the famous Paris Symphonies. At the same time, profitable business connections were established with French publishing houses (Nadermann, Willmann, Sieber, and others). Haydn's compositions were frequently performed in the French capital and the well-known composer, Luigi Cherubini, who heard them there, was so deeply impressed that he became one of the master's most enthusiastic admirers.

The year 1781, which brought Haydn the letter from Monsieur le Gros and the present from the king of Spain, also saw the beginning of the master's direct connection with England. The eminent violinmaker, William Forster, applied to the British ambassador in Vienna for help in securing Haydn's works for his newly established publishing house. The ambassador, General Jermingham, was successful, and within six years Forster published no less than one hundred and twenty-nine works by Haydn, among them eighty-two symphonies, for which he paid considerable sums. Forster's example was followed by the firm of Longman & Broderip. When the Professional Concerts were founded in 1783, Lord Abingdon tried to induce Haydn to take over their direction. Haydn declined, as giving up the service of his prince appeared to be out of the question, while on the other hand, leave of absence would certainly not have been granted to him by his patron. So the directors of the Professional Concerts had to be satisfied with William Cramer, who opened the series with a Haydn symphony. By that time the master's work had already gained a predominant place in English musical life and there was hardly an important concert or solo recital without some number by the composer of Eszterháza. His quartets were frequently played, since the Prince of Wales set the example in his own chamber music, in which he performed the violoncello part. Various music managers flooded Haydn with invitations. A particularly enterprising publisher,

[11] *See* M. D. Herter Norton, "Haydn in America," *Musical Quarterly* (April, 1932).

John Bland, took the trouble to travel from London to Eszterháza
to obtain new works and to persuade Haydn to visit England. The
master presented Bland with two autographs. One was the cantata
Arianna a Naxos, the other the string quartet, Op. 55 No. 2. About the
latter work Bland used to tell an amusing story which brought it
its peculiar nickname of the Razor Quartet. He said that he had
visited Haydn just when the master was shaving with a very blunt
razor and exclaimed in despair, "I would give my best quartet for a
good razor." Thereupon Bland rushed to his room and brought his
own excellent set of razors. Haydn was delighted and scrupulously
kept his promise, for the Razor Quartet was certainly among the
best he had written. As regards Bland's urgent invitation, Haydn
saw no possibility of acceptance, but it is certain that the personal
contact with the English publisher greatly increased his interest in
the musical life of London.

Nor was England the only foreign country that invited the master.
In Italy also Haydn was a great favorite. The Philharmonic Society
of Modena elected him a member in 1780, thus putting to shame the
Viennese Tonkünstlersocietät. King Ferdinand IV of Naples, a passionate lover of music, commissioned in 1786 several concertos for his
favorite instrument the *lira organizzata* (cf. p. 258). The works that
Haydn wrote satisfied the king so completely that he urgently invited the composer to visit his court. Haydn felt much inclined to do
so for he had always longed to go to Italy, but again he saw no chance
of accepting the invitation.

All in all royalty was gracious to the son of the wheelwright. Frederick William II of Prussia, an excellent violoncello player,[12] sent
Haydn a magnificent diamond ring worth three hundred ducats.
Haydn was delighted with the gift and made a habit of wearing the
ring when he composed an important work. Carpani even declares
that when the master forgot to put on the ring no ideas came to him.

Another royal admirer of Haydn was the Russian Grand Duchess
and subsequent Empress Maria Fedorovna, who took lessons from
him while visiting Vienna in 1782 and as late as 1805 sent him a valuable ring in thanks for his new songs for three and four voices. Such
proofs of success naturally gave Haydn a great deal of gratification
and he did his utmost to satisfy the constantly growing demands from

[12] Mozart wrote for the king his last three quartets; Beethoven dedicated his two
violoncello sonatas, Op. 5 to him.

foreign publishers, showing no small business acumen in his intercourse with various clients. But his great fame did not in the least turn his head. He remained the same kind and simple man whose "eyes beamed with benevolence" (Dies), and he never forgot his humble origin. "I have had intercourse with emperors, kings, and many a great personage," he remarked once to Griesinger, "and have been told by them quite a few flattering things. For all that, I do not care to be on intimate terms with such persons and prefer to keep to people of my own station."

Naturally enough, Vienna could not but be influenced by the attitude of the whole musical world. The publishing firm of Artaria & Company entered into a close business connection with Haydn and did much to promote the master's fame in his own country. In 1781 when Artaria published a collection of pictures of the greatest men of the time, they included the portrait of Haydn by Johann Ernst Mansfeld.[13] The composer was, as he wrote to them, "exceedingly pleased . . . and the prince felt even more strongly on the subject."[14] Although certain court circles in Vienna still maintained their old attitude, the number of Haydn's friends in Vienna steadily increased. They belonged mostly to the lower aristocracy or to the wealthy middle classes whose role in Austria's musical life was acquiring more and more importance.

Among them were the sisters, Franziska and Marianne von Auernbrugger, to whom Haydn dedicated six piano sonatas, and about whom he wrote to Artaria:[15] "Their style of playing and their genuine insight into music equaled that of the greatest masters." An important personality was the high official, Franz Bernhard von Kees, and in his home orchestral concerts of amateurs regularly took place. Both Mozart and Haydn considered it an honor to have their new works performed in the von Kees house and we understand their attitude when we read in a letter from Mozart to his father[16] that his symphony had been executed by forty violins, ten violas, eight violoncellos, and all the wind instruments doubled. Another friend was Hofrat Greiner who chose the texts for Haydn's songs. Haydn also liked to visit the Anglo-Italian composer, Stephen Storace, at

[13] It was reproduced in 1784 in the *European Magazine* (London) with a biography of the "celebrated composer."
[14] Letter of June 23, 1781.
[15] Letter of February 25, 1780.
[16] Letter of April 11, 1781.

that time living in Vienna, and his sister, the charming Nancy, who sang the role of Susanne at the first performance of *Le Nozze di Figaro*. The Irish singer Michael Kelly, tells us in his *Reminiscences* of a chamber music party in Storace's home, when the quartets were played by no lesser masters than Dittersdorf, Haydn, Mozart, and Vanhall, while Paisiello and the Italian poet, Abbate Casti, were among the listeners. There was also the music-loving merchant, Johann Michael Puchberg, who besides being an unfailing friend to Mozart (which of course spoke in his favor from Haydn's point of view) helped Haydn with financial matters. Puchberg and Haydn were the only people whom Mozart invited to the first rehearsals of his opera *Così fan tutte*.

Haydn made other friends by joining the Order of Freemasons in 1785, a step which he probably took on the recommendation of Mozart and Puchberg, who were both ardent freemasons. The lodge Zur wahren Eintracht of which Haydn was a member, enjoyed a very high reputation. The master probably became a freemason mainly for the pleasure of associating with men of high culture. Unlike Mozart, his works do not reflect in any way the influence of masonic ideas, which were really alien to the orthodoxy of Haydn's religious faith.

But, with the possible exception of Mozart's house, there was no place in Vienna that proved so attractive to Haydn as the home of Peter L. von Genzinger, a very successful doctor, who had been Prince Eszterházy's physician for many years. Both the doctor and his charming wife, Marianne, an excellent singer and pianist, were real friends of music. On Sundays the musical élite of Vienna used to assemble at the Genzingers' home for performances of the first quality. Haydn, who naturally knew Prince Eszterházy's physician well, attended these gatherings whenever he was in Vienna and they meant a great deal to him. Here he found an atmosphere which seemed like the fulfillment of his old dreams: a comfortable, pleasant home; a woman of high culture who took the keenest interest in every one of his new compositions and who at the same time was so thoughtful a hostess that she prepared his favorite dishes; children gifted for music whom he could guide. The Genzinger home offered him all that he had missed throughout his married life. He basked in this congenial atmosphere, only to feel all the more strongly the misery of his lonely existence when he returned to Eszterháza.

Fortunately for us, letters were exchanged between Haydn and Marianne von Genzinger after she had sent him in January, 1789 a pianoforte arrangement of an andante from one of his symphonies which she had made herself, and which, according to Haydn, was an excellent piece of work. Among the personal documents that have come down to us from Haydn, there is probably nothing more important than his letters to Marianne. The master ordinarily found it difficult to get away from the florid and stilted style of his time. When he wrote to Marianne, however, the words seemed to come from his very heart and they convey to the reader the impression that he is actually hearing Haydn talk to his dear friend. Most revealing is the long letter that he wrote to his "much esteemed and kindest Frau von Genzinger" on February 9, 1790, after a visit to Vienna:

Well here I sit in my wilderness; forsaken, like some poor orphan, almost without human society, melancholy, dwelling on the memory of past glorious days. Yes, past, alas! And who can tell when those happy hours may return—those charming meetings where the whole circle has but one heart and one soul—all those delightful musical evenings which can only be remembered and not described? Where are all those inspired moments? All gone—and gone forever. You must not be surprised, dear lady, that I have delayed writing to express my gratitude. I found everything at home in confusion; for three days I did not know whether I was Capellmeister or "Capell-servant." Nothing could console me; my apartment was all in confusion; my pianoforte, which I formerly loved so dearly, was perverse and disobedient, and irritated rather than soothed me. I slept little, and even my dreams persecuted me, for when I fell asleep and was under the pleasant illusion that I was listening to *Le Nozze di Figaro,* the blustering north wind woke me and almost blew off my nightcap. I lost twenty pounds in weight in three days, for the effects of the good fare at Vienna had disappeared on the journey back. Alas! alas! thought I to myself, when forced to eat at the tavern a slice of a fifty-year-old cow instead of your admirable beef, an old mutton with turnips instead of a ragout with little forcemeat balls, a tough grill instead of a Bohemian pheasant, Hungarian salad instead of good juicy oranges, and dry apple fritters instead of pastry. Alas and alas thought I to myself, would that I now had many a tidbit that I despised in Vienna! Here in Eszterháza no one asks me, "Would you like chocolate with or without milk? Will you take coffee with or without cream? What can I offer you, my good Haydn? Will you have vanilla ice or strawberry?" If only I had a piece of good Parmesan cheese, particularly in Lent, to enable me to swallow more easily the black puddings! Today I gave our porter a commission to get me a couple of pounds.

Forgive me, dear lady, for taking up your time in this my very first letter by so wretched a scrawl and such stupid nonsense; you must forgive a man spoilt by the Viennese. Now, however, I begin to accustom myself by degrees to country life, and yesterday I rehearsed for the first time, and somewhat in the Haydn style too.

No doubt you have been more industrious than myself. The pleasant adagio from the quartet has probably now received its true expression from your fair fingers. I trust that my good Miss Peperl [Marianne's daughter] may be reminded of her master by often singing the cantata *Arianna a Naxos,* and that she will pay particular attention to distinct articulation and correct vocalization, for it would be a sin if so fine a voice were to remain shut-up in her chest. I beg, therefore, for a frequent smile or else I shall be much vexed. I also advise master François [the eldest son] to cultivate his musical talents. Even if he sings in his dressing gown, it will do well enough, and I will often write something new to encourage him. I again kiss your hands in gratitude for all the kindness you have shown me, and am unchangeably while life lasts,

Yours, etc.

HAYDN

Soon after this letter was written an event occurred which was bound to increase Haydn's depression. Princess Maria Elisabeth, the wife of his patron, died on February 15th. Haydn described the gloomy atmosphere at Eszterháza in the following letter which also shows that he kept his friend informed of what was happening to him:

March 14, 1790

MOST VALUED, ESTEEMED, AND KINDEST FRAU VON GENZINGER,

I ask your forgiveness a million times for having so long delayed my answer to your two charming letters. This has been caused not by negligence (a sin from which may Heaven preserve me so long as I live), but by the pressure of business that devolved upon me on behalf of my gracious prince in his present melancholy condition. The death of his wife has overwhelmed the prince with such grief that we have been obliged to use every means in our power to rouse him from his profound sorrow. I therefore arranged for the first three days a selection of chamber music, but no singing. The poor prince, however, the first evening, on hearing my favorite adagio in D, was affected by such deep melancholy that it was difficult to dispel it by other pieces. On the fourth day we had an opera, on the fifth a comedy, and afterwards our daily theater as usual. We were also commanded to study Gassmann's old opera *L'amor Artigiano*, as our master had recently expressed a wish to hear it. I composed three new arias for it which I will shortly send you, not on account of their beauty, but to demonstrate my industry. You shall receive the new symphony I promised in April, so that it may be performed at the Kees' music party.

You must now permit me to kiss your hands gratefully for the rusks you sent me, which came exactly at the right moment, when I had just finished the last of the others. That my favorite *Arianna* has been successful at Schottenhof [17] is delightful news to me, but I recommend Miss Peperl to pronounce her words clearly, especially in the phrase *che tanto amai*.

As I feel sure, dear lady, that you take an interest in everything that concerns me (far greater than I deserve), I must let you know that last week I received a present of a handsome gold snuffbox, of the weight of thirty-four ducats, from Prince Öttingen-Wallerstein, accompanied by an invitation to pay him a visit this year, the prince defraying my expenses. His Highness is desirous of making my personal acquaintance (a pleasing fillip to my depressed spirits). Whether I shall be able to make up my mind to the journey is another question.

I beg you to excuse this hasty scrawl.

I am always, etc.

HAYDN

P.S. I have just lost my faithful coachman; he died on the 25th of last month.

The question has often been asked whether Haydn was in love with Marianne von Genzinger. It is not easy to answer. Marianne certainly showed in her letters no more than friendliness. They leave indeed the impression on one's mind that she was always on guard to convey by her words nothing but great esteem. Haydn doubtlessly felt much more strongly and it would not be surprising if he had been in love with this charming admirer of his art who, at the time when these letters were exchanged, was only in her middle thirties. There is a postscript to his letter of June 20, 1790 in which he exclaims:

[17] The Genzingers' residence.

Oh, how I wish that I could only play over these sonatas once or twice to you; how gladly would I then reconcile myself to remaining for a time in my wilderness. I have much to say and to confess to you, from which no one but yourself can absolve me.

When writing a sonata specially for her, he called her attention in particular to the adagio adding, "it has a deep significance which I will analyse for you when opportunity offers." On another occasion, when a letter that he had written to her went astray and they suspected that it had been abstracted by some curious person, Haydn reassured his friend in the following words:

> You need be under no uneasiness, dear lady, either as regards the past or the future, for my friendship and esteem for you (warm as they are) can never become reprehensible since I have always in mind my respect for your elevated virtues, which not only I, but all who know you, must reverence. Do not let this deter you from consoling me sometimes by your charming letters as they are so needed to cheer me in this wilderness and soothe my deeply wounded heart. Oh, that I could be with you, dear lady, even for a quarter of an hour, to pour forth all my sorrows, and to receive comfort from you! Well, as God pleases! This time also will pass away and the day return when I shall again have the inexpressible pleasure of being seated beside you at the pianoforte, hearing Mozart's masterpieces, and kissing your hands from gratitude for so much pleasure.

This letter gives a clear picture of what Marianne meant to him. Here was a woman to whom he could, as he wrote, "pour forth his sorrows," who understood and comforted him.

But why should Haydn have needed comfort at that time? Why was "his heart deeply wounded"? To all outward appearances he was leading a highly satisfactory existence. His fame by far exceeded anything he might have hoped for in his proudest dreams; indeed there was probably no living composer with a more widespread reputation. He had an excellent and well-paid position. His health was good, his productivity in fullest bloom. The unhappiness of his married life was a burden he had become used to carrying, and all the more so since he and his wife now mostly lived apart. Still, many remarks in his letters point to an increasing moodiness and dissatisfaction, which are always ascribed to the same reason. In his autobiographical sketch of 1778, he had proudly said of his position: "Capellmeister to his Highness Prince Eszterházy, in whose service I hope to live and die." Now he wrote (June 27, 1790): "I am doomed to stay at home. It is indeed sad always to be a slave." Other similar outbursts could be mentioned, showing that Haydn had ceased to be happy at Eszterháza. It was natural for him to long for Vienna where he could enjoy the inspiring company of Mozart and the wonderful sympathy of Marianne von Genzinger. Moreover, the various invitations to foreign countries that reached him were a great temptation and made the master increasingly restless. But these were only symptoms of a more deeply rooted trouble. Haydn had outgrown Eszterháza. The various problems that had confronted him in his position there had ceased to interest him. Even his attachment to his beloved prince had somewhat diminished. Haydn, now a man of nearly sixty, like a person of half his age, craved for change, new tasks, new experiences. With the sure instinct of genius he felt that the immense creative forces still slumbering in him could be released only by a clean-cut break with the way of life that for nearly thirty years had been dear to him.

Chapter 7

SWEET LIBERTY

1790 — 1792

WHEN Haydn was writing his melancholy letters during the spring and summer of 1790 he could not have guessed how soon the dreary monotony of Eszterháza would become only a memory. In the autumn of that year things began to happen with a speed that he had never before experienced. Prince Nicholas, the beloved patron whom Haydn would never have been able to leave, died on September 28, 1790, thus bringing to an end the fundamental reason for his staying at Eszterháza. Fortunately for Haydn and for the history of music, Prince Anton, who succeeded Prince Nicholas, did not share his father's interests. He immediately dismissed all the musicians with the exception of Haydn, Tomasini, and a few instrumentalists who were to carry on the church services. Haydn's old patron and friend had bequeathed to him a yearly pension of a thousand florins, to which Prince Anton added four hundred florins, thus keeping the master nominally in his service but at the same time leaving him perfectly free to do whatever he wished. Haydn jumped at this opportunity and without making any further plans, rushed off to Vienna. Indeed, he was so anxious to get away from Eszterháza that he left behind most of his belongings. Hardly had he moved into an apartment in the house of his friend, Nepomuk Hamberger, when various offers were made to him. Prince Anton Grassalkovics, a son-in-law of Haydn's deceased patron and also a great lover of music, wanted him to come to his court at Pressburg. Such an offer naturally did not tempt Haydn, since it would have meant exactly the same kind of life he had been leading at Eszterháza. King Ferdinand IV of Naples, who had come to Vienna for the triple marriage of two of his daughters and a son to members of the Habsburg family, repeated with great urgency his former invitation. While Haydn was still weighing the pros and cons of this proposition, he was swept off his feet by the bearer of a third proposal. One day a stranger appeared in his room and introduced himself with the blunt words: "My name is Salomon. I have come from London to fetch you; we shall conclude our accord tomorrow." In fact, a detailed agreement was instantly worked out by Salomon. Haydn was to receive three hundred pounds for a new opera to be written for the impresario Gallini, the same sum for six new symphonies, two hundred pounds for the copyright of them, another two hundred for twenty new and smaller compositions to be performed by him at twenty concerts, and a guarantee of two hundred pounds for a benefit concert. On account of these twelve hundred pounds Salomon proposed to deposit five thousand florins with the Viennese bankers, Fries & Company.

Italy or England, which was it to be? Haydn was confronted by a crucial problem. For many years he had cherished the dream of traveling to the classical land of opera. Again and again he had suggested such a trip to his patron, always to be put off with some excuse or other. Now, however, when the decision rested entirely with himself, Italy seemed much less glamorous. His interest in composing operas had waned considerably—partly because of the supremacy of Mozart's masterpieces—and he felt keenly that instrumental music was his particular language. In this field, England with its large and excellently trained orchestras was definitely the leader. Moreover, as in the case of Prince Grassalkovics' offer, there was the question of personal freedom, which had become extremely vital for Haydn. At the court of a king he would again have to wait in antechambers, conform to strict etiquette, and, in short, be treated once more as an upper servant. So Haydn chose England, in spite of all the problems connected with such a venture. In a way, to go to England required more courage than a journey to Italy; it was, to a far greater extent, a step into the unknown. Haydn spoke and wrote Italian fluently and was used to working with Italian singers. But he did not know a word of English, and had no chance of becoming even slightly conversant in it before reaching that country. The journey itself was more complicated too, for it entailed the dreaded crossing of the Channel, which, even a hundred years later, deterred a less intrepid nature, that of Johannes Brahms, from accepting an honorary degree at

Cambridge. In Haydn's time, crossing the Channel was certainly no minor venture, even for people brought up near the sea. There was the tragicomic experience of Dr. Burney for instance. After leaving Calais on a stormy December day he had been "so nearly annihilated by his sufferings," that on arriving at Dover, he had not enough energy left to move. Some time later, when he came out of his torpor, he found himself, to his unspeakable horror, on the way back to France. Haydn may have heard stories of this kind. Even if he had not, his Viennese friends did not restrain themselves from pointing out all the dangers awaiting a man fifty-eight years old starting for the first time on a great journey. But all their Cassandra-like cries were in vain, for it was the very novelty of the prospective experiences that attracted Haydn. He was brimful of energy, in excellent health, and felt himself able to cope with any difficulty. So, when Mozart exclaimed: "Oh, Papa, you have had no education for the wide world, and you speak so few languages," Haydn answered serenely, "But my language is understood all over the world."

In his attitude Haydn was greatly sustained by Salomon who became Haydn's shadow in his anxiety not to lose this invaluable prize. They got on very well together, in Vienna as well as in London, so that at a much later date Haydn spoke of Salomon as "his dearest friend." It therefore seems appropriate to say a few words about the artist who played an important part in the history of music by taking Haydn to England.

Johann Peter Salomon was born in 1745 at Bonn, the birthplace of Beethoven and it is worthy of record that for some time the Salomons shared a house with the Beethoven family. In 1816, Beethoven wrote to Ferdinand Ries: "Salomon's death grieves me deeply, for he was a noble-minded man whom I remember well ever since I was a child." Salomon was an eminent violinist who filled various positions in Germany and then went to England in 1781 where he soon won success and a great reputation. A correspondent of the *Berliner Musikzeitung*,[1] after praising Viotti as the greatest living violinist in Europe, declared that Salomon almost equaled him as a virtuoso, although not as a composer. In 1786 Salomon began to give subscription concerts, competing with the older series of the Professional Concerts. He had been an ardent admirer of Haydn for a long time and it was for these concerts that he wanted to engage the master. It chanced

[1] (June 29, 1793).

that he was at Cologne, on his way to Italy, when he heard of Prince Nicholas Eszterházy's death and taking the next coach, he rushed to Vienna and carried Haydn off in triumph.

Despite Haydn's eagerness for the great adventure, it was by no means easy for him to tear himself away from Vienna where he was bound by many ties. There was Marianne von Genzinger, whom he had so greatly pined for at Eszterháza. How delightful it was now to go regularly to her lovely home, to have long and friendly chats, and to make music together! Haydn's sad feelings in leaving this cherished friend are expressed in his "Farewell Song" written for Marianne. The author of the words is not known, but it would seem not unlikely that Haydn had them written on his explicit instructions by some literary friend, possibly Hofrat Greiner. Such words as "now when we have just begun to know each other well we have to part" and "think of me when sea and land are between us," [2] are too pertinent to be found in the poem of a stranger. This little song so charged with tenderness and gentle melancholy must have touched Marianne deeply.

It was probably easier to leave Luigia Polzelli, for whom his passion had somewhat subsided during recent years. Luigia of course, had also lost her position at Eszterháza and moved to Vienna. Her husband was failing rapidly and died in a hospital a few months after Haydn's departure. She depended mainly on Haydn's financial support, and would have liked very much to go to England with the master, but this was out of the question for so mediocre a singer and Haydn much preferred to get engagements for her in Italy.

Finally there was the parting from his beloved Mozart. They spent the last day together, both deeply moved. When they said goodbye, Mozart exclaimed with tears: "I am afraid, Papa, this will be our last farewell." Little did either of the friends guess the terrible truth in these prophetic words!

On December 15, 1790 Haydn and Salomon set forth on their journey, which was made as rapidly as possible for the manager was anxious to start the preparations for his subscription series. Only two stops of any length were made, one at Munich, the other at Bonn where Haydn was received very charmingly by the elector (who

[2] *"Kaum dass man sich kennen soll, muss man auch schon wieder scheiden."*—*"Denke meiner, wenn . . . uns trennen Meer und Land . . ."*

apparently did not share his brother's [3] dislike for the master's music). On New Year's Eve the travelers arrived at Calais and Haydn, in a short note to Marianne, described himself as "very well, although somewhat thinner, owing to fatigue, irregular sleep, and eating and drinking so many different things." Appropriately enough, it was on New Year's Day that Haydn started his life in the British capital. The journey itself seems to have been but moderately unpleasant and unless Haydn was boasting to his friend, this old man, who had never seen the sea before, had stood on firmer sea legs than most of his fellow passengers. Anyway, this is how he described the great event to Marianne: [4]

I must now tell you that on New Year's Day, after attending early Mass, I went on board at 7:30 A.M., and at 5:00 in the afternoon arrived safe and well at Dover, for which Heaven be praised! During the first four hours there was scarcely any wind and the vessel made so little way that in that time we went only one English mile. Fortunately, toward 11:30 such a favorable breeze began to blow that by 4:00 o'clock we had come twenty-two miles. I remained on deck during the whole passage, in order to gaze my fill at that huge monster, the ocean. So long as there was a calm I had no fears, but when at length a violent wind began to blow, rising every minute, and I saw the boisterous waves rushing on, I was seized with slight alarm, and a little indisposition likewise. But I overcame it all and arrived safely in harbor without being actually sick. Most of the passengers were ill and looked like ghosts. I did not feel the fatigue of the journey until I arrived in London but it took two days before I could recover from it. But now I am quite fresh and well, and occupied in looking at this mighty and vast town of London, its various beauties and marvels causing me the most profound astonishment.

Haydn's "astonishment" can well be imagined. What his young friend, the Czech composer, Adalbert Gyrowetz, expressed in his autobiography (written in the third person) may also reflect the older master's attitude: "The first moment Gyrowetz stood on English soil, he felt as if he were seeing a new world. Everything was different: a different air, a different architecture, different regulations, different customs, the highest degree of cleanliness in everything, and quite different people." And Gyrowetz had traveled a great deal through Italy and France, whereas Haydn had never before been beyond a

[3] Emperor Joseph II.
[4] Letter of January 8, 1791.

small section of his own country, a territory corresponding in area approximately to the state of Connecticut!

It was not only the strangeness of English life that made Haydn's head whirl; it was rather the size of London and its enormous traffic. The figures relating to London's population interested him tremendously. We find twice in his diary [5] a remark that "in thirty-one years 38,000 houses had been built in London"; once he mentioned that in 1791, 22,000 persons died in London; another time he made a note that the city consumed annually 800,000 cartloads of coal. The size of London as compared to Vienna fascinated and at the same time frightened him. "The noise in the streets and the cries of the common people selling their wares" seemed "unbearable" to him. As to the traffic, we can well imagine what Haydn felt if we refer to a letter that Horace Walpole wrote in 1791 to Miss Berry:

> Though London increases every day, the town cannot hold all its inhabitants, so prodigiously is the population augmented. I have twice been going to stop my coach in Piccadilly, thinking there was a mob, but it was only nymphs and swains sauntering. The other morning I was stopped five times before I reached Northumberland House, for the tides of coaches, chariots, and phaetons are endless. Indeed, the town is so extended that the breed of chairs is almost lost, for Hercules and Atlas could not carry anybody from one end of this enormous capital to the other.

Added to these difficulties was the strange tongue. Perhaps the master was right in assuming that he, with his music, could make himself understood everywhere but it was another matter for him to understand others. This old man, with the soul of a youth, was filled with insatiable curiosity regarding all aspects of English life and he did not like being left out of anything at all. John Taylor in his *Records of My Life* describes a dinner party at the house of the singer, Madame Mara, which was attended by the satirist Dr. John Wolcot (Peter Pindar), and the violoncellist, John Crosdill,[6] and continues:

> Before the wine was removed, Mr. Salomon arrived and brought Haydn with him. They were both old friends of Madame Mara. Haydn did not know a word of English. As soon as we knew who he

[5] There exist three diaries from the English visits. Two, preserved by the National Library, Vienna, refer to his first stay; one, in the Mozarteum, Salzburg, refers to the second. There must have existed also a second notebook of the second visit, from which Griesinger brought excerpts, but it cannot be traced today.

[6] Crosdill was the violoncello teacher of the Prince of Wales.

was, Crosdill proposed that we should celebrate the arrival of Haydn with "three time three." This proposal was warmly adopted and commenced, all parties except Haydn standing up. He heard his name mentioned but not understanding this species of congratulation, stared at us in surprise. He was so confused by this unexpected and novel greeting that he put his hands before his face and was quite disconcerted for some minutes.

Incidents like that must have happened often enough. Haydn, of course, did his best to study English and in the "spring mornings," he used "to walk in the woods alone with his English grammar," [7] but still it was a continuous strain for him to follow and take part in the conversations of his new English friends.

The numerous old acquaintances that Haydn renewed in London were a great help. The British capital attracted artists and virtuosos from all corners of the earth. When Haydn visited there it was one of the most important centers of music although the British composers of the time could not compare with those of Vienna. Still, the most eminent musicians flocked to England, received great honors and excellent salaries, and helped to build up a musical life which, in volume at least, was quite dazzling. Many of these artists had been in Vienna and with these Haydn naturally established contact.

There was Adalbert Gyrowetz, whom Haydn had met years before at the private concerts of their common friend, Hofrat von Kees.[8] Gyrowetz had arrived in London two years before Haydn; he was a great success and moved freely in society. According to his autobiography, he helped Haydn greatly by introducing him to the right people.

Mention has already been made of Gertrude Elisabeth Mara, a singer of German origin who captivated London by the "irresistible fire, dignity, and tenderness of her vocal appeal" (Gardiner) at the Handel Festival of 1784. Madame Mara had been in Vienna in 1780, after escaping from Prussia, where King Frederick II had held her almost as a captive because of his enthusiasm for her art. Haydn admired her and was glad to have Salomon engage her for appearances at his own concerts.

[7] Letter to Marianne dated September 17, 1791.
[8] Gyrowetz describes his first meeting with various masters at the von Kees house as follows: "Haydn smiled a bit roguishly, Dittersdorf was serious, Albrechtsberger quite indifferent, Giornovichj somewhat somber though noblehearted, and Mozart the kindest of all."

The distinguished Croatian violinist, Giovanni Mane Giornovichj, who according to Dittersdorf, played "with art and heart," was also known to our master from his participation in the von Kees concerts.

One of the most successful pianists in London was Muzio Clementi. Haydn had probably met him in 1782 when Clementi came to Vienna for his contest with Mozart on the pianoforte and Clementi apparently was fond of Haydn for he presented him with a goblet made of cocoanut shell, adorned with rich silver ornaments.

Haydn also had friendly relations with the Czech pianist, Jan Ladislav Dussek, who lent him his own excellent piano when the master moved to a more rural apartment in Lisson Grove. In a charming letter to Dussek's father [9] Haydn described the son as "one of the most upright, moral, and, in music, most eminent of men."

Stephen and Nancy Storace were delighted to meet Haydn again for he had visited them and played chamber music at their home in Vienna. The master's diary, in mentioning a dinner with them on June 3, 1792, adds the obscure remark "sapienti pauca," which probably meant that the food offered was not too plentiful. Michael Kelly, the Irish tenor, had also returned to London from Vienna and was among the Storaces' circle of friends. He probably was not too great a creative musician—this is implied at least by Sheridan's remark that "Kelly composed his wines and imported his music"—but he was a pleasant companion and Haydn could chat with him about their various mutual friends in Vienna.

And of course there was the Cramer family from Mannheim, and although they belonged to the rival camp of the Professional Concerts, they were great admirers of the master and promptly established contact with him. The youngest son, John Baptist (composer of the well-known *Études*) became an especial favorite of Haydn.

Another man who, although not personally known to Haydn, had been corresponding with him for some time, was the great musicologist, Dr. Charles Burney. He welcomed the master with an enthusiastic poem and one of Haydn's first visits was to Chelsea College where the English scholar held the post of organist.

Such was the circle of fellow musicians who gathered around Haydn, a circle that was to be greatly widened during the following eighteen months. And there was always Salomon, who helped Haydn get a footing in the strange and fascinating new world into which he had been plunged.

[9] Letter of February 26, 1792.

To find one's way through the intricacies of London's musical life, with all its different currents and undercurrents, was indeed not easy and Haydn needed Salomon's guidance. A preview which appeared on December 30, 1790, in the *Morning Chronicle* may help us to get some idea of the number of musical events in the British capital:

> The musical arrangements now being made promise a most harmonious winter. Besides two rival opera houses, a Concert [meaning a whole series] is planned under the auspices of Haydn, whose name is a tower of strength, and to whom the amateurs of instrumental music look as the god of the science. Of this concert Salomon is to be the leader and Madame Mara the principal singer.
>
> The Professional Concerts under the able conducting of Cramer, are to be reinforced by Mrs. Billington, assisted occasionally by Mr. and Mrs. Harrison.
>
> The Ancient Concerts under the patronage of their Majesties will continue soon after the queen's birthday, with Cramer as their leader and Storace as the principal singer. The Ladies' Subscription Concerts are to be continued as usual on Sunday evenings by permission (we hope) of his Grace the Archbishop of Canterbury.
>
> There will be oratorios twice a week at the theaters of Drury Lane and Covent Garden during Lent.
>
> These, with the Academy of Ancient Music will constitute the principal public musical entertainments of this winter.

Five different subscription series of orchestral concerts! An amazing quantity of music to be offered to a city of less than a million inhabitants. And all this was eagerly absorbed. Most of the concerts were crowded; thus, on the very day when Haydn's sensational first concert took place, oratorio performances in the two theaters also had very full houses. Present-day historians might find the artistic standard of the London audiences of 1791 not high enough—Marion Scott, for instance, in her delightful study "Haydn in England" [10] warns us against mistaking quantity for quality. Anyway, it cannot be denied that the Londoners of Haydn's time loved music very much and that it was natural for them to hear a good deal of it and, if we may believe Gyrowetz,[11] also to perform it. To be sure, the element of competition played some little part in rousing the public's interest

[10] *Musical Quarterly* (1932).
[11] He writes in his autobiography: "The girls are mostly musical and either well versed in the pianoforte or in singing, and know how to spend their evenings very pleasantly in this way. The men, however, are slightly or not at all musical, but they love to listen to music."

in the various concerts. There was, for instance, a fierce rivalry between the English and the Italian opera (Covent Garden versus the Pantheon), between the Professional Concerts and the Salomon series, rivalries in which the press took a very active part. But this was a common occurrence in the eighteenth century and London certainly took such matters no more passionately than Paris did. Leaving aside those snobs who went to the concerts only for the sake of fashion or faction, there remained enough sincere music lovers to give Haydn the satisfaction of being truly valued and understood.

Returning to that memorable New Year's Day, 1791, when Haydn set foot on English soil, we find the master spending his first night at 45 High Holborn, the home of John Bland, owner of the Razor Quartet. Haydn's host received him with open arms and good pea soup (which meant much to our master for in a letter to Marianne he pined for her delicious soups). Mrs. Bland may have somewhat disconcerted this lover of female beauty at first sight for she was "short and fat, pitted with smallpox and on the whole the most inharmonious-looking person that can be imagined." [12] Later, however, Haydn was to share the general verdict that "when she sang, she threw a charm and magic on all she did that was perfectly entrancing."

The next day Haydn moved to a "neat, comfortable, though very dear" lodging provided by Salomon in the house where he lived himself (18 Great Pulteney Street, Golden Square). The Italian landlord was an excellent cook and Haydn would have liked to enjoy the meals he offered in the sole company of Salomon, so as gradually to get his bearings. This was not to be, however, for Salomon had paved the way for Haydn extremely well. The newspapers made much of his arrival; the Austrian and Neapolitan ambassadors called, and when Haydn wrote to Marianne on January 8th, he confessed that he had "already dined out six times" in this first week and that he could be invited every day if he chose.

Besides making social contacts Haydn was anxious to get a true impression of English musical life. He attended various concerts, at which great honors were bestowed on the illustrious guest, and the impressions he received from the size and quality of the English orchestras were responsible for various alterations he made in the works he had brought with him.

[12] See Henry Phillips, *Musical and Personal Recollections* (London: 1864).

Eighteen days after his arrival he made his real debut in society. He was invited to the court ball given in honor of the queen's birthday and to the amazement of the guests was greeted very respectfully by the Prince of Wales, although he had not yet been presented at court. Haydn was very favorably impressed by this "handsomest man on God's earth" as he described him to Marianne.[13] Indeed, the appearance of the future George IV must have been dazzling even to one used to Prince Eszterházy's splendor, for on this occasion he wore diamonds worth some eighty thousand pounds. The next day Haydn's interest in the prince was further heightened, for when he was invited to take part in one of the famous musical evenings at Carlton House, the residence of the prince, he found that his host possessed "an extraordinary love of music and a great deal of feeling." [14] The chamber music, played by Haydn, Salomon, Giornovichj, and sung by the Italian tenor, Davide, took place in the small music room, the "jewel" of Carlton House. Again Haydn's impressions may best be expressed in the words of Horace Walpole: "In all the fairy tales you never were in so pretty a scene. Madam, I forgot to tell you, how admirably all the carving, stucco, and ornaments are executed, but whence the money is to come, I conceive not—all the tin mines in Cornwall would not pay a quarter."

The prince's gigantic debts were known even to Haydn. He mentioned the fact to Marianne, adding anxiously: *"Nota bene,* this is *entre nous."* He need not have worried on this account, as the prince's financial problems were a common topic of conversation. But although his Royal Highness was generally considered to be "above a low attention to pecuniary matters" [15] Haydn was one of the very few musicians rewarded adequately by the prince. On his return to Vienna, he sent a bill for one hundred guineas as the honorarium for twenty-six appearances at Carlton House and obtained prompt payment.

Haydn, by the way, seems also to have enjoyed the fare offered by his royal host. Anyway, he took pains to note in his diary the recipe of the Prince of Wales's punch as follows: "one bottle champagne,

[13] Letter dated December 20, 1791.
[14] The following story mentioned by Pohl proves the prince's musical aptitude. When he was three years old, he heard the violinist, F. H. Barthélémon, and was so impressed by the "harmonics" the artist produced that he exclaimed: "There must be a flute hidden in the violin," and eagerly tried to find its hiding place.
[15] Letter of Elizabeth Montagu, the "Queen of the Bluestockings" dated June 4, 1795.

one bottle burgundy, one bottle rum, ten lemons, two oranges, a pound-and-a-half of sugar."

While the master was starting on an extremely successful social career under the auspices of the Prince of Wales, he was at first prevented from appearing in public in his real capacity. Salomon, though most anxious to open his concert series at the earliest possible moment, found himself unable to carry out his intention. For the first concert he had engaged the singer, Giacomo Davide, the "first tenor of his time," as Lord Mount Edgcumbe described him. Signor Davide, however, was under contract to make his first public appearance in the Italian opera at King's Theater and since (for reasons to be mentioned later) that performance could not take place, Salomon was twice forced to postpone his concert. This was most fortunate for the rival enterprise, the Professional Concerts, which started on February 7th. Considerately a symphony and a quartet by Haydn were performed and the composer received a free ticket of admission to all the concerts. Haydn went and declared that he had never heard a symphony of his played so well. In spite of this exchange of courtesies, Salomon's rivals were not above circulating rumors injurious to the visiting composer. Remarks could be overheard or read in certain newspapers that Haydn, although undoubtedly a great composer, was after all, an old man whose powers were exhausted and who was bound to disappoint the high expectations of British friends of music. Haydn could not help being aware of such undercurrents. He tried not to let them discourage him and with characteristic persistence, used the extra time to rehearse most carefully, playing important passages to the orchestra on the violin and gradually imbuing them with a perfect understanding of his ideas and wishes.

Finally when the great day came he swept the London audience completely off its feet. The concert took place on March 11th at the famous Hanover Square rooms, the scene of so many great events in music. Opened in 1775 by Johann Christian Bach, they were destined, after Haydn's triumphs, to witness the spectacular appearances of Liszt, Rubinstein, Mendelssohn, Joachim, and many others. Haydn's audience was a very brilliant one: the ladies all in hoops, the gentlemen in full dress with swords, the solo performers preceded by the sword-bearer who girded them in front of the audience with a special weapon. The artists Salomon had engaged were of the first class and earned much applause. The climax was reached with Haydn's new symphony in D major (No. 93). At the special request of the composer it was played as the first number of the second part, Haydn hoping that by this time the many latecomers would be in their seats. The orchestra was much stronger than the Eszterházy ensemble. It contained some forty players including sixteen violins, four violas, three violoncellos, and four double basses. Salomon was the leader, playing on a Stradivarius instrument that had previously belonged to Corelli, and Haydn conducted from the harpsichord. Dr. Burney, attended the concert and described the reaction of the public in the strongest words he could think of, speaking of Haydn's "electrical effect on all present" and of "such a degree of enthusiasm as almost amounted to frenzy." The adagio of the symphony had to be encored and this made Haydn so proud that he asked Griesinger to make a note of this "unusual occurrence" for his biography. March 11th definitely assured Haydn's success in English musical life, and it is significant that the *Morning Chronicle* ended its report with the words: "We cannot suppress our very anxious hope that the first musical genius of the age may be induced by our liberal welcome to take up his residence in England."

The succeeding concerts of the series, taking place from March to June, were a continuous triumph; the peak was reached with Haydn's benefit concert on May 16th when he earned three hundred and fifty pounds, almost double what had been guaranteed to him.

The brilliant success won in the Salomon concerts had far-reaching consequences. It increased Haydn's confidence in himself enormously. He had, of course, before his journey to London, received numerous proofs of his outstanding reputation in various countries. Still, it is one thing to read an enthusiastic letter and another to experience directly the response of a huge and brilliant audience. This was a novel sensation for the master, used to performing his works mostly to a very small and intimate circle of musical connoisseurs. The frenzied applause he was given by the exacting audience of the world's largest capital did not go to his head; it was only a challenge for him to offer London the very best he could give. Haydn's creative powers were taxed to the utmost, and the result took the form of the twelve London Symphonies (six of them written for his first stay in London, six for his second) in which Haydn's music for orchestra attained its very climax. For these masterworks the musical world has to thank London; it is indeed doubtful whether Haydn's genius would ever have unfolded so brilliantly without the stimulus of his English adventures.

On the other hand, Haydn's presence in London gave British music an inspiration and impetus of the greatest value which ultimately reached far beyond the frontiers of Great Britain. Musicians who had the privilege of playing under him, or at least, of becoming acquainted with the master's interpretation of his own works, traveled from London to the New World taking with them an insight of how Haydn's works should be performed. There is a direct line from Haydn to some of the pioneers of American musical life, such as Graupner, Menel, Hewitt, and Bergmann.

Haydn's triumph was crowned, so to speak, at the instigation of the faithful Dr. Burney, when he was invited in July, 1791 to the Oxford Commemoration in order to receive the honorary degree of Doctor of Music. Unlike Handel or Brahms, who received a similar invitation from Cambridge, Haydn went and was immensely fêted. Three concerts took place on this occasion with brilliant soloists, among them "little Clement" for whom Beethoven was to write his violin concerto. As a thesis Haydn was obliged to offer an older symphony because he arrived too late to rehearse with the orchestra the new work he had brought. The symphony in G major (No. 92) composed in 1788 was chosen, and this was henceforth named the Oxford Symphony. Later Haydn sent the university as his "exercise" a three-part canon cancrizans, "Thy Voice, O Harmony." Haydn felt strange in his Doctor's gown of cherry and cream-colored silk, which he had to wear for three days, but neither was he above a bit of naïve pride. "I only wish my Viennese friends could have seen me," he wrote to Marianne. In his diary he commented on the event in these words only: "I had to pay one-and-a-half guineas for the bell peals at Oxforth (sic!) when I received the Doctor's degree, and half a guinea for [hiring] the gown. The journey cost six guineas." This matter-of-fact statement is not surprising, as Haydn never expressed any personal feelings in his notebook but confined himself to jotting down mere facts. A letter to Marianne on the event mentioned by Haydn apparently did not reach her. To his biographer, Dies, however, Haydn stressed the importance of the degree, to which he owed, as he declared, "much, I might say everything, in England; for thanks to it I met the first men and was admitted to the most important houses." Although this seems to be somewhat exaggerated, it is certain that the man, who still remembered so well how he had striven desperately as a penniless youth to instruct himself in all that Reutter failed to teach him, felt satisfaction in signing his letters with the words "Doctor zu Oxford." After being acclaimed as a fellow scholar by one of the oldest universities of the world, it was easy for Haydn to disregard those critics in the German-speaking countries who had found his music too light and not learned enough.

Strangely, there is no comment in Haydn's notebook on the exquisite buildings of Oxford. Perhaps he was too much occupied with rehearsals and social functions to take in all the beauty around him. That he observed such things when traveling in a more leisurely way, is shown by his account of Cambridge, which he visited in November of the same year:

> Each university has at the back of it a very roomy and beautiful garden, besides stone bridges, in order to afford passage over the stream which winds past. King's College Chapel is famous for its carvings. It is all stone and so delicate that nothing more beautiful could have been made of wood. It has already endured four hundred years, yet everybody judges its age at about ten years because of the firmness and peculiar whiteness of the stone.

At this time, when Haydn was reaping the greatest triumphs as a symphonic composer, his efforts in the domain of opera were doomed to failure. According to his contract with Sir John Gallini, he worked during the first part of his stay in London on the opera *L'anima del filosofo*, based on a book by Badini. He had completed the work (having written one hundred and ten pages, which is hardly less than the scores of all the first six London Symphonies) when it turned out that Gallini was unable to perform the opera, for reasons beyond his control. The old Italian opera at the Pantheon was supported by the king and the management exerted all its influence to prevent a second Italian opera from being established in the King's Theater. Although the Prince of Wales espoused Gallini's cause, the Pantheon's adherents pointed out that two Italian opera houses were not needed. Haydn's opera was to be performed in May but after long controversies Gallini was refused a license for opera altogether. When Haydn was conducting the first rehearsal, officials appeared and forced him to stop after forty bars had been played. Gallini had to be content with arranging entertainments of music and dancing, using the soloists he had engaged and frequently Haydn's music, such as the chorus "The Storm" (on words by Peter Pindar, pseudonym for John Wolcot). There was now no opportunity for a performance of *L'anima del filosofo;* nevertheless Gallini paid the agreed sum for the composition. The master naturally regretted having spent so much time on this work, but it seems that he was not specially interested in it, for he never had it performed elsewhere. As for Gallini, who had paid three hundred pounds without being able to produce the opera, no pity need be wasted on him, for in spite of various accidents during his career as a manager, he left the tidy sum of £150,000.

Although Haydn's creative output in the field of opera came to an abrupt end in England, it was in this country that he received the incentive to enter a new field. Here again, we have to thank London for a most decisive influence on Haydn's work.

In 1784 a Handel Commemoration on a gigantic scale took place in Westminster Abbey, celebrating the centenary of that master's birth. Its success was so great that similar performances were arranged in the three succeeding years. Then there followed an interval of four years, after which a Handel Festival of the same kind took place in May, 1791, with Haydn among the enraptured audience. William Gardiner gives a lively description of the scene:

> On entering the Abbey I was filled with surprise at the magnitude of the orchestra; it rose nearly to the top of the west window and above the arches of the main aisle. On each side there was a tier of projecting galleries and I was placed in one of these. Above us were the trumpeters and appended to their instruments were richly embossed banners worked in silver and gold. We had flags of the same description which gave the whole a gorgeous and magnificent appearance. The arrangement of the performers was admirable, particularly that of the sopranos. The young ladies were placed upon a framework in the center of the band in the form of a pyramid, as you see flowerpots set up for a show. This greatly improved the musical effect. The band was a thousand strong, ably conducted by Joah Bates upon the organ. The orchestra was so steep that it was dangerous to come down and some accidents occurred, one being of a ludicrous nature. A person falling upon a double bass, as it lay on its side, immediately disappeared; nothing was seen of him but his legs protruding out of the instrument. For some time no one could assist him for laughing. Haydn was present at this performance and

with the aid of a telescope, which had been placed on a stand near the kettledrums, I saw the composer near the king's box. The performance attracted persons from all parts of Europe and the demand for tickets was so great that in some instances a single one was sold for twenty pounds.

The female fashions of the day were found highly inconvenient, particularly the headdresses, and it was ordered that no caps should be admitted of a larger size than the pattern exhibited at the Lord Chamberlain's office. As everyone wore powder, notwithstanding a vast influx of hairdressers from the country, such was the demand for these artists, that many ladies submitted to have their hair dressed the previous evening and sat up all night to be ready for the early admission in the morning.

We do not know how familiar Haydn was with Handel's oratorios before he came to England, but certainly he had never heard anything like the performance in Westminster Abbey. Although Hadow contends that the number of 1,068 performers frequently mentioned is exaggerated, it still must have been gigantic. Listening to the immortal masterworks performed by the enormous musical body in one of the loveliest churches of the world, feeling the veneration with which Handel's music was received "in a silence almost devotional" (Mount Edgcumbe) by an audience taught by their king to see in this music the most sublime achievement, Haydn was so deeply moved that at the "Hallelujah" chorus he burst into tears, exclaiming: "He is the master of us all." He was tremendously impressed at finding Handel's oratorios still so alive in the hearts of the English people and he may have conceived at that time the plan of trying his hand at an oratorio.

There was another occasion in the following year when Haydn was again deeply stirred by great choral masses. This time he wrote in his diary: "No music has ever moved me so much in my life," which is the only emotional utterance in the entire notebook. Haydn referred here to the annual meeting of the charity children at St. Paul's Cathedral, when he heard four thousand children sing a hymn by the organist of the cathedral, John Jones. (Haydn's profound emotion was shared, many years later, by Hector Berlioz and his companion, the tenor, Gilbert Duprez, who "wept and raved.")

Truly, England had revealed to Haydn what the human voice in great numbers can accomplish. The consequences of such experiences were to manifest themselves later when he had regained firm ground under his feet. At the moment he was unable to start on any new experiment in composition, for he was too much absorbed by the various aspects of the fascinating new country which he was determined to explore as fully as he possibly could. Through the summer and autumn, when concert activities had ceased, he traveled and visited and had a wonderful time. This does not mean that he stopped working, for he had to prepare for the next season, but that he was free to go wherever he pleased without asking anybody's permission and to indulge in any passing whim. In a way it was the first vacation for this man of fifty-nine. The following outburst in a letter [16] to Marianne is characteristic: "Oh, my dear good lady, how sweet is some degree of liberty! I had a kind prince, but was obliged at times to be dependent on base souls. I often sighed for release and now I have it in some measure. I am quite sensible of this benefit, though my mind is burdened with more work. The consciousness of being no longer a bond servant sweetens all my toil."

Some of the visits Haydn paid at this time are mentioned in his diary. For instance we find the following entry: "In the month of August I journeyed at noon in an East India merchantman with six cannon. I was gloriously entertained. In this month, too, I went with Mr. Fraser on the Thames from Westminster Bridge to Richmond, where we had dinner on an island. We were twenty-four persons and a band of music." (How Haydn, with his deep love of nature, must have enjoyed the picnic in such a beautiful spot!)

For five weeks he was "very well entertained" in the house of the rich banker, Mr. Brassey, teaching his daughter at the same time. His hosts, with typical English tact, left him alone as much as he chose and Haydn describes his life to Marianne in these words: "I have been residing in the country, with a banker, whose heart and family resemble the Genzingers' [what higher compliment could he pay to the Brasseys?], and where I live as if I were in a monastery." After the noise of London, which caused our master much suffering, the quiet and peace of the English country must have done him a great deal of good. Unfortunately a letter from his patron caused him some worry. Prince Eszterházy complained of his long absence, and exacted, as Haydn described it, "his speedy return in the most absolute terms" because he wanted him to compose an opera for a fête

[16] Letter of September 17, 1791.

planned in honor of the emperor. Haydn could not comply with the
request because he had already concluded a contract with Salomon
for the coming season. He had to inform the prince accordingly,
which was not easy for a man used to obeying every demand coming
from an Eszterházy, and he expected his dismissal and the cancella-
tion of his pension. None of this happened, however, as even an un-
musical Eszterházy, like Prince Anton, was too conscious of the
renown that his connection with the world-famous composer gave
him to desire to sever it.

In September Haydn again took up his residence in London but, as
during the months before the New Year concert life was almost stag-
nant, he frequently interrupted his work to make visits and trips to
the country, or to attend important official functions. The diary
devotes a long description to the dinner of the new Lord Mayor on
November 5th which Haydn attended, sitting at the second table
with Mr. Silvester, the "greatest lawyer and first alderman of London." Haydn was naturally interested in the music played on this
occasion, and his comments are none too flattering, though quite
amusing. Mentioning the small hall where he first watched the dancing, he wrote:

> Nothing but minuets are danced in this room; but I could not stay
> longer than a quarter of an hour. First, because of the heat caused
> by so many people being crowded into so small a room; secondly,
> because of the wretched dance music, two violins and one violoncello
> composing the whole orchestra. The minuets were more Polish than
> German or Italian. Then I went into another room that looked more
> like a subterranean cave. There the dance was English and the music
> was a little better because there was a drum that drowned the blun-
> ders of the fiddlers. I went on to the great hall where we had dined;
> here the music was more tolerable. The dance was English but only
> on the elevated platform where the Lord Mayor and the first four
> members had dined. The other tables were all newly surrounded by
> men who, as usual, drank right lustily all night long. The most singu-
> lar thing of all, however, was the fact that a part of the company
> danced on without hearing a note of the music, for first at one table,
> then at another, some were howling songs and some drinking toasts
> amidst the maddest shrieks of Hurrah! Hurrah! and the swinging of
> glasses.

Very different is the description of the three days during which
Haydn stayed at Oatlands, the castle where the Duke of York was

spending his honeymoon. The bride of seventeen was a daughter of the music-loving King Frederick William II of Prussia (whose beautiful ring Haydn valued so much). It gave her the greatest pleasure to meet the composer whose music she knew quite well and Haydn was received in the most gracious way by the young couple as well as by the Prince of Wales, who was responsible for the invitation. He wrote about it to Marianne: [17]

> The duchess is the most charming lady in the world, possesses much intelligence, plays the piano, and sings very pleasingly. She remained beside me from ten o'clock at night, when the music began, until two hours after midnight. No compositions were played but Haydn's. I directed the symphonies at the piano. The sweet little lady sat close beside me at my left hand and hummed all the pieces from memory, having heard them often in Berlin. The Prince of Wales sat on my right and accompanied me very tolerably on the violoncello. They made me sing too. The Prince of Wales is having me painted just now [18] and the portrait is to be hung in his private sitting room.

The same month Haydn visited Sir Patrick Blake at Langham, but in spite of having traveled a hundred miles, he left after three days to attend the performance of Shield's comic opera *The Woodman* at Covent Garden. The magnet that drew him was the celebrated singer, Mrs. Billington, whom Kelly described as "an angel of beauty and the St. Cecilia of song." These words faithfully reflect the verdict of the majority of Londoners, at least of the male sex. In point of fact, Sir Joshua Reynolds painted Elisabeth Billington as the saintly musician. Haydn, according to the report of Carpani, visited the artist while he was working on the picture and pointed out that a strange mistake had been made. "You have painted her listening to the angels, but you should have represented the angels listening to her." Although the story in this form is inaccurate, as the portrait was painted in 1790 before Haydn arrived in England, it is not unlikely that our master made the remark when seeing the completed picture. Nice compliments like that were what endeared Haydn to the ladies. When a scandalous book, the so-called *Memoirs of Mrs. Billington* appeared, his diary commented indignantly on the "shameless exposure" and continued: "It is said that her character is far from faultless, but

[17] Letter of December 20, 1791.
[18] Haydn's portrait by John Hoppner is now in the collection of Buckingham Palace.

nevertheless, she is a great genius, and all the women hate her because she is so beautiful."

Haydn's caustic report on the performance itself is rather interesting:

> She [Mrs. Billington] sang timidly this evening, but very well. The first tenor has a good voice and a fairly good style but he uses the falsetto to excess. He sang a trill on high C and ran up to G. The second tenor tried to imitate him but could not master the change from the natural voice to the falsetto; besides he is very unmusical. He creates a new tempo, now three-quarter then two-quarter, and cuts his phrases wherever he pleases. But the orchestra is used to him. The common herd in the galleries, as is the case in all theaters, is very impertinent and the performers are obliged to give encores according to its noisy wishes. The parterre and all the boxes frequently have to applaud a great deal to secure a repetition but they succeeded this evening with the duet in the third act, which is very beautiful. The dispute lasted nearly a quarter of an hour before the parterre and boxes triumphed and the duet was repeated. The two performers stood in a fright on the stage, now retiring, now again coming to the front. The orchestra is sluggish.

Haydn's admiration for Reynolds's St. Cecilia by no means made him less sensitive to other beautiful women. Among the music that the master took back from England was a song which he commented upon: "This song is by Mrs. Hodges, the loveliest woman I ever saw in my life, and a great pianoforte player." Again, when Haydn visited his great admirer, Mr. Shaw, in December, 1791 he found his hostess to be the most beautiful woman he ever saw. How pleased he must have been when he noticed that this attractive lady had prepared a special homage for him. She, her daughters, and all the ladies present "wore on their headdresses a pearl-colored band embroidered in gold with the name of Haydn, while Mr. Shaw wore the name worked on the ends of his collar in the finest steel beads." (Diary.) One can well imagine how Haydn basked in this atmosphere of beauty and admiration and how he repaid it in his particular way. Perhaps he sat down at the pianoforte and sang gay songs to them, with the humor that English people could appreciate so well.[19]

There were certainly quite a few of such innocent friendships with

---

[19] According to Gyrowetz, it was this singing that made Haydn so popular with his English hosts.

beautiful women, but they did not prevent the inflammable **master** from enjoying a more significant romance as well. This time the story can be followed only in the letters of the lady. Haydn copied them faithfully into his notebook and what happened to the originals is not known, but it may be that the lady wanted them returned to her when Haydn left England. None of the master's answers have been traced, nor is there any mention of the affair in his diary, except for a note of the lady's address. Many years later, Haydn showed the letters to Dies and remarked: "They are letters from an English widow in London who loved me. Though sixty years old, she was still lovely and amiable and in all likelihood I should have married her if I had been single." There must be an error in this statement, made by either Dies or Haydn, whose memory at that time was not as good as it had been. Haydn, indeed, was sixty when he became attached to the widow, but his partner was certainly considerably younger. She was a Mrs. Schroeter, the widow of Johann Samuel Schroeter, who had been music master to the queen and the first exponent of skilled pianoforte playing in England. Dr. Burney, mentioning the musician Schroeter in *Rees's Cyclopedia*, described his wife as "a young lady of considerable fortune." As Schroeter was only thirty-eight when he died in 1788, his wife would have been eighteen years his senior to conform to Dies's description and certainly not "a young lady" when she married him. It seems more likely that the amiable English widow was about the same age as Marianne von Genzinger. Both ladies had in common a great love of music, and while Marianne arranged Haydn's works for the piano, Mrs. Schroeter did copying for the composer. Here the similarity ends, however, for the English widow did not show any of Marianne's reserve. There is preserved, for instance, the following love letter, copied in the original spelling from Haydn's diary:

My Dear:

   Enclosed I send you the verses you was so kind as to lend me, and am very much obliged to you for permitting me to take a copy of them. Pray informe me how you do, and let me know my Dear Love: when you will dine with me. I shall be happy to see you to dinner either to morrow or Tuesday whichever is most convenient to you. I am truly anxious and impatient to see you and I wish to have as much of your company as possible: indeed my Dear Haydn I feel

for you the fondest and tenderest affection the human heart is capable
of, and I ever am with the firmest attachment my Dear Love
most Sincerely, Faithfully and most affectionately

Yours

Sunday Evening June 10. 1792

After the last Salomon concert, Mrs. Schroeter wrote:

My Dear:

I can not close my eyes to sleep till I have returned you ten thousand thanks for the inexpressible delight I have received from your
ever Enchanting compositions and your incomparably charming performance of them. Be assured my Dear Haydn: That among all your
numerous admirers no one has listened with more profound attention, and no one can have such high veneration for your most brilliant talents as I have. Indeed my Dear Love no tongue can express
the gratitude I feel for the infinite pleasure your Music has given me:
accept then my repeeted thanks for it; and let me also assure you,
with heartfelt affection, that I shall ever consider the happiness of
your acquaintance as one of the chief Blessings of my life, and it is
the Sincere wish of my heart to preserve to cultivate and to merit it
more and more. I hope to hear you are quite well, shall be happy to
see you to dinner and if you can come at three o'clock it would give
me great pleasure, as I should be particularly glad to see you my
Dear before the rest of our friends come. God bless you my Dear:
I ever am with the firmest and most perfect attachment

Yours

Wednesday night June 6th 792

Mrs. Schroeter liked to mother the master a little. She was always
inquiring about his sleep and his health, and on April 19, 1792 she
wrote: "I am told you was five hours at your Study's yesterday; indeed
my D.L. I am afraid it will hurt you. . . . I almost tremble for your
health. Let me prevail on you my muchloved Haydn not to keep to
your study's so long at one time. My dear love if you could know how
very precious your welfare is to me. I flatter myself you wou'd endeavor to preserve it, for my Sake as well as your own."
This sounds as if the lady were pretty sure of Haydn's affection,
and indeed there is no reason to assume that the master did not

respond to the lovely widow's feelings. According to the letters, Haydn must have been a fairly frequent visitor at No. 6 James Street, Buckingham Gate, and the music lessons that first took him there were probably soon considered unimportant.

During the time that Haydn was living through this delightful romance, he regularly exchanged letters with his old love, Luigia Polzelli. Parts of them have already been quoted and it cannot be denied that they are ardent in tone. Luigia was at that time in Italy and was very anxious to go to London where her sister was living. This of course was the last thing that Haydn wanted, for both personal and professional reasons. It seems probable that in order to dissuade her and at the same time extinguish her innate (and probably well-founded) jealousy, Haydn expressed more passion than he really felt. He sent her money in answer to her requests and gladly declared himself willing to have her elder son, Pietro, join him in London.

Evidently the situation was emotionally none too easy for Haydn and it was further aggravated by sundry venomous letters from his wife, for apparently she also had got wind of Haydn's recent successes with the fair sex. In a letter to Luigia Haydn reacted with these strong words: "My wife, that infernal beast, wrote me so many things that I was forced to answer that I was never coming back. To this letter she paid attention." [20]

Although there were enough entanglements of the heart to disturb Haydn during the second part of his sojourn in London, they were still of minor importance compared to the strain that he labored under at that time in his artistic career. The Professional Concerts twice sent a deputation to the master with the object of inducing him by the offer of a much higher salary to go over to their camp. When they found that nothing could shake Haydn's determination to keep his word to the man who had brought him to England, they changed their tactics. Rumors began again to circulate against Haydn, to such an extent that they reached even the ears of such good Viennese friends as Hofrat von Kees and Marianne von Genzinger. Finally the bomb exploded; the English public was informed that, in view of Haydn's advanced age and inability to create important new music, the Professional Concerts had had the good fortune to engage his young pupil, the outstanding composer, Ignaz Pleyel. Musical London was tremendously stirred by this news and

[20] Letter of January 14, 1792.

violent partisanships were formed. All drawing rooms rang with
heated discussions as to who was the better composer, Haydn or
Pleyel. Today it is not easy to envisage the "murderous harmonious
war" (Haydn) between the two composers in the right light. No one
plays music by Pleyel, whom we know only as the founder of a celebrated pianoforte factory, an improver of the mechanism of the harp,
and as the first publisher to produce a complete edition of Haydn's
quartets. In the eighteenth century, on the other hand, many people
valued Pleyel's compositions very highly, especially when the composer was young. Even Mozart wrote about Pleyel's first quartets
that "They are very well written and very agreeable. It will be a
happy thing for music if, when the time arrives, Pleyel should replace
Haydn for us." [21] One cannot therefore blame the London public
too much for taking the contest between Haydn and Pleyel seriously
and awaiting the outcome with eager anticipation. What satisfied
the English sense of "fair play" was that Haydn and Pleyel remained
personally on the best of terms. The day after Pleyel's arrival they
dined together; they spent New Year's Eve in each other's company;
they attended each other's concerts, and Pleyel, according to Haydn,
displayed so much modesty that he gained his teacher's goodwill
anew. But in spite of this pleasant personal relationship between the
two contestants, which Haydn, world-wise and shrewd as he was,
would have kept up under any circumstances, the old master must
have felt deeply hurt by the whole matter. Even if Pleyel, who perhaps had come to London unaware of the implications of his engagement, were not to blame, it was an insult to consider the young
musician worthy of entering into competition with Joseph Haydn;
an insult of which Haydn was fully aware, although he rarely showed
it. For instance there is the story told by John Taylor of a dinner with
Haydn, Salomon, and Dr. Wolcot. The latter was tactless enough to
praise Pleyel's "genius" in the most enthusiastic terms. Haydn, at
first, graciously agreed. Finally the doctor's rapture was too much
for him and he remarked "with considerable warmth" : "But I hope
it will be remembered that he was my pupil." And once he wrote
to Marianne: "Pleyel's presumption is criticized everywhere."

Pleyel had one advantage; he was an unusually prolific composer.
As Haydn informed Marianne: "He brought with him a number of
new compositions, which were, however, written long ago! He ac-

[21] Letter to his father dated April 24, 1784.

cordingly promised to produce a new work every evening. On seeing this, I could easily perceive that there was a dead set against me, so I also announced publicly that I would likewise give twelve different new pieces. In order to keep my promise and to support poor Salomon, I must be the victim and work perpetually. I do feel it, however, very much. My eyes suffer most, and my nights are very sleepless." [22] And in another letter he exclaimed: "Never in my life have I written so much in one year as during the last, and it has indeed utterly exhausted me." [23] There are more complaints about being quite worn out with fatigue. The amazing thing is that nothing of this weariness can be felt in the works Haydn wrote under this strain, the Surprise Symphony being one of them.

The London audience, in spite of the preceding venomous campaign against the composer, could not help being completely overwhelmed by these works. In the concert of February 27th two movements of the symphony in D (No. 96) were encored, and the *Morning Chronicle* declared: "The concert was exceedingly spirited, and was distinguished above all common competition by the overture of the matchless Haydn." In the fourth concert again two movements (of symphony No. 98) had to be repeated. The music lasted until midnight and the *Morning Advertiser* reported that "Haydn shone with more than his usual luster." On the sixth evening the enthusiasm of the Londoners reached a climax when the Surprise Symphony had its first rendering. And so it went on, a series of triumphs for Haydn. On April 24th he wrote to Marianne: "In spite of the great opposition of my musical enemies, who are so bitter against me, more especially leaving nothing undone with my pupil Pleyel this winter to humble me, still, thank God! I may say that I have kept the upper hand." When the twelve concerts for which he had contracted were over (one day before the tenth, the indefatigable master had conducted his own most successful benefit concert), Salomon went on to add a thirteenth on June 6th and finished the season, according to the *Morning Herald,* with the "greatest éclat."

Fourteen important concerts consisting to a great extent of Haydn's own compositions seem a pretty big program for one season, but by no means did they cover all his appearances in public. He conducted Salomon's benefit concert and those for his "brother in af-

[22] Letter of March 2, 1792.
[23] Letter of January 17, 1792.

fection," the violinist, Barthélémon; for the pianist, Haessler; for Madame Mara; for the vocalists, the sisters Abrams, and many others. His creative activity was not confined to the music for the Salomon concerts and the opera. Other new works owed their origin to friendships that Haydn made in London. There was, for instance, Anne Hunter, who was married to John Hunter, the famous surgeon and anatomist. She showed him some of her poems and he set them to charming music. Another time he heard of the financial worries of the music dealer, William Napier. In order to help this impoverished musician, Haydn arranged Scottish folk songs for him, adding preludes and postludes, and an accompaniment of piano, violin, and violoncello. The works brought both the publisher and arranger the benefits of an enormous success and greatly enhanced Haydn's popularity in the British Isles.

Finally, there was a certain amount of teaching to be undertaken. Besides such nominal pupils as Mrs. Schroeter and other ladies, there were the pianist, Thomas Haig, and the composer, John Callcott, who really did study under the master.

How Haydn managed to get all this work done, and done so brilliantly, and at the same time to lead a very active social life; how, in spite of the tremendous forces released in his creative activity he was still able to muster the emotional capacity for love and friendship, is hard to understand. Several factors may have contributed to produce the rare phenomenon of a man of sixty with the creative power and zest for living of a person half his age. During the long and undisturbed years at Eszterháza, when Haydn was not living to the utmost of his capacity in many respects, he stored tremendous reserves of energy for the years to come. (A lesser artist might have reacted differently, and probably would have aged prematurely in such an existence of unvarying routine.) Another important factor was Haydn's excellent physique. During the eighteen months he spent in England, in spite of the difference in climate, the unfamiliar food, frequent travels, and long hours Haydn was generally in very good health. He once complained of "English rheumatism" (against which he wrapped himself from head to foot in flannel), and once he noted in his diary that he had had to be bled, but that was all. His discomforts from a polypus in the nose, inherited from his mother, were as old as Haydn himself. John Hunter almost used force to persuade Haydn to have an operation, but when the master was seized by strong assistants to be tied to a chair, he screamed and struggled so vigorously with hands and feet that the surgeon had to give up.

When the concert season was over the "worn out" composer still used every available chance to see and enjoy interesting sights in England.

On June 4, 1792, he went to Vauxhall where the birthday of the king was celebrated, and apparently liked it very much. "The place and its diversions have no equal in the world," he writes. "There are one hundred and fifty-five dining booths scattered about, all very neat, and each comfortably seating six persons. There are large alleys of trees, the branches meeting overhead in a splendid roof of foliage. Coffee and milk cost nothing. You pay half a crown for admission. The music is fairly good." He also explored the country around Windsor and of Windsor itself he mentions in his notebook the "very old but splendid chapel" and the "divine view from the terrace." But while there are a few lines dealing with this subject, Haydn devotes more than six hundred words to a description of the races at Ascot Heath, which he attended on June 14th. It must have warmed the hearts of his English friends to notice Haydn's eager interest in this national event. Here he saw eye to eye with them, just as he did in his passion for hunting and fishing. The following excerpt from Haydn's report shows what interested him most:

In the first heat there were three riders who were compelled to go around the course twice without stopping. They did it in five minutes. No stranger would believe it unless he were convinced by observation. The second time there were seven riders and when they approached some fell back, but never more than about ten paces and when one thinks the one rider who is about to reach the goal will be the first, at which moment large bets are laid on him, another rushes past him with inconceivable force and reaches the winning post. The riders are very lightly clad in silk, each of a different color, to make it easier to recognize them and all lean as greyhounds. The horses are of the finest breeds, light, with very slender legs, the manes plaited into braids, the hoofs very neat. As soon as they hear the sound of the bell they dash off with the greatest force. Every leap of the horses is twenty-two feet long. These horses are very costly. A few years ago the Prince of Wales paid eight thousand pounds for one and sold it again for six thousand. But the first time he won fifty thousand pounds with it. I saw eight heats the first day, and in spite of a heavy rain there were two thousand vehicles, all full of people, and three times as many people were present on foot. Besides this there are all kinds of puppet plays, ciarlatanz (sic!), conjurors, and buffoons performing during the races, and in a multitude of tents food and all kinds of wine and beer. . . .

The next day the indefatigable traveler went to Slough to meet William Herschel. Haydn was very much interested in this German musician who discovered the planet Uranus in 1781 after working on astronomy as a hobby, and was now universally acclaimed as an astronomer. The main attraction for Haydn was of course Herschel's gigantic telescope. Before it was raised skywards Herschel's most prominent visitors were allowed to take a walk through the enormous tube. In 1787 King George III and his retinue did so and the monarch was delighted thus to be able to show the Archbishop of Canterbury "the way to Heaven." [24] Haydn had to content himself with gazing at the monster, the measurements of which he faithfully put down in his notebook. Apparently he was much impressed by Herschel's ability to "sit from five to six hours under the open sky in the severest cold."

Now the time for Haydn's departure was approaching, much to the distress of Mrs. Schroeter, to whom "every moment of his company was more and more precious." There were many other people who also wanted to keep the master in England. Haydn, while quite willing to return to London, found it imperative to go home for the time being, so that he could put his affairs in order and straighten out matters with Prince Eszterházy who had summoned him to Frankfort, where he was to attend the coronation of the Emperor Francis II.

So Haydn got his trunks ready and made various purchases for his Viennese friends, such as scissors, needles, knives, spectacles, steel chains, the prices of which he carefully noted in his diary. He also took pains to jot down anecdotes that might amuse the people at home, such as the following: "An archbishop of London asked Parliament to silence a preacher of the Moravian creed who preached in public. The vice-president answered that it could easily be done: only make him a bishop, and he would keep silent all his life."

Until the last moment the round of social functions went on. On June 22nd Haydn gave a dinner at Parsloes for the Musical Graduates' Society and Salomon had to be invited as an interpreter, "Dr.

[24] *See* Cecil Roberts, *And so to Bath* (London: 1940).

Haydn having not made sufficient progress in the English language."
Next day he attended a dinner for one hundred and eighty persons
which the Duchess of York gave under a tent in her garden. After that
it was time for him to take leave of his numerous friends but he promised to return before long to the country that had received him so
hospitably and had given him the most exciting time of his life.

Chapter 8

VIENNA OR LONDON?

1792 — 1795

No PERSONAL documents are available about Haydn's return journey from London. We know that he again stopped at Bonn, where he had spent such pleasant hours eighteen months previously. The elector Maximilian had already left for the coronation at Frankfort, for which Haydn was also heading, but the elector's orchestra invited the master to a breakfast at Godesberg, that charming village overlooking the Rhine where the residents of Bonn still like to take their guests. On this occasion Haydn had a long talk with the young Beethoven, whom he may have met on his first visit to Bonn. The musician of twenty-two showed the master a cantata (probably the cantata on the death of Emperor Leopold II) which Haydn praised greatly. Beethoven was planning to go to Vienna to study under Haydn and it was arranged that he should do so as soon as he could get leave from the elector, who had undertaken to bear the expenses of the young musician's journey.

Haydn then proceeded to Frankfort, not without some misgivings as to his reception by Prince Anton Eszterházy, since he had been forced to ignore the prince's earlier request for a speedy return. To his relief, however, the prince was so engrossed by the splendors of the coronation of Emperor Francis II, that he merely remarked: "Oh, Haydn, you could have saved me forty thousand florins!"

The man who arrived in Vienna in one of the Eszterházy carriages on July 29, 1792, was rather different from the Haydn who had left the imperial capital only nineteen months before. He had tasted both delirious success and freedom. A highly renowned university had awarded him the degree of Doctor of Music. The Prince of Wales and other members of the highest British nobility had shown him great respect and friendliness. The newspapers, though sometimes critical in their attitude, had dealt with him and his music as providing news of importance and he had earned a considerable amount of money. Now he had returned to the city that had witnessed his rise from the humblest beginnings. How would Vienna receive the new Dr. Haydn?

The official circles of the capital proved to be most disappointing. No newspaper took the trouble to mention the master's return. No concerts were arranged in his honor. The Austrian court gave no sign of recognition to the composer who had contributed so immensely to the fame of Austrian music. In contemporary diaries, which Botstiber has searched carefully, Haydn's name hardly ever appears. What a contrast to the frenzied attention given to him in London! In private life things were of course different, for his old friends were delighted to welcome Haydn home. Still, there was one gap, never to be filled, that greatly marred Haydn's joy in his Viennese circle. Mozart was dead! The news had reached Haydn in London and at first he tried not to believe it, for rumors of that kind were not always trustworthy. (Haydn himself had been declared dead in 1778.) When he could doubt the fact no longer, it became, even for a man of Haydn's deeply religious feeling, a trial of faith to reconcile himself to the premature passing of this genius. In January, 1792 he wrote to their mutual friend, Puchberg: "I was for some time quite beside myself about his death. I could not believe that Providence should so quickly have called an irreplaceable man into the other world. Have the kindness, dear friend, to send me a list of Mozart's works not yet known here, and I will do my utmost to push them in the interest of the widow. I wrote to the poor woman three weeks ago, telling her that when her dear son was old enough, I would teach him composition without payment as well as I could, so as to replace his father to some extent." Haydn was not able to interest the British public in Mozart; at that time very few cared for him (among them, characteristically, was the Prince of Wales, who even owned the autograph of *La Clemenza di Tito*). We know, however, that when consulted by the music dealer Broderip in the presence of Dr. Burney regarding the purchase of a Mozart manuscript, Haydn exclaimed with the greatest emphasis: "Do buy it by all means. He was truly a great musician. Friends often flatter me that I have some genius, but he stood far above me." Truly, Haydn suffered deeply in losing this unique artistic friend, a loss that became still more evident to him amidst the old, familiar surroundings. Even with the healing influence of time the wound inflicted by Mozart's death did not cease to hurt. As late as 1807, when some friends mentioned the name of Mozart, Haydn burst into tears, exclaiming: "Forgive me, I must ever, ever weep when I hear the name of my Mozart."

On his return to a city that in a strange way seemed to have become different, Haydn felt more than ever the need of friends who really stood close to him. His wife, of course, was not among them. Time and distance had done nothing to soften the animosity between them. Frau Haydn's letters, in which she reported poisonous gossip against her husband by people dear to him (among them even Mozart!) could not improve their relationship, nor did Haydn particularly care for her suggestion that he buy her a house in Vienna which she might use as a dower house. The house itself, which Frau Haydn insisted on showing him, pleased the master well enough, because of its "quiet and secluded location." As he could now afford to do so, he bought it in August, 1793, after careful negotiations, and had it repaired and a second story added, but he did not fulfill his wife's wishes to make her the owner of the property.[1]

No, it was not to Frau Haydn, but to Marianne von Genzinger that he turned again "for comfort." With her he felt at ease. In her home he was sure of never-failing, sincere interest. To her he played his new works; to her he described what he had seen and heard in England. Only two short notes of the autumn of 1792 have been preserved, for there was now no need for correspondence. Then, all of a sudden, a catastrophe shook Haydn's existence. On January 26, 1793 Marianne died, at the age of thirty-eight, leaving five children. Through her death Haydn lost the best friend he had at that time. None of his other old acquaintances could replace her. The master, who had experienced the bliss of a really understanding and warmhearted friend only in his late years, now experienced a terrible loneliness that surrounded him like a wall. With Marianne's death, something went out of Haydn's life, never to be recaptured. A certain sarcasm in his nature began to show, an asperity of which the diary of his second trip to London offers many instances.

[1] The house situated in Vienna's sixth district, at 71 Untere Steingasse, now 19 Haydngasse, has been preserved by the city of Vienna as a Haydn Museum.

The loneliness Haydn was now suffering could not be dispelled even by the two interesting pupils who were then constantly in touch with the master. Young Pietro Polzelli came to stay with the Haydns and the composer, besides teaching him, helped him to get well-paid lessons, and certainly enjoyed his company. His relation to the other pupil is not so easily described. Ludwig van Beethoven arrived in Vienna shortly after Haydn, and started at once to take lessons, for which the master asked a nominal fee of eight groschen per hour. They met fairly frequently, and Beethoven's memorandum book contains such entries as "chocolate twenty-two times for Haydn and myself," and "coffee six times for Haydn and myself."

As early as 1787 Beethoven had paid a short visit to Vienna in order to meet Mozart. It was his great wish to study with this master but before this intention could be carried out he was recalled to Bonn, and by the time he was ready to visit the Austrian capital again, Mozart had died. Beethoven decided to study with Haydn instead, but it seems probable that he always regarded Haydn as a sort of understudy for Mozart. Such an attitude is also expressed by Count Waldstein, who wrote the following words of farewell in Beethoven's album on October 29, 1792:

DEAR BEETHOVEN,

You are traveling to Vienna in fulfillment of your long-cherished wish. The tutelary genius of Mozart is still weeping and bewailing the death of her favorite. With the inexhaustible Haydn she has found a refuge, but no occupation, and she is now waiting to leave him and associate herself with someone else. Labor assiduously and receive Mozart's spirit from the hands of Haydn.

Beethoven, of course, never revealed anything of the kind to Haydn; on the contrary, he went out of his way to win the friendship of the world-famous master. Nevertheless, it is possible that Haydn, a very keen observer of men, realized the young man's true feelings. At all events the deep sympathy and understanding that, in spite of very different temperaments, drew Mozart and Haydn irresistibly together, were entirely lacking in the relationship between Haydn and Beethoven. It was not the difference in their ages that was the real barrier, for Haydn loved, and was loved by, young people. Nor, as has been sometimes assumed, were Beethoven's revolutionary tendencies in music abhorrent to Haydn. On the contrary, everything new interested Haydn and there are proofs enough in his last works that he was in complete sympathy with the newly rising romantic school. But Beethoven, headstrong and prone to suspicion, was not easy to get on with, and often irritated Haydn. His youthful arrogance was particularly hard to be borne by a man of Haydn's age and the older master used to refer jokingly to Beethoven as "that Great Mogul." In addition to these intangible personal differences there developed a dissatisfaction about the method of instruction that was shared by teacher and pupil alike. Beethoven wanted to study strict counterpoint as carefully as possible, for he felt that only a thorough mastery of the regular rules would entitle him to vary them in his compositions. Haydn therefore set him to work on the old textbook he himself had studied, Fux's *Gradus ad Parnassum,* but in the forty years since the master had pored over this manual it had naturally lost much of its significance for him. It is not surprising that Haydn at the zenith of his fame and creative power found the correction of such elementary exercises rather tedious. Absorbed in his own thoughts and problems, he did not give to the work of instruction the necessary attention, and overlooked mistakes that Beethoven made. The pupil became suspicious of his teacher's competence, and complained of it to the renowned pianist, Abbé Gelinek, who introduced him to Johann Schenk, a composer of successful Singspiele and a pedantic music teacher as well. Schenk was tremendously impressed by Beethoven's improvisations on the piano and went to call on the young genius the next day. "On his writing desk," he tells in his autobiography, "I found a few passages from his first lesson in counterpoint. A cursory glance disclosed the fact that, brief as it was, there were mistakes in every key. Joseph Haydn, who had returned to Vienna, was intent on utilizing his abilities in the composition of large masterpieces, and thus laudably occupied he could not well devote himself to the rules of grammar. I was now eagerly desirous to become the helper of the zealous student, but before beginning my tuition I made him understand that our co-operation must be kept a close secret. In view of this I recommended him to copy every exercise that I corrected, so that Haydn would not recognize the handwriting of a stranger when the exercise was submitted to him." And so it was done. Beethoven, for the sake of appearances, continued going to

Haydn for instruction, but his real teacher at that time was Schenk. The young musician cannot be blamed for his duplicity; he was anxious to study counterpoint thoroughly but could not risk offending Haydn. On the other hand, the older master's behavior is also understandable. As Schindler put it: "The eminent composer can be a good adviser on special cases, but he simply is not a teacher in the real sense of the word; that is, one who leads the student on with patience and devotion from easy to difficult problems." Nevertheless Haydn and Beethoven kept on quite friendly terms and even when, a few years later, Schenk's secret was divulged by Gelinek, after a disagreement with Beethoven, there never occurred any outward break in the relations of the two composers. Beethoven dedicated to Haydn his piano sonatas, Op. 2, for which, as for all other compositions of the Rhenish master, the old composer had the greatest praise. He found only Beethoven's trio, Op. 1 No. 3 in C minor too original and revolutionary to be understood by the great public, and therefore advised the young man to delay its publication until he had made a name for himself. The suspicious Beethoven saw in that advice a proof that Haydn was not well disposed toward him, and was even jealous, thus totally misjudging his teacher's character. The idea of envying a composer almost young enough to be his grandson would have seemed ridiculous to Haydn who, after winning great triumphs in England, was at last receiving proofs of unusual admiration at home. In 1793, to the old master's tremendous gratification, Count Harrach erected in the composer's birthplace a monument in honor of this greatest son of Rohrau.

No, Haydn was not jealous of the younger generation. On the contrary, he got genuine satisfaction out of their achievements and missed no opportunity to encourage them. A charming proof of this is offered by his letter to the operatic composer, Joseph Weigl, Jr., the son of his old friend, the violoncellist of the Eszterházy band, Joseph Weigl:

Vienna, January 11, 1794

Dear Godson,

When I took you in my arms shortly after your birth, and had the pleasure of becoming your godfather, I implored omnipotent Providence to endow you with the highest degree of musical talent. My fervent prayer has been heard. Yesterday, on hearing your *Principessa d'Amalfi,* I felt the warmest sympathy with the well-merited applause bestowed on it. Persevere, my dear godson, in this genuine style, that you may again show foreigners what a German can accomplish. Keep a place in your memory withal for an old boy like myself. I love you cordially, and am, dearest Weigl,

Your sincere friend and servant,

JOSEPH HAYDN

When Haydn wrote this letter he was in the midst of his preparations for a second journey to London. A new agreement had been concluded with Salomon in the summer of 1793, according to which Haydn was to conduct six newly composed symphonies in the English capital. The financial terms are not known, but it seems certain that they were at least equal to those of the first contract. It is natural that Haydn should choose to revisit London, a city in which he had enjoyed so much success and appreciation. There was now very little to attract him in Vienna or Eisenstadt either, where he spent part of the time with Prince Eszterházy, for the castle of Eszterháza was abandoned after the death of its creator, not to be used again for a century. But, although the prince had no real use for him and remunerated him insufficiently, he did not like to see his Capellmeister go, and it was difficult for Haydn to get leave again. At last he succeeded and the day of departure was fixed for January 19, 1794. This time he could not rely on Salomon's help on the journey. At first, he wanted one of his pupils, Polzelli or Beethoven, to accompany him, but after giving the matter more thought, he came to the conclusion that these young musicians would not have his welfare as much at heart as his trusted servant, Johann Elssler, so he wisely decided to take Johann to London with him. Young Elssler, another of Haydn's godsons, was the son of Prince Eszterházy's music copyist, who helped Haydn with the first catalogue of his works (cf. pp. 183). Born in 1769, Johann lived with Haydn during his youth, and rendered him excellent service as a copyist, secretary, and general factotum. It speaks in favor of both master and servant that in spite of their being constantly together, Elssler's admiration for Haydn was boundless. There is even a report that the factotum, when he thought himself unobserved, worshiped with a censer before Haydn's portrait as if before an altar. The lack of a woman's care in the aging master's life was, to a great extent, made up for by Elssler's constant devotion and thoughtfulness. To this excellent man, incidentally, a place of honor is due, not only as the faithful servant, secretary, and copyist of Haydn, but as the father of the great dancer, Fanny Elssler.[2]

On January 19, 1794, the two travelers set forth in a coach provided by Baron van Swieten, director of the Vienna court library and an ardent lover of music, who was later to play an important part in Haydn's life. A halt was made at the well-known watering place, Wiesbaden, about which Dies tells the following pleasant story. At the inn Haydn heard the strains of the andante from his Surprise Symphony issuing from another room. He followed the sound, to find a group of Prussian officers gathered around the pianoforte and enjoying the beauties of this, by now very popular, masterpiece. When Haydn introduced himself, the Prussians could not believe the composer of so youthful a tune to be this aged man. They were at last convinced when Haydn proudly took out of his trunk the letter bearing the signature of their own king, Frederick William II, that had accompanied the diamond ring so highly treasured by the master.

About the journey no word from Haydn himself has been preserved, and our information regarding this second visit to England is altogether poor compared to that about the first journey. It should not be inferred that less happened to him, or that his experiences did not seem so interesting, but the incentive to describe his impressions in letters had vanished with the loss of his most sympathetic listener, Marianne. There was now really no single person to whom he cared to write any detailed account of his life in England. His notebook again confines itself to the jotting down of facts interesting to the master for one reason or another, but no word of a more personal nature has come down to us. Taken as a whole, the diary of this second journey is more censorious in tone and the comments on other artists are none too flattering.

Haydn's first appearance in London had been announced for February 3rd. But again, to continue the old tradition, the concert had to be postponed, as Haydn arrived on February 4th and a soloist engaged by Salomon, the celebrated basso, Ludwig Fischer (who had sung Osmin in the Vienna premiere of Mozart's *Die Entführung aus*

[2] Recently (*See* Larsen, *Drei Haydnkataloge in Faksimile,* p. 33) it has been alleged that Elssler may have appropriated some of Haydn's manuscripts not quite honestly. So far this has not been proved and it seems possible that the old and extremely forgetful composer sometimes gave his faithful factotum a manuscript without keeping the fact in mind.

dem Serail) was also late. The first concert therefore took place on February 10th, and Haydn was received with the old enthusiasm and admiration, this time marred by no opposition whatever, as the Professional Concerts had been given up in 1793. There was, however, a difference in the attitude of the London audience toward the master. Haydn was greeted like an old and highly treasured friend, while the element of sensation so characteristic of his first appearance was lacking. The reporter of the *Oracle* therefore, writing about Salomon's opening night, confined himself to this comment: "We must of necessity be brief. And after all it may be best, when the chef-d'oeuvre of the great Haydn is the subject. 'Come then, expressive Silence, muse his praise.' Viotti gave a concerto, simple and affecting, like his genius. Mara sang, *c'est assez dire.*" But if Haydn did not supply as much material for the newspapers as he had three years before, the acclaim given to him was by no means less frenzied; indeed, if possible, it was even more so. A letter written on March 25th by the London correspondent of the *Journal of Luxury and Fashion,* Weimar, gives a lively description of the general reaction to Haydn's music:

> But what would you now say to his new symphonies composed expressly for these concerts and directed by himself at the pianoforte? It is truly wonderful what sublime and august thoughts this master weaves into his works. Passages often occur that render it impossible to listen to them without becoming excited. We are altogether carried away by admiration and forced to applaud with hand and mouth. This is especially the case with Frenchmen, of whom we have so many here that all public places are filled with them. You know that they have great sensibility and cannot restrain their transports, so that in the midst of the finest passages in soft adagios they clap their hands in loud applause and thus mar the effect. In every symphony of Haydn the adagio or andante is sure to be repeated each time, after the most vehement encores. The worthy Haydn, whose personal acquaintance I highly value, conducts himself on these occasions in the most modest manner. He is indeed a goodhearted, candid, honest man, esteemed and beloved by all.

This love and esteem were felt also by the members of his orchestra who enjoyed Haydn's sense of humor and friendly ways. On the other hand, they were not above playing little jokes on him. Young George Smart, for instance (the future Sir George, friend of Beethoven,

Weber, and Mendelssohn), liked to remember how he showed Haydn the "English way of playing the drums." At a rehearsal, when the drummer was absent, Smart, a violinist, volunteered to take his part, although he had never played the instrument before. Naturally he did not produce quite the desired effect. Haydn let it pass, but after the movement was finished, he went to Smart and remarked politely that in Germany the drumstick was used in such a way as not to check the vibration. Then, adopting his usual method of demonstrating his intentions on the instrument, he took the drumstick and showed himself, to the astonished orchestra, as an excellent drummer. Smart was quick to see where he had failed and exclaimed: "Oh, very well, if you like it better that way we can do it so in London too."

The Salomon series again gained added luster by the engagement of excellent soloists. The great violinist, Viotti, has already been mentioned. Very successful also was the blind glass harmonica virtuoso, Marianne Kirchgaessner, whom Mozart admired so much that he wrote for her an Adagio and Rondo for Harmonica and Strings, K. 617. (Incidentally, it was in London that this unfortunate musician, who had been blind since her fourth year, was given an eye lotion that enabled her to distinguish the color and shape of objects.) Dussek again frequently appeared in the series, as did the popular singer, Maria Hester Parke, who was also a good pianist. Madame Mara was engaged again and Haydn continued to take an interest in her, although he did not always approve of her behavior. This is proved by a curious item in his notebook. It seems that the singer and her husband, Johann Mara, a talented but dissipated violoncellist, were not exactly in accord. As the oboist, W. T. Parke, expressed it in his *Musical Memoirs:* "Mr. Mara loved her and his bottle equally, and frequently broke the head of one and cracked the other." In writing about the singer's benefit concert on March 24, 1795, after mentioning the various artists, Haydn continued: "When the concert was over, Madame Mara gave a supper in the adjoining room. After midnight Mr. Mara stepped in quite boldly and asked for a glass of wine. Madame Mara knowing what madness might result therefrom, appealed to her lawyer who was sitting at the table, and this man said to Mr. Mara: 'You know our laws, you will be kind enough to leave this room, otherwise you'll have to pay two hundred pounds tomorrow.' The poor man left the party. Next day, Madame Mara, his wife, traveled to Bath with her *cicisbeo,* but I think her obstinacy makes her ridiculous to the whole nation." It seems that in spite of the notorious faults of the husband, Haydn was definitely on his side.

While his feelings for the singer were of a mixed nature, Haydn wholeheartedly enjoyed the intimate friendship that during this second stay in England he established with Domenico Dragonetti, "Il Patriarca dei Contrabassi." Dragonetti's never-paralleled mastery of his instrument fascinated Haydn as it did everybody else. The Italian virtuoso, playing on a double bass built by Gasparo da Salò, the teacher of Amati, could apparently express anything he wished on the unwieldy instrument. Haydn must have chuckled when Dragonetti told him how, by imitating a terrific thunderstorm on the double bass, he made all the monks in a Paduan monastery jump out of their beds one night. And the fact that Dragonetti collected dolls and operatic scores with the same fervor was something that Haydn, who loved puppets so much himself, could well understand.

The English composer, William Shield, was also among Haydn's new friends. They spent a few days together at Taplow, and Shield declared that on this occasion he had learned more about music than he had in years of study. This shows that if Haydn did not have to follow a textbook on counterpoint implicitly, he was a pretty good teacher.

Haydn again had some real pupils and received a fee of one guinea a lesson. An entry in his diary throws a side light on teaching conditions at that time: "If a singer, pianoforte or dancing master asks half a guinea for his lesson, he requests before the first lesson an entrance fee of six guineas. This is done because during the winter many Scottish and Irish people, out of pride, have their children taught by the best masters, and in the end find themselves unable to remunerate them. But the entrance fee is dispensed with if the master asks for a whole guinea. This, however, has to be paid at every lesson." [3]

The name of Lord Abingdon frequently appears in Haydn's notebook. This musical enthusiast was among the first amateurs who tried to bring the master to London. He now endeavored to direct Haydn's interest toward the composition of an oratorio, showing him an English translation of John Selden's *Mare Clausum* as a possible

---

[3] This is quoted by Griesinger in his biographical sketch in *Allgemeine Musikalische Zeitung* (1809) and probably was contained in the fourth diary of Haydn which has disappeared.

libretto. Haydn actually started working on it, but after composing
a bass aria and a chorus, he gave it up, feeling that he had too little
knowledge of English to justify his composing an oratorio to a text
in that language. Haydn and the aristocratic lover of music even collaborated in producing "Twelve Sentimental Catches and Glees"
which, according to the frontispiece, were melodized by the Earl of
Abingdon, while the accompaniments for the harp or pianoforte were
written by "the celebrated Dr. Haydn." In the privacy of his notebook, however, Haydn could not help making fun of the musical accomplishments of his friend. He quoted the following epigram:

> King Solomon and David led merry, merry lives
> With many, many lady friends and many, many wives.
> But when old age came creeping on, with many, many qualms,
> King Solomon wrote the Proverbs and King David wrote the Psalms.[4]

He added: "My Lord Abingdon sets it to music, but miserably. I do
it a little better." Another story connected with his friend is set down
by Haydn with evident enjoyment: "Lord Abingdon had an organ
built in the church on his estate. When the bishop of the diocese
heard of it, he reproved the nobleman in a letter for having done so
without obtaining a faculty, which is not allowed in England. Whereupon he received the following answer: 'The Lord gave it—the Lord
can take it away.' This is very ambiguous, but very good." Another of
his hosts whose love of music was mentioned by Haydn was Lord
Aston,[5] whom he visited at Preston, in the township of Hitchin, Hert-
fordshire.

Haydn, however, did not confine himself to intercourse with noblemen. How he became attached to a music dealer by the name of
Howell is described by William Gardiner:

> One morning a neat little gentleman came into his (Howell's)
> shop and asked to look at some pianoforte music, and he laid before
> him some sonatas by Haydn which had just been published. The

[4] The German version noted by Haydn is much more outspoken.
[5] This must have been Walter Aston (d. 1805), in early life a watchmaker who
claimed the title of Lord Aston of Forfar in the Scottish peerage. According to *The
Complete Peerage,* there was some doubt whether, under the laws of succession, he
and his immediate forebears were entitled to this peerage, and he was not allowed to
vote in the election of Scottish peers to the House of Lords. However, in 1769 George III
granted him a pension of three hundred pounds per annum under the title of Lord
Aston of Forfar. The *Gentleman's Magazine* described him thus: "His Lordship, who
had been in trade in the early part of his life was an inoffensive man of a rather convivial
turn."

The Eszterházys' castle at Eisenstadt—view from the park

The *Bergkirche* in Eisenstadt where Haydn conducted his own masses

An opera performance in the theatre of Eszterháza, supposedly Haydn's *L'Incontro Improvviso* (1775). Haydn at the harpsichord. (Painter unknown)

stranger turned them over and said: "No, I don't like these." Howell
replied: "Do you see they are by Haydn, Sir?" "Well, Sir, I do, but I
wish for something better." "Better," cried Howell indignantly, "I am
not anxious to serve a gentleman of your taste," and was turning away
when the customer made it known that he was Haydn himself.
Howell, in astonishment, embraced him and the composer was so
flattered by the interview that a long and intimate friendship followed.[6]

Some of Haydn's friends were not connected with music at all. We
read, for instance, in his diary: "Mr. March is at the same time dentist,
coachbuilder, and wine merchant. He is eighty-four, keeps a young
mistress, and has a daughter of nine who plays the piano quite well.
I dined frequently with him. As a dentist he earns two thousand
pounds a year; each carriage brings at least five hundred pounds; as
a wine merchant he does not, I think, make so large an income."
But what about Mrs. Schroeter? Did their friendship continue?
There are no letters to help us get a clear answer to this question. It
may be that this time Haydn omitted to make copies or that they
were included in his fourth notebook, which has not been preserved.
Certainly the pleasant rooms Haydn occupied this time, at 1 Bury
Street, at the corner of King Street, opposite the St. James's Theater,
were near Mrs. Schroeter's house. Pohl may be right in his assumption that they were chosen by the lady herself. Furthermore, on his
return to Vienna, Haydn dedicated his trios, Op. 82 to Mrs. Schroeter,
and her name appears again in 1800 among the subscribers to *The
Creation*. There is no reason to assume that the feelings of either
had changed in the course of years. When we hear that Haydn left
the scores of his last six symphonies "with a lady in England," it seems
likely that the recipient of these treasures was his fervent admirer,
Mrs. Schroeter.[7] Probably she again contributed much to making
Haydn's stay in the British capital a happy one.
On his second visit Haydn was again most anxious to get to know
the various aspects of life in England. When the concert season was
over, this indefatigable man of sixty-two made frequent journeys and

[6] Gardiner does not give a date for this occurrence and it cannot be ascertained
whether it happened during the first or second visit to England.
[7] On the other hand Elssler wrote in 1811 to Breitkopf & Härtel that he had the
manuscripts of six out of the twelve London Symphonies. *See* W. Schmieder, "Joseph
Haydn's Kopist und Bediensteter schreibt einen Brief," *Allgemeine Musikzeitung*
(1937).

took an avid interest in all the new sights and facts that came his way. His notebook affords much information regarding different kinds of ships, chiefly in connection with a visit to Portsmouth. He visited the palace of Hampton Court and the beautiful park there reminded him of Eszterháza; he was conducted through the Bank of England, and later wrote a detailed report about it. When staying with Sir Charles Rich, whom he found a "rather good violoncellist," he examined the ruins of the famous Abbey at Waverley, and described his reaction in the following words: "I must confess that whenever I saw this beautiful wilderness, my heart felt oppressed at the thought that all this had once been subject to my own religion." He enjoyed trips to Cowes, Newport, Winchester (whose "beautiful Gothic cathedral" he praised), and Southampton. Mentioning the Isle of Wight in his diary, he extols the "most magnificent view of the sea" from the governor's green villa. The following remark in the diary also probably refers to this lovely island: "There is a story that Julius Caesar, on his flight, came by chance to the island and exclaimed: 'This is indeed the home of the Gods!'"

No such enthusiastic words were uttered by Haydn in connection with operatic conditions in London. Here is a story that the composer jotted down in his diary [8] with evident disgust: "Dr. Arnold [9] composed an opera for Drury Lane Theater. As the manager was afraid the work might not be successful, Dr. Arnold agreed to have it performed three times at his own expense. He spent more than seven hundred pounds on it; the manager, however, paid a crowd of people to hiss the opera off each time. Finally, Arnold handed the work to the manager who had it performed, after a few alterations, with better costumes and decorations, and within a year earned twenty thousand pounds on it. The publisher alone netted five thousand pounds, but the poor composer lost seven hundred. Oh, rascals!" Haydn expressed himself in even stronger words after a visit to the Haymarket Theater on July 29, 1794: "There they perform just as miserable trash as at Sadler's Wells. A fellow sang an aria so dreadfully and with such extravagant grimaces that I began to perspire all over my body. But he had to repeat the aria. *Oh, che bestia!*"

Any unpleasant memory of that evening was quickly dispelled by

---

[8] Again quoted by Griesinger. Cf. note 3.

[9] Dr. Samuel Arnold, composer, court organist, and conductor of the Academy of Ancient Music.

Haydn's visit to Bath, which took place only four days later and proved to be the most delightful experience of the summer. In this highly fashionable watering place there lived many distinguished musicians who were anxious to meet Haydn, the most desirous being the famous tenor Venanzio Rauzzini, about whom the composer Naumann said: "He sings like an angel and is also a remarkable actor." Haydn wrote a long description of the trip in his diary, part of which reads as follows:

> On August 2, 1794 I left for Bath at 5:00 A.M. in the morning and arrived at 8:00 P.M. I stayed with Mr. Rauzzini, a very famous musician who was one of the greatest singers of his time. He has been living there for nineteen years, supports himself with Subscription Concerts in the winter, and also gives lessons. He is a very good and hospitable man. His summer house, where I stayed, lies in a very lovely site on a hill that overlooks the whole city. Bath is one of the most beautiful towns in Europe, all the houses being made of stone. The stone is quarried in the near-by hills and it is so soft that it can be easily cut into all shapes, and is very white. The longer it is out of the earth, the harder it becomes. The whole town lies on a hill, and therefore there are few coaches, but there are plenty of chairs in which one can be carried a good distance for sixpence. There are many beautiful squares with the most excellent houses. I made the acquaintance of Miss Brown, an amiable discreet person and a good pianist. Her mother is a very beautiful woman. . . .

The delight with which Haydn was received in the watering place is apparent from the welcome in the Bath *Herald and Register:* "Oh, had I Jubal's lyre, I would sweep the strings till Echo tired with repeating—Haydn treads upon Bathonian ground! Had this place, previous to his arrival, been the seat of discord, it must now be lulled into peace by the God Harmony—while every individual who hath music in his soul must exclaim with enthusiasm: *Erit mihi magnus Apollo!*" At a later date the paper also published a French poem by a refugee in honor of the "immortal master."

Haydn had his own method of thanking his hosts for a charming reception. When Rauzzini showed him the tomb of his beloved dog Turk, in his garden, bearing the somewhat misanthropic inscription "Turk was a faithful dog and not a man," Haydn composed a four-part canon on these words and the grateful recipient added it to the epigraph. For the renowned musician, Dr. Henry Harington, founder

of the Harmonic Society of Bath, Haydn composed the music to a
poem *What Art Expresses* that the doctor had written in the Austrian
master's praise.[10] This collaboration between the two musicians
caused Clementi to make the following rather involved statement:
"The first doctor [Harington] having bestowed much praise on the
second doctor [Haydn], the said second doctor, out of doctorial gratitude, returns the first doctor thanks for all favor received, and praises
in his turn the said first doctor most handsomely."

After three delightful days Haydn went on to Bristol, which he
also describes in his diary, praising the beautiful view from the hill,
and remarking on the numerous churches, all in "the old Gothic
style."

On returning to London in the autumn of 1794, Haydn began to
make intensive preparations for the coming season. This time conditions were somewhat changed. Salomon suddenly decided not to
continue his subscription series—why, is not known—but perhaps
the whole matter had lost some of its attraction when there was no
rival to fight. Be that as it may, he agreed to Haydn's being engaged
for a new enterprise, the Opera Concerts, in which series he himself
frequently appeared as soloist. The new concerts were arranged on
the largest scale known at that time. The performances took place
every two weeks in the great new concert hall of the King's Theater.
Viotti was the artistic director and Haydn shared the conductorship
with Vincenzo Federici, who for three years had been accompanist at
the Italian opera in London. The orchestra, led by the violinist William Cramer, comprised no less than sixty players. The composers engaged, other than Haydn, were Muzio Clementi, Francesco Bianchi,
and Vicente Martin y Soler (composer of the once successful opera
Una Cosa rara immortalized in the second act of Mozart's *Don Giovanni*). The soloists included the greatest artists available, among
them Brigida Banti, who had come to London in 1794. This former
street singer enjoyed a tremendous success, and the words of Lord
Mount Edgcumbe reflect only the general attitude: "In her, genius
supplied the place of science, and the most correct ear, with the most
exquisite taste, enabled her to sing with more effect, more expression,
and more apparent knowledge of her art, than many much better

[10] The composition has a rather strange form. The theme is first sung by a solo voice,
then taken over by a mixed chorus, then follow variations for the piano. *See* the introduction to the Collected Edition of Haydn's songs, p. xv.

professors. Her voice had not a fault in any part of its unusually extensive compass." Haydn wrote an aria for her, which she performed at his benefit concert, but according to Griesinger, he noted in his diary (in English) that she "song (sic!) very scanty," which again proves that at that time there were very few artists who earned Haydn's full approval. He also found the oboist, Giuseppe Ferlendis, who made his London debut in this benefit concert, "mediocre." But even if the master did not feel quite happy about the soloists, he could not help admitting that the benefit concert was a brilliant success. He remarked in his diary: "The hall was filled with a distinguished audience. The whole society was extremely pleased, and so was I. I netted four thousand florins on this evening. This one can make only in England." Altogether the Opera Concerts were received so enthusiastically that instead of the projected nine concerts, eleven had to be given. Details of their programs are now not ascertainable, but it is known that the tenth, eleventh, and twelfth of Haydn's London Symphonies had their first performances in this series.

During this, his last London season, Haydn was in even closer touch with the court than in the preceding years. It seems surprising that the master, in spite of his outstanding success, had never yet been introduced to the king, but George III was so passionately devoted to Handel's works that he took little interest in contemporary music. By now, however, Haydn had become so beloved in England that the monarch could no longer overlook his presence. The oboist, William Thomas Parke, tells about the first meeting in his *Memoirs:*

The Duke of York gave a grand concert of instrumental music at York House, at which their Majesties and the princesses were present. Salomon led the band and Haydn presided at the pianoforte. At the end of the first part of the concert Haydn had the distinguished honor of being formally introduced to his Majesty, George III, by the Prince of Wales. My station at the time was so near to the king that I could not avoid hearing the whole of their conversation. Among other observations, his Majesty said: "Dr. Haydn, you have written a good deal." Haydn modestly replied: "Yes, Sire, a great deal more than is good." His Majesty neatly rejoined: "Oh, no, the world contradicts that." After his introduction, at the queen's desire, Haydn sat down to the pianoforte and, surrounded by her Majesty and her daughters, sang and accompanied himself admirably in several of his canzonets.

From that day on Haydn was frequently invited by the queen to her musicals at Buckingham House. He was treated most graciously and the queen gave him the manuscript of Handel's oratorio in German *Der Erlöser am Kreuze*. The Prince of Wales also continued to see and hear Haydn frequently. When he gave a brilliant concert and supper in honor of the king's first visit to Carlton House, the music consisted almost entirely of Haydn's works, with Haydn directing from the piano. According to Parke: "The magnificence of the scene on this occasion was truly fascinating. The splendor of the dresses and the elegance and beauty of the ladies all combined to strike the beholder with admiration and delight."

On April 8, 1795 the wedding of the Prince of Wales with the Princess Caroline Amalia Elisabeth of Brunswick took place. It was of course impossible for Haydn to take part in the ceremony, for it had to be entrusted to the official court musicians. He was asked only to help solve a certain problem arising from the participation of three different musicians and he reports on it in his diary as follows:

> On the 21st of January I dined with Dr. Parsons and during dinner a dispute arose as to which of the three doctors, Parsons, Dupuis, or Arnold, should conduct Handel's "Anthem" at the wedding of the Prince of Wales. Dr. Parsons is conductor of the king's band, the other two are organists of the royal chapel. In England the organist is, however, the head in all churches, and the singers are subordinate to him. Each of the three wanted to beat time. When I was forced to express my opinion, I said: "The younger organist should play the organ, the other conduct the singers, while Dr. Parsons should conduct the instrumental performers." This did not suit them so I left the blockheads and went home.

In spite of the negative attitude of the three musicians concerned, Haydn's advice was followed at the ceremony. Only three days later, the master was invited by the newly married couple to a musical party, about which he remarks in his diary: "An old symphony of mine was given, which I accompanied on the piano; then a quartet; and later I had to sing German and English songs. The princess sang with me and played a concerto on the pianoforte quite well." (The description recalls the musical soiree at Oatlands arranged by the newly married Duke and Duchess of York four years previously, but how much warmer had been Haydn's praise of the "sweet little lady" then! Was this because of his preference for the daughter of the king of Prussia, or was it just another symptom of the composer's general disillusionment?)

It seems that various members of the royal house made efforts to keep Haydn permanently in England. According to Griesinger, the queen offered him a residence at Windsor for the summer, adding, with a mischievous glance toward the king: "Then we can make music tête-à-tête." The king declared that he was not jealous of Haydn, and also extended a most cordial invitation to the composer. Nevertheless, Haydn refused, giving various reasons, among them even his attachment to his wife (!) who, he said, would be unwilling to make so long a journey.

At first sight it does not seem easy to understand Haydn's attitude. England was giving him so much—much more indeed than Vienna had ever done. He was the central figure of London's musical life; no other composer's works were performed so frequently, or with greater applause. Respect and admiration were paid to him as the "God of musical science," while to the Viennese he was still nothing more than the court conductor of a Hungarian magnate. The income he made in England was most satisfactory too, a matter that was anything but unimportant to one who had actually known utter poverty. Personally, life in England suited him well enough, for he had quite a few good friends there, probably not less than in Vienna, and many people seemed only too anxious to make his stay in London enjoyable. If, in spite of all these advantages, he decided to return to Austria, he had good reasons for doing so.

Being the musical hero of London was gratifying, even fascinating, but also fatiguing. Haydn was living, as it were, under continuously high pressure. To produce that "electrical effect" as Burney terms it, on a large and exacting audience demanded the utmost concentration and vitality, and called for an effort that could not be maintained indefinitely. The constant demands for new works, even with their enthusiastic reception, which had inspired Haydn to his greatest achievements, would have drained him of his creative power in the long run. Haydn instinctively felt that now it would be better for him to stand no longer in the limelight. Age was beginning to tell, and although he did not consider his creative work finished, he felt that it was imperative to economize his strength. A quiet life in England seemed out of the question; there was too much to do and see. Moreover, any real relaxation appeared impossible in a country where he still had a difficulty in understanding the language. The thought of his own little house in the quiet suburb of Gumpendorf drew him away; there at least he might be able to lead a secluded life, devoted mainly to his art which he now craved.

There was yet another consideration influencing him. Prince Anton Eszterházy had died a few days after Haydn's departure from Vienna. His successor, another Nicholas, was following the tradition so gloriously established by his grandfather, Prince Nicholas, the Magnificent. He had written to Haydn that he planned to restore the former orchestra and asked the master to take over the leadership again. The composer consented, for after so many years of service for the family it was inconceivable to him that another should preside over the Eszterházy orchestra. It would be wrong, however, to see Prince Eszterházy's offer as the main attraction that drew Haydn back to Austria. At that time he had become independent enough, both in character and financial status, to choose the kind of life best suited for his art and it will be seen that even as an employee of Prince Nicholas Eszterházy he gave but a small part of his time and his interests to the service of his patron.

Leaving England, and this time he knew it was for good, was by no means easy, so Haydn lingered on and on. On May 4, 1795 his benefit concert took place; on May 29th he directed two of his symphonies in a concert of Madame Dussek. After that he was free to go home, but he stayed on until August 15th, eager to catch another and yet another glimpse of this English life that had become so dear to him.

His English admirers were not aware of Haydn's inner struggles; to them the matter had a different aspect. The king had invited Haydn to take up his residence in England and the master had refused. The court was disappointed and rather offended, and characteristically, no member of the royal family, except the faithful Duchess of York, appeared at Haydn's benefit concert. The newspapers ceased to mention his name, aware perhaps of the court's changed attitude, but his personal friends remained faithful to him. As happened before Haydn's departure from Vienna in 1790, a farewell song was exchanged between a lady and the master. This time, however, the positions were reversed. It was the lady, Anne Hunter, who wrote the poem *O Tuneful Voice*, deploring that the composer's "accents which still vibrated in her heart" were to be heard no more. Haydn, pleased with his friend's tender words, did not hesitate to set to music the poem written in his own praise. He received various parting gifts, among them a talking parrot (which was auctioned off for 1,400 florins after Haydn's death), a beautiful cocoanut goblet from Clementi, and a silver goblet with a very respectful inscription from the Reverend W. D. Tattersall, to whose *Improved Psalmody* Haydn had contributed six melodies. The master's trunks were fairly bulging with musical compositions; according to his own list in the diary copied by Griesinger he had written no less than 768 pages of music during his two visits to England. Nor was the money he took home a mean amount. He had once more earned 1,200 pounds for concerts, lessons, and symphonies, and to this was added the considerable income from other works, fees for appearances at Carlton House, and other sources. But the fruits of his stay in England cannot be expressed in figures alone. Haydn's mental outlook had been immensely widened, his self-confidence had tremendously increased; and, if, at the age of sixty-two, he felt impelled to leave the country that had given him so much, it was not the quiet repose of old age to which he was looking forward. Life in England was too exciting and exhausting for him; he needed now the seclusion necessary for starting on new artistic ventures.

Chapter 9

"SO MUCH YET TO BE DONE . . ."

1795 — 1801

BY THE end of August, 1795, Haydn was back again in Vienna and this time things looked more promising for him than they had on his return from London three years previously. A new head of the Eszterházy family was awaiting the Capellmeister's return so that musical activities worthy of the traditions of Nicholas, the Magnificent could be arranged. Haydn had his hands full in reorganizing the orchestra and making all necessary preparations for a brilliant debut of the new *capelle*. The occasion was a grandiose performance on January 4, 1796 of the opera *Penelope* by Antonio Draghi. The audience was dazzled not only by excellent singers from the Vienna opera but also by costly fireworks. The event took place in the prince's Viennese palace. Fortunately for Haydn, his new patron, Nicholas II, was by no means enamored with the castle of Eszterháza and much preferred spending the winter months in the imperial capital, and the summer and autumn at Eisenstadt. In this respect the prince's wishes coincided fully with those of his conductor.

Unfortunately this was nearly the only point on which the prince and Haydn saw eye-to-eye, for on the whole, their relationship was not too pleasant. Of the four Eszterházy princes with whom Haydn was connected, the last, under whom the master served for fifteen years, was the hardest to satisfy. His predecessor had merely been uninterested in music, a state of affairs that Haydn could not really resent. With Nicholas II it was different. In many respects he, like his grandfather, was a passionate patron of the fine arts. He spent enormous sums in adding to his collections; he engaged well-known artists, such as the painter Franz Roesler and the sculptor Antonio

Canova; he greatly embellished the castle and park of Eisenstadt; and he had excellent troupes of actors. He professed a love of music and showed himself generous to some composers. It is recorded, for instance, that on a visit to Paris he gave Cherubini a ring worth four thousand thalers. But he would not have dreamed of making such a gesture to Cherubini's idol, Joseph Haydn. The truth was that he did not really care for the old composer's works. His musical interest was centered almost exclusively in church music. One of his favorite composers was Haydn's former "teacher," K. G. Reutter, whose pompous, and at that time entirely outmoded, compositions he could not hear too often. He also admired Michael Haydn because he had written some important church music and he probably thought more highly of this minor composer than of the "Father of the Symphony." On the other hand it was flattering to his vanity to have attached to his court a composer whose services made him the envy of many a potentate and therefore, of course, he kept Haydn as his Capellmeister. At first the prince paid the composer only the old salary of 1,400 florins (which Haydn had received from Prince Anton without doing any work), nor did he strain himself in pretending an interest or sympathy for the master that he did not feel. Contemporaries describe the prince's nature as worthy of an "Asiatic despot." His lack of tact and feeling of superiority in his intercourse with composers is well revealed in his behavior to Beethoven. At the prince's request, Beethoven wrote his first great work of sacred music in 1806–7, the *Mass in C major,* which ranks among the foremost works of the kind written in that period. After the performance the prince merely remarked to the composer, who had already proven his genius with the Eroica Symphony, *Fidelio,* and other works: "But, my dear Beethoven, what is this that you have done here again?" Whereupon the outraged composer left the castle. Prince Nicholas II seems not to have been ruffled even by the new ideas released through the French Revolution. He was as complete an autocrat as his grandfather had been but lacked the latter's charm, kindliness, and genuine understanding of music.

This placed Haydn in a difficult position. Willing as he had been to overlook the despotism of Nicholas, the Magnificent, who for all his shortcomings had been truly attached to the master, he felt much less inclined to put up with it from a man half his age, and one who often did not understand what he was talking about. Once Haydn even

went so far as to express this. When the prince uttered some unjustified criticism at a rehearsal, Haydn burst out with: "Your Highness, it
is *my* job to decide this," whereupon Nicholas indignantly went out of
the room, leaving all the musicians "horror-stricken." Nor did Haydn
lose any opportunity of impressing on his patron that he felt his salary
was inadequate. This is revealed in the following letter which shows
that the composer possessed a keen sense of business. Prince Eszterházy had as major-domo a certain Johann Alois Luegmayer, who had
the good luck to be married to a niece of Haydn. The spendthrift
nephew took ample advantage of this relationship, for he liked to contract debts in the name of his famous uncle and he was so successful in
these manipulations that, according to Haydn's own testimony, Luegmayer received from him in the course of years some six thousand
florins. Eventually even Haydn, to whom the integrity of his family
mattered greatly, lost patience. When informed by the prince's administration that his account was being charged with new debts of
the major-domo, he not only refused to pay them, but also boldly
changed from defensive to offensive tactics. This is the way he expressed himself in an undated letter, written probably in 1796 or
1797:

To the Managers of Prince Eszterházy's Estate:

I see from the papers forwarded to me, and the enclosure from his
Highness, Prince Eszterházy's Estate Office, that in consequence of
Luegmayer's *inability* to pay his debt, I am expected to do so. Pray,
why? Because I am supposed to be *able* to pay. Would to God this
were the case. But I swear by the Kyrie eleison, which I am at this
moment composing for my fourth prince, that since the death of my
second prince of blessed memory I have fallen into the same state
of inability as Luegmayer himself, only with this difference; he has
descended from a horse to the back of an ass, whereas I have remained on the horse, but without saddle or bridle. I beg therefore,
gentlemen, you will at least have patience till I have finished the
"Dona nobis pacem," and till the prince's major-domo Luegmayer
shall have ceased to receive his salary from the poorly paid music director Haydn (who has spent thirty-six years in the princes' service)
and shall begin to receive the salary justly due to him from his most
gracious prince. For surely nothing can be more sad or incongruous
than that one servant should pay another servant; that is, the Capellmeister pay the major-domo. If I should presently, by my own efforts

(for flatter or beg I cannot) or by the voluntary impulse of my gracious prince, be placed in a better position, I will not fail to comply with the above demand.

Yours, etc. . . .

Usually, however, Haydn managed to restrain himself and found a better method of reaching the prince's ear. He went to Princess Hermengild, the wife of Nicholas II, who liked and admired the master greatly, and eventually she smoothed out matters for him. For instance, he resented not being addressed with the courtesy due a Doctor of Music of Oxford and it was the princess who saw to it that no one at court should speak of the composer curtly as "Haydn" without a prefix, and that official letters addressed to him were full of the flourishes accorded a person of distinction. In the course of years the princess also obtained several increases of salary for the composer, as well as other favors such as the regular delivery of wine from the princely cellars.

Altogether Haydn, although not enjoying the work for his fourth prince, did not resent it too much since his duties were not particularly heavy. His main obligation was that of regularly composing new masses for his patron. This he did, and six masterworks were written for this purpose. Apart from that, Haydn's most important duty was to be on hand for festive occasions when the prince wanted to show off his famous conductor, as he did, when the Archduke Joseph, the Palatine of Hungary, visited Eisenstadt twice in 1797, and the emperor and empress once in 1800, events that were celebrated with the traditional Eszterházian splendor. For the ordinary routine work there was a substitute, Johann Fuchs, a member of the orchestra, as Haydn himself felt entitled to give most of his time to occupations not connected with the service of his prince; occupations that were to assume a paramount importance during the years to come.

The composer had returned to Vienna teeming with energy and the work to be done for his narrow-minded patron was but a poor outlet. While still in London, Haydn is said to have declared: "I want to write a work which will give permanent fame to my name in the world." The unforgettable experience of the Handel Commemoration in Westminster Abbey had convinced the composer that an oratorio was best suited to link his name indissolubly to the future. In addition to this consideration, Haydn's constant urge to experiment with new ways of expression drove him toward the oratorio. After writing the London Symphonies he felt that he had reached a summit never to be surpassed by him in this type of music. Orchestral composition offered no further attractions to him, and although he was in his middle sixties, he felt eager to measure his strength by a new genre, one in which he had not as yet proved his mastery.

That Haydn chose the Creation for a subject is again due to England. There are various reports about it. It seems that Salomon gave the master a libretto that a man by the name of Lidley [1] had compiled for Handel from Milton's *Paradise Lost*. On the other hand, according to Purday,[2] the violinist Barthélémon, one of Haydn's great friends, when asked to suggest a suitable subject for an oratorio, pointed to the Bible and exclaimed: "There! Take that, and begin at the beginning." It does not seem impossible that both stories are true. Haydn, influenced by Barthélémon, may have mentioned his intention to Salomon who then procured the libretto which Haydn took with him to Vienna. This book was in English and the composer, who was determined to compose a German text, needed a translator. Chance helped him to find the right man.

Vienna had among its musical amateurs of noble birth, a baron of Flemish origin whose hobby was the oratorio, especially the works of Handel. His name was Gottfried van Swieten, prefect of the Vienna court library and president of the educational commission. His father, Gerhard van Swieten, had played an important part at court as the favorite physician of the Empress Maria Theresa. The son chose a diplomatic career, and from 1771 to 1777 was ambassador to the court of Frederick the Great of Prussia, where he became acquainted with north-German music. Here for the first time he heard the name of Johann Sebastian Bach and his curiosity was stirred to such an extent that he traveled to visit Bach's son, Philipp Emanuel in Hamburg and bought from him several manuscripts and copies of works by the cantor of the Thomasschule, together with some music by Emanuel himself. When he returned to Vienna he was probably the only person in the city who owned a copy of the *Well-Tempered Clavier*. On the other hand, in 1769 the baron had visited Eng-

---

[1] Tovey (*Essays in Musical Analysis*, V, 119) suggests that Lidley might be a misprint for Linley, father of the well-known violinist, Thomas Linley, and the singer Elizabeth Ann Linley (Mrs. Sheridan).

[2] This information was given to C. F. Pohl by Sir George Grove, who had it from Purday's son.

land, where he became an ardent admirer of Handel. He took home
the scores of some of Handel's greatest oratorios, and thenceforth
considered it his mission to propagate the music of Handel and Bach
in the Sunday morning musicals, which he arranged in the magnificent baroque hall of the court library. As there was no organ available, the baron made one of the regular guests, Wolfgang Amadeus
Mozart, reorchestrate various Handel oratorios by substituting wind
instruments for the organ. Van Swieten also induced the young composer to arrange some Bach fugues for string trio or quartet with the
addition of introductory adagios, and by drawing Mozart's attention
to baroque music, he exercised an important influence on the composer's artistic development. Beethoven too was patronized by the
baron and repaid him by dedicating his first symphony to him. Van
Swieten was a composer himself, and although his orchestral works
were "as stiff as their composer" (Griesinger), his symphony in E♭
enjoyed the undeserved privilege of being attributed to Haydn for
a long time. Altogether the baron was not what one would call a lov-
able person. He was obstinate, despotic, and despite his considerable
wealth, decidedly close-fisted. It was he who, when approached on
Mozart's death by the destitute widow, advised Constanze to bury
the master in a pauper's grave, so as to save expense. Culturally his
influence was sometimes anything but beneficial, and, according to
Riemann, the Vienna court library suffered under his leadership
greater damage than from wars or fires. He gave orders for the re-
moval of everything that "merely gratified the imagination or was a
scholastic luxury," and by so doing he had many priceless incunabula
destroyed.

Nevertheless, in spite of his faults, Gottfried van Swieten was the
right man for Haydn. He was much more than a mere translator,
and in the chapter dealing with Haydn's last period of composition,
the baron's share in Haydn's oratorios will be pointed out. What
concerns us here is the fact that van Swieten, through his influential
position, gave the works the best possible start. In those times composers as a rule did not write an important work unless it was commissioned. Even Haydn, in spite of his enormous fame and secure
financial position, would probably have been reluctant to do so. Had
he stayed in England, he might have written such an oratorio for
Salomon or Gallini. To whom could he turn in Vienna, where busi-
nesslike concert enterprises in the English manner were hardly

known? At this point van Swieten stepped in. He got together a group of twelve music-loving noblemen and each guaranteed a contribution of fifty ducats to defray the expenses of performance and pay an honorarium to the composer. Thus Haydn had firm ground under his feet, and started on the composition of *The Creation,* to which he devoted most of his time and energy during the following years. The work progressed slowly, for as Haydn remarked, he "spent much time over it, because he intended it to last a long time."

These years devoted to the composition of *The Creation* were among the richest and happiest in Haydn's life. He was fully absorbed by a task in which, perhaps better than ever before, he could express the innermost forces of his nature. Haydn had always been deeply religious and free from doubt and skepticism and was really sincere when he wrote the words *Laus Deo* at the end of each of his compositions. In spite of life's darker sides, which were well known to one who had led quite an unsheltered life from his earliest childhood, the world seemed a very good and beautiful place to Haydn. To some slight extent, each of his works was a Creation, expressing praise and thankfulness to the Heavenly Father. Now he could do so on a much larger scale and with a freedom he had never had in the composition of a mass, and at the same time he had a chance to depict in sounds the beauties of nature, which delighted this passionate hunter and fisherman so much. When he worked on this oratorio, Haydn felt uplifted and in close communion with his Creator. "Never was I so devout," he said, "as when composing *The Creation.* I knelt down every day and prayed to God to strengthen me for my work." He remarked to Carpani that when he felt his inspiration flagging, he "rose from the pianoforte and began to say his rosary." He "never found this method to fail."

The effect that Haydn wanted to achieve with this work cannot be better expressed than in the words that the Princess Eleonore Liechtenstein used in a letter to her daughter about *The Creation:* "One has to shed tender tears about the greatness, the majesty, the goodness of God. The soul is uplifted. One cannot but love and admire." [3]

April 29 and 30, 1798, were exciting days for the Viennese. Although only invited guests were admitted to these first performances of *The Creation* at the palace of Prince Schwarzenberg, a tremendous crowd of onlookers gathered outside the building. The market stalls

[3] *See* Pohl and Botstiber, *Joseph Haydn,* III, 130.

on the Neuer Markt (or Mehlmarkt) where the palace (demolished
in 1893) was situated had to be removed, and twelve policemen and
eighteen mounted guards were stationed to keep order in the walk-
ways to the house. The privileged who were allowed to enter consisted mostly of the nobility, among them, as Princess Liechtenstein
records, "all the elegant Polish, English, and Viennese ladies." Carpani also relates: "I was present, and I can assure you I never witnessed such a scene. The flower of the literary and musical society
of Vienna was assembled in the room, which was well adapted to
the purpose. The most profound silence, the most scrupulous attention, a sentiment, I might almost say, of religious respect prevailed
when the first stroke of the bow was given." On this occasion the
master was not his usual placid self. "One moment," he said later, "I
was as cold as ice, the next I seemed on fire. More than once I was
afraid I should have a stroke." The musicians were of the first rank.
Haydn himself conducted in the modern way with a baton, as was
customary for choral performances. At the piano sat the court composer Salieri. The soprano part was sung by Christine Gerardi, whom
a contemporary critic describes as follows: "Flexibility and beauty
of voice, a lovely figure, expressive features, and lustrous eyes give
vigor to each of her words and grace to every sound rising from her
throat." [4] The male soloists were Ignaz Saal, bass of the court opera,
and Mathias Rathmayer, professor of the Theresian Academy, whose
beautiful tenor voice Princess Liechtenstein praised. Success was
overwhelming and far beyond expectation. Most of the listeners may
have felt like the Viennese correspondent of the *Neuer teutscher Merkur,* who wrote: "Three days have gone since that enrapturing evening, and still the music sounds in my ears and in my heart; still the
mere memory of all the flood of emotions then experienced constricts
my chest."

Furthermore, Haydn had good reason to be well satisfied with the
material success. Not only did his aristocratic patrons pay him the
agreed honorarium, but in addition they presented him with the entire receipts from the admission fees. But this was only the beginning. For years *The Creation* was to prove so unfailing an attraction
that the proceeds from it, mostly given to charitable institutions, by
far surpassed even the receipts from the London benefit concerts that
had once seemed so extraordinary to Haydn.

[4] In *Neuer teutscher Merkur* (May 3, 1798).

As early as May 7th and 8th of the same year the work was again played at the Schwarzenberg Palace. Suddenly, however, the exertion of these last years made itself felt; Haydn broke down and had to spend some time in bed. For while his absorption in the congenial task of composing *The Creation* brought the greatest happiness to the master, it also imposed on him a tremendous strain. On many occasions physical weaknesses checked the flow of his inspiration and caused Haydn to despair and when he had recovered and could go on with his work, a certain lack of confidence in what he was doing taxed his strength as the writing of symphonies or string quartets had never done. A letter which the master addressed to Breitkopf & Härtel on June 12, 1799 is very significant in this respect. Although written one year after the memorable first performance of *The Creation,* it still vividly reflects the strain of the past years of composition and shows that Haydn was not certain even then how the more conservative critics would receive the work that was now to be circulated in print throughout the musical world:

> My business unhappily expands with my advancing years, and it almost seems as if, with the decrease of my mental powers, my inclination and impulse to work increase. Oh God! how much yet remains to be done in this splendid art, even by a man like myself! The world, indeed, daily pays me many compliments, even on the fervor of my latest works; but no one can believe the strain and effort it costs me to produce them, inasmuch as time after time my feeble memory and the unstrung state of my nerves so completely crush me to earth, that I fall into the most melancholy condition. For days afterwards I am incapable of formulating one single idea, till at length my heart is revived by Providence, and I seat myself at the piano and begin once more to hammer away at it. Then all goes well again, God be praised! I only wish and hope that the critics may not handle my *Creation* with too great severity and be too hard on it. They may possibly find the musical orthography faulty in various passages, and perhaps other things also, which for so many years I have been accustomed to consider as minor points, but the genuine connoisseur will see the real cause as readily as I do, and willingly ignore such stumbling blocks. This, however, is entirely *entre nous;* or I might be accused of conceit and arrogance, from which, however, my Heavenly Father has preserved me all my life long.

Writing a full-sized oratorio with such painstaking care would be a heavy task for any artist in his later sixties, but Haydn by no means

confined himself to this work. During these same years he wrote
two large masses, a vocal arrangement of the *Seven Last Words,* a
concerto for keyed trumpet, some of his very best string quartets,
three trios with piano, and his own favorite, the national hymn "Gott
erhalte," which more than anything else enhanced the master's popularity in his own country. Again the impulse to compose the Austrian
hymn came from England. Noticing the deep impression produced
in London whenever "God Save the King" was played, Haydn felt
that in the distressed times of the Napoleonic Wars Austria also
needed a patriotic song. Here too van Swieten proved of service in
the realization of the master's idea. He discussed it with the imperial
chancellor, Count Saurau, who gladly took up the project and commissioned a poet by the name of Leopold Haschka to write a suitably
patriotic text. In January, 1797 Haydn set it to music and on February 12th, on the birthday of the emperor, the hymn was sung in all
the theaters of Vienna as well as of the Austrian provinces. The enthusiasm aroused by the new hymn was tremendous and the following little story throws a sidelight on its fast-growing popularity. A
wealthy Englishman, who seemed to have stepped out of a fairy tale,
offered to provide trousseaus for twenty-four engaged couples in
Vienna who did not have enough money to be married and thus make
their marriages possible. The fortunate young people were all married simultaneously at St. Stephen's and then liberally entertained at
Jahn's, the court caterer. Music was provided by a military band
which, upon urgent request, had to play three times in succession the
national hymn introduced to the Viennese only two days earlier.

Haydn received from the emperor a gold box with the monarch's
portrait. The composer would have considered a decoration a more
appropriate gesture of thanks for this national hymn that so greatly
built up public morale at a time when this was sorely needed. But
even though the Emperor Franz and his second wife, another Maria
Theresa, felt much more friendly toward the master than their predecessors on the Habsburg throne, the grant of such an honor simply
did not occur to them. In spite of the innumerable tributes of admiration that Haydn received in his old age, the award of a decoration
from a court was not among them.

But there were other honors bestowed on him. One came from
Sweden, when the Austrian composer was made a member of the
Royal Music Academy. Another one, awarded in Vienna, had a sym-

bolic significance, as it annulled an injustice under which Haydn had long smarted. The Viennese Tonkünstlersocietät had coolly rejected Haydn's application in 1778 but now offered him membership as "perpetual assessor" with exemption of any admission fees. This was quite an unusual procedure, as the Societät, whose main function was to insure musicians and their families, was naturally dependent on the payments of its members. The musicians, however, felt it imperative to make an exception in the case of Haydn, in order to obliterate their former shortsightedness. In so doing they not only gave great pleasure to the old master, but also brought important material benefits to the institute. From that time on Haydn showed himself most generous to the Societät. Shortly after his election he gave them the music to his new vocal version of the *Seven Last Words* and he himself conducted two brilliant performances, thus assuring unusually high receipts. How little Haydn spared himself when there was a chance of helping the Societät is revealed in his calendar for March, 1799. The month was mainly devoted to rehearsals of *The Creation,* for it was to be performed for the first time in a theater open to the general public on March 19th. In addition to this task, the burden being increased by two performances of the oratorio on March 2nd and 4th at the Schwarzenberg Palace, Haydn conducted performances of the *Seven Last Words* for the Societät on the 17th and 18th, the two days immediately preceding the great event. Nevertheless, on March 19th he showed no signs of fatigue, and the first public performance of the oratorio brought him a sensational success. Indeed, so thrilled were the Viennese about the event (it drew the greatest crowd ever seen in the Burgtheater) that they hardly seemed to notice the Russian army under Suvarov that was passing through the capital on the same day. The receipt of 4,088 florins actually surpassed the fees that the most popular Italian stars were earning in Vienna, and the whole amount went to Haydn, as van Swieten's group was again defraying the expenses. The soprano singer was the seventeen-year-old Therese Saal, whose father, Ignaz Saal, performed the bass solos. One critic wrote of her performance: "The part of Eve in Haydn's *Creation* will hardly ever be sung again with such warmth, delicacy, and devout simplicity."

As a Christmas present for the Societät Haydn conducted two performances of his *Creation* on December 22 and 23, 1799, and thereby again greatly improved the institute's financial status. On this occasion a critic of the *Allgemeine Musikalische Zeitung* wrote: "Haydn's gestures were most interesting to me. With their aid he conveyed to the numerous executants the spirit in which his work was composed and should be performed. In all his motions, though anything but exaggerated, one saw very clearly what he thought and felt at each passage." From that time forward it became the custom for Haydn to let the Societät perform his great oratorio, usually under his own direction. In a letter that the publisher, George Thomson wrote to Haydn's friend, Mrs. Hunter, he remarked: "Haydn wrote me lately that in three years 40,000 florins had been raised for the poor families of musicians by the performances of *The Creation* and *The Seasons* at Vienna."

One year after the first public performance in Vienna, the oratorio was heard in London, and in this event the rivalry between competing impresarios played an important part. This time it was a race between Salomon and Ashley,[5] since both had ordered the score from Haydn. The unlucky Salomon decidedly came out second. Not only did he have to pay the outrageous sum of £30.16.0 for postage when the score arrived, while Ashley's expenses for delivery through the courier of the British Legation amounted to only £2.12.6, but what was worse, Ashley was far quicker in presenting the oratorio. *The Creation* was performed by him at Covent Garden on March 28th, only six days after receipt of the score, while Salomon followed on April 21st. The amazing speed of Ashley's production was due mainly to the excellent organization of the copyist, Thomas Goodwin, who had to get one hundred and twenty parts copied out in so short a time. When praised for his efficiency, Goodwin remarked: "Sir, we have humbly emulated a great example; it is not the first time that the Creation has been completed in six days." In spite of all his ill luck, Salomon's performance united, as a critic remarked, "in the overcrowded hall all of London's most distinguished friends of music." In the same year a performance of *The Creation* took place at the Three Choirs' Festival in Worcester.

Paris followed London's example a few months later. Interest in Haydn's compositions had been steadily increasing here and the French friends of music desired that the composer himself conduct his oratorio. This attitude was rather remarkable in view of the almost

[5] John Ashley directed the Lent oratorios at Covent Garden inaugurated by Handel. He began directing them in 1795.

continual state of war in those years between France and Austria; however, if the French were magnanimous enough to forget political controversies for the sake of good music, the Austrian police definitely did not adopt this attitude. When Pleyel, who had settled in Paris and become a French citizen, was sent to Vienna by the *Opéra* in the summer of 1800 to present in person the French invitation to Haydn, and possibly carry him off as Salomon had done ten years previously, the Austrian authorities did not allow the musician, lest he might be a spy, to cross the border from Germany. All the endeavors of Haydn and the publishing house of Artaria proved to be of no avail and Pleyel had to return to Paris without having accomplished his mission. At first Haydn felt greatly tempted to go to Paris, for he had not forgotten how delightful it was to travel in a foreign country. In the end, however, he decided against it, and the Paris performance took place on December 24, 1800, under Steibelt's direction. Unfortunately the attention of the audience was greatly distracted by the news that Bonaparte, then First Consul, who was attending the concert, had just escaped a bomb attempt on his life in the Rue Nicaise. In spite of this drawback the musicians were so enthusiastic about *The Creation* that they had a large gold medal engraved in commemoration of the event. This medal, designed by Gatteaux, was presented to Haydn one year later and gave him immense pleasure.

Although Haydn would certainly have enjoyed a visit to Paris, he was wise not to have yielded to the temptation. His physical strength might have been unequal to the exertion, for since the spring of 1800 his health had not been satisfactory. Early in April he had been seized by a "rheumatic head fever" that kept him in bed and at first looked so serious that, according to Straton's letter to Thomson, the Viennese "were not altogether devoid of alarm in regard to his recovery." Although by the end of April, Haydn was allowed to get up, his convalescence proceeded very slowly. Throughout the summer at Eisenstadt he was tired and dispirited and it was not until August 2nd that he was able to write to Luigia Polzelli that he was feeling better.

This breakdown, which was far worse than the one two years before, was not surprising. Indeed it is rather to be wondered at that it had not occurred earlier. Haydn had been absorbed in too many activities. He had even, for the first time, tried his hand in business by being his own publisher. He collected the subscriptions for the score of

The Creation himself, and with his characteristic politeness, in many cases took pains to write detailed answers. The subscribers' list to be found in this first edition of the oratorio is illuminating in many respects. That both Austria and England claimed Haydn as their own is shown by the illustrious names heading the list: the Austrian Empress and various Archdukes of the house of Habsburg, the King and Queen of England, the Prince and Princess of Wales, the Duchess of York, and the Princesses Augusta, Elisabeth, Maria, Sophia, Amalia. About half of the remaining subscriptions came from England. Among them were the names of many persons who had become Haydn's friends during his stay in the British capital, like Bartolozzi, Barthélémon, Salomon, Mrs. Schroeter, the Misses Abrams, Sir Patrick Blake, Lady Rich, and Haydn's colleagues in the Doctorate of Oxford, Dr. Arnold, Dr. Aylwood, and Dr. Ayrton. In addition there was a surprisingly large number of members of the British nobility, and characteristically, many of the subscribers were women. Apparently the memory of Haydn's earlier social success was still very much alive. Among the Austrian subscribers we also find many aristocratic music lovers, names like those of the Princes Lichnowsky, Kinsky, and Liechtenstein, all familiar to us from Beethoven's dedications. Germany too was represented by various princes and duchesses. Looking over this imposing list, the son of the modest wheelwright must have felt great satisfaction. But when the preparatory work was done and the score of the oratorio securely launched, Haydn entrusted the firm of Artaria with the distribution of the work, recognizing that his time might be spent in a more congenial way.

The passion for production was not exhausted by the completion of *The Creation* and the constant awareness of "so much to be done" drove the old master on inexorably, heedless of his diminishing physical strength. He was now almost exclusively absorbed in creative work. An interesting document preserved in the Mozarteum of Salzburg, and entitled *Daily Schedule of the late Herr von Haydn* [6] (possibly written by Elssler) gives some details of the composer's way of life. It runs as follows:

In the summertime he rose at 6:30 A.M. First he shaved, which he did for himself up to his seventy-third year, and then he completed

[6] It was customary in the Austrian Empire to employ the word "von" (abbreviated "v.") in addressing every person of good standing, although it was rightfully confined to the nobility.

dressing. If a pupil were present, he had to play his lesson on the piano to Herr von Haydn, while the master dressed. All mistakes were promptly corrected and a new task was then set. This occupied an hour and a half. At 8:00 o'clock sharp, breakfast had to be on the table, and immediately after breakfast Haydn sat down at the piano, improvising and drafting sketches of some composition. From 8:00 to 11:30 his time was taken up in this way. At 11:30 calls were received or made, or he went for a walk until 1:30. The hour from 2:00 to 3:00 was reserved for dinner, after which Haydn immediately did some little work in the house or resumed his musical occupations. He scored the morning's sketches, devoting three to four hours to this. At 8:00 P.M. Haydn usually went out and at 9:00 he came home and sat down to write a score or he took a book and read until 10:00 P.M. At that time he had supper which consisted of bread and wine. Haydn made a rule of eating nothing but bread and wine at night and infringed it only on sundry occasions when he was invited to supper. He liked gay conversation and some merry entertainment at the table. At 11:30 he went to bed, in his old age even later. Wintertime made no difference to the schedule, except that Haydn got up half an hour later.

Griesinger amplifies this schedule by telling us that every evening Haydn carefully went through the household accounts in order to keep his servants in their bounds. On the other hand, he liked to play cards with them on winter evenings, and he got much amusement from seeing their delight when they won a few pence from him. Haydn, fully absorbed in creative work, probably enjoyed intercourse with such simple people as a relaxation. On the whole, this way of life left but little scope for close relationships of any kind, and indeed there is not much to relate about Haydn's personal activities during these years. From 1797 he lived in his own house, doubly enjoyable since his wife was hardly ever there. Frau Haydn, who was suffering from severe rheumatism, spent most of her declining years at the sulphur springs of the little town of Baden, where she died on March 20, 1800. The event probably meant little to her husband for he had become used to a sort of bachelor existence, and was well looked after by Elssler and the cook, Anna Kremnitzer. There was one person, however, who was sent into a flurry of excitement by the news of Frau Haydn's death. Luigia Polzelli was again living in Vienna, although not in the service of Prince Eszterházy, for Haydn's influence with this patron was apparently insufficient to obtain her an engagement.

Luigia lost no time in reminding Haydn of his former promise to marry her when he was free. The old composer did not like the idea at all; he felt too settled in his ways for any further matrimonial experiments. All that mattered to him was to pass the remainder of his life in so smoothly ordered a routine as would be instrumental in conserving his creative powers. When Luigia found it was impossible to change his attitude, she made him sign the following document:

> I, the undersigned, promise Signora Luigia Polzelli, in case I should marry again, to take nobody else for wife other than the above-mentioned Luigia Polzelli; and if I remain a widower, I promise to leave to the above-mentioned Luigia Polzelli after my death a pension of three hundred florins in Vienna currency for so long as she lives. Valid before any judge, I sign

> JOSEPH HAYDN
Maestro di Cappella to his Highness
> Vienna, May 23, 1800   *the Prince Eszterházy*

Luigia, on her side, did not promise anything. Thus, with Haydn's pledge safely in her pocket, she saw no reason for remaining single. She therefore married an Italian singer, Luigi Franchi and they went to Italy. The old master, while not feeling jealous, did not like to be imposed upon, and therefore, in his will reduced the promised pension to half the amount.

So Luigia Polzelli gradually faded from Haydn's life, and no other woman appeared to take her place or that of Marianne von Genzinger. As the above-mentioned *Daily Schedule* testifies, Haydn still had some pupils. He had lost the one to whom he had been particularly attached. Pietro Polzelli, Luigia's eldest son, died in 1796, at the early age of nineteen. His place was taken to some extent by Sigismund Neukomm, who worked for seven years under Haydn and became attached to him. In 1799 Anna Milder (the first to sing the part of Leonore in Beethoven's *Fidelio*) also became a sort of pupil. Haydn found that the girl of fourteen had a voice "as big as a house" and handed her over for instruction to Neukomm, probably taking an active interest in the singer's development. When she won her first laurels in 1803 Griesinger wrote: "Her voice sounds like pure metal and as her teacher Neukomm is schooled by Haydn, she produces long vigorous notes without flourishes and exaggerated ornaments."

The name of Griesinger has been frequently mentioned in this book. From 1799 he was in close contact with Haydn and his letters as well as his *Biographical Notes on Joseph Haydn* based on direct information from the composer (who was quite aware of his friend's intention to use this material in a book) are among the most valuable sources of information for the Haydn biographer. Georg August Griesinger, after studying theology, came to Vienna in 1799 as tutor to the children of the Saxon ambassador, Count Schönfeld. In 1804 he became secretary of the Saxon Legation and in 1806 its councilor. Griesinger was known to Gottfried Härtel, the head of the publishing house of Breitkopf & Härtel, Leipzig. The publisher was most anxious to establish business contacts with Haydn, but having found out that the master, overburdened with work, was slow in answering letters, he hoped for better results through an intermediary and asked Griesinger to undertake the task. Härtel's idea proved to be excellent and fruitful. Griesinger was delighted to have an opportunity of meeting the world-famous composer, whom he described after his first visit as "a cheerful and still well-preserved man, and to all his colleagues a model of modesty and simplicity." Haydn immediately took a fancy to the young man who understood how to humor him and thus obtained important contracts for the Leipzig publisher. (On the other hand presents from Breitkopf & Härtel, such as a diamond ring, Indian-silk handkerchiefs, waistcoats of English cashmere, and colored silken hose pleased the old man immensely.)

Another publisher, who also used a personal emissary, was George Thomson of Edinburgh, who asked Mr. Straton, and subsequently Mr. Stuart, both of the British Legation, to negotiate with Haydn for arrangement of Scottish folk songs to be published by him. Haydn approved the suggestion and in the course of the years adapted some two hundred and fifty airs for Thomson, for which, according to the publisher's statement, he received £291.18.0. No friendship, however, developed between Haydn and Straton, who apparently did not have much use for musicians. The following passage in a letter from Straton to Thomson reveals a feeling of superiority that made a closer relationship with the composer impossible:

> Haydn called here yesterday and mentioned that he had already written to you and also begun the composition of the accompanyments to the Scotch airs (15 in number) that you had sent him through me. He seemed desirous of having rather more than two Ducats for each air, but did not precisely insist upon this point, which

I therefore left undecided exhorting him to proceed with his composition as speedily as its nature as well as that of his other occupations will admit of. This he solemnly promised but said that he could not possibly determine a period for finishing the airs in question. Upon the whole he appears to be a rational animal, whereas all that can be said of the other, I mean Koz(eluh),[7] is that he is a Bipede without feathers.

There were other English visitors to Austria who saw in Haydn much more than a "rational animal." In September, 1800, Admiral Nelson and Lady Hamilton paid a visit to the Eszterházys at Eisenstadt. Haydn asked his publisher Artaria to send him a copy of his cantata *Arianna a Naxos* because Lady Hamilton wanted to sing it. Griesinger reports about the event to Breitkopf: "In Lady Hamilton Haydn found a great admirer. She visited the Eszterházy estate in Hungary but paid little attention to its splendors, and for two days did not budge from Haydn's side." There is also an unconfirmed story that Nelson asked for Haydn's pen and in exchange gave the master his valuable gold watch.

In the same year the Bach biographer and musicologist, Johann N. Forkel, visited the composer and brought him a poem that the famous poet, Christoph Martin Wieland, had written on hearing *The Creation.*

Haydn was happy to be reminded of the years in London by visits from his good friends, Domenico Dragonetti, the double-bass virtuoso, and the young Johann Baptist Cramer. Michael Haydn's short visit to Vienna also gave both brothers much enjoyment. To Michael, who had lived in Salzburg since 1762, a trip to the capital was about as exciting and as important as the London visits had been to his brother. He kept a diary of all he saw and did, and after the lapse of a year, he tried to revive the memory of all those delightful experiences by rereading his notebook.[8]

Although Joseph enjoyed such pleasant episodes, his main interest always lay in composition. The year 1798, the year of the first performance of *The Creation,* also saw the completion of the *Nelson Mass,* and 1799 that of the *Theresa Mass.* During these same years

[7] Leopold Anton Koželuch, the successor of Mozart as Viennese court composer, also arranged Scottish airs for Thomson.
[8] This is mentioned in a letter from Michael to Joseph Eybler, dated November 5, 1799. *See* Pohl and Botstiber, III, 133. Joseph Eybler was an intimate associate of both Haydn and Mozart and studied under Albrechtsberger.

Haydn composed two string quartets, Op. 77, for Prince Lobkowitz, and some small vocal works such as the thirteen vocal duos, trios, and quartets, written according to the composer's words, *"con amore* in happy hours, without being commissioned." All this happened, as it were, on the fringe of his creative life, the center of which was fully occupied after the completion of *The Creation* by another oratorio, *The Seasons*. The impulse for the composition of this oratorio came from van Swieten who, after winning so many laurels with Haydn, was anxious to continue on this path. He translated James Thomson's poem *The Seasons* and adapted it as a libretto for an oratorio, giving Haydn minute instructions as to the sequence of arias and recitatives. Haydn, although he considered the guidance of the composer by the poet to be quite in order, did not feel so happy as when he composed *The Creation*. The imitation of natural sounds and voices, such as the song of birds and the roll of thunder, which had long been familiar in music, gradually became unacceptable to certain aesthetic circles. Their rejection of such devices made the old master uncertain of his work in composing music to a libretto that seemed urgently to call for them. Haydn naturally blamed van Swieten for any passages in his score that seemed to savor of such devices, and there are records about various disparaging remarks that he made about the libretto. When he had to compose the trio in praise of Industry, he observed that, while he had always been very industrious himself, it had never occurred to him to set industry to music. When correcting the proofs of the pianoforte adaptation of the work, he wrote against No. 22: "This whole passage imitating a frog has not flowed from my pen. I was forced to write down this Frenchified trash. With the whole orchestra the miserable idea easily disappears, but it cannot be so treated in the piano score." Unfortunately, through an indiscretion, the German critic, Johann Gottlieb Spazier, got hold of Haydn's own comments and used them in his review as an argument against van Swieten's text. The baron was furious and promised to rub this remark into Haydn with "salt and pepper." Two weeks later, however, Griesinger was able to report to Breitkopf & Härtel that the storm had passed. After all, van Swieten was too happy basking in the sunshine of Haydn's triumphs to sever so important a connection.

In point of fact, *The Seasons* achieved a triumph. Amazingly enough the completed work, in its freshness of inspiration, revealed no trace of the physical handicaps and difficulties that the composer had suffered while writing it. Haydn won the battle, but the price he had to pay was tremendous. His health was now definitely shattered, for as he said himself, *"The Seasons* has finished me off."* Still, stubborn like so many of his forefathers, Haydn doggedly continued doing what he felt to be essential and the very months before the first performance of the work show him trying to continue his active life in the face of increasing physical failings. In January, 1801, when war was again ravaging unhappy Austria, Haydn helped to raise money for the wounded. A performance of *The Creation* conducted, according to Rosenbaum,[9] by the composer "with youthful fire," netted 7,183 florins for the good cause, and a concert in which Haydn and Beethoven co-operated with Christine Gerardi, who first sang the part of Eve, brought in as much as 9,000 florins. But in February, 1801 Haydn was again laid up with "rheumatic head fever." This kept him inactive until the middle of March. Still, on March 29th and 30th he again conducted his *Seven Last Words* for the Societät and, above all, he was burdened with the exacting preparations for the production of *The Seasons.* Again Prince Schwarzenberg had the privilege of being host for this important event, which took place on April 24, 1801, and was repeated on April 27th and May 1st. The soloists were the same as for the first public performance of *The Creation* and again produced a great effect. As for the reaction of the listeners, the correspondent of the *Allgemeine Musikalische Zeitung* describes it with these words: "Silent reverence, amazement, and loud enthusiasm alternated, for the powerful appearance of colossal visions, the immeasurable abundance of splendid ideas surprised and overwhelmed the boldest expectations."

Shortly afterwards, the Empress Maria Theresa insisted on having a performance of *The Seasons* at court, to be followed the next day by *The Creation.* In both oratorios the empress sang the soprano solos "with much taste and expression, but a small voice," according to Haydn. These events occurred on May 24th and 25th, and four days later the first public production of *The Seasons* took place in the Redoutensaal. Haydn had reason to be well satisfied with the finan-

---

[9] J. C. Rosenbaum, official in the service of Prince Eszterházy, kept a diary that affords much interesting information about Haydn after his return from London. The unpublished manuscript is preserved in the National Library in Vienna (New Series, 194–204). Rosenbaum was married to Haydn's godchild, the singer of the Vienna opera, Therese Gassmann.

cial result for, in addition to the receipts of 3,209 florins, he was presented with an honorarium of six hundred ducats by the group of aristocrats who also paid all the expenses. But it is doubtful whether the composer was much impressed by this fact, although as a rule, he showed an increasing eagerness to earn large sums in his old age. He was now too weary, too exhausted from the unending struggle between his urge to create and his worn-out body. His thoughts were moving more and more toward the ultimate goal, and on June 5, 1801 Griesinger wrote to Leipzig: "Haydn has just drafted his last will."

Chapter 10

RETIRING FROM LIFE

1801 — 1809

HAYDN'S last will, which he worked on from June to December, 1801, is an interesting document, for it throws light on certain traits in his character. It is the testament of a man of means, for when Haydn died he left bonds to the value of 15,450 florins, property that, when auctioned off, brought 23,163 florins, and a house that was sold for 17,100 florins, all told the equivalent of about 27,000 dollars, which of course meant much more at that time than the same amount would today. But the man who had risen so high in the world did not forget his humble origin. Although he had left his father's house at the age of five, and had never since been more than an occasional visitor to it, he retained a deep-rooted attachment to his widely branched family. For a man who hardly knew what it was like to grow up in the midst of brothers and sisters, such an existence was imbued with a certain nostalgic fascination. Possibly he felt close to his relatives because he had never been obliged to live with them, had never suffered the fate of other growing artists, to be hampered by the family's narrow-mindedness and lack of understanding. He had always relied on himself alone. Throughout his life he hardly ever received a favor from any relative, though he had assisted dozens of them materially. In many villages near Eisenstadt and Eszterháza there dwelt nephews and nieces of Haydn who had settled in the neighborhood mainly because of their generous uncle. Haydn loved visiting them, and again and again he became the godfather of their children and helped one or another to set up business or get good training in a trade. A charming instance of Haydn's family sentiments is recorded by Carpani. Once a year Haydn invited all his

159

relatives of the neighboring villages to the little town of Bruck an der Leitha where he gave them a feast in the best inn, presented each with a small sum of money, and on parting embraced each and extended a cordial invitation for the next year. "Haydn called this family gathering his day of grandeur and went to it happily and proudly." While writing his testament, he saw himself as if again presiding over such a family gathering and made the greatest effort to remember everyone and to distribute his riches fairly. So the last will of the world-famous composer provided, for the most part, legacies to hard-working artisans. A shoemaker, a blacksmith, a silversmith, a tailor, a saddler's wife, four workmen, and two lacemakers are among the legatees.

On the other hand, various bequests to women who were not related to him point to the master's interest in the fair sex. It is much to be regretted that at the present time there is no possibility of following up these interesting clues. The only legatee whom we know even a little about, is "Babett," or, Barbara Pilhofer, first soprano at the Eszterházy court. But there are also legacies to Mesdemoiselles Anna and Josepha Dillin, to the blind daughter of the choirmaster at Eisenstadt, to the four daughters of the wigmaker Sommerfeld of Pressburg, to the daughter of the bookkeeper Kandler, and others. Most tantalizing is the provision of a thousand florins for Mademoiselle C. Czech, waiting woman to Princess Grassalkovics. The princess was the daughter of Prince Nicholas, the Magnificent and it seems possible that she employed a girl from her father's estate as a waiting woman who might have known Haydn well. (Was she the predecessor of Luigia Polzelli?) The entry, however, was crossed out by Haydn, just as he has canceled the bequest to his first love, the sister of his late wife. Whether or not Haydn acted thus because these women died after he had drawn up his testament is not known. The legacy to Luigia Polzelli has been previously mentioned. Haydn left her an annuity of one hundred and fifty florins and remarked: "I hereby revoke the obligation in Italian, signed by me, which may be produced by Mademoiselle Polzelli; otherwise so many of my poor relations, with greater claims, would receive too little."

Other important legacies were left to the master's faithful servant, Johann Elssler, to the cook, and to the housekeeper. But it was to Haydn's two brothers, Michael and Johann, that the two largest sums of four thousand florins each were bequeathed. Of these brothers

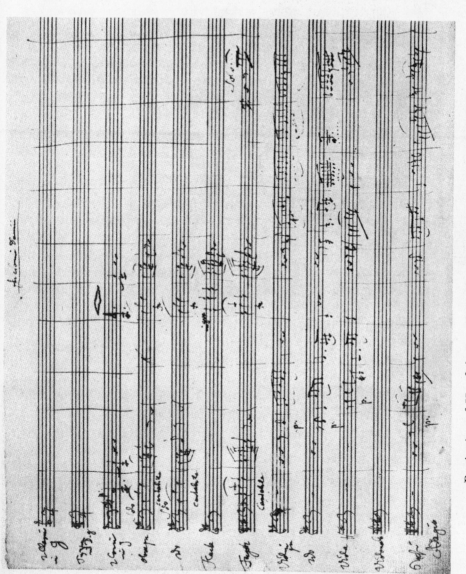

Beginning of Haydn's Symphony No. 94, "The Surprise" (1791)

Prince Nicholas Eszterházy II, Haydn's fourth patron in this family

Haydn's baryton and square piano in the museum of the Society of Friends of Music in Vienna

Johann was probably the nearer to the composer's heart, because it had fallen to Haydn to look after him, since at the age of twenty-two and after the death of their father, Johann had joined his brother in Eisenstadt. Although trained as a wheelwright, Johann became a tenor singer in the church choir, but his musical accomplishments seem to have been very modest, for in spite of his brother's influence, he never rose from this inferior position throughout the forty years of his service. As his salary was very small, he was mainly dependent on Joseph and his distinguished brother helped him continually, found pupils for him, and for twenty-five years sent him every summer to the sulphur springs of Baden near Vienna, where Johann had to take the cure.

Thus to set his house in order was no sad task for Haydn. Rather it afforded him satisfaction, for his heart was warmed by the thought of how much his financial assistance would mean to some of these humble people. His health improved while he was engaged in the task; indeed, it seemed in those summer days of 1801 as if he had recovered from the "terrible worry and torture" of composing *The Seasons*. He went again to Eisenstadt and was industriously working on a new composition for his prince, the so-called *Creation Mass*. On September 11th he wrote to an unknown friend: "Poor old boy that I am, I have just come to the end of my new mass which is to be produced the day after tomorrow." Again this splendid work reveals no signs of fatigue and in addition to its composition Haydn continued to arrange Scottish songs for Thomson.

His contented state of mind was also due to various proofs of worldwide recognition that reached him during this year. From Amsterdam came a letter announcing that the society Felix Meritis had made him an honorary member. From Paris there arrived Gatteaux's beautiful medal. Haydn cherished it immensely and told his prince that he would bequeath the medal to him, provided he could be assured that it would be kept in the Eszterházy treasury. Nor was this the only tribute that the master received from France in 1801. In December he was elected an *associé étranger* to the class of fine arts of the Institut de France, and this time a medal was engraved by Dumarest. This great honor caused some disappointment and bitter remarks in England, for Sheridan had been an unsuccessful candidate for membership. It would be wrong, however, to deduce from outbursts of indignation in some parts of the press, a changed attitude among British music lovers toward Haydn. When, at about the same time, the sculptor Grassi made busts of the composer in two different sizes five of each size were immediately ordered from England.

While the entire world was paying homage to Haydn, there were still fellow countrymen who did not even know him by name. This is revealed by a rather absurd episode which happened in July, 1801. The little town of St. Johann in Bohemia wanted to hear *The Creation*. Rehearsals were started under the auspices of the music-loving pastor, who applied to the Prague consistory for permission to perform the oratorio in an old unused church. Strangely enough, the reply was negative. The indignant citizens then tried to build an improvised concert hall, but when this plan proved to be impracticable they decided to have the performance in the old church in spite of the prohibition issued by the authorities. The good pastor was abducted in a carriage, so he would not be held responsible for the violation of the decree from Prague, and the citizens duly had their performance of *The Creation*. Another pastor, hearing about the matter, delivered a fulminating tirade against the desecration of the church by the performance of the work of a "heathen" (the German word for "heathen" having the same sound as the name of the composer). Naturally the pastor of St. Johann became worried about the reaction in Prague and appealed to Haydn. The master, in a reply [1] written to the pastor, said that the whole strange story "did no credit to the head and heart of its originator" and continued: "At all times the Creation has been considered the loftiest, most awe-inspiring picture for mankind. To accompany this great work with suitable music could certainly have only the effect of increasing the holy emotions in man's heart and making him more sensible to the goodness and power of the Creator. How could this stirring of divine emotions be a desecration of the church?" Finally Haydn promised to intercede, if necessary, with the emperor, who had always listened to the oratorio with the deepest emotion. We do not know the outcome of this storm in a teacup, but it is to be hoped that the persons responsible for it did not persist in their ridiculous persecution.

The report of a *Creation* performance in another little circle was likely to make Haydn forget the annoying incident. In the small

[1] The letter is dated "Eisenstadt, July 24, 1801." Cf. *Allgemeine Musikzeitung* (1874), No. 3.

German town of Bergen on the North Sea island of Rugen, enthusiastic music lovers got together and performed Haydn's oratorio with
a very modest number of players. So great was their delight and
gratitude that they felt bound to express them to the composer. Coming from the heart, this expression moved Haydn deeply, and he
answered with one of the most charming letters of thanks he ever
wrote:

Vienna, September 22, 1802

GENTLEMEN:

It was indeed a most pleasant surprise to me to receive such a
flattering letter from a place where I could have no idea that the
fruits of my poor talents were known. When now, however, I see that
not only is my name familiar to you, but that my compositions are
performed by you with approval and satisfaction, the warmest wishes
of my heart are fulfilled; and these are to be considered by every
nation into which my works penetrate as a not wholly unworthy
priest of this sacred art. You reassure me on the point so far as regards
your fatherland and, still further, you give me the pleasant convic-
tion (which cannot fail to be a most welcome consolation of my
declining years) that I am often the enviable source from which you,
and so many families susceptible of true feeling, derive pleasure and
enjoyment in domestic life. What happiness does this thought cause
me! Often, when contending with the obstacles of every sort that
interfered with my work, often when my powers both of body and
mind were failing and I felt it a hard matter to persevere in the
course I had entered on, a secret feeling within me whispered, "There
are but few contented and happy men here below; everywhere grief
and care prevail; perhaps your labors may one day be the source
from which the weary and worn, or the man burdened with affairs,
may derive a few moments' rest and refreshment." What a powerful
motive for pressing onwards! And this is why I now look back with
heartfelt and cheerful satisfaction on the work to which I have devoted so long a succession of years and such persevering efforts and
exertions. And now in the fulness of my heart I thank you for your
kindly thoughts of me, and beg you to forgive the delay of my answer.
Feeble health, the inseparable companion of the grey-haired man
of seventy, and likewise pressing business have until now deprived
me of this pleasure. Perhaps nature may yet accord me the gratification of composing a little memorial of myself to send you from which

you may gather the feelings of a gradually decaying old man who would fain, even after death, survive in the charming circle of which you draw so pleasing a picture. I have the honor to be, with the highest consideration,

Your obedient servant,

JOSEPH HAYDN

The references in this letter to declining years, feeble health, and decay are very significant. At that time Haydn was already prone to stress these points, a tendency that was to increase in the years to come. While up to his return from England the composer had felt younger than his actual age, the opposite was happening now. He did not yet stop working; indeed, the summer of 1802 saw him "laboring very wearily" (as he termed it) on his last mass. In addition he was engaged on the quartet, Op. 77 No. 3 and in adapting Scottish folk songs for a new publisher, Whyte of Edinburgh, who paid him a thousand florins for fifty songs. Official duties kept him busy as well and documents in the Eszterházy archives contain various reports by him on engagements of new musicians, on dismissals, and examinations of singers. But it was clear that old age was beginning to bear heavily on the man who had led so extremely industrious a life. He was not really ill, except for the discomfort caused by his old enemy, a nasal polypus which, according to Griesinger, made him "grumpy and uncomfortable." (Now he probably regretted having refused so vehemently the help offered him by the celebrated surgeon, John Hunter in London.) But he grew increasingly weary and fits of dizziness often prevented him from working at the piano. The prince, aware of the state of affairs, began to look for an adequate substitute, and as he was mainly interested in church music, he sought for an expert in this kind of composition. His choice fell at last on Michael Haydn who, after the capture of Salzburg by the French in 1800, had been robbed of his entire property, and like his patron, the archbishop, had lost his position. History seemed to repeat itself. Would the younger brother supplant Joseph at the court of Prince Eszterházy as he had done at St. Stephen's? It is doubtful whether Joseph, enjoying such enormous fame, admitted even to himself any anxiety in this regard. Subconsciously, however, certain memories still rankled and so Joseph thought it his duty to warn Michael of the intrigues at the Eszterházy court; he felt his candid brother was no match for these intrigues. We do not know whether these warnings influenced Michael, but in any case he refused at the last moment, alleging that he could not bear to leave Salzburg, and preferred to accept minor posts there. The prince was disappointed and abandoned his search for the moment. He appointed Johann Fuchs, who had really done the work for the past years, as vice-conductor, while Tomasini was to be responsible for the chamber music in Haydn's absence. At last, in 1804, at Haydn's recommendation he engaged Johann Nepomuk Hummel, a pupil of Mozart, as concertmaster and composer, and it was Hummel who actually took over the master's duties. Under Haydn's successor there were constant conflicts and scenes between the members of the orchestra. Gone was the spirit of friendly co-operation which had characterized this ensemble. The melancholy contrast between the Haydn and the Hummel eras throws a striking light on "Papa" Haydn's genius in handling his "children" and getting the best out of everyone through kindness, intelligence, and firmness.

But what happened at this period among the musicians of the prince was of little concern to Haydn, as he felt himself more and more engulfed by physical infirmities, so much so that eventually he could not even go to Eisenstadt in the summer. At first he fought with some of his former energy against his ailing body and in December, 1802 he wrote to Ignaz Pleyel: "I only wish I could throw off ten years of my life so that I might be able again to show you something new from my work. Perhaps this may yet be possible after all." The succeeding months, however, were spent by the composer, after recovering from a bad cold, in complete inactivity, and only in June, 1803 could Griesinger report that the master, thanks to the good weather, was again improvising a little on the piano. At that time Haydn started on his last quartet; however, only two movements were ever completed.

In the same year the master made his last appearance as a conductor when he performed the *Seven Last Words* for the benefit of the civic Hospital of St. Mark, a charitable institution in which he took a great interest. From then on he was more and more confined to his house and hardly ever seen in public. Even when special homage was to be paid to him on his seventy-third birthday (in 1805), he could not attend the celebration. The scene was the first appearance in public of young Wolfgang Mozart (*fils*), who was to perform among other works a cantata he had composed to words by Griesinger in honor of Haydn's birthday. It was planned that Haydn should introduce the young musician to the audience, but finally the project had to be abandoned as it was feared the excitement would be too much for the invalid master.

The short walks, which were all Haydn could manage with his badly swollen legs, were taken in his own little garden, supported and almost carried by the faithful Elssler. Once the actor August Wilhelm Iffland saw Haydn returning from a stroll in his garden with flowers in his hands, and the old man, who "clearly took comfort in their fragrance" remarked to his guest that "he had attended to his devotions in nature."

Now that the composer definitely felt that the period of his creative work was over, he liked to look back on his former achievements and was anxious to see a catalogue of his life's work prepared. With the help of earlier lists, a thematic catalogue intended to embrace all works composed by Haydn in the last fifty-five years was compiled in 1805 and written out by Elssler. Although the list is incomplete and not free from errors, it is one of the most valuable sources for research on Haydn's music.

Haydn spent his last years in increasing bodily discomfort and they cannot be called happy ones. They differed too completely from his former way of life to satisfy him and his forced inactivity weighed heavily on him. For instance Carpani describes his mood as a "habitual state of sadness" and an "absorption in the melancholy sentiment that life was escaping him." Still, there were brilliant patches even in this shadowy existence. Haydn was fortunately spared the tragic fate of other aging masters, who were forgotten even in their own lifetimes. On the contrary, evidence of his outstanding reputation again and again broke the dreary monotony of an invalid's life. He even experienced the strange sensation of reading obituary notices about himself. In 1805 the rumor spread all over Europe that Haydn had died. In England the *Gentleman's Magazine* announced the master's death and the publisher Thomson wrote a letter of condolence to the Viennese bankers, Fries & Company, who had handled his business with Haydn. In Paris the greatest consternation prevailed. Cherubini wrote a cantata on Haydn's death and Kreutzer composed a violin concerto based on themes from Haydn's works. A special memorial concert with these works and Mozart's

Requiem was planned for February, 1805, when good news from Vienna put a stop to the undertaking.

Haydn was rather amused by the whole matter. He signed a letter to Thomson "to prove that he was still of this base world," and when he heard about the plans in Paris, he remarked: "The good gentlemen! I am greatly indebted to them for the unusual honor. Had I only known of it in time, I would have traveled to Paris to conduct the *Requiem* myself."

High tribute was projected to be paid to the dead composer, nor is this surprising. After all, it has always been so. It is far more rare to see a living composer as greatly honored as was Haydn. In 1803 he had been awarded the gold "Salvator" medal by the city of Vienna, and one year later the city nominated him an honorary citizen. The French, in spite of the honors previously awarded, still felt that they had not done enough for so great a master. In 1805 a diploma of membership was handed him from the Paris Conservatory, another in 1807 from the Société académique des enfants d'Apollon, both accompanied by gold medals. In the following year the Philharmonic Society of St. Petersburg followed the example of Paris. It is not surprising that the old master, when he was feeling particularly low and depressed, should have taken out the box holding his medals to draw encouragement from these visible signs of his success.

Of course he derived an even greater pleasure from displaying them to his guests and this was usually part of the ceremonial observed with visiting strangers whom the name of Haydn had drawn to the little house in the quiet Viennese suburb. These visits meant much to the invalid, and although they sometimes tired him greatly, he would not have missed them for anything. He was always ready to receive anyone who might drop in unannounced. He once remarked to Dies: "You seem to be surprised that I am fully dressed, although I am ailing and weak and cannot go out. My parents trained me strictly as a child to be clean and orderly, and these two qualities have become a second nature to me." But the simple wheelwright and Count Harrach's cook would never, in their wildest dreams, have thought of seeing their Sepperl attired on an ordinary working day in the manner that the Czech musician, Johann Wenzel Tomaschek describes: "Haydn sat in an armchair, very much dressed up. A powdered wig with sidelocks, a white neckband with a gold buckle, a white richly embroidered waistcoat of heavy silk, in the midst of which shone a splendid jabot, a dress coat of fine coffee-colored cloth with embroidered cuffs, black silk breeches, white silk hose, shoes with large silver buckles curved over the instep, and on the little table next to him a pair of white kid gloves made up his attire." [2]

The year 1805 was particularly rich in interesting visitors. The pianist, Marie Bigot (to whom Beethoven gave the autograph of his Sonata Appassionata), delighted Haydn so much with her interpretation of his own works that he exclaimed: "My dear child, you have not only played this, you have composed it." The visit of the violinist, Pierre Baillot, may have left a less pleasant memory, for when the friendly host opened his arms the impetuous Frenchman embraced him with such violence that he almost knocked out the old master's last two teeth. Another visitor from France was Haydn's former pupil and later competitor, Ignaz Pleyel, now a successful publisher. He had greatly pleased the master by his model edition of Haydn's complete string quartets. Pleyel was accompanied by his son, Camille, who described the visit as follows in a letter to his family, dated June 16, 1805:

> We found him very weak; the face, it is true, has hardly changed, but he can scarcely walk and when he speaks for some length of time, he completely loses his breath. He told us that he was only seventy-four years old [as a matter of fact, Haydn was seventy-three!], and looks indeed as if he were eighty, so weak is he. We found him holding a rosary in his hands, and I believe he passes almost the whole day in prayer. He says always that his end is near, that he is too old, and that he is useless in this world. We did not stay long because we saw he wished to pray. I embraced him and kissed his hand which gave him great pleasure. He has a very pretty and well-furnished house, but it seems that he does not see any one. [Here Camille was definitely mistaken!]

The most welcome of all his guests from France proved to be Luigi Cherubini, who took the opportunity of calling on his beloved "Father" when he was invited to produce his operas in Vienna and they spent many happy hours together. Haydn found Cherubini a "handsome little man full of distinction" and gave him the autograph of his symphony No. 103 (with the Drum Roll). He wrote under his name 'Giuseppe Haydn' the words: *Padre del Celebre Cherubini ai*

---

[2] *See* Libussa, *Jahrbuch für 1846,* p. 330.

24to di Feb. 806. At every opportunity the younger composer expressed his deep reverence for Haydn and two years after his departure from Vienna he wrote: "Since I had the bad luck to leave you, dear Father, I have been continuously ill with nervous attacks. They have prevented me from working and trying to imitate you, oh dear Master of us all." [3]

Viennese friends of course continued to visit Haydn, and above all Griesinger, who, as he wrote to Breitkopf, could not bear to give up these visits, although the old man was growing weaker from day to day. He tried to get whatever information he could from the composer for his proposed book, and the same was done by a new friend, the painter, Albert Christoph Dies, who paid all together thirty calls and set down the contents of his conversations in his *Biographische Nachrichten von Joseph Haydn,* published in 1810. Haydn did not object to the inquisitiveness of his friends. He lived more in the past than in the present and evidently enjoyed looking back on the struggles of his childhood and youth.

Another welcome visitor was Magdalene von Kurzböck, an excellent pianist, to whom the master dedicated his last piano sonata (No. 52 in E♭ major) and his last piano trio (E♭ minor, Peters Edition, No. 18).

Sometimes Haydn had the pleasure of seeing his dear Princess Eszterházy in his house. It was she for instance who brought the deeply moved master the sad news of the death of his brother Johann in May, 1805. She was, as Haydn said, like a good angel to him, and thanks to her influence, her husband now showed himself much more gracious to the invalid composer and increased his salary in 1806 to 2,300 florins. Moreover the prince offered him the use of his carriage and paid the accounts of his doctor and apothecary, all of which Haydn greatly appreciated.

On no other occasion did the love and respect shown to the composer become more apparent than at the remarkable performance of *The Creation* in Italian on March 27, 1808. The concert was planned in celebration of Haydn's approaching seventy-sixth birthday. The master was formally invited, and in view of the mild weather, his physician allowed him to leave the house. Prince Eszterházy was—of course!—prevented from attending the performance because of important business but he sent his carriage and

[3] Letter of April 26, 1808.

Haydn rode slowly to the university. A huge crowd, which had to be kept in order by military guards had gathered in front. Members of the high nobility as well as distinguished musicians, among them Beethoven, Salieri, Hummel, and Gyrowetz, received the master, who was carried in an armchair into the beautiful lecture hall. On his appearance a flourish of trumpets and drums was sounded, mingled with jubilant exclamations: "Long live Haydn!" The master was seated among the highest aristocracy, next to Princess Eszter-házy, who wrapped the old man in her own shawl when she noticed him shivering a little. Many other ladies followed her example, and soon Haydn was covered with the costliest of garments. The French ambassador, noticing with pleasure that Haydn was wearing the gold medal from the Concerts des Amateurs on his coat, exclaimed: "This medal is not enough; you should receive all the medals that are distributed in the whole of France." Poems in German and Italian were written for the occasion and were handed to the master by his friends, Magdalene von Kurzböck, and the Baroness Spielmann. The conductor was Salieri; at the leader's desk sat the famous virtuoso, Franz Clement, who thus repaid the master for having conducted the benefit concert for the boy of eleven in London. The audience was in an unusually receptive state of mind. When thunderous applause followed the words "Let there be light—and there was light," Haydn lifted his hands upwards and exclaimed: "Not from me, from thence comes everything." The reception given to him and his work moved the master indescribably. Indeed, he was so shaken that it was thought advisable not to let him stay on after the interval. Everybody present realized that the days on earth of the frail old man were numbered. The people thronged around him with tears in their eyes, shaking his hands and embracing him. Beethoven at this moment behaved not at all like a "Great Mogul," for he knelt down before Haydn and fervently kissed the hands and forehead of his old teacher. Only in broken sentences could Haydn express his thanks and good wishes, but before he was carried out, he lifted his hand as if to bless the whole assembly.

The Princess Eszterházy had the scene painted by Balthasar Wigand and mounted on a costly box which she gave to the delighted master. It contained a sumptuous album with the most cordial inscriptions from the princely family and was furnished with elegant writing equipment and all kinds of useful instruments in fine English steel and gold.⁴ After Haydn's death, the princess acquired the box again for the sum of four hundred florins, and later gave it to Franz Liszt. Eventually it became the property of the Museum of the City of Vienna.

When Cherubini heard of the performance, he wrote: "I have learned with inexpressible satisfaction of the honors paid to you at the University of Vienna when they performed your immortal *Creation*. I wept with joy and wished I had been there to join in offering my share of incense."

This was Haydn's last public appearance. Before long political conditions made festivities of the kind impossible, as Austria again became the scene of a devastating war. Decisive battles were fought in the spring of 1809 and the French army came nearer and nearer to Vienna. These were indeed dark days for the invalid master. His greatest concern was in the revision and alteration of his last will. In the years that had passed since he first drafted it, Haydn's two brothers, Johann and Michael, and his sister, Anna Maria, had died. The master, while leaving most of the legacies unaltered, made his only surviving nephew, Mathias Frölich, his principal heir. Mathias had been trained as a blacksmith at Haydn's expense and lived in the village of Fischamend near Vienna. One year after his uncle's death he settled down at Rohrau where he stayed for the rest of his life and had the pleasure of witnessing the first Haydn Commemoration in 1841, which took place in the master's native village. Whether Mathias was worthy of his uncle's inheritance is open to doubt. Schmid's information that he kept a piano owned by his uncle in a loft and used it as a flour-bin, does not impress us too favorably. Be this as it may, Mathias did not derive from his uncle's rich bequest the benefit that Haydn had fondly imagined. Owing to the inflation following the Napoleonic Wars, the money Mathias inherited lost its value almost entirely and the principal heir of the wealthy composer died a poor man.

Six weeks before his death Haydn called his servants and his grand-niece, Ernestine Juliane Loder, who was looking after him, into his room and read them his will, for he wished to know whether they were satisfied with its provisions. All of them heartily thanked him with tears in their eyes. By the beginning of May the French had

⁴ *See* the description by J. F. Reichardt in *Vertraute Briefe geschrieben auf einer Reise nach Wien* (1810), new edition by Gustav Gugitz (Munich: 1915).

captured some of the western suburbs of Vienna and made the castle of Schönbrunn their headquarters. Haydn's house was perilously near the enemy and Magdalene von Kurzböck entreated him to move to her house in the center of the city. Haydn refused, for he felt unequal to coping with any change in his life. On May 12th the great bombardment of the city started, and a cannon ball fell with a tremendous noise quite near Haydn's house. The house shook as in an earthquake and Haydn's entourage were scared out of their wits. Not so the old invalid, who exclaimed above the uproar: "Children, don't be frightened; where Haydn is, nothing can happen to you." (Marion Scott very aptly called this "sublime illogicality" the "Nelson touch in Haydn.") For twenty-four hours the bombardment went on, shattering the poor old man's nervous system. When Vienna capitulated and quiet was restored, the invalid, at whose doorstep Napoleon had placed a guard of honor, was unable to recover. He suffered no pain, but his strength was ebbing away. On May 26th kind fate still allowed him a great joy. A French officer of hussars, by the name of Clément Sulemy, called and after conversing with the master about his *Creation,* sang to him the aria "In native worth." According to a letter from Andreas Streicher [5] (who got the report from Elssler), he sang in "so manly, so sublimely a style, and with so much truth of expression and real musical sentiment that Haydn could hardly restrain his tears of joy and assured the singer as well as the people in his house that he had never before heard the aria sung in so masterly a manner. After half an hour's visit the officer mounted his horse in order to go against the enemy." (Schnerich contends that Sulemy fell soon afterwards in the battle of Aspern.) On the same day Haydn called his people to the piano and played for the last time his favorite, the Austrian hymn. In those days of Austria's collapse, the act had an unusual significance. Haydn, playing it three times in succession, put into the immortal tune all that he felt for his unhappy country, and although his strength nearly failed him, he achieved an "expressiveness that surprised even himself." [6] But on the next day he could rise no more. A second doctor was called in for consultation, but was unable to suggest anything to combat the quickly progressing exhaustion. The master seemed to be quite happy and when asked how he was feeling, whispered: "Children, be

[5] Streicher's letter to Griesinger is dated July 2, 1809.
[6] Elssler's letter to Griesinger, dated June 30, 1809.

comforted, I am well." Nevertheless the periods of unconsciousness increased and on May 31, 1809, shortly after midnight, he went "blissfully and gently" to sleep, to wake no more.

Austria, in the throes of a deadly struggle, could not pay the departed the honors that unquestionably would have been extended to him in normal circumstances. Indeed, there was so great an upheaval in the town that the news of Haydn's death was hardly circulated before the funeral. Carl Rosenbaum, ex-secretary of Prince Eszterházy, commented on the event as follows in his diary: "Haydn lay in his large room, dressed in black, not disfigured at all. At his feet were placed the seven medals from Paris, Russia, Sweden, and Vienna. After 5:00 o'clock he was borne in an oak coffin to the Gumpendorf Church, carried around it three times, blessed and carried to the Hundsturm Cemetery. Not a single Viennese conductor accompanied him." However, Rosenbaum could not deny that the official obsequies, which took place on June 15th, were "very solemn and worthy of Haydn." Members of the French army alternated with grenadiers of the municipal militia to form a line around the catafalque. The medals were placed in front of it and among them the little ivory tablet with Haydn's name which had been handed to the master as a free pass to the London concerts.[7] High-ranking French officials, generals, and officers as well as the whole cultured world of Vienna were present. The music was chosen very fittingly for the occasion, for it was the *Requiem* by his beloved Mozart that Vienna's musicians played on taking leave of Joseph Haydn.

[7] According to Griesinger, Haydn was particularly impressed by this courtesy and laid stress on the fact that nothing of the kind had ever been shown him in Vienna.

Chapter 11

AN INCONGRUOUS POSTLUDE

IN THE year of Haydn's death Prince Eszterházy applied for permission to have the body exhumed and moved to Eisenstadt. But presently the whole matter slipped his memory, and although he received the permission, no action was taken. Haydn's tomb remained neglected, until in 1814 the master's devoted pupil, Sigismund Neukomm, on returning to Vienna from France, had a simple marble tablet erected bearing as an inscription Haydn's favorite quotation from Horace *non omnis moriar* set as a five-part riddle canon. The prince continued to ignore the question of Haydn's last resting place until in 1820 he was reminded of his obligations by Adolphus Frederick, Duke of Cambridge. This distinguished visitor observed, after attending a gala performance of *The Creation* given in his honor at Eisenstadt: "How fortunate was the man who employed this Haydn in his lifetime and now possesses his mortal remains." Prince Eszterházy did not care to contradict his guest's assumption but he gave orders immediately for the body to be brought to Eisenstadt and for it to be buried in the English fashion in the Bergkirche, where Haydn had so often performed his own masses. When the coffin was opened for identification, the horrified officials found no head on the body, only the wig. Inquiries soon brought an explanation of the mystery. Two students of Gall's and Spurtzheim's work on phrenology, namely Haydn's friend, Carl Rosenbaum, former secretary of Prince Eszterházy and Johann N. Peter, the administrator of a penitentiary, bribed the gravedigger and stole Haydn's head a few days after the funeral, in order to "protect it from desecration." Peter had a black

174

wooden box made with glass windows and decorated with a golden lyre in which the skull was placed on a white silk cushion trimmed with black. When Haydn's body arrived in Eisenstadt without the head, the prince was furious and sent the police to Peter, who said that he had given the skull to Rosenbaum. A search in the latter's house did not yield any result, as Rosenbaum's wife, the singer Therese Gassmann, hid the skull in her straw mattress and lay down in bed. The outraged prince now tried bribery and his emissary promised Rosenbaum a large sum if he would deliver the skull, whereupon the skull of an old man was handed to the prince and buried with Haydn's body. Not unnaturally Prince Eszterházy did not keep his promise of a reward, but neither had the wary ex-secretary acted honestly, as he had not delivered the right skull. On his deathbed Rosenbaum gave Haydn's skull to Peter and made him promise to leave it in his will to the museum of the Society of Friends of Music in Vienna, the owner of a great number of valuable Haydn relics. And that is where Haydn's skull has been reverently preserved since 1895,[1] and has been shown by the author of this book in prewar times to countless admirers of Haydn.

[1] The authenticity of the skull of the Society of Friends of Music was proved beyond any doubt by Joseph Tandler, in "Ueber den Schädel Haydns" Mitteilungen der anthropologischen Gesellschaft (Vienna: 1909).

Part Two

WORKS

Introduction

THE SOURCES

THE student who undertakes the compilation of a work dealing with the music of Joseph Haydn is faced with difficulties that it would be hard to overestimate. Collected editions have been made of the works of Bach and Handel, Mozart and Beethoven, Schubert and Schumann, Mendelssohn and Chopin, Berlioz and Brahms. Even the compositions of the lesser known old masters, Josquin des Prés, Palestrina, Lasso, Monteverdi, Lully, and others have been painstakingly collected and published. No such edition, however, exists for the creator of the Clock and Surprise symphonies. It is true that a definitive Collected Edition of Haydn's works was begun in 1907, when it was estimated that it would comprise some eighty volumes. So far ten of them have appeared and if the edition continues to be produced at this rate, we may look forward to its conclusion in a little less than three hundred years.

Catalogues of Haydn's works have repeatedly been made. Their contents, however, are so widely conflicting that instead of clarifying the situation they have rather added to the confusion. Two examples will illustrate this.

The older biographers of Haydn, following the lead of the composer's own catalogue, state that the master wrote 118 symphonies. This figure was increased to 144 by Leopold Schmidt, to 149 by Alfred Wotquenne, and to 153 by Sir Henry Hadow. In 1907 Eusebius Mandyczewski, using extensive preparatory work by Carl Ferdinand Pohl, reduced the number of symphonies to 104, contending that all other so-called Haydn symphonies were either not symphonies or not by Haydn. He pointed out that suites, overtures, and concertos had been enumerated among Haydn's symphonies and that in many other cases the master's authorship could not be established authentically. It seemed as if Mandyczewski's work had definitely clarified an important part of the Haydn researches. His list, which opens the volumes of symphonies in the Collected Edition, was generally adopted and for more than twenty years it remained unquestioned. Therefore, the declaration in 1932 by Adolf Sandberger, famous for his researches on Haydn's string quartets, that Mandyczewski's list ought to be scrapped promptly because it omitted at least seventy-eight symphonies came as a great shock. According to Sandberger, a number of the symphonies that Mandyczewski considered as dubious or false are clearly genuine, while other authentic Haydn symphonies were not even known to Mandyczewski.[1] One of the foundations of the Haydn researches erected slowly and painstakingly by Pohl and Mandyczewski seemed about to collapse. Nobody, therefore, was much surprised when in 1938, under the auspices of the eminent Sir Donald Tovey, a "rediscovered" symphony was printed under the name of Joseph Haydn, although an autograph score clearly proved that all movements but one were by the master's younger brother, Michael.[2]

Another case of mistaken identity took a rather surprising turn. In 1936 Ernst Fritz Schmid edited the Göttweig Sonatas which he considered to be unknown pianoforte sonatas by Joseph Haydn; but in the very next year he had to confess that instead of Haydn, one of his lesser contemporaries, the publisher Franz Anton Hoffmeister, was the real author of these compositions. Also the *Requiem* edited by Schmid under Haydn's name turned out to be the work of a minor composer.

The reason for this situation is no less fantastic than the situation itself. It can be expressed in a brief sentence: Haydn was too famous. During the end of the eighteenth century and the beginning of the nineteenth there was a continual demand from amateurs and professional organizations all over the world for new compositions by Haydn. The master did all in his power to satisfy these urgent calls,

---

[1] Sandberger's theory was contested by other scholars. Cf. articles by Jens Peter Larsen in *Acta Musicologica and Zeitschrift für Musik* (1935–37).

[2] The editor, Hans Gál, explained his attitude in a number of spirited articles in the *Daily Telegraph* (October–December, 1938). See also H. Gál, "A Rediscovered Symphony by Haydn," *Monthly Musical Record* (January, 1939) and Marion M. Scott, "Mi-Jo Haydn," *Monthly Musical Record* (March–April, 1939).

but his creative output was never able to keep pace with the unend-- ing stream of orders. Haydn often sold the same work to both private persons or organizations and to publishers in different countries. The Paris Symphonies, for instance, were sent to Paris for performances in the Concerts de la Loge Olympique and were sold later to the publishers Imbault in Paris, Artaria in Vienna, and Forster in London. Somewhat different is the case of the symphonies written for Prince Ernst of Oettingen-Wallerstein. In 1787 this ardent music lover asked Haydn for three symphonies that "besides himself nobody else must own." When the music was delivered the delighted prince sent the master a heavy gold snuffbox filled with fifty ducats. Soon after, however, these same symphonies mysteriously found their way to different publishers, such as Hummel in Amsterdam, André in Offenbach, Le Duc in Paris, and Forster in London. We cannot avoid the suspicion that Haydn secretly connived at these publica- tions. If so, he was but following a custom usual in the eighteenth century. One of the most puzzling problems created by the enor- mous demand for Haydn's music is that of the piano trio in C major (No. 12 of the Peters Edition). The composer sold this work to For- ster in London in 1784 and it was also printed by Artaria in Vienna. Nevertheless in 1803 the master rather surprisingly informed Breit- kopf & Härtel that this trio was not his own work but a composition by his brother, Michael. This is a case of Haydn versus Haydn and it seems not unlikely that the composer, hard pressed for new com- positions, sent to the publishers a work by his younger brother.

But with all his shrewdness and even with the use of petty devices Haydn was never able to satisfy all the publishers. Soon these disap- pointed men found an easy way out of their difficulties. They pro- duced their own Haydn compositions. The number of works by other composers published during Haydn's lifetime under his name is ex- cessive. Jens Peter Larsen points out that the so-called Haydn sym- phonies in his Op. 9, 12, and 13, printed in Paris, contain sixteen works of which only three are authentic Haydn compositions. The case of his string quartets is even worse. Op. 18, 21, and 28 contain eighteen pieces, not one of which is genuine. It is known that For- ster in London, although a personal friend of Haydn, printed in- discriminately both authentic and spurious Haydn symphonies. The Czech composer, Gyrowetz, tells us in his autobiography that when he arrived in Paris in 1789 he was surprised to find his own symphony in G major printed under Joseph Haydn's name. The outraged composer went to the publishers, who excused themselves by saying that they had bought the symphony from the violinist Tost, a member of the orchestra at Eszterháza. In this particular case the publishers probably acted in good faith as they knew of Tost's connection with Haydn's orchestra and the violinist had sold them genuine symphonies together with the counterfeit one.

It is not easy to determine in every case who was really responsible for the fraudulent use of Haydn's name. Very often the publishers were the culprits; sometimes, however, copyists in Vienna or even members of Haydn's orchestra were approached, and these men were often more interested in gaining substantial fees than in scrupulously observing the truth. It was much easier to take a composition by Vanhal, Dittersdorf, Gyrowetz, or Michael Haydn and change the name on the title page than to obtain a new work from Haydn himself, who had the inconvenient habit of disposing of every composition even before it was put on paper.

Neither the dubious nor the outright false compositions of Haydn were always printed. Before 1780 in particular, music was often reproduced by professional copyists. How important this form of reproduction was is shown by the fact that between 1760 and 1787 the publishing house of Breitkopf & Härtel issued no less than twenty-five thematic catalogues of "musical works that have not been made public through printing" and were "now to be had in correct manuscript copies." [3] The name of Haydn appears frequently in these catalogues, but they are a source both of information and of confusion, for again only part of the compositions listed under the master's name were really written by him. Haydn, however, may have felt a certain consolation in the fact that he was by no means the only composer whose name was falsely used. In his article on Sammartini,[4] Georges de St. Foix proved that of the four symphonies listed under the name of Sammartini in the Breitkopf catalogue of 1762 only two were by the composer himself, the third and fourth being by Martinelli and Pergolesi respectively.

Thus it is certainly not easy to form a correct idea of what Haydn actually wrote; yet on the other hand, the problem does not present insurmountable obstacles. Great though the difficulties are, they can

[3] Cf. Kathi Meyer's interesting study in *The Musical Quarterly* (April, 1944).
[4] In *Sammelbände der Internationalen Musikgesellschaft* (1914).

be overcome. Undoubtedly there are sources above suspicion that must be carefully studied by anyone making a comprehensive research.

Among the best sources are Haydn's autographs. If a work is in the master's own script, written with his characteristic thin and energetic notes on a sheet of paper showing one of the familiar watermarks, there is hardly any room for doubt. This is especially so if one finds written at the beginning the typical *Di me Giuseppe Haydn,* together with the date of composition, and at the end *Finis. Laus Deo* (The end. Praise the Lord). All together there are more than forty autographed symphonies, six overtures, over two dozen string quartets, some thirty *divertimenti* for different ensembles, a dozen piano compositions, six concertos, most of the operas, ten masses, and many smaller instrumental compositions. They amount to over one hundred and sixty autographs and this seems a considerable number in itself, although it is pitifully small compared with Haydn's vast output in all fields of composition.

Most of these manuscripts are to be found in the library of the Princes Eszterházy in Budapest, Hungary. The vast collection accumulated during the many years of Haydn's activities in the service of this family was increased by the wholesale purchase of the music and books left by Haydn after his death. No other collection can boast of so many precious Haydn relics as this library, which has become the traditional center of Haydn research. On a smaller scale, though still of great importance, are the Haydn collections of the State Library in Berlin and those of the Society of Friends of Music and the National Library in Vienna. Valuable Haydn compositions are also preserved in the British Museum in London and in the Bibliothèque du Conservatoire and the Bibliothèque Nationale, both in Paris. These collections must be consulted not only for autographs but for all problems concerning Haydn, for in them more than three fourths of all the material for the study of his compositions have been preserved.

Fortunately, autographs are not the only sources of our knowledge of the extent of Haydn's works. Catalogues made or authorized by the composer himself help us to distinguish between the trustworthy and the spurious in both old printed music and manuscript copies. Perhaps the most important of these lists is the so-called *Entwurf Katalog* (draft catalogue) written mainly by Haydn himself or by his copyist, Joseph Elssler, and now preserved in the State Library in Berlin. This most authoritative catalogue lists on seventeen sheets the thematic beginnings of compositions by Haydn, thus making the identification of these works possible. According to the investigations of Jens Peter Larsen the draft catalogue was started by Haydn, with the help of Elssler, in 1765 and continued somewhat intermittently until 1777, after which date only a few additions were made at rare intervals. For the period from 1765 to 1777 it provides an invaluable source of information.

Better known than this early list is the famous thematic *Verzeichnisz aller derjenigen Compositionen, welche ich mich beyläufig erinnere von meinem 18ten bis in das 73ste Jahr verfertiget zu haben* (catalogue of all those compositions that, as nearly as I can remember, I composed between my 18th and 73rd year). It was written by Johann Elssler—Joseph's son—who became Haydn's faithful copyist after his father's death. This most important catalogue is preserved in the Eszterházy collection at Budapest. With its one hundred and twenty-three pages, filled with many hundreds of themes of Haydn's compositions, it is an impressive document and would seem to be admirably suited for solving all problems of the Haydn research. Unfortunately, however, the memory of the man of seventy-three left much to be desired, and all the friends who visited him in 1805, the year of the completion of this catalogue, agreed that Haydn's mental recollections were far from trustworthy. He and Elssler used the best sources at their disposal for this work, the above-mentioned *Entwurf Katalog,* autographs and other manuscripts from Haydn's collection, and reliable printed editions authorized by himself. But in spite of their great efforts this catalogue is far from being satisfactory. While it affords no actual evidence that Haydn included works by other composers, it nevertheless contains many mistakes. Among the operas, for instance, a work called *L'Infedeltà fedele* (*Faithful Unfaithfulness*) is listed. This title sounds strange and actually Haydn never wrote any opera by that name. The two rather similar titles of Haydn's operas, *La Fedeltà premiata* (*Faithfulness Rewarded*) and *L'Infedeltà delusa* (*Faithlessness Deluded*), may have been responsible for this mistake. Among the masses the so-called *Little Organ Solo Mass* is quoted twice: once with bars three and four of its beginning, as *Mass No. 4* and then with bars one and two, as *Mass No. 13.* In the list of the symphonies Haydn and Elssler quote as No. 17 the first movement and as No. 91 the second movement of the same symphony (No. 34 of the Collected Edition). Similarly they note as No. 32 the slow introduction and as No. 100 the following allegro of one symphony (No. 54 of the Collected Edition). Worse than these mistakes is the fact that many of the works listed in the catalogue are not to be found in any library; probably they were lost during one of the fires that ravaged both Eszterháza and Eisenstadt. On the other hand, a number of Haydn's compositions, the authenticity of which cannot be doubted, are missing from the Haydn-Elssler catalogue. Especially for the period before 1765 and for occasional compositions, such as the little pieces for musical clocks, or the Lira Concertos, the list of 1805 is not a reliable source.

This catalogue, made under Haydn's personal supervision, is essential to research, but if it is to be used to good advantage a clearheaded criticism of its contents is as necessary as the study of supplementary material.[5]

Authentic contemporary editions also furnish important sources of information about Haydn's music. Not all the publishers and copyists were pirating Haydn. Many of them were authorized by the master himself and in some cases we know that he personally supervised the publication of the music. Early editions of this type must certainly be considered as fully reliable. Among these authentic prints the editions of the Viennese publishers, Artaria & Company, are of special importance. Between 1780 and 1790 one hundred and fifty-seven works by Haydn, both original compositions and arrangements, were published by Artaria. Of equal rank are the editions of the Paris Symphonies by Imbault, Paris, for which Haydn furnished the autographs. After Haydn visited England, business connections with London publishers predominated. He worked with William Forster, Longman & Broderip, John Bland, William Napier, George Thomson, and others. At the beginning of the nineteenth century it was a German firm that printed the greatest amount of Haydn's work. From 1800 to 1806 Breitkopf & Härtel in Leipzig published twelve installments of the so-called *Oeuvres complettes*. The master at first did not

[5] Larsen (cf. Bibliography) edited facsimile editions of the draft catalogue as well as of the Haydn catalogue of 1805 (omitting only the Scottish songs). His publication also contains the so-called *Katalog Kees*, a list of Haydn's symphonies belonging originally to his friend, Court Councilor von Kees. It was used by the master and Elssler as a basis for the list of the symphonies in the catalogue of 1805. In an appendix Larsen listed a great number of additional compositions, the authenticity of which is still uncertain.

answer the publishers' written inquiry as to whether or not he would agree to the publication of such an edition. But when Griesinger gave his services as an intermediary and called on the old composer, Haydn gladly gave his consent. The *Oeuvres complettes* were, of course, not a collected edition in the modern sense. They contained only compositions for piano alone or works with piano, such as songs and piano trios, and even these types of composition were by no means complete.

Haydn's former pupil Ignaz Pleyel supplemented these Breitkopf editions by publishing simultaneously in Paris a *Collection complette des Quatuors d'Haydn*. It was an excellent edition of all the string quartets and became the basis of most of the later printings.[6]

Among the Haydn publishers, the master himself must not be forgotten. Occasionally Haydn tried to tackle the business end of composition, but he never kept at it for any length of time. In 1799 the publication of *The Creation* was announced by the composer himself, but soon after the master entrusted Artaria with at least part of the distribution. And in 1801 the plates and remaining copies were all sold to Breitkopf & Härtel.

As a last source of information on the extent of Haydn's work there remain the authentic manuscript copies of his compositions. If the work of a copyist is supplemented by Haydn's own writing, for instance, in his corrections or signature, there can be no doubt that the master approved of it. The Wolf Museum at Eisenstadt possesses a score of Haydn's opera *Armida* written by an unknown copyist but containing many annotations and corrections by Haydn himself. This and other similar manuscripts must certainly be considered as authentic. The same may be said of such manuscripts as display the familiar handwritings of the master's favorite copyists, the Elsslers, father and son, or his pupils, Polzelli and Neukomm. Even if the identity of the writer is unknown, the mere fact that an eighteenth-century manuscript can be traced back to Haydn's own library or to that of Prince Eszterházy can be considered as a fair proof of its authenticity.

The field of research on Haydn will remain dangerous and difficult ground as long as the several hundreds of spurious compositions have

---

[6] The list of the string quartets in Haydn's catalogue of 1805 is also based on the Pleyel edition.

not been scientifically investigated. Only when this is done will a modern thematic catalogue of the master's compositions and a collected edition of his works be possible. The Second World War has destroyed any hope for a speedy solution of these problems.

The reader may be perplexed to find in the following chapters the symphonies quoted according to the Collected Edition, the string quartets with their opus numbers, the piano trios after the Peters Edition, the baryton trios after Haydn's own catalogue. Such discrepancies are unavoidable as long as there is no catalogue of Haydn's works of the type of Köchel's *Verzeichnis* of Mozart's works.

This book makes no attempt to deal with all the works of Haydn. Such an endeavor would be impossible under present conditions and include all the authentic works that are important for the outlining will be impracticable for a long time to come. It tries, however, to of Haydn's artistic personality.

Chapter 12

YOUTH

The First Period: 1750 — 1759

THERE is nothing sensational about Haydn's early compositions. Unlike the precocious geniuses of the eighteenth century—a Pergolesi or a Mozart—who died at an early age, or the masters of the romantic period, who wrote some of their best works at the beginning of their careers, Haydn developed with the utmost slowness. If an accident had caused his death when he was thirty-one years old, the age at which Schubert died, he would not have written a single work capable of bringing him lasting fame. Like Handel and Verdi, Haydn composed his greatest masterpieces during the latter part of his life. He was nearly sixty when he wrote his first London Symphony and over seventy when the two great oratorios, *The Creation* and *The Seasons* were completed.

Hardly any of the young musician's first attempts pointed to future greatness. In the compositions written before 1760 Haydn followed the model of the "preclassical" school. He was just one of the many exponents of the *style galant* and by no means the most important.

In order to understand the position of the young composer it is necessary to look back at the general evolution of music during the second quarter of the eighteenth century.

Even before Johann Sebastian Bach wrote his most important works a strong reaction had set in against the style of the great old master of baroque music. "The essence of the new artistic creed was," as Paul Lang points out, "an urge for liberty: liberation from the rules that had become stereotyped, from the stylistic conventions that had become rigid, from the artistic forms that had become immutable." [1] The new rococo period tried to supplant majestic splendor by graceful delicacy. Whereas baroque art had striven toward a powerful unity of form, the younger generation preferred looseness and variety. Music had changed the buskins of pomposity for the dancing slippers of the *style galant*.

This revolutionary movement originated mainly with the Italians, Austrians, and Bohemians born during the first quarter of the eighteenth century. The "preclassical" composers, as they were frequently called, stood midway between the baroque and the classic masters. They were fifteen to thirty years younger than Bach and fifteen to thirty years older than Haydn. This "preclassical" school disliked every type of polyphonic writing. Strict counterpoint was practically eliminated and so were the forms of the Italian *sonata da chiesa* and the French *ouverture* which included as a rule a fugue. On the other hand the sinfonia, the artless curtain raiser of the Italian opera, consisting of a fast, a slow. and another fast movement, now came into frequent use as a separate instrumental piece. Its popularity was matched only by the suite, a set of pieces of dance character. Both these forms exhibit the easy gaiety and the colorful variety so dear to the rococo period.

It was not long before the sinfonia and suite began to attract and influence each other. A great number of hybrid forms resulted from the combination, one of which was to become of outstanding importance. About 1740 the Viennese composer, Georg Matthias Monn, wrote a sinfonia consisting of an allegro, a slow aria, and a final allegro; between the last two movements he inserted a minuet taken from the suite of dances. But the possibilities of the newly created form were, at least in Vienna, not immediately realized. Monn and his contemporary, Georg Christoph Wagenseil, still preferred the sinfonia in three movements to the cycle of four movements.

Even more important than the shaping of a new instrumental form was the development of its first movement into the so-called sonata form. The beginning of this process was to be observed as far back as the baroque period and was not completed until about the year 1770. The aim of this evolution was to create, as an analogy to the three movements of the sinfonia, three sections in its first movement. An "exposition" displayed the themes, a "development" treated them in a varied way and modulated to distant keys, and a "recapitulation"

[1] *Music in Western Civilization* (New York: 1941), p. 533.

brought a restatement of the first section. Even the exposition itself was in three parts, for between the main theme at the beginning and the concluding theme, a subsidiary theme was inserted. These transformations were made with a view of giving greater solidity and poise to the levity of the sinfonia form. For no sooner had the massive grandeur of the baroque style been overcome than a new process of complication set in, and it is significant of the German mentality that German composers took the lead in this movement. Joseph Haydn's work carried the development to a climax; but he was only continuing a process begun by the previous generation.

This leads to the question, who were Haydn's immediate predecessors? It seems almost as difficult to determine the origin of Haydn's orchestral style as it is to ascertain the true origin of his family. Hugo Riemann [2] tried to prove that Haydn was a disciple of such Bohemian and Austrian composers as Franz Xaver Richter (b. 1709), Ignaz Holzbauer (b. 1711), and Johann Stamitz (b. 1717), living at Mannheim in southwestern Germany. Fausto Torrefranca [3] and Robert Sondheimer,[4] on the other hand, considered that certain Italian composers, especially Giovanni Battista Sammartini (b. 1701), exercised a decisive influence in the development of the classical style. But it is hardly to be doubted that Guido Adler and Wilhelm Fischer [5] were correct when they stated that Haydn carried on from where such other Viennese composers as the younger Georg Reutter (b. 1708), Georg Christoph Wagenseil (b. 1715), and Georg Matthias Monn (b. 1717) left off. Haydn may have known of the Mannheim group and of various Italian composers, but as their style differed so little from that of the Viennese masters there was no need for him to draw from foreign sources what he was able to find at home. It is true that young Haydn used the Mannheim *walze* (road roller), a melody rising by steps with a simultaneous crescendo and the accompaniment of a pedal point; he liked sudden changes from forte to piano, from strong sections in unison to soft harmonized sections. He employed subsidiary themes in the minor with their characteristic imitations, and the "rocket" themes that suddenly rise from a low to a high range. But all these devices were the general prop-

[2] See *Handbuch der Musikgeschichte* (Leipzig: 1922), II, 3 and Preface to *Denkmäler deutscher Tonkunst*, second series, III, 1, VII, 2, VIII, 2.
[3] "Le origini della Sinfonia," *Rivista Musicale Italiana* (1913).
[4] "G. B. Sammartini," *Zeitschrift für Musikwissenschaft*, III (1920–21).
[5] See Adler's and Fischer's works in the Bibliography.

erty of the time and Haydn did not need to go to Mannheim or Milan to become acquainted with them; he found them right on his doorstep, in the city where he grew up. In those few cases, however, in which Viennese "preclassical" composers differed from their contemporaries, Haydn always tended to identify himself with the Austrian tradition. Like Monn and Wagenseil, the young master wrote in turn symphonies in three and in four movements; like these Austrian composers he used recapitulations that brought in a complete restatement of the material of the exposition. On the other hand Haydn did not follow Stamitz and other early symphonists in their penchant for incomplete recapitulations.

While young Haydn favored in his orchestral music the sinfonia form with slight influences from the suite, his works for pianoforte and his chamber music were based on the suite form with slight influences from the sinfonia. The composer employed here the *divertimento*, the *partita*, or the *cassazione*, sets of pieces in which the use of the same key and the dance character prevailed, with one or more movements displaying the simple sonata form. In these pieces Haydn closely followed the "preclassical" style. His minuets, for instance, with their typical motion in triplets and formalistic cadences clearly show the rococo spirit.

In discussing the works in such an order as to begin with the compositions written for small ensembles and gradually proceeding to those written for bigger groups of instruments, we must first speak of the sonatas for pianoforte. It must be emphasized here that the clavier used by Haydn was the same instrument that Mozart also employed for his keyboard compositions: the pianoforte. Although some of the earliest of Haydn's sonatas may also be played on the clavichord (the favorite instrument of Philipp Emanuel Bach), and most of Haydn's concertos on the more powerful harpsichord, Haydn's main instrument was certainly the delicate *hammerclavier* of the eighteenth century. The words *per il cembalo* or *pour le clavecin* on some of the old manuscripts or printed editions must not lead us to believe that the composer actually wrote these compositions for the harpsichord. *Pour le clavecin ou fortepiano* was a standard indication on clavier compositions of the period and is found even on a number of Beethoven's piano sonatas. The fact that during the last years of his life Haydn owned a precious English harpsichord made by Burkat Shudi and John Broadwood has no connection with his clavier compositions. From this harpsichord the master conducted symphonies or other large ensemble works, but it was not used as a solo instrument for his sonatas.

Haydn wrote piano sonatas from early youth to old age. The Collected Edition, revised with great care by Karl Päsler, contains fifty-two sonatas, of which Nos. 1, 2,[6] and 4 may have been written during Haydn's first period of composition. The first sonata shows the composer completely absorbed in the Austrian art of Georg Christoph Wagenseil. The use of the same tonality in all three movements of each piece, the name *partita*, the inclusion of a minuet with a trio in the minor key, the Alberti basses, the occurrence of melodies that seem to have been conceived first for the violin and later arranged for the pianoforte, and the clear separation of the three themes in the exposition of the first movement are typical of the Viennese piano style of the rococo period. On the other hand, the second sonata shows some marks of the influence of Philipp Emanuel Bach which was to assume much larger proportions in the years to come. The syncopations and unison passages, the passionate and quite personal character of its largo with the sudden contrasts in mood are unmistakably of north-German origin. But there is no doubt that at this early age Haydn's art grew primarily out of the soil of his native country. Although in the fourth sonata some technical details, such as the division of passages between the two hands, still remind us of Bach, the predominantly Austrian character, especially conspicuous in the minuet and trio, shows the true origin of the work.

No other type of Haydn's chamber music equals in importance his compositions for strings alone. The author has attempted to prove [7] that the origin of the string quartet is to be found in the four-part instrumental compositions by Austrian and German composers of the early seventeenth century, such as works by Peuerl, Posch, Schein, Hausmann, Franck, and Staden. These compositions are definitely intended for performance by string instruments; the thematic material is evenly distributed between the four parts, the thematic invention is simple, almost like a folk song, and the technique of

---

[6] The authenticity of Nos. 1 and 2 could not be definitely established, but the author considers it as very likely that these two works are genuine.

[7] In a paper read in New York at a meeting of the American Musicological Society in 1943. (Cf. Karl Geiringer, "Paul Peuerl" in *Studien zur Musikwissenschaft*, vol. XVI.)

composing variations is expertly handled. Not much imagination is needed to see in these pieces early precursors of the classical string quartet. But this type of composition came to an end around 1620, because of the degeneration of the tenor part, which was assigned to the viola. The quartet was thus transformed into a trio sonata consisting of two violins and figured bass, the latter to be executed by a violoncello and a keyboard instrument which improvised chords to fill the gap between the two treble instruments and the bass. (This trio sonata was, therefore, in reality a sort of keyboard quartet.) For a hundred years the trio sonata prevailed as the main form of chamber music and all the great masters of baroque music, like Corelli, Purcell, Handel, and Bach wrote pieces for this ensemble. Nevertheless, during the first half of the eighteenth century it was gradually pushed into the background. Alessandro Scarlatti's *sonate a quattro* which, according to Edward J. Dent, were written between 1715 and 1725, were again real string quartets, reinstating the former viola part in substitution for the part filled by the keyboard instrument. The new string quartet of the eighteenth century soon became very popular, especially in Germany, as compositions by Franz Xaver Richter, Johann Zach, Philipp Emanuel Bach, Joseph Starzer, and others can prove. But in all these works, and in the quartets of young Haydn as well, the viola part was still dependent on the violoncello which was frequently figured, thus implying that the addition of a keyboard instrument was optional. The close relationship to the old trio sonata was herewith established. Haydn followed the general trend of his time. He wrote trio sonatas before attempting the string quartet, as it never occurred to the young composer to deviate from established conventions.

Haydn's trios for two violins and violoncello which are apparently based on the baroque form of the trio sonata belong to the composer's earliest attempts in the field of chamber music. Haydn lists in his own catalogue twenty-one of these pieces, of which Nos. 15–20 appear as early as 1763 in a Breitkopf & Härtel catalogue and were probably written around 1750. The rather thin texture of the compositions and the occasional crossing of the part of the first violin with the bass (noticeable even in the trio No. 2, written after 1760) indicate that a keyboard instrument, doubling the bass of the violoncello in the lower octave and filling the gaps between the middle parts, is to join the ensemble, changing the string trio into a keyboard quartet. These compositions, with their rather trivial melodies built on the triad display the simple and gay character of the *style galant.*

More important than the trios are Haydn's string quartets for two violins, viola, and violoncello. Whenever the master's music is mentioned we like to think of his quartets and there is every reason for doing so. Although Haydn wrote a great many, all are interesting and at least half are unquestioned masterpieces; they were declared unequaled by Goethe who was not even particularly interested in Haydn.

There is still another reason why the string quartet plays so important a role in Haydn's musical evolution. The composer was in his early twenties when he wrote his first quartet and he had passed his seventieth birthday before he began to work on his last, which proved to be the ultimate significant composition Haydn was ever to write. No other form of music occupied the composer for an equal length of time.

We do not know the exact number of Haydn's string quartets. In the master's own catalogue of 1805, eighty-three are enumerated but among these are included seven arrangements of a sacred piece for orchestra called *The Seven Last Words of Our Saviour on the Cross,* which won so much favor that Haydn included arrangements of it in both his piano works and his string quartets. These eighty-three works actually comprise only seventy-six quartets and even this figure is not correct, for the composer omitted works he had written in his youth. Nos. 1–4 and 6–12 of Haydn's own list (usually known as Op. 1 Nos. 1–4, Op. 1 No. 6, and Op. 2 Nos. 1–6) belong to the master's first period of composition. A twelfth quartet in E♭ major, known as "No. O" was erroneously listed by Haydn among the *Divertimenti auf verschiedene Instrumenten.* Early editions of Haydn's six string quartets forming Op. 1, such as those printed by J. J. Hummel, Amsterdam; Longman & Broderip, London; and Bremner, London, include this quartet "No. O" together with the quartets, Op. 1 Nos. 1–4 and Op. 1 No. 6 of Haydn's list. Later editions, however, such as that of La Chevardière, Paris, omitted the quartet in E♭ major, replacing it by the quartet, Op. 1 No. 5 which belongs definitely to the period after 1760, and is probably an arrangement of a symphonic work with oboes and French horns (cf. p. 207). Haydn himself, using for his catalogue the list of Pleyel's Collected Edition of the string quartets, did not enumerate "No. O" among the quartets, but only among the *divertimenti* and the nineteenth century completely overlooked the modest creation. Oddly enough, after more than a century of ob- livion, it was rediscovered on the occasion of Haydn's two hundredth birthday, simultaneously by Miss Marion Scott and the author, each working independently and unknown to the other. Miss Scott edited the work for the Oxford University Press and the Geiringer edition was published in Nagel's *Musikarchiv*.

It is probable that further quartets of the young Haydn will come to light, but it is fairly certain that no great surprises are to be ex- pected and that we now know of all the important quartets of the master.[8]

Just as uncertain as the exact number of the early quartets are the dates of their composition. Haydn's friend, Griesinger, contends that the master's first quartet was written in 1750. Pohl, the great Haydn biographer, considers this too early and assumes that the quartets, Op. 1, 2, and 3 of Haydn's own list were written about five years later. As no original manuscripts of the early quartets have been pre- served, the years of their composition cannot be exactly determined. On the other hand, there is no doubt that the quartets, Op. 1 No. 5 and Op. 3 Nos. 1–6 are far more mature than the aforementioned quartets, Op. 1 Nos. 1–4, Op. 1 No. 6, Op. 2 Nos. 1–6, and the "No. O." Op. 1 No. 5 and Op. 3 definitely belong to the phase of transition, after 1760, while the other twelve quartets clearly show the style of Haydn's youth, before 1760. In this connection it should be men- tioned that the Breitkopf & Härtel catalogue of 1765 lists the quar- tets, Op. 1 Nos. 1–4, Op. 1 No. 6, Op. 2, and "No. O," but not Op. 1 No. 5 and Op. 3. If the publishers had known the better and more mature compositions they would certainly have enumerated them in preference to the weaker ones. The fact that they did not do so proves that they had seen only the twelve earlier pieces and that the quartets, Op. 1 No. 5 and Op. 3, composed at a later date, had not then traveled from Eisenstadt to Leipzig.

The *quadri* and *cassazioni,* as the Breitkopf catalogue calls the earliest quartets, show quite clearly the influence of the suite. They are always in the major key and contain five movements, two of them minuets. The order of the movements is well balanced and symmetri-

[8] Larsen (*Drei Haydnkatalogue,* p. 126) lists twenty-six quartets that are to be found in different Austrian and German collections under Haydn's name and do not appear among the eighty-three of the list of 1805. A critical investigation, which has not been attempted so far, is likely to establish the genuineness of some of them.

cal: allegro (or presto), minuet, adagio, minuet, presto (or allegro molto). Slight variations of this scheme are to be found in Op. 1 No. 3 and Op. 2 No. 6 in which the first and third movements change places. The majority of the movements in each quartet preserve the same key except that for the trios of the minuets, in compliance with the Viennese tradition, the tonic minor is preferred, while the slow movements are written in the subdominant, the dominant, or again in the tonic minor. Within this rigid scheme, however, Haydn displays a surprising variety of details indicating both the richness of his imagination and the rather immature state of his technical knowledge. The treatment of the sonata form differs in practically each of the first movements, sometimes two, sometimes three, or even four themes being introduced. A proper development of themes, in the manner of Haydn's mature style, is not to be found in any of these early compositions. But the composer conscientiously tried to make a choice of themes for the second parts of his sonata forms, usually giving preference to the second or third melody over the main theme. An interesting experiment in form is shown in the quartet, Op. 2 No. 3 in which the trio of the second minuet consists of a theme with three rather free variations.

These early string quartets need not necessarily be performed by four players only; the execution by a small orchestra of stringed instruments is correct, as the difference between chamber and orchestral music is not manifest in this first period. Nevertheless, the first signs of a genuine string quartet style are to be noticed already. It is true that the viola frequently uses the same rhythm as the violoncello and even plays in octaves with this instrument; true that the composer occasionally concentrates the whole of the melodic life in the first violin part, so that the adagio of Op. 2 No. 2, for example, with its six-four chord for the cadenza near the end resembles a concerto rather than a quartet. There are also many dialogues between the two violins, reminding us of the technique of the old trio sonata. At the same time the crossing of the parts of second violin and viola, as we find it in the second trio of Op. 2 No. 5, and the transparent style of the third movement of Op. 1 No. 3, in which all four instruments are granted an equal share of the thematic material, give a fair promise of future achievements.

The contents of the quartets are simple and gay, with a preference for melodies resembling folk songs of Austrian character. An exception is found only in the adagio of Op. 2 No. 4, the passionate ardor of which reminds us of the north-German art of Philipp Emanuel Bach, with which Haydn had just become acquainted. A movement of similar character is the above-mentioned largo of the second piano sonata, which was probably written about the same time.

In the seventeen-fifties Haydn also wrote a quintet for strings in G major. Although this work exists in different versions, the *a cinque* of Haydn's own catalogue (No. 2 of the *Divertimenti auf verschiedene Instrumenten*) indicates that the quintet is an original one and also settles the old argument as to whether or not Haydn ever wrote a quintet. The six movements of the composition again show the character of the suite. Most of the movements are in the same key, simple in form and of a light and graceful character.[9]

A transitional phase, coming between the works in three to five parts and the symphonies, is represented by the six scherzandi for flute, two oboes, two horns, two violins, and bass. They are little pieces in four short movements (allegro, minuet, andante or adagio, presto) that probably would not have been attributed to Haydn if the master himself had not listed one of them (the scherzando in A major) on the first page of his draft catalogue.

Of a more brilliant character is a nonet for two oboes, two horns, two violins, viola, violoncello, and double bass written before 1757 and listed as No. 20 of the *Divertimenti auf verschiedene Instrumenten* in Haydn's catalogue of 1805. This composition has the same arrangement of its five movements as the early string quartets. In an old manuscript the work is called *concertante* as the composer shows a marked tendency to let each of the nine instruments have an interesting and independent part; the oboes particularly have attractive passages.

A similar transitional character can also be noticed in Haydn's concertos of this period, which are written mainly for keyboard instruments and small orchestra. In his own catalogue Haydn listed four concertos for the clavier (or organ) but according to subsequent research he probably wrote ten or twelve such compositions.[10] Whereas the early string quartets occasionally assume the character

[9] There is also a string sextet or double trio called Echo which is sometimes attributed to Haydn but is of too inferior a quality to be seriously connected with his name.

[10] See Hans Engel, *Die Entwicklung des deutschen Klavierkonzertes* (Leipzig: 1927).

of concertos, the first concertos for keyboard instruments show a definite leaning toward chamber music. The musical form is remarkably well developed, but nowhere is there any display of technical brilliance. The origin of the keyboard concerto from the violin concerto, so clearly shown in Bach's compositions, is also noticeable in Haydn's works. As a rule, the left hand of the solo instrument doubles the bass and the right hand alone is melodically independent. Sometimes both hands participate in brilliant scale runs or triad passages. The Organ Concerto in C major of 1756 is typical of these early works. The composition appears both in Haydn's draft catalogue and in old manuscripts preserved in the Austrian monasteries of Melk and Göttweig; however, it appears as a concerto for the clavier and in fact, does not differ in the least from contemporary pianoforte concertos. The importance of the solo instrument is still diminished by a comparatively large orchestra (strings, two oboes, two trumpets) and the composition is much more like a piece of ensemble music than a real concerto.

Closely related to these early concertos are a number of *divertimenti* for the clavier and varying groups of instruments, such as violin, two horns and bass, or two violins and bass. Haydn's catalogue of 1805 lists four of these works, but Larsen enumerates no less than twenty,[11] many of them—as is characteristic of Haydn's early compositions—existing in different versions. Of these works, which may be considered equally as chamber music or as concertos, at least half should prove to be authentic compositions but since these unassuming pieces have only historical interest now, a closer examination does not seem necessary.

In discussing Haydn's symphonies we can use as a basis the excellent list provided by Eusebius Mandyczewski in 1907 and printed in the symphony volumes of the Collected Edition. In spite of many attempts to make the list seem unreliable, no conclusive evidence against it has been found so far. It is true that Mandyczewski did not always have access to the best sources for his edition, so that the musical text of the symphonies is not authentic in every detail; still the list of works, which was the basis of his edition, stands up remarkably well even in the light of the most recent research. The main corrections needed in this catalogue concern the chronological

[11] *Drei Haydn Kataloge*, p. 127, No. V.

order (cf. p. 212), since Mandyczewski entered some works, whose dated autographs he did not know, in the wrong places in his list. Thus symphony No. 40, according to the original manuscript, was written in 1763 and therefore ought to follow symphony No. 13 of the same year; No. 49 belongs to the year 1768 and should follow No. 35; the Paris Symphonies Nos. 83 and 87 were written in 1785 and accordingly should be inserted between Nos. 81 and 82.[12]

In his First Symphony, written in Lukavec in 1759, Haydn certainly did not establish himself as a great innovator. The work is still in three movements without a minuet. It begins with the fashionable "roller" and introduces a subsidiary theme in the minor key with imitations, typical of the Viennese "preclassical" composers. The wind instruments (two oboes and two horns) are employed mainly to increase the sonority of the full orchestra; no use is made of them in the piano passages or in the slow middle movement. A *continuo* instrument, such as the harpsichord, is essential for filling the occasional gaps between the melody and the bass.

In his works for the stage Haydn began his career as a close adherent to the Viennese tradition and Joseph Felix Kurz-Bernardon, the Viennese actor and author of farces, became his librettist when the composer was only nineteen. A truly Austrian book, filled with merry gaiety and coarse realism, delightfully ridiculing the stilted style of the serious opera, was used by the composer in his first work for the stage, a Singspiel entitled *Der krumme Teufel* (based on Lesage's *Le Diable Boiteux*). Haydn's music to this comedy is lost. In an interesting study Robert Haas suggests [13] that Haydn was attracted by the subject and in 1758 worked on a new version of the same libretto, called *Der neue krumme Teufel;* this composition, however, seems to be lost also. On the other hand, Haas assumes that young Haydn kept up the connection with Kurz-Bernardon during the intervening years, occasionally writing music to other comedies by the poet-actor. If these different theories are correct, it may be presumed that a collection of *Teutsche Comedie Arien* in the Vienna National Library, containing texts by Kurz-Bernardon from the years

[12] According to the procedure introduced by Alfred Einstein in the third edition of Köchel's Mozart catalogue, symphony No. 40 might be numbered 13a, No. 49 would be 35a, and the symphonies Nos. 83 and 87 would be Nos. 81a and 81b.

[13] "Die Musik in der Wiener Stegreifkomödie," *Studien zur Musikwissenschaft* (1925).

1754 to 1758 and set to music by anonymous composers, contains pieces by Haydn. Volume XXX/1 of the *Denkmäler der Tonkunst in Oesterreich* offers a valuable selection from this collection. The arias, duets, trios, and quartets of this volume are imbued with a healthy earthiness and keen wit, displaying a surprising sense of musical form, so that it does not seem altogether impossible that young Haydn contributed his share to the collection.

Another of Haydn's earliest dated compositions, besides the Organ Concerto in C major, is his first *Salve Regina* in G major. Both these works, according to their autographs in the possession of Breitkopf & Härtel, Leipzig, were composed in 1756. The *Salve Regina* is scored for solo soprano and contralto, two violins, organ, and bass. It is a short, very unpretentious piece in three movements, showing in its typically Italian melodies the influence that Haydn's new teacher, Porpora, exercised on the responsive mind of the young composer.

In his settings of the Mass Haydn naturally followed models that he had studied as a choirboy at St. Stephen's. They were by such composers as the two Reutters, father and son, Antonio Caldara, and Johann Joseph Fux, the great master of counterpoint; possibly also by older musicians like Johann Stadlmayr and Christoph Strauss. The style of these composers had its roots in Italy. The solid texture and the tendency to assemble solo voices, vocal *tutti*, and orchestral instruments in individual choirs, which are used alternately, point to the styles of Venice and Rome. The display of arias and duets with brilliant coloratura and the use of operatic effects, however, show the influence of Neapolitan music but these devices of south-Italian art had been used in Austria for over a century, with the result that by Haydn's time their origin was all but forgotten.

The first *Mass in F major* (Novello Edition No. 11) written at the beginning of the seventeen-fifties is one of the most important works of Haydn's early youth. It is a so-called *missa brevis*, a concise composition of the Mass text, using a very small accompanying orchestra. This work is written for two solo sopranos, a four-part chorus, two violins, organ, and bass (an ensemble very similar to that used for the *Salve Regina*). The words are crowded together as much as possible and in order to abbreviate the composition, occasionally the four voices sing simultaneously different sections of the liturgical text.

Only in the Benedictus given to the two solo sopranos is the melodic impulse allowed to develop freely. This little duet and the coloratura of the solo voices display the influence of the Neapolitan school. Remarkable is the composition of the Kyrie which, just as in later masses by Haydn and in Beethoven's first mass, is also used for the "Dona nobis pacem." The words of the Kyrie eleison (Lord have mercy on us) were set to a melody with a folk song character; the music showing so carefree and gay an attitude that it hardly seems appropriate to the solemn words of the prayer. This brings us to an important feature of Haydn's church music, which must be understood in order to appreciate the master's sacred works. Haydn's "attitude toward religion was not gloomy and repentant, but gay, reconciled, and trustful and this character is also to be found in his compositions for the church." (Griesinger.) To Haydn's pious optimism a prayer for mercy seemed to involve a grant of this request and he felt justified in beginning and ending his mass in a spirit of gay confidence. Haydn made hardly any distinction between sacred and secular music; as a painter of the Renaissance period did not hesitate to give to the Madonna the features of some girl he knew personally, so Haydn applied the principles of instrumental music to his mass by starting and ending with an allegro. As Alfred Schnerich, the champion of Haydn's church music, explains,[14] this can also be defended from a liturgical point of view, since the congregation ought to be received as well as dismissed in a spirit of joyousness.

But it seems hardly necessary to say so much in defense of this first mass. Haydn himself was always fond of the work of his early youth and as an old man he took it up again, adding wind instruments to the modest score.[15] "What I like particularly in this little work," he confessed to the painter Dies, "is its tunefulness and a certain youthful fire." No modern critic can be so sophisticated as not to acknowledge these merits in the unpretentious composition.

[14] See his *Messe und Requiem seit Haydn und Mozart* (Vienna: 1909).
[15] This arrangement which is traditionally ascribed to Haydn was probably merely supervised by him. The manuscript of the later version in the Eszterházy library shows the parts of the original composition written by Haydn's copyist Elssler, while those for the wind instruments were inserted by his pupil, Polzelli.

Chapter 13

A PHASE OF TRANSITION

The Second Period: 1760 — 1769

It is a new Haydn that we meet after the composer became conductor for the Princes Eszterházy. No longer was he the poor and unimportant musician making a scanty living by teaching youngsters or playing in third-rate bands. The Haydn of the seventeen-sixties was a successful man who occupied an important post and was held in high esteem by both his superiors and his subordinates.

Haydn could now work regularly with a group of well-trained singers and players. He could study at the closest range the possibilities of each instrument and the human voice; he could hear each of his compositions almost before the ink of the manuscript was dry. Some young composers of our time, who almost despair of ever hearing their symphonies performed, would give years of their lives for such an opportunity.

Slowly, gropingly Haydn was now finding a way toward the expression of his own true self. During the first ten years of his appointment as conductor for Prince Eszterházy he made it his object, with that infinite slowness and carefulness so characteristic of all his actions, to master the overpowering influence of the past. He was no longer satisfied to be just one among a large number of insignificant composers. We watch his first timid attempts not to be influenced by others, but to be himself—Joseph Haydn. There was, to be sure, no deliberate effort to shelve the past but while preserving on the whole the musical language of the "preclassical" composers, Haydn became increasingly anxious to imbue it with his own personality. The sixties of the eighteenth century were for him essentially a phase of transition. Old and new elements were more closely interwoven than in

202

any other period of Haydn's artistic evolution; and while the man of thirty was discovering himself the world was slowly becoming aware that a genius was living and maturing in the remoteness of the Hungarian plains.

In his sonatas for the pianoforte of the second period the influence of the past seems at first particularly strong. Up to No. 16 of the Collected Edition the character of the suite is predominant; the minuet is never missing and in most sonatas the same tonality is preserved in all movements; however, the air with variations in No. 15 represents a new type of movement.

Undoubtedly Haydn's early piano sonatas are influenced by his ensemble music. There are many sections that seem as if they were really meant for violin and figured bass and it is not at all surprising that some of these sonatas were also printed "with the accompaniment" of a violin or a violin and violoncello. Some passages are definitely inspired by the technique of the violin, and the frequent changes between high and low registers suggest the arrangement for pianoforte of an orchestral composition.

At the same time these sonatas are not lacking in clear indications of future trends. In addition to the imitations of string instruments, there are freely modulating passages, especially in the development sections, that exhibit a definitely pianistic character. Yet more important is the fact that Haydn was already striving toward the unity and concentration of form so characteristic of the best among his mature compositions. In the first movement of No. 3 the continuous use of triplets, sometimes in the bass and sometimes in the treble, gives the work considerable uniformity. (As such a homogeneous construction is inconceivable in the composer's first period, it seems likely that No. 3 is a later composition than the less mature sonata No. 4.) In No. 10, the second subject is closely related to the first and it remains for the third to bring in new melodic material, a procedure that was to become important in Beethoven's compositions.

The closer we come to Haydn's third period, the clearer the indications of the influence of Philipp Emanuel Bach become. No. 19, of 1767, was even considered by an English periodical [1] to be a parody of the style of the Hamburg master. According to the author of the article, Haydn wanted thus to revenge himself for the unfriendly attitude that Bach assumed toward him. A refutation of this statement

[1] *The European Magazine* (London: October 6, 1784).

was made by Bach himself when he declared most emphatically in an article for a Hamburg paper [2] that he and Haydn were the best of friends and that all assertions to the contrary were to be considered as mere lies. Still it cannot be denied that a certain similarity exists between Haydn's sonata No. 19 and Emanuel Bach's piano compositions. The transparency of the two-part writing in the work of the younger composer, the accompaniment of melodies in high register by low-pitched basses resting on accented beats of the measure, the dramatic development in the first movement, the broad baritone melody of the subsidiary theme in the second movement, and most of all, the unrelenting intensity of feeling permeating the whole work all show Haydn as a diligent disciple of Johann Sebastian's great son.

Haydn's trios for piano, violin, and violoncello belong, in a way, to his piano music. The keyboard instrument is completely dominant, while the use of the violin and especially of the violoncello seems more or less optional. Nos. 19 and 26 of the Peters Edition, which will be used for quotations since the Collected Edition has not yet dealt with this class of Haydn's compositions, were written during the master's second period.

Here again the character of the suite is quite clearly expressed. No. 26 in F major is in three movements, all being in the same key; the second is a minuet, the third an adagio with variations. The violoncello part is practically identical with that of the bass of the piano and its sole function is to increase the volume. The part of the keyboard instrument is not lacking in purely pianistic effects, such as the crossing of hands in the development section of the first movement. The violin—although retaining a certain amount of independence—exhibits none of the technical brilliance to be found in the first violin parts of Haydn's string quartets of the same period. Rather similar is No. 19 in G minor. But, as is customary in compositions in the minor mode, the character of the suite is not so clearly revealed. The finale (presto) brings us an attractive example of the contrasts between forte passages in unison and harmonized piano passages which were so dear to both Haydn and Mozart. (Compare the beginning of the Jupiter Symphony.)

Among the trios for two violins and violoncello the pieces Nos. 1–4,

[2] *Hamburger Unpartheiische Correspondenz,* No. 150 (1785).

8, 10, and 12 of Haydn's own list belong to the master's second period. They are musically far more attractive than the earlier works of this type and show clearly that Haydn wrote them after he had entered the service of Prince Eszterházy. The first violin parts, which ascend nearly up to c^4 and frequently introduce double stops, indicate that Haydn had in mind the brilliant violinist Tomasini when he wrote these movements. But the substance of the trios has also changed. The pastoral character of the deeply felt adagio in No. 2, the ardent passion in the adagio in B minor in No. 3, and the frequent daring modulations all show that Haydn had begun to outgrow the superficiality of the rococo style.

These trios for two violins and violoncello were succeeded by trios for baryton, viola, and violoncello which Haydn wrote for Prince Nicholas Eszterházy, the enthusiastic devotee of the baryton. This unusual stringed instrument is a relative of the bass viola da gamba. Six or seven gut strings extend over its finger board and about twice as many metallic strings are stretched behind the neck, and consequently cannot be reached by the bow. These metallic strings serve a double purpose. They sound in sympathy with the gut strings when the latter are played by the bow and they can also be plucked by the thumb of the left hand. Pizzicato and arco notes must be played simultaneously, which makes any performance on the instrument clumsy and difficult. In consequence the baryton never attained great popularity and its use was always confined to a small circle.

Contemporary sources vary in their estimates of the merits of the instrument. Whereas Friedrich August Weber, a physician who was one of the most spirited musical writers of the time, praised it saying, "One seems to hear the gamba and harp at the same time," and confesses that he was "moved to tears" by its sounds,[3] Dr. Burney, in discussing the performance of the baryton virtuoso, Andreas Lidl, who had been in the service of Prince Eszterházy before going to London, writes: "Mr. Lidl played with exquisite taste and expression upon this ungrateful instrument, which has the additional embarrassment of base [sic] strings at the back of the neck and he accompanied himself with these; an admirable expedient in a desert, or even in a house, where there is but one musician, but to have the bother of accompanying yourself in a great concert, surrounded by idle per-

[3] *Musikalische Zeitung* (1788).

formers who could take the trouble off your hands, and leave them more at liberty to execute, express, and embellish the principle melody, seemed at best a work of supererogation." [4]

Haydn listed in his own catalogue no less than one hundred and sixty-five compositions with the baryton, among them one hundred and twenty-five trios for baryton, viola, and violoncello. Twelve other little *divertimenti* for two barytons and bass, not listed by Haydn, are to be found in autograph in the Eszterházy collection. Although the composer considered that the baryton compositions were written mainly for the use of his prince and did not care to see them widely distributed in print, about two-thirds of the pieces seem to have survived either in the original form or as arrangements.[5] The most important among them are the one hundred and twenty-five baryton trios and, according to Mandyczewski, over a hundred of these are still preserved; Oliver Strunk points out that today eleven probably are to be found only in the Library of Congress in Washington.[6]

The earliest of the baryton trios were probably written in 1762 when Prince Nicholas succeeded to the family title; the last dated autographs are of the year 1775. Pohl suggests that the first forty-eight pieces of Haydn's catalogue of 1805 were written between 1762 and 1767, the next twenty-four (Nos. 49–72) before 1769, the following twenty-four (Nos. 73–96) before the end of 1770, and the last twenty-nine (Nos. 97–125) between 1771 and 1775.

The form of the baryton trios shows a certain resemblance to that of the trios for two violins and violoncello. The pieces for baryton, viola, and violoncello are mostly in three movements with a minuet in the middle or at the end, and the second movement is usually in a key closely related to the other movements. Quite a number of fine specimens are to be found in this collection, showing that Haydn gave of his best even when he did not expect his compositions to be heard outside the court of his prince. Nearly every trio has an interesting little detail, such as the charming melody for baryton in the adagio of No. 1, the attractive changes of dynamics in the minuet

[4] *See* Burney, *A General History of Music* (1789).

[5] This fact ought to be stressed for in 1904 William Henry Hadow wrote in the *Oxford History of Music* (V, 41) about Haydn's baryton compositions: "This vast mass of music has wholly disappeared, except three *divertimenti* and a few inconsiderable fragments."

[6] According to Strunk (cf. Bibliography), this library owns eighty-two of Haydn's trios for baryton, viola, and bass in copies made by Louis Picquot (the biographer of Boccherini) and acquired in 1906 by the library.

of No. 34, the pretty variations in No. 38,[7] the humorous minuet *alla zoppa* (limping minuet) in No. 52, the unusual way in which the baryton in the adagio of No. 56 alternatingly assumes the role of a bass and of a melody instrument, the remarkable changes between plucked and bowed baryton passages in the trio of the minuet of No. 57, and again the pizzicato of the baryton in the trio of the minuet of No. 61. Although the best baryton trios were written during Haydn's third period, these earlier pieces are not lacking in charm.

Haydn's string quartets of the seventeen-sixties are probably the only compositions of this period that still enjoy a certain amount of popularity, at least with ambitious amateurs.

Probably the earliest quartet is Op. 1 No. 5 and this work is entirely different from the other quartets of Op. 1. It has only three movements (allegro, andante, allegro molto) and no minuet. The first and last movements breathe a festive, slightly impersonal character, and as the work exists also in a version with two oboes and two horns, its relation to the sinfonia, the instrumental introduction to the Neapolitan opera, becomes quite apparent. There is little of the intimate character of the other early string quartets in this work.

Rather different from this composition are the quartets, Op. 3 Nos. 1–6 (Nos. 13–18 of Haydn's list). With a single exception (Op. 3 No. 4 has no minuet and consists of two movements only) they still follow the form of the suite, but unlike the earlier quartets they have only one minuet, thus sacrificing the idea of symmetrical construction to that of variety. Four works of this group (Nos. 1, 3, 5, 6) show the new form in four movements that was to become so important in the future.

There are a great number of attractive details that surprise the music lover in this Op. 3. In No. 1, the interesting sound effects in the trio of the minuet and the touching fervor of the melody in the following serenata are not surpassed in any of Haydn's mature compositions. Quite remarkable also is the rondo finale of this quartet. The last entry of the theme reaches a climax by the simple expedient of putting the melody in octaves to be played by both the viola and first violin, whereas previously the first violin had played it alone.

[7] The theme of these variations has been used again in Haydn's set of variations for piano duet entitled, Il Maestro e lo Scolare of 1778 (cf. Weigl, *Handbuch der Violoncell Literatur*, 1929).

In No. 2 the *fantasia con variazioni* is the most remarkable movement. As in other early variations by Haydn, the bass of the theme is retained throughout the whole piece, giving the movement a basic consistency. The same striving for unity of form is also shown in the first movement of No. 3, which adheres strictly to a single, permanently recurring motive. In the finale of No. 4 Haydn proves to be an expert in the style of the Italian comic opera. In two places short adagio sections are followed by lively presto passages. Pergolesi's immortal Serpina, who interrupts her outbursts of hypocritical sadness with expressions of merry insolence,[8] seems here to be peeping over Haydn's shoulder. The scherzando and the presto finale of No. 5 are also masterpieces of the *buffo* style. These movements are the quintessence of impishness and mischief, while the andante cantabile of the same quartet, a counterpart to the serenata in No. 1, reveals a simplicity, innocence, and ardor that make the great popularity of the movement easily understandable.[9]

While the quartets forming Op. 3 were written at the beginning of Haydn's second period of composition, the following six pieces (Nos. 19–24 of Haydn's list) known as quartets, Op 9, were composed in 1769. In this cycle the use of four movements, with a minuet as the second one, has become the rule. In the movements in the sonata form the development section assumes an increasing importance. Whereas in the first movement of Op. 3 No. 4 the exposition was nearly three times as long as the development, both sections in Op. 9 No. 2 are almost equal in length. At the same time the developments begin to outgrow the traditional sequences and modulations; they show, as for example in the first movement of Op. 9 No. 4, a subtle sense of discrimination between ideas more or less suitable for elaboration. At the same time the composer tries to express a greater intensity of feeling. The fervent ardor that seemed like an episode in Op. 2 No. 4 attains increasing importance in Op. 9. There cannot be any doubt that these works foreshadow the master's Storm and

---

[8] Cf. *La Serva Padrona*, Intermezzo II, aria "A Serpina penserete."

[9] The string quartet in E major, which E. F. Schmid published in 1935 from the manuscript parts owned by the monastery of Göttweig, Austria, shows a certain similarity to the quartets, Op. 3. It will, however, require further research to determine whether it is one of Haydn's genuine works. The quality of the composition does not seem quite on the same level as that of the quartets, Op. 3 and it is hard to believe that, in spite of the enormous demand for Haydn's string quartets during the master's lifetime, this piece completely escaped attention. Up to the present, not a single early print, nor even a second early copy has been found.

Stress period. Some forebodings of this may be found in the first movement of No. 1, with its use of the minor key and of syncopations in the subsidiary group of themes and with the surprising hold over the six-five chord. More obvious still are these tendencies in the adagio that precedes the cantabile of No. 2, in which the tension of an impassioned introduction is resolved into a melody of profound sadness. This applies also to the first movement of the dramatic quartet No. 4 in D minor; the chromaticism, syncopations, and pauses seem like a challenge to the levity of the rococo period. In the ardent minuet of this quartet, the grand pause on the first beat of the third bar is easily recognizable as one of Philipp Emanuel Bach's favorite means of expression. But the antithesis of this mood, uncontrollable mirth, is also beginning to gain in importance. The same D minor quartet contains in its finale certain sections that foreshadow Beethoven's most inspired scherzos.

A peculiarity of this cycle, as well as of the following six quartets, is the brilliant character of the first violin part with its difficult runs and double stops, and its predilection for the highest registers. An explanation for this tendency is easily found in the fact that Haydn then had at his disposal a player of unusual technical gifts, Luigi Tomasini, the first violinist of the prince's orchestra. It must not be overlooked, however, that the personal and somewhat rhapsodical character of the music really calls for a certain display of virtuosity. Looking at the problem from this angle, it would seem as if Tomasini had been the ideal interpreter rather than the instigator of the brilliant parts for the first violin.

The next group comprises a number of smaller works for either string and wind instruments or wind instruments alone. They are compositions marking the transition toward symphonic music. Haydn himself had in his thematic catalogue a group of *Divertimenti auf verschiedene Instrumenten* which are for the most part the pieces that are to be discussed here.

A characteristic of the various compositions in this class is an inexhaustible interest in sound effects; musical color is so important for the composer that it even, for a short time, obscures his interest in form. These *divertimenti* provide Haydn with a training field for the use of orchestral instruments, particularly the wind section. At first, however, his experiments produced but scanty results; for

example, in the version existing of the string quartet, Op. 2 No. 3 with
two French horns, the horns are mainly used as filling (ripieno)
instruments. In the adagio, just as in Haydn's first symphonies, they
are omitted altogether. Similarly in the *divertimento* for two oboes,
two horns, and two bassoons, written in 1760 (Haydn's catalogue
No. 15) the horn has not outgrown the role of a mere reinforcement
of the *tutti* passages. A change is noticeable only in the Menuetto,
Trio, and Finale for two horns and strings (not in Haydn's catalogue; autograph in the State Library, Berlin), written during the
early sixties. Here the musical ideas seem to have grown out of the
technical possibilities of the horn (in bars 5 and 6 the string bass is
playing a real horn motive). Stronger still is this tendency in the
divertimento for horn, violin, and violoncello dating from 1767 (not
in Haydn's catalogue; autograph formerly in the possession of Edward Speyer, England). In its theme and variations the horn has
some really interesting technical problems to master and occasionally
the instrument's part as the ardent singer of German romanticism is
foreshadowed.

As for the woodwind instruments, the octet for two horns, two
English horns, two violins, and two bassoons of 1760 (Haydn's catalogue No. 16) exploits with rare skill the colorful quality of the gentle,
melancholy English horn. Sound effects of great beauty are realized
particularly in the adagio of this piece.

The favorite form of these *divertimenti* is the variation. Haydn
entrusts in each successive variation a different instrument with the
leading part, thus varying the musical color simultaneously with the
melodic line. A good example of this procedure may be found in
the *cassazione* for flute, oboe, two violins, violoncello, and bass, with
the andante *Mann und Weib* (husband and wife), which was composed in the middle sixties (Haydn's catalogue No. 11). Here the lead
is given to the first violin in the theme, to the violoncello in the first
variation, to the flute in the second, to the second violin in the third,
to the oboe in the fourth, and again to the first violin in the fifth;
however, in the last three variations the instruments more or less
blend together, with no special one entirely taking the lead.

Such an employment of the instruments brings elements of the
concerto into the *divertimento*. This is revealed with particular clarity in the *cassazione* for flute, oboe, two violins, violoncello, and bass,
written at the beginning of the sixties (Haydn's catalogue No. 1).

It frequently shows, as in a *concerto grosso,* a real *concertino* of flute, oboe, and first violin, to which a proper cadenza is entrusted in the slow movement.

Six quartets for flute, violin, viola, and violoncello published as Op. 5 are listed in Breitkopf & Härtel's catalogue of the year 1770. Although it is not possible to prove the authenticity of these compositions, which are not contained in Haydn's own *Verzeichnis,* Carleton Sprague Smith is inclined to consider them as genuine in view of their similarity to Haydn's early instrumental compositions, especially his string quartets. These pleasant, though unimportant, pieces exist in versions with one or two minuets (four or five movements).

The close relation between Haydn's piano concertos and his chamber music, noted during the fifties, remained unchanged in this period. Thus the piano (harpsichord) concertos in C major of 1760 and 1764 (autographs in Eszterházy library) were called *divertimenti* by the master himself and their piano parts are hardly more brilliant than that in one of his piano sonatas. It must always be kept in mind that among Haydn's earlier compositions a rigid distinction between concertos, chamber music, and orchestral works is impossible.

Three violin concertos in G major, B♭ major, and C major have been reprinted in recent times; however, only one of them, the concerto in C major (Haydn's catalogue No. 1), composed *per il Luigi Tomasini,* is definitely authentic. The concerto in G major was, according to Pohl, written in 1768 but it is probably an earlier composition. The concentration of the thematic life in the parts of the accompanying orchestra and the small share accorded to the solo instrument in the development of the main ideas seem to prove this. More significant still is the very simple technical equipment of the violin part, which hardly ever oversteps the first three positions, and a predilection for subsidiary themes in the minor. Quite different is the concerto in C major and the stylistically related concerto in B♭ major, both written before 1770. In these the violin competes with the orchestra in the elaboration of the themes and the double stops, big skips, fast runs, and melodies in the highest register offer a more gratifying task to the skill of the soloist. Even so these works are not really interesting for player or audience and fail to make a lasting impression.

In 1937 Helmut Schultz edited the double concerto for violin and piano (or harpsichord) in F major, which Haydn himself had listed (without theme) in his draft catalogue and Breitkopf & Härtel had announced in 1766 in their catalogues. Schultz's edition was based on old parts in the State Library, Berlin and on a score in the State Library, Dresden. The concerto is an unassuming work, showing clearly the origin of this type of composition in the baroque double concerto for two violins. The violin and the keyboard instrument carry the themes alternatingly; in the piano part the melody is practically always entrusted to the right hand, while the left hand has a typical *continuo* part, doubling the bass and introducing notes to fill in the harmony.[10]

In Haydn's concerto for the French horn of 1762 (autograph in the library of the Society of Friends of Music, Vienna) the difficult technical problem of writing a concerto for a brass instrument that was not yet equipped with valves seems to have inspired the master. The many gaps between the different notes of the horn are barely noticeable; the melodies are adapted to the possibilities of the instrument and the expressive music displays all shades of emotion, from powerful energy to tender longing.

Among Haydn's symphonies of this period, No. 2, of 1760, shows no improvement over No. 1 of the preceding year. This work, which uses only two horns in the wind-instrument section, exhibits throughout the characteristic features of the first period. In the slow movement, since only the two outer parts are written down, the improvisation of the middle part by a keyboard instrument is essential.

Before continuing with the analysis of the symphonies written during the second period (Nos. 2–40 and No. 49 of the Collected Edition), a reference to the chronological order of the symphonies in the list by Mandyczewski is necessary. It was pointed out in the last chapter that the date of composition of Nos. 40 and 49 were earlier than assumed by Mandyczewski. Whereas in the case of these two symphonies the autographs provide the necessary evidence, an examination of the style of the compositions proves, in at least three more cases, that symphonies whose numbers were far too high were

[10] The oboe concerto which has recently been published under Haydn's name is probably not a composition of the master. Pohl knew the work but refused to include it in his biography, although it was his general policy to mention even the doubtful compositions. *See also* Larsen, *Die Haydn-Ueberlieferung*, pp. 286–7.

entered in Mandyczewski's list. This applies to No. 33 ("before 1767"), which uses wind instruments only as a reinforcement to the *tutti* passages and omits them in the slow movement as well as in the trio of the minuet, and to No. 39 ("before 1770") with a slow movement that requires the filling chords of a *continuo* instrument for a performance.

Haydn's Third Symphony of 1761 for the first time has a subsidiary theme in the dominant major. In this work the light rococo spirit of previous compositions is replaced by a rather rigid and polyphonic style. The first movement shows a strongly contrapuntal tendency, the minuet—the great innovation of the symphony!—furnishes canonic imitations, and the finale shows a real double fugue. It is the first of a number of symphonies that display a contrapuntal style. Thus No. 40 has a fugue as its final movement, No. 22 (The Philosopher) uses the *canto fermo* technique in its first movement, and No. 26 (Lamentatione or Weihnachts Symphony) displays the *canto fermo* technique in both its first and second movements. Haydn may have been stimulated to produce these works by a desire to impress his superior, Capellmeister Gregor F. Werner, a master of the contrapuntal style, with his own technical skill.

In the year 1761 five more symphonies were probably written in addition to No. 3 and this year definitely marks the beginning of a new phase in Haydn's symphonic output. For the first time No. 5 uses the wind instruments in the slow movement; they are even entrusted with short solo passages. Still more important are Haydn's attempts to enrich the rather brilliant and impersonal character of his early symphonies by the introduction of elements of the concerto and of the suite. The most remarkable products of this experiment are the symphonies Nos. 6–8 known as Le Matin, Le Midi, and Le Soir dating from 1761. In Le Midi the presence of two slow movements, following each other in immediate succession appears to be most unusual. But a closer examination reveals the true meaning of this arrangement: the first slow movement is a sort of dramatic accompanied recitative, the second a beautiful aria of a lyric character. In both pieces (as in Spohr's violin concerto No. 8, *in modo d'una scena cantante*) a solo violin is used for the declamation as well as for the aria. In a truly romantic way Haydn introduces the vocal form of the aria into his symphony, giving the part of the singer to a violinist. Le Matin, Le Midi, and Le Soir are based on a poetical program which Hermann Kretzschmar has attempted to interpret. Such clearly defined pieces as the sunrise in the introductory adagio of Le Matin, the amusing parody of a solmization class in the slow middle movement of the same work, and the effective thunderstorm, *la tempestà*, in Le Soir made his task much easier.

Solo instruments are widely distributed through these three symphonies. Le Matin uses in its slow middle movement a solo violin; in the trio of the minuet a solo bassoon and a solo violoncello; and in its finale a solo flute, violin, and violoncello. In Le Midi and Le Soir the genuine *concertino* of two violins and violoncello used by Corelli and Handel alternates with the ripieno instruments. In later symphonies of this period the influence of the concerto is also noticeable; a solo flute is used in the slow movements of Nos. 24 and 30 and a solo violin and solo violoncello appear in the slow movement of No. 36. A good example of the graceful art of orchestration acquired by Haydn in the seventeen-sixties is provided by the adagio of No. 31, *Auf dem Anstand—mit dem Hornsignal* (on the lookout —with the horn signal) with its delightful combination of the tones of the horns and the solo violin. In this work Haydn used four rather than the traditional two horns. Two instruments are in the key of D and two in the key of G so that their notes may supplement each other.[11] (This expedient had to be used since the valves of the brass instruments were unknown.) The symphony No. 31, an interesting precursor of Haydn's famous La Chasse, contains many attractive passages for the wind instruments and it seems hardly surprising that a theme with variations, the favorite form of the suite, is used as its finale.

Haydn's tendency to unify certain movements of his works, so obvious in most types of his instrumental output, is particularly strongly developed in his symphonies. Apart from the predilection for contrapuntal forms mentioned before, occasionally, as in the first movement of No. 28, a whole movement in sonata form grows out of a single motive. The mature tendency to develop the subsidiary theme out of the main idea is already noticeable; in the first movement of No. 39, for instance, the contrasting idea appears only in the epilogue. The principle of the eighties of providing each musical instrument with a fair share in the thematic development of the musical material is foreshadowed in the beginning of symphony No. 37.

[11] As early as 1723 Handel used in *Giulio Cesare* two horns in G and two in D.

In the finale of No. 36 Haydn was so anxious to give thematic material even to the accompanying parts that his exposition assumed certain aspects of a development; accordingly the real development seems all but superfluous and is six bars in length. Johannes Brahms, who was a great admirer of Haydn and followed his example in many respects, used a rather similar device in the finale of his First Symphony. It brings so many elements of the development into the exposition as to make possible the omission of the middle part of the sonata form.

The subject matter of the symphonies is at first merry and carefree, with a rather robust popular note in some of the minuets. The pleasure in little "surprises," in sudden unexpected changes of a slightly humorous character is already evident. At the same time a quality of grave seriousness is by no means absent. It is indicated in No. 3 and even more clearly expressed in the first movement of No. 22. Here the grave notes of the *canto fermo* intoned by horns and English horns (replacing the oboes) create an atmosphere foreshadowing the solemn passages of Mozart's *Magic Flute*. There are also early signs of the *Empfindsamkeit* (sensitiveness) of the Storm and Stress period. No. 16, written about 1764, has as a main theme a sequence of wailing "sighs," prepared dissonances introduced on the strong beat and resolved by stepwise progression downward on the weak beat. To emphasize the unusual character of these "sighs," Haydn introduces them in the bass. Probably in the following year the tragic symphony No. 26 in D minor was written. From the stirring syncopation of the beginning to the passionate lament of the minuet this work strikes the note of suffering and despair. Of the double name (Lamentatione or Weihnachts Symphony) under which the work is usually known, the first alone seems to be justified. The *canti fermi* used show a definite resemblance to the Gregorian chants sung during Holy Week; however, there seems to be no noticeable sign of any Christmas spirit. Perhaps a pastoral movement, intended as the last movement of the work, has been lost. It hardly seems possible that the minuet with trio, which now ends this symphony in three movements, can be the finale Haydn had in mind for so important a work. The symphony No. 39 in G minor was also written before 1770 and in its first movement it anticipates the mood of suffering and grief in Mozart's string quintet in the same key. The climax of these efforts to give greater depth of feeling to his symphonies is

reached in No. 49 of the year 1768, with the characteristic name of
La Passione. This work displays, particularly in its second movement
in F minor, a feverish fierceness of expression that few musical or
poetical works of the eighteenth century surpassed.

Although the master's string quartets and symphonies of the second period offer, in spite of all their indisputable beauties, more
promise than real achievement, Haydn's operas of the second period
are equal, if not superior, to his later output.

Very little can be said about the Italian comedies *La Marchesa
Nepola, La Vedova, Il Dottore, Il Sganarello,* all written in 1762 for
the festivities in honor of Prince Nicholas becoming reigning head
of the family, for all these works have been lost with the exception
of four insignificant arias and one recitative from *La Marchesa
Nepola.*

More interesting is the Italian *Acide* (*festa teatrale*) written in the
same year for the festivities accompanying the wedding of the
prince's eldest son. Part of this score has also been lost; nevertheless,
enough remains to give a good idea of the character of a work that
is concerned with a subject treated by Handel some forty years
earlier. Haydn's work gives a rather long-winded account of the love
story of Acis and Galatea and the murder of the handsome shepherd
by the giant Polyphemus. The intervention of the traditional *Deus
ex machina,* in this case the sea-goddess Thetis, makes possible the
happy ending that an eighteenth-century audience expected. The
hero Acis, after being murdered, returns to life as a fountain and—
as a fountain—joins vigorously in the final quartet, which is the only
ensemble of the whole opera! The music follows closely the style of
the Italian *opera seria,* containing numerous *secco* recitatives and
isolated recitatives with the accompaniment of the orchestra. It keeps
pedantically to the *da capo* aria trimmed with ornate coloratura,
never attempting to reach more dramatic spheres. The overture in
three movements conforms to the shallow type of the symphony of
the Italian opera. The melodies are merry, gay, and rather trivial.
This overture is nothing but a glorified signal to indicate the beginning of the performance, a piece that might easily be replaced on the
modern stage by the ringing of a bell. As this overture has no connection whatever with the opera, there is no objection to its being
performed as a separate instrumental piece without any reference

to the stage work. In fact, this has often been done; conversely, the eighteenth century did not hesitate to use symphonies that were composed as separate instrumental pieces as overtures to vocal compositions.

The unnatural character of the *opera seria* ultimately provoked in Italy a reaction that led to the composition of gay and popular works. Haydn also felt the attraction of this type and his opera *La Canterina* (*The Songstress*), composed in 1766, is no mythological drama but rather a lively farce taken from everyday life. It is an intermezzo, similar in character to Pergolesi's *La Serva Padrona*. There is no overture and its two parts are meant to be performed in the intermissions of a three-act serious opera. *La Canterina* is the first of Haydn's operas of which a complete score has been preserved. It is also the earliest of Haydn's dramatic compositions that even in our days can be enjoyed without reserve.

No one could uphold the morality of the plot for the young vocalist Gasparina sees no impropriety in encouraging two lovers at the same time. Her double-dealing is discovered, and this places her in a very embarrassing position but she is clever enough to know the well-worn trick of threatening to commit suicide and pretending to faint, whereupon the fury of her lovers gives way to compassion. They repent of their anger and once more shower gifts upon her. The music is simple and graceful, following, like the libretto, the tradition of the Italian intermezzo. The composer replaces the schematic construction of the *opera seria* by a freer and more lively dramatic spirit. The undramatic *da capo* aria is avoided; instead there is a preference for Logroscino's trick of introducing recitatives into the aria. The very first aria of the work is interrupted and concluded by a recitative. Accents of tragedy are used only for the purpose of burlesquing the pathos of the *opera seria*. Gasparina's aria in the second act, intended to move the heart of her infuriated lover, assumes by the use of the somber English horn, the key of C minor, the tremolo of the strings, the "sighs," and augmented intervals of the melody a mood of exaggerated grief, easily recognized as a parody. The fits of despair of the lovers, produced by Gasparina's fainting, are of a similar nature. Such agitated syncopations and wild runs were used in the *opera seria* in moments that decided the life and death of the heroes. In the quartet that concludes the first act Haydn attempted what Mozart was to accomplish in his great masterpieces: the simultaneous expression of the personality of each of his characters, without violating the musical beauty of the whole. The fury of the singing teacher, the cowardice of the second lover, the despair of Gasparina, and the impudence of the duenna all find expression in this charming piece of music. In spite, or perhaps because, of its great simplicity, *La Canterina* is a really effective stage work. The author of this book has been responsible for a number of performances in Austria, Germany, Switzerland, Belgium, England, and the United States and at all presentations this early product of Haydn's dramatic art has been received with delight.

Lo Speziale (*The Apothecary*), written in 1768, carries on the tendencies of *La Canterina*. In this opera in three acts, based on a libretto by Goldoni, as many as three suitors compete to win the love of pretty Grilletta. Sempronio, an old apothecary, who is thinking too much of distant countries and not enough of his business, wishes to marry his ward Grilletta; Mengone, a serious young man, is inspired by his love for the young girl to enter the apothecary's shop as a clerk; and the bold and frivolous Volpino tries to win Grilletta's love through his pert little improvisations. Sempronio and Mengone are tenors; the part of Volpino, like that of Cherubino in Mozart's *Figaro*, is for a soprano, to be sung not by a man but by a disguised woman. Between these four characters, two sopranos and two tenors, the comedy is enacted and eventually the faithful Mengone wins Grilletta's hand.

Haydn succeeded in making *Lo Speziale* a true musical comedy. The conceit of narrow-minded Sempronio, whose knowledge is based mainly on newspaper reports, is beautifully described in his very first aria. Mengone's aria in A major paints the sufferings of indigestion and the soothing effect of rhubarb with a daring realism that makes the piece hardly suitable for a refined audience. Very different is the attitude of the young man in the trio at the end of the first act. Here Grilletta and Mengone whisper tender words of love while the old man meditates on war in the Far East (a conflict that seemed fantastic and improbable in Haydn's time), but as soon as the apothecary leaves the room the flame of suppressed passion starts to blaze. The bold impudence of Volpino is well expressed in his aria in E major of the second act. There is an interesting detail in this number that deserves special attention. When Volpino mentions Grilletta's lovers he sings a tune that reappears in the quartet finale of the act as soon as the names of the apothecary and the two young men are uttered. It is probably the first, though by no means the only, time that Haydn used the technique of the "leading motive." In this finale, Sempronio dictates to the two suitors, disguised as lawyers, his marriage contract with Grilletta. While pretending to repeat the words, they really burlesque them, changing every sentence to their own purposes. A tender melody of the oboe accompanies the main part of this scene. Repeated changes of tempo and the introduction of roguish, but also affectionate, mirth make this piece one of the most attractive numbers of ensemble music in the pre-Mozart *opera buffa*.

Unfortunately a small part of this score has also been lost. The arrangement of the opera by Robert Hirschfeld that is ordinarily used in modern performances interpolates in its place a duet from Haydn's *Orlando Paladino*. While this seems to be a fairly good way out of a difficult situation, other changes made in Haydn's original version have gone too far, one instance being the replacement of the tenor Sempronio by a baritone.

Haydn's early cantatas are closely related to his early operas. Both the *Eszterházy Cantata*, written in 1763–64 for Prince Nicholas' name day, and the *Applausus*, composed in 1768 for the inauguration of a new prelate in the Austrian monastery of Göttweig, closely follow their Neapolitan models. The two works consist of a succession of *da capo* arias introduced by recitatives and only rarely interrupted by ensemble numbers or choruses. In the *Applausus*, the text of which is written in Latin, the conversation conducted by the four Cardinal Virtues and Theology about the merits of life in the seclusion of a monastery is of such a dry and abstract quality that the composer found it extremely difficult to get any inspiration from the words. A happier choice of subject is that of the earlier work, which assumes a heroic note in its glorification of Haydn's beloved prince. Here the composer was really in sympathy with his theme and in consequence the aria in D minor "Quanti il mar," for instance, has the quality of an inspired passion. The accompaniment in fast-moving sixteenth notes describes the roaring of the ocean and at the same time reflects a deep emotion, while the wide intervals of the melody display an unusual fervor. Arias of an equally impressive character are, however, not too frequent in these two works. It is true that the instrumentation offers some variety; true that the formal construction is not lacking in attractive detail (especially so in the almost strophic chorus No. 4 of the *Eszterházy Cantata*). Yet it must be admitted that the composer's approach to his subject was slightly mechanical. Here Haydn followed a certain tendency of Neapolitan art to manufacture rather than to create music.

The composer was unable to be present at the first performance of his *Applausus* and therefore accompanied the score with a memorandum enumerating his wishes about its production and the following are the main features of the ten points on which he laid most stress in this remarkable document:

1. The composer asks that his indications of tempo be carefully observed and that, in accordance with the festive character of the text, the allegros be taken a little faster than usual.

2. As an overture the allegro and andante of any symphony may be used; its finale is to be replaced by the first ritornello of the cantata.

3. In the recitatives the instrumentalists should come in immediately after the vocalist has finished, but on no account is the vocalist to be interrupted, even if such a procedure were prescribed in the score.

4. The composer requires the dynamic signs to be strictly observed and points out that there is a great difference between piano and pianissimo, forte and fortissimo, crescendo and sforzando.

5. He professes to have been annoyed often by musicians who neglected his slurs and warns the violinists to avoid such an "unpleasant and faulty" way of playing.

6. He wishes the viola part to be performed by two musicians, "as the middle parts are sometimes more important than the melody," and he adds the interesting remark: "It can be seen in all my compositions that the viola rarely doubles the bass."

7. He advises the copyist to write out the part so that not all the violinists would have to turn the pages at the same time, as this reduces the volume of sound of a small ensemble.

8. He requests a good and slow diction of the soloists, so that every syllable may be understood.

9. He hopes that at least three or four rehearsals be given to his composition.

10. He recommends the addition of a bassoon to the violoncello

and double bass as this makes the bass of the composition more distinct than in a work that is scored only for string basses. He asks the musicians to work hard on the production in their own and in his interest, and concludes: "If I have failed to guess your taste it must not be taken amiss, as I did not know the performers or the locality. My ignorance of these matters has really made the work hard for me."

This is a document of unusual importance. Not only does it show what a good music director Haydn was—many of his wishes are still expressed by twentieth-century conductors—but it indicates his progressive attitude as a musician. His request for strict observation of the dynamic indications, the emphasis put on the importance of middle parts, the desire for a lively tempo: all these show that Haydn was anxious to fight the obsolete traditions of the past.

Among Haydn's smaller church compositions two offertories that adapt music from the *Eszterházy Cantata* to the liturgical text in Latin should be mentioned. An independent composition is the first *Te Deum* in C major written before 1765. The relation of the first chorus "Te Deum laudamus" to the following tenor solo "Tu Rex Gloriae" by means of the same impetuously rising motive in thirty-second notes shows the hand of a master. The transition from a trio of solo voices to the full chorus at "Per singulos dies" anticipates the contrast between solo and *tutti,* which Haydn was to use so effectively in his later church compositions. A very poetical thought is expressed at the end of the work where the music to "Non confundar in aeternum" is immediately added to the motive of "In te Domine speravi" as a sort of counterpoint. Haydn's attitude in religious questions is shown by this little detail. To put one's hope in the Almighty is identical with the certainty of salvation.

Just as in Haydn's operas and cantatas of the seventeen-sixties, so in his settings of the Mass the influence of the Neapolitan style is strong. The master's second composition of this kind, the *Great Organ Mass* (Novello No. 12) of 1766, is a brilliant *missa solemnis* differing in style from the modest *missa brevis* in F major of the first period. It calls for a four-part chorus, four solo singers, string instruments, an obbligato organ part, two English horns, trumpets, and horns. The parts of the vocal soloists are enriched with coloratura like the arias in a Neapolitan opera and the organ part is also embellished with brilliant ornaments and runs. Some numbers of the mass, such as the beautiful "Qui tollis," exhibit a distinct tendency to express the meaning of the words in music, but on the whole Haydn was more interested in the musical possibilities that a composition on so large a scale offered than in the interpretation of the mysteries of the text of the Mass. It even seems possible that the composer used in this mass sundry numbers that he had originally written for an altogether different work. The "Dona nobis pacem" with its careless declamation and very loose connection between music and words certainly supports such a theory; however, this would not have been an unusual procedure for a composer brought up in the traditions of the eighteenth century.

Chapter 14

STORM AND STRESS

The Third Period: 1770 — 1779

THE AUTHOR of a short article on Haydn printed in 1766 [1] called the master's music "charming, ingratiating, engaging, naturally humorous and enticing." If the man who wrote these words had read them again a few years later he would have found them surprisingly inadequate, for by then Haydn's music had lost most of the characteristics he had mentioned. The composer had grown tired of the charm and gracefulness of rococo music, so dear to him in his earlier days. To express personal feelings and strong emotion now seemed one of the main aims of Haydn's art and his creative activity experienced what the great French scholar of Mozart, Theodor de Wyzewa, called "a romantic crisis."

It has been shown in a previous chapter that the impulse to such a change came to Haydn from outside. The slogan "back to nature," which implied a return to sincerity of feeling, originated with Jean Jacques Rousseau and German literature and music accepted it eagerly. In the early seventies of the eighteenth century Goethe wrote his *Sorrows of Young Werther* and its unrestrained emotionalism moved people all over the world to bitter tears, even suicide. About the same time the young Mozart wrote his first G minor symphony (K. 183, not to be mistaken for the great symphony K. 550 of 1788), a surprisingly deep and moving work for a boy in his teens.

No musician felt the importance of the new movement more keenly than Joseph Haydn for it opened his eyes to all those qualities that had so far been lacking in his music. It is true that even during the sixties the composer's work exhibited attempts at introducing a more

---

[1] *Wiener Diarium* No. 84, *Anhang* "Gelehrte Nachrichten," XXXVI. *Stück.*

emotional musical language, but it was only after 1770 that this tendency broke forth with full power. At that time the composer of Eszterháza found himself in complete accord with the best tendencies of his time and there was no reason for him to suppress his passionate feelings any longer.

As always in outbreaks of a revolutionary character, the reaction against the past went beyond the mark. Haydn's *Sturm und Drang* (Storm and Stress), as the movement was frequently called in Germany, reached its climax in 1772, a year in which works of a strangely exaggerated character were created. In the following years Haydn's compositions gradually assumed a more normal aspect, although the aftereffects of the "romantic crisis" were destined to be felt all through the seventies. Just as the French Revolution, despite its aberrations, made an essential contribution toward the formation of human society, so the crisis of the Storm and Stress period through which Haydn passed played a vital part in his development and the attainment of his full maturity. It was indispensable to him as an antidote against the excessive lightness of the rococo style.

The movement toward subjectivity and sentimentality brought Haydn closer and closer to the *Empfindsamkeit* that Philipp Emanuel Bach had revealed in his compositions more than twenty years previously. But Haydn did not really copy Bach. The relation between the two masters was not so much that of teacher and pupil as that of two artists who for a short time were pursuing the same artistic goal. The study of Bach's compositions helped Haydn overcome a deficiency in his own compositions and as soon as he had succeeded in so doing he freed himself from the overpowering influence of the older master.

The pianoforte sonata No. 20 of 1771 shows Haydn in the midst of his "romantic crisis." In this composition, the master's only piano sonata in C minor, all the formal restraints of the *style galant* are broken and passion and subjective feeling triumph. The finale of the C minor sonata is no longer a carefree affair, destined solely to dismiss the listener in a gay mood; it becomes the climax of the whole work and is imbued with dramatic tension. The beginning of the development exhibits Haydn's art as constituting a link between the music of Bach and that of Beethoven. The contrapuntal style used in the elaboration of the main theme, the daring modulation to Bb

Haydn, waxbust, 1790

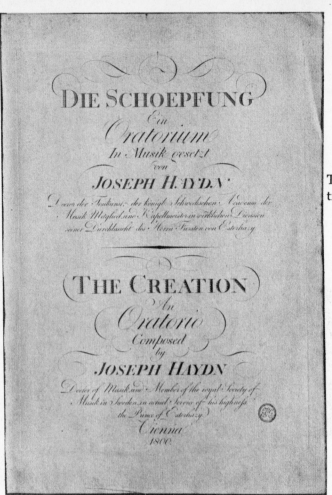

Title page of the first edition of "The Creation," 1800

The Haydn house in Vienna where he spent the last years of his life

minor, and the sudden change from tragic feeling to a completely lighthearted mood points both into the past and into the future.

The six following sonatas written in 1773 were rather different from the work composed two years earlier. As a reaction against the previous subjectivism, Haydn's style was, at least temporarily, becoming less personal. No strong expression of feeling is noticeable here. These six sonatas contain only two real adagios and in No. 26 the slow movement is replaced by a minuet. The insignificant·finale of the same sonata is certainly different from the remarkable last movement of No. 20. At the same time a tendency may be noticed to make the form of the sonata increasingly compact. In No. 24 the adagio leads straight into the finale and in No. 30, of 1776, the dividing lines between the movements are omitted altogether. As the last two movements of this sonata stand in a certain rhythmical relation to each other, the connection is particularly strong. Within individual movements also the subjects are intimately linked together and often grow out of the germ cells of a few basic motives. The first movement of No. 21, for instance, is based entirely on a dotted march-rhythm and a motive in sextuplets; its subsidiary theme is, as a matter of course, derived from the main subject. A fairly frequent use is now being made of polyphonic devices. In No. 25 the finale is a canon; in No. 26 the minuet and trio are composed *al rovescio*, each being designed to be played at first forward, the way they are written, and next backward as a "crab canon."

The piano sonatas written after 1775 again display the "sensitiveness" of the Storm and Stress period, although not with the same intensity as the C minor sonata. Three sonatas of this time were written in the minor key. No. 32 in B minor, of 1776, brings in the development section of the finale a remarkable contrapuntal elaboration on the theme. The unexpected, rumbling unison of the coda furnishes a good example of Haydn's sense of humor. At the beginning of sonata No. 34 in E minor, written in 1778, bass and melody answer each other in a rather original way. (Beethoven attempted a similar device in the first movement of his string quartet, Op. 18 No. 5.) The very first theme of the sonata No. 36 in C♯ minor, written before 1780, displays an unconventional contrast of moods between its different fragments. The second movement of this sonata is a gay scherzando in two-four time, the finale a minuet in C♯ minor with a trio in C♯ major. Although the use of a minuet as the last movement of a sonata reminds one of the old suite form, the inversion of the traditional key relation (minuet in the minor, trio in the major) and the personal expression of this movement with its now vigorous, now tender melodies, offers a striking contrast to the *style galant* of the previous period.

Particularly charming are the sets of variations that Haydn often introduced as finales to his sonatas. The composer was continually experimenting with fresh possibilities. In Nos. 27 and 28 a passage in the minor key is suddenly inserted into a set of variations in the major; in No. 29 the minor passage is used to separate the theme from its variations; in No. 33, as well as in the first movement of No. 40, a theme in major and a theme in minor are varied in turn. The technique of the variation is also applied occasionally to the rondo form. Haydn now wrote rondos in which, as in the works of Philipp Emanuel Bach, each entrance of the main theme displays new figurations, and even the episodes are variations of the main theme. It is most remarkable that the second movement of No. 36 and the first movement of No. 39 grow out of the same theme. In an *avertimento* preceding the publication of the sonatas through Artaria & Company in Vienna in 1780, the master himself stated: "Among these sonatas are two movements that begin with the same theme. . . . The composer explains in advance that he has done this on purpose, modifying the continuation of the movement in each case." Haydn was obviously interested in the problem of developing two different movements from a single theme. The movement in A major displays a light, frisking gaiety; whereas that in G major, in spite of its buoyancy, distinguishes itself by a vigorous and expressive introduction.

Related to the piano sonatas are the pieces for musical clocks. Pater Primitivus Niemecz, Prince Eszterházy's librarian, was an expert in constructing organs that were played mechanically. So great was his reputation that his instruments were exported even to England. Niemecz built three clocks equipped with tiny mechanical organs, the first in 1772, the other two in 1792 and 1793. In these he used only music composed by his friend and teacher, Joseph Haydn. Haydn gave the organ of 1772 to the wife of his friend, the Austrian court conductor, Florian Gassmann, at the christening of their daughter Anna. The gift was received with the greatest enthusiasm and the family still treasures the little instrument which has a weak but light, gay, and very clear tone. Ernst Fritz Schmid who edited these compositions for the first time has compiled thirty-two pieces, partly from autographs of Haydn and old manuscripts and partly from notes written down while the tunes were played by the instruments. By making slight alterations he has adapted them for the piano. They are short and unpretentious though very charming pieces. The sixteen numbers in the clock of 1772 (Nos. 2, 6, 8, 11, and 13–24 of Schmid's Edition) contain one piece with a middle part in F minor *all'Ongarese* (No. 14), a Russian dance (No. 16), and a fugue (No. 24), compositions very characteristic of the period in which the clock was built. The Russian dance is based on a composition by the violinist Giornovichj; this same composition was also used later by Beethoven as a theme for his Twelve Variations in A major. Owing to the character of its accompaniment, the Gassmann family gave the piece the nickname of The Bagpipe. In a similar way No. 6 was named The Call of the Quail and No. 18, Gossips at the Coffee Table. The minuet, No. 11, was slightly changed and later used by Haydn for the minuet in his string quartet, Op. 54 No. 2, composed about 1789.

Apparently Haydn did not write a piano trio during the first half of the seventies. The master had no use for this still undeveloped genre in a period when he was indulging in a personal expression of his feelings. Neither the antiquated dependence of the violoncello on the bass of the piano part nor the constrained role of the violin attracted him; nor was he sufficiently interested in this type of composition to try to reform it.

It was probably because of orders only that in the second half of the seventies Haydn wrote two trios (Nos. 27 and 28 of the Peters Edition). They are not particularly interesting works and hardly differ at all from his earlier compositions in this field.

However, the six sonatas for violin and viola are on quite a different level; in all likelihood they were composed during the first half of the seventies. Here the master revived the old style of the solo sonata with *basso continuo*. The whole of the melodic life is concentrated in the violin part, while the viola provides the basis for the harmonic support. The violin displays the inventive power and brilliant conception to be expected in a composition of the seventies and were it not for the poor treatment accorded the viola part, these sonatas would have to be counted among Haydn's representative compositions of this period. It might be worth while to use this viola part as the bass for a newly made piano accompaniment; a set of rather interesting violin sonatas could thus be produced, which might easily take the place of the inferior sonatas for violin and piano published under Haydn's name (cf. p. 275).

The most interesting of Haydn's trios for baryton, viola, and violoncello were composed during his third period of composition. The attractive contrapuntal treatment of the trio of the minuet in No. 84 in Haydn's list (written about 1770), the fascinating variations in No. 95 (about 1770) and No. 111 (about 1773), the unusual intensity of the adagio in No. 96 (about 1770) are examples of the many beauties to be found among these charming pieces.

Haydn also used the music of some of his baryton trios for other compositions. In 1781 when Prince Nicholas returned from a trip to Paris Haydn greeted him with a chorus "Al tuo arrivo felice," which had been arranged from one of the prince's favorite pieces, the allegretto of No. 116. Similarly the composer made a vocal arrangement, "Dei Clementi," from the adagio in No. 115 to celebrate the recovery of his prince from a serious illness. Practically all the baryton trios were also arranged for violin, viola, and violoncello so that they could be performed on the usual stringed instruments. Most modern editions publish the pieces in this version.[2]

Haydn wrote twelve string quartets during his third period of composition. The six quartets, Op. 17 (Nos. 25–30 of Haydn's list) were finished in 1771, the six Sun Quartets, Op. 20 (so called because of the lovely symbol of the rising sun on an old edition) in the following year.

The adagio of Op. 17 No. 5 shows how closely Haydn approached the art of Philipp Emanuel Bach during this period. Like the middle movement of the northern master's first Prussian Sonata for clavier, this adagio has a dramatic scene with recitatives and ariosos. The austere sternness in the beginning of the adagio of Op. 17 No. 1 and still more, the bold harmonies in the slow movement of Op. 17 No. 3 also show the north-German influence. In the first movement of Op. 17 No. 5 Haydn wrote a development that was longer than the exposition. He carried on with tendencies begun at an earlier period; at the same time these tendencies harmonized with Bach's aim to give

---

[2] Cf. Strunk, "Haydn's Divertimenti for Baryton, Viola, and Bass," *Musical Quarterly* (1932), XVIII, 248. To these may be added trios Nos. 82 and 96 edited by the author of this book for Hansen (Copenhagen: 1933) and *Zeitschrift für Musik* (1932) respectively.

greater solidity and concentration to the works. The unexpected pianissimo ending of the finale of Op. 17 No. 2 is true Haydn, but it also reminds us of the pleasure Bach took in sudden surprises.

These quartets are full of interesting effects of timbre. In the adagio of Op. 17 No. 2 Haydn introduced a theme first on the two highest strings and then repeated it immediately on the G string. In the trio of the minuet of Op. 17 No. 3 the second violin was given the melody while the first accompanied. Haydn apparently took into consideration the fact that the player who usually performed a part of minor importance assumed in the long run a quality of tone different from that of the leader of the ensemble.

Rousseau's movement of "back to nature" resulted in a general reawakening of the interest in national folk music. Haydn showed himself in complete sympathy with this tendency. In the minuet of Op. 17 No. 1, for instance, lively skips of the octave and tenth exhibit the character of the lighter type of Austrian popular music, while the last subject in the finale of Op. 17 No. 6 shows clear traces of the Hungarian atmosphere in which Haydn had lived since he was twenty-eight years old.

The date of composition of the Sun Quartets, Op. 20 is incorrectly given or not mentioned at all in most books on Haydn and it should be pointed out that according to the autograph, which was formerly in the possession of Johannes Brahms and was bequeathed by him to the Society of Friends of Music in Vienna (the institution that also owns the autographs of Op. 17), these quartets were composed in 1772. Brahms, who was a great admirer of Haydn's quartets and owned a miniature score of the complete "eighty-three," was very fond of this manuscript. He carefully compared the printed with the written edition and marked in the miniature score all the deviations from the original.

In the Sun Quartets (Nos. 31–36 of Haydn's list) all the features of the quartets, Op. 17 are intensified. The designation *affettuoso,* found twice in the directions for the tempo of slow movements, is characteristic of the whole series. In his aim to avoid the shallow frivolity of the rococo style Haydn adopted a "learned" attitude and introduced the architectural form of the fugue into the finales of three of the six quartets in this series. In a naïve way he boasted of his scholarly achievements. The fugues were inscribed *a due, a tre,* and *a quattro soggetti,* the canon cancrizans ("crab canon") was pointed out by *al rovescio,* and the *stretto* by *in canone.* This is more the attitude of a student of counterpoint doing an exercise for his teacher than that of a great master. Apparently the fugue did not seem quite the natural form to our composer for expressing his feelings. It may be pointed out that Haydn's string quartets with fugues were by no means isolated in this period of Storm and Stress. In 1773 Florian Leopold Gassmann, the composer of the operetta *La Contessina,* wrote six quartets, each of which contained two fugues; in the same year Mozart (influenced by Haydn) finished six quartets, twice using fugues as finales. On the other hand Philipp Emanuel Bach, who was so highly admired by Haydn, was somewhat prejudiced against contrapuntal devices. The use of the fugue is not the only instance of Haydn's return to baroque means of expression. The adagio of No. 2, with the unusual name *capriccio,* has an introduction of four bars and its weighty unison is reminiscent of the ritornello in a concerto of the Bach-Handel period.

Haydn's marks were now far more explicit than ever before. We find such directions as *allegro di molto e scherzando* or *mancando* (dying away).

The Haydn of the Storm and Stress period was more daring in the choice of keys than most composers of the time. The use of C♯ minor and C♯ major in the piano sonata No. 36 was certainly a proof of boldness, and accordingly, it seems hardly surprising that the Sun Quartets should display a predilection for the minor mode; No. 3 is in G minor, No. 5 in the then unusual key of F minor, and in the other works modulations into the minor are frequent. Excluding the first violin, the violoncello becomes the melody instrument in these quartets; in the beginning of No. 2 and in the fourth variation of No. 4 a role of unexpected importance is entrusted to it. The national element is again conspicuous in these pieces and Haydn openly confessed his predilection for the music of the Hungarian gypsies in the *menuetto alla zingarese* and the following *presto e scherzando* of No. 4. This finale is certainly one of the most fiery and at the same time one of the most amusing pieces that Haydn ever wrote.

The composer liked to reveal his sense of humor in still another way. At the end of the fugue that forms the finale to No. 2 he wrote the Latin words: *Laus omnip. Deo. Sic fugit amicus amicum.* (Praise to the Almighty Lord. Thus one friend runs away from the other.)

This is certainly an apt description of the fugue where the themes appear repeatedly in the different voices as if fleeing from each other.

Haydn's six *divertissements à huit parties concertantes* (for flute, two horns, string quartet, and bass) were probably written in 1775 as ensemble pieces with baryton. In order to make these compositions available to a wider circle Haydn replaced the baryton with a flute, transposing the part up an octave when necessary. In this form the compositions were published by Artaria in 1781 as Op. 31. The master's earlier *divertimenti* consisted of as many as five movements but these pieces have no more than three; however, there is a great variety of forms within them. Both No. 2 and No. 6 contain a set of variations in which the theme is repeated after each variation and a little coda is attached at the end. The result is one of the many different mixtures of the rondo with variation forms that Haydn liked a great deal. In the development section of the initial movement in No. 1 the thematic material is allotted impartially to all the instruments, thus showing that we are approaching the master's period of full maturity. Nos. 4 and 5 contain minuets, each with two trios, a form that is just as frequent in the nineteenth century as it is rare in the eighteenth. The subject matter of these pieces reveals their origin in Haydn's Storm and Stress period. They are imbued with severe dignity, passionate fervor, and dramatic intensity. Particularly expressive are the remarkable adagios in Nos. 1 and 2.[3]

Among Haydn's concertos for the clavier those in F major and G major (Haydn's catalogue Nos. 2 and 3) probably were written in the seventeen-seventies. Even though it appears quite difficult sometimes to distinguish in Haydn's first two periods between clavier concertos and *divertimenti* with a clavier obbligato, the third period at last produced concertos worthy of this name. The F major concerto is rather conventional in its musical language and old-fashioned in its technique. On the other hand, in the G major concerto the increased impetus of the passages and the occasional use of full chords show Haydn's effort to endow the part of the soloist with at least a moderate amount of brilliance. The expression of heroic defiance in the first movement proves this work to be a product of the

---

[3] The second and third movements of the *divertissement* No. 1 were edited by the author as "Adagio and Presto" (London: Novello, 1940).

Storm and Stress period. The final rondo brings the entrances of the tutti-ritornello on different degrees of the scale, thus displaying a certain similarity to the form of the Vivaldi concerto and it surprises us both by its bold modulations and the inexhaustible imagination that continually finds new ideas for the retransitions to the main theme.

As Haydn's second concerto for the French horn was first announced by Breitkopf & Härtel in 1781, it also was probably a work of the third period. Although no conclusive proof for the authenticity of this composition can be furnished, its musical similarity to the first concerto for the horn makes Haydn's authorship almost certain. It is a more mature and musically more interesting composition and preference is justly given to the later work. If it is played in the right chamber music style, this unusual concerto is bound to interest any audience.

Like most other types of Haydn's instrumental music, the symphonies show a decrease in number and an increase in quality during the seventies. Against some forty symphonies written in the sixties we find in the seventies only about thirty. The same tendency is evident in later decades; about twenty symphonies were composed in the eighties and twelve during the first half of the nineties. These figures clearly show the general trend of development in Haydn's art.

In the third period Haydn's symphonic style was determined by a striving for truth and strength of expression. The composer wrote works that almost remind us of Beethoven, so obvious is their emphatic diction. The powerful unison at the beginnings of Nos. 46 and 53 and the first and last movements of No. 44 express the unbending energy characteristic of this period. This symphony No. 44, known as Trauer-Symphonie (Symphony of Mourning) laments the death of a hero. Haydn wanted its beautiful adagio in E major, in which the dramatic impetus of the first and last movements is replaced by a gentle expression of grief, to be played at his own funeral service.

The changed feeling in this period made Haydn eager to find new means of expression. Particularly daring is his choice of keys. One symphony is in C minor (No. 52), another in E minor (No. 44), a third in F# minor (No. 45), and a fourth even in B major (No. 46). In the finale of No. 46 Haydn introduced a little reminiscence of the preceding movement (a minuet) just before the beginning of the coda. This seems to foreshadow the cyclical form, so important in the nineteenth century.

Perhaps the most unorthodox of these symphonies is also the most important. This is the famous Farewell Symphony (No. 45, autograph in the Eszterházy library, Budapest) of 1772. In this work the "back to nature" results in a process of simplification. The orchestra of strings, two oboes, and two horns [4] is no larger than that of the very first symphony. The initial movement has only about thirty bars of real development, while the exposition is more than twice as long. This short development ends dramatically on a general pause and a new melody of heavenly calm, not used in the exposition, is now presented. At the end of this lovely section, which is as long as the development itself, the recapitulation begins. In an earlier symphony (No. 42, composed before 1771, autograph in the Eszterházy library, Budapest) Haydn corrected a few measures of the original manuscript and remarked: *"Dieses war vor gar zu gelehrte Ohren"* (This was for too scholarly ears). In the Farewell Symphony also it seems as if Haydn tried to avoid making too learned an impression, or rather that he wanted, as Beethoven expressed it, to write music that "comes from the heart, let it go to the heart." An adagio in A major and a minuet in the unusual key of F♯ major are followed by a presto finale. This presto has as a coda an adagio, resuming the tempo and key of the slow second movement (compare the similar construction in symphony No. 46!). According to the poetical program one instrument after another becomes silent in this long, drawn-out coda. By the end only one first and one second violin are left and they finish the movement pianissimo on a sixth chord. From an artistic point of view this adagio ending of a symphony in several movements was even bolder than Haydn's attempt to teach his inconsiderate prince a lesson.

In the symphonies of the early seventies a certain display of contrapuntal technique can be observed. No. 44 possesses a canon in its minuet; in No. 47 the minuet and trio are *al rovescio*. The second movement of No. 47 is constructed in double counterpoint at the octave. Here we have the same combination of such contrasting elements as free expression of personal feeling and polyphonic severity which we found in the string quartets of this period.

[4] Bassoons may have been used as a reinforcement of the parts of the violoncellos and basses but they have only a few independent bars in the last movement.

Haydn's innate pleasure in the use of unexpected ideas grew particularly strong during the seventies of the eighteenth century. Examples from the Farewell Symphony have already been mentioned. In the first movements of Nos. 43 and 55 the main theme appears in the tonic soon after the beginning of the development. But this apparent recapitulation turns out to be merely a deception; presently the merry game of the development starts all over again with increased intensity. Even the famous "Surprise" to which Haydn owed so much of his popularity in England had made an earlier appearance. The first movement of No. 60 brings after a diminuendo a sudden loud *tutti,* in which the timpani greatly contribute to the intensity. The same work, a sort of suite based on Haydn's incidental music to the comedy *Il Distratto,* contains in its adagio a sudden fanfare and its affinity to some sort of a program is obvious. The finale of this symphony embodies a joke that was certain to amuse any audience in the eighteenth century. After a grand pause of the whole orchestra Haydn required the violinists to retune their instruments. The E, A, and D strings proved to be correct. But when they tried the G string they found to their dismay that its pitch was no longer G, but had gone down to F. Disregarding the listening audience, the players raised the lowest string again to G; whereupon they continued as though nothing at all had happened. To play wrong notes purposely in order to produce a humorous result is one of the oldest and most effective comic devices. Haydn did this in the second movement of Le Matin, Mozart in his Ein Musikalischer Spass (K. 522).

The symphony nicknamed Il Distratto is a work of the year 1775. By that time the climax of the Storm and Stress movement had passed and Haydn gradually returned to his former path, though he had almost been lured away by the "romantic crisis." Problems of musical form regained much of their previous interest for him. In the first movement of No. 54, for instance, he connected the slow introduction thematically with the following allegro quasi presto. The composer again showed a preference for the highly artistic form of the variation with frequent changes of major and minor within the same set. In No. 55, Der Schulmeister (The Schoolmaster), Haydn even used two sets of variations, one in the slow movement and another in the finale. Particularly interesting is the symphony No. 69, Laudon, named in honor of the great Austrian Field Marshal Ernst Gideon Laudon. Its first theme is practically identical with the first theme of the symphony No. 48, Maria Theresa, written a few years earlier. At about the same time Haydn did something similar in his compositions for the pianoforte. He wanted to show that the main problem in a composition was how to deal with a theme, not how to invent it; it is the same idea that Beethoven brought to full development.

Haydn now also showed greater interest in the wind instruments. In No. 54 the main theme of the allegro was entrusted to bassoons and horns. The effects that Haydn produced by entrusting the violins with a melody and accompanying them in the lower octave by bassoons are rather interesting (cf. the third movements of Nos. 54 and 66). A particularly wide field of activity was offered to the woodwind as well as to the brass section in the numerous movements in variation form.

No. 67, composed "before 1779" seems like a stranger among the symphonies of this period and may have been composed earlier, in the real Storm and Stress years. The first movement introduces, like the Farewell Symphony, a new idea in the development section; moreover, its finale is crammed with musical themes to such an extent as to replace the sonata form by the three-part song form, the middle part introducing a new idea, new tempo, and new rhythm. Near the end in the parts of the strings the second movement of this remarkable symphony contains the surprising direction *col legno del arco.* Instead of the hair, the wooden part of the bow is to be used, to give an insubstantial and ghostlike quality to the tone.

During Haydn's third creative period the majority of his works for the stage, six in all, were written and performed at Eszterháza. They are:

Le Pescatrici (The Fishermaids), 1770, libretto by Goldoni

L'Infedeltà Delusa (Unfaithfulness Deluded), 1773, librettist unknown

L'Incontro Improviso (The Chance Meeting), 1775, text arranged after the French book of Dancourt by Karl Frieberth

Il Mondo della Luna (The World of the Moon), 1777, libretto by Goldoni

La Vera Costanza (True Constancy), 1776–79, libretto by F. Puttini and P. Travaglia

L'Isola Disabitata (The Deserted Island), 1779, libretto by Metastasio.

With the exception of *L'Isola Disabitata*, which has the rather non-committal designation of *azione teatrale*, all are called burletta or *dramma giocoso* and are comic operas. But these comic operas are different from similar works of the sixties. They are more ambitious and increased prominence is given to the music. It is not surprising that in the long run the superficial gaiety of *La Canterina* (*The Song-stress*), which offered no scope for any deeper musical expression, was no longer able to satisfy the artistic leanings of a Haydn than was the shallow pathos of the *opera seria*. The composer now tried to combine both comic and serious elements; the beginning of such tendencies could be noticed in *Lo Speziale* (*The Apothecary*). In the seventies Haydn's comic operas were increasingly permeated with warmth and tenderness, his gay characters were more and more contrasted with serious and dignified figures and thereby a type of seriocomic, or mixed opera was created, a type that Mozart was to develop to perfection. It was no mere accident that Goldoni, the Venetian poet mainly responsible for the division into *parte serie* and *parte buffe* (serious and comic characters), should have supplied the libretto for three of Haydn's operas.

A similar distinction is clear in the music too. The language of the serious characters is practically that of the great *opera seria* of Naples. Preference is given to the big arias in three-part form, with rich coloratura and frequent repetitions of the text. The recitative accompanied by the orchestra is used in moments of dramatic tension. The *parte buffe*, however, employ the two-part song or the strophic form, simple melodies with folk song tendencies and free from flourishes and coloratura.

Haydn's tendency to attach increased importance to the music may be seen in the growing use of ensembles. In Eszterháza he had no chorus at his disposal; therefore he combined his soloists into quartets, quintets, and occasionally even septets and octets. Of special importance are the finales which show the composer at the height of his dramatic mastery. The tempo, the rhythm, the key, and the number of singers are constantly varied but the musical unity is always maintained. In each finale a great climax is reached after several interruptions. In some of these operas Haydn included purely instrumental numbers of an illustrative or "programatic" character and also some ballets.

It is interesting to analyze Haydn's arias of the seventies. At first they show, like the arias of Hasse, a great similarity to the forms of instrumental music. In two-part arias in the major the first part modulates to the dominant; in two-part arias in the minor, to the relative major. The second part begins like a *da capo* and keeps the tonic up to the end. In arias in three-part form the first part assumes the function of an exposition and the third part that of a recapitulation; the middle part rarely brings any contrasting new idea, but consists as a rule of a sort of development of the text and music of the extreme parts.

Toward the end of this period Haydn occasionally discarded this principle. Arias in three, four, and five different parts, sometimes interspersed with recitatives, were now used. The form of these arias was dictated by the exigencies of the libretto rather than by musical considerations. Haydn began to realize the deep truth of Gluck's axiom, that in the opera music always has to serve the drama and never to dominate it.

The first of these mixed operas, *Le Pescatrici*, introduces one serious couple, Prince Lindoro and his bride, Eurilda, and two lively pairs: the fishermen Burletto and Frisellino and their sweethearts, Nerina and Lesbina. The contrast between the couples is likewise shown in the choice of voices. The prince is a bass, Eurilda a contralto; whereas the merry couples consist of sopranos and tenors. The first act of the work is an excellent example of the pleasure Haydn took in ridiculing the stiffness of the *opera seria*. In a solemn manner Lesbina praises her own beauty and this part of her aria in B♭ major would be quite in place in any of the great operas of Naples. But suddenly her roguish temperament gets the better of her and in conformity with the best traditions of the *opera buffa*, she calls her rival all sorts of names. It is interesting to note that in Pergolesi's lovely intermezzo, *La Serva Padrona*, an aria of Serpina displaying a similar character is in the same key of B♭ major. Haydn apparently knew the work of the great Neapolitan composer well.

Besides effective arias a considerable amount of ensemble music is used in this work. The first act has two quartets, a sextet, and a septet. *La Canterina* and *Lo Speziale* employed four vocalists but now even seven were not enough for Haydn; in the introduction to the third act he used several choristers besides the regular cast.

L'Infedeltà Delusa of 1773 was performed during the Empress

Maria Theresa's visit to Eszterháza. Its somewhat weak libretto deals with the triumph of true love over all obstacles; the number of ensembles is small and most pieces are arias, though of a rich variety of expression. True dramatic passion as in the arias of the serious heroine, Sandrina, is replaced by insolent mirth in those of the gay and energetic Respina. An interesting feature in the bass aria of Nanni is the introduction of a violoncello obbligato. (Such association of a solo instrument and a voice of the same range is often seen in compositions of Johann Sebastian Bach.) One number of the opera, the aria "Come piglia si bene la mira" is available in a modern edition.[5] It deals with a favorite subject of the rococo period, describing how Cupid, in spite of the bandage over his eyes, does not fail to pierce the heart of his victims. Although the piece abounds in coloratura the expression is warm and deeply felt.

In the Turkish opera *L'Incontro Improviso* Haydn dealt with a subject that had been previously used by Gluck and was to be treated a few years later by Mozart. Therefore in the German version of the work, edited by Helmut Schultz, the opera was called *Die Entführung aus dem Serail,* giving it the same name that Mozart used for his *Seraglio* in 1781. In Haydn's opera Calandro, a real *basso buffo,* and his servant Osmin are comic parts while the noble Rezia and the Sultan of Egypt represent completely serious characters. It is interesting that, according to the fashion of the time, the clergy are ridiculed in the person of the roguish monk Calandro. The score is full of charming details. Ali, for instance, sought by the Egyptian soldiers, disguises himself as a painter. He shows the officers a number of pictures and describes their subjects to them. The ensuing aria in D major thus illustrates a magnificent Italian banquet, a sweetly murmuring little brook, and an appalling battle scene with the discharge of muskets and guns. Exquisite effects of tone color are attained in the trio "Mi sembra un sogno" for three sopranos accompanied by muted strings, English horns, and French horns. Another remarkable number is an orchestral interlude in the third act in which such conventional Turkish instruments as the triangle and the tambourine are used to portray the atmosphere of an oriental fairy tale. The opera has three important finales, the most interesting being that of the second

[5] The aria was edited in 1932 by the author under the title of "Amors Pfeil" ("Cupid's Arrow") with both Italian and German text.

act, which consists of three sections contrasting in tempo and rhythm. It is preceded by a duet in E major, which together with this finale forms a sort of larger unit.

Il Mondo della Luna of the year 1777 is based on a libretto by Goldoni and is related in its content to *Lo Speziale*, the first Goldoni opera composed by Haydn. The apothecary Sempronio in the earlier work is crazy about geography and Bonafede, the father of two pretty daughters, is all too fond of astronomy. His excessive interest in the world of the moon is destined to become his undoing; thinking that he lives on that distant satellite, he consents for his daughters to marry suitors whom he would never have approved on earth. This rather amusing farce was very popular in the eighteenth century and composers such as Galuppi, Piccini, Gassmann, and Paisiello successively set it to music. Haydn's opera has recently been translated into German and reprinted in a modern edition.[6] *Il Mondo della Luna* includes an unusually large number of instrumental movements. In the first act a short orchestral piece leads us into the world of the moon and three times the trusting Bonafede looks through a telescope prepared by a fraudulent astronomer, Ecclitico. On each occasion the same instrumental piece is played, only to be interrupted by a *recitativo secco* and an arietta in which Bonafede explains what he sees. The orchestration changes after each observation; for its original appearance Haydn used strings in the instrumental piece and oboes, horns, and strings in the arietta. At the first repetition in both pieces flutes are added. Bonafede's last observation was particularly unpleasant, which induced Haydn to add bassoons to his orchestra and to change the key of the piece from D to E♭. The prelude to the second act describes the pompous entry of the sovereign of the moon. At the beginning of the first finale the sensations of flying are painted with realism by the orchestra and an accompanying ballet is introduced. Haydn was obviously following the tradition of Gluck's reformed operas composed for Vienna, in which descriptive orchestral preludes and ballets were of great importance. Strangely enough the overture to the opera which is in one movement only, has no direct connection with the work that it precedes. According to the custom of the time Haydn also used it for other purposes; the overture to *Il Mondo della Luna* is identical with the first movement of the symphony No. 63,

[6] *Die Welt auf dem Monde,* edited by Treichlinger and Lothar in 1932.

La Roxolane [7] (the symphony owes its name to the French song "La Roxolane" which is used as a theme for variations in the allegretto movement).

The opera *La Vera Costanza* was composed for Vienna and shows an interesting relationship to a work by Mozart. By an odd coincidence the heroine, who rises from humble beginnings to the position of countess, bears the name Rosina and like the Countess Rosina in Mozart's *Le Nozze di Figaro,* she is devoted in deep love and faithfulness to her husband, although the count, heedless of his own gallant adventures, torments her with his unfounded jealousy. The tender and sensitive Rosina has as a counterpart the merry Villotto, who tries to win her love. *La Vera Costanza* is perhaps the most mature of Haydn's comic operas for the new and dramatic form of its arias is indeed remarkable. The count's aria (No. 8) in the first act is introduced by an accompanied recitative in preparation for the tempestuous atmosphere of the first part of the aria; the second section brings by an abrupt change of mood a tender adagio, inspired by the thought of his beloved. Irritated by a motion of his clumsy rival the count suddenly starts; another recitative accompanied by the orchestra leads to the third part of the aria, bringing in new thematic material. The count's overwrought state of mind could not be better expressed than by the free form of this passionate piece and a similar feeling is also expressed in the count's solo (No. 15) in the second act. An accompanied recitative built on the thematic material of the first part of the aria is followed by an intricate vocal number consisting of not less than five sections. These sections contrast in tempo, rhythm, and character and are interspersed with occasional recitatives. In these two numbers Haydn succeeds in presenting a vivid picture of the weak and unstable character of the count. The finales, too, reveal the hand of the mature artist: the first consists of seven contrasting parts in different keys related to each other; the number of singers gradually increases from three to seven; and in the second finale nine sections can be distinguished. At the beginning one singer and one sleeping person are on the stage but at the end all the seven characters take part. The composer gives a great amount

---

[7] Pohl (II, 283) and Mandyczewski (No. 12 of the list of Haydn's overtures) are wrong in considering as the overture to *Il Mondo della Luna* a piece that contains three different numbers of the opera. Pohl's mistake is all the more surprising as the correct statement is given by him on p. 267 of the same volume. (*See* Bibliography for Pohl reference.)

of variety to these finales without ever endangering the continuity of the plot and the musical unity. Obviously, when he was composing this work Haydn had the rich resources of the opera in the imperial capital in mind.[8]

La Vera Costanza showed Haydn's growing interest in the serious opera but he took a more important step in the same direction in L'Isola Disabitata. This is a real opera seria, based on a simple and short drama of the great Pietro Metastasio. Costanza, separated by pirates from her husband Ernesto, lives with her sister Silvia on a deserted island until finally, after many years, she finds her beloved spouse again. The work shows that the composer knew Gluck's operas and allowed himself to be influenced by them. It is hardly due to mere chance that Haydn called L'Isola Disabitata an azione teatrale, the same designation that Gluck had used for his Orfeo ed Euridice. The recitativo secco accompanied by the harpsichord only is banished from Haydn's opera as it was from Gluck's work. It is replaced by a carefully designed recitative accompanied by the orchestra and fills the greatest part of the score. Unity between the different scenes is achieved through the use of simple and constantly recurring motives. While the recitative is sometimes transformed into a real arioso, the arias themselves are unaffected and powerful, without an excessive development of the musical element. To some extent, however, Haydn deviated from this rule in the arias of Silvia, which he wrote for Luigia Polzelli. In these lovely pieces the master attained a tenderness of expression reminiscent of Mozart. It is a pity that he included only a single ensemble number, the final quartet, in the score; a fire, which shortly before had ravaged the theater at Eszterháza, may have been responsible for such economy. As Haydn did not have a real stage at his disposal he had to be satisfied with four singers only and to abstain from the use of ballets or changes of scenery. There is only one instrumental number in this opera, the overture, whose slow introduction uses the same main idea as the following allegro. This fast movement gains in unity through the prevailing accompaniment in eighth notes. After a short contrasting allegretto in G major the first allegro returns as a kind of coda. Haydn meant to describe in the restless allegros the terrible existence

[8] The overture to La Vera Costanza appeared together with other numbers from the opera in 1782 as a sinfonia published by Artaria & Company, since Haydn liked to form suites out of the most successful numbers of his works for the stage. (Cf. his symphony No. 60, Il Distratto.)

on the desolate island, while the allegretto voiced the hope of the eventual union of the loving couple.

Mention should also be made of the little German puppet opera *Philemon und Baucis,* which was performed in 1773 on the occasion of Empress Maria Theresa's visit to Eszterháza. Unfortunately, only a single canzonet of Philemon and the overture [9] to the opera have been preserved. The overture consists of two movements only, since, according to a custom of the period, instead of the finale the introduction to the first vocal number of the score was used. Both movements have passages full of tenderness, showing that in the overture too the composer made an attempt to illustrate the moving idyll enacted by the frail puppets.

It is very doubtful whether Haydn is really the composer of the incidental music to Shakespeare's *King Lear* though it has often been attributed to him.[10] The old parts of the work contained in the library of Eszterháza do not mention the name of Haydn and a copy of the composition in the library of Schwerin names W. G. Stegmann as the real composer.[11]

Haydn composed no cantatas during his third period of composition, but in the years 1774–75 he wrote an even bigger work. It was his first oratorio, *Il Ritorno di Tobia* (*The Return of Tobias*), based on a book by Giovanni Gastone Boccherini (the autograph of the second part is preserved by the Society of Friends of Music in Vienna). This work still adheres to the model of the Neapolitan vocal style. Even a cursory glance at the many arias with the abundant coloratura discloses the influence of Italian art. At the same time the intricacy of the musical craftsmanship and the close connection between words and music give this oratorio a character all its own. The libretto differs favorably from the typical Neapolitan oratorio text; instead of the traditional and feeble allegories a definite plot is established, a plot that is by no means lacking in dramatic episodes, such as his parents' meeting with Tobias whom they had thought dead, the miraculous healing of old Tobit's blindness, the revelation of the

[9] Even the authenticity of the overture can be questioned.

[10] The author previously shared the opinion of such experts as Jahn, Pohl, and Mandyczewski in believing this very interesting piece to be a true Haydn work. However, now he feels inclined to consider it as a spurious composition.

[11] See Otto Kade, *Katalog der Musikalien der Schweriner Regierungsbibliothek* (1893), II, 255; *also* Robert Heger, "Die Musik zum Trauerspiel König Lear" in *Oesterreichische Kunst* (1932) and Larsen, *Die Haydn-Ueberlieferung.*

archangel's identity, and his return to heaven. This oratorio, written for Vienna, follows the best musical traditions of the Austrian capital. The Habsburgs always preferred a more severe musical style and accordingly, oratorios in Vienna were kept free from the aberrations of Neapolitan music. Haydn himself was striving in his Storm and Stress period for an expressive musical language; now he was emotionally qualified to write a work in accord with the exacting tradition of Viennese art. The remarkable overture of the work consists of a largo in C minor, the lofty character of which reminds us of Gluck, and an *allegro di molto* in C major in sonata form. The slow introduction is thematically related to the first chorus *Pietà d'un infelice* while a spiritual affinity exists between the allegro of the overture and the final chorus of the work. In this overture Haydn deals with the main idea of the oratorio: out of sorrow and darkness a way is leading to happiness and light. In Beethoven's C minor symphony the basic idea is not very different.

The arias frequently renounce the stereotyped *da capo* form. They show the same strong influences of the sonata form that were to be noticed in the opera arias. There are two contrasting ideas in the first part of the aria. The middle section brings the development of feeling and action and the last part once more recapitulates it. Dramatic and musical points of view are in complete accordance here. In her first aria, for instance, the mother of Tobias deplores the weakness of her husband. In the initial section the achievements of the warrior and peasant are glorified and then, after a modulation to the dominant, the passivity of the husband is lamented. In the second (development) section in the minor the passionate reproaches increase. Anna cannot help remembering once more (recapitulation) the gallant warrior and the diligent peasant, both of them so sadly contrasting with her husband.

The recitatives too are most carefully treated. The shy and delicate portrait of Tobias' young wife in No. 8 of the first part, or the healing of blind Tobit in No. 7 of the second part are strikingly depicted, surpassing by far the average recitatives of the period.

The most important numbers of the score, however, are the choruses. At first the work contained three choruses only, one each at the beginning and end of the first part and one as the finale of the second part. For a performance in 1784 Haydn added two more choruses, one in each part. Most effective in the first number is the combination of solo voices and chorus, as well as the use of the instruments to which the melody is frequently entrusted, while the chorus provides the harmonic basis. The last number is in a sort of rondo form. Again and again the chorus repeats its moving supplication *Rendi a Tobit la luce, o della luce autor* (return the light to Tobit, Creator of the light), interrupted only by the five soloists who send their individual prayers to the heavenly Father. Particularly dramatic is the moment when the humble wailing *mire le calde lacrime* (notice our scalding tears) suddenly changes into the passionate outcry *odi le nostre voci* (listen to our voices). Perhaps the most important of the ensemble numbers is the "Storm Chorus" which Haydn wrote in 1784 for the second part. The effective contrast between pictures of darkest horror and heavenly peace makes this piece equal to the best creations of the mature Haydn.

Three years before the master's death, Haydn's pupil, Ignaz Neukomm, arranged *Il Ritorno di Tobia* on behalf of the composer. Some of the unnecessary repetitions of the text and excessive coloratura were then eliminated. Neukomm's changes and enlargements of the orchestration, however, might well have been avoided for they coarsened some charming details of Haydn's original instrumentation. Even if the pupil acted in full conformity with Haydn's own wishes it is doubtful whether the composer himself, after the passing of more than thirty years, was able to conjure up the atmosphere of the original work in order to judge the merits of the "improvement" of his composition. (It is equally doubtful whether Brahms's remodeling of his early piano trio, Op. 8 or Wagner's later Paris version of *Tannhäuser* really helped the original compositions.)

Another of Haydn's compositions of this period also exists in more than one version. It is the *Salve Regina* in G minor (No. 6 in Haydn's catalogue) which he wrote for four solo voices, organ, and a few instruments. Later editions replaced the organ by different wind instruments such as oboes and bassoons, or clarinets, and divided the vocal sections between chorus and soloists. Like the first *Salve Regina* this work is in three movements. The voices are predominant while the instruments mainly support and strengthen them. It is an attractive composition, showing clearly the characteristic Viennese version of the Italian style used in this period for the master's sacred and oratorio compositions.

An old copy of the *Salve Regina* contains the following chronogram in the form of a Latin verse:

oro te, o pIa, o DVLCIs VIrgo,
Vt assIstas CoMposItorI

If the capital letters are considered as Roman figures and added up, they give 1771, the year in which the work was written.

More important than the *Salve Regina* is Haydn's only *Stabat Mater* (No. 2 of the oratorios in Haydn's catalogue) written around 1773. It is characteristic of the composer that he set to music this text full of grief and sadness during his Storm and Stress period. The music certainly reflects the passion and sensitiveness that dominated Haydn's feelings at this time. Minor keys, particularly the sadly sweet G minor, chromatic progressions, "sighs," syncopations, and sudden dynamic changes create an atmosphere of restlessness and suffering in keeping with the character of the text. One of the most impressive numbers of this score is the solo quartet with chorus, "Virgo virginum praeclara." The lead is given to the soloists while the chorus—in a sort of antiphonal style—has short phrases only. The words of the soloists, for example, *passionis fac consortem—fac ut portem Christi mortem—fac me plagis vulnerari* are interrupted again and again by the one word *fac* sung like an urgent shout by the chorus. Movements of a somewhat similar nature are to be found among J. S. Bach's works (cf. *The Passion According to St. Matthew*, aria with chorus, No. 79). Haydn gave the composition more variety and dramatic fire than the rather monotonous text would seem to admit.

Two short masses also belong to the early seventies. Schnerich was certainly right in asserting that the *Missa St. Joannis de Deo,* also known as the *Little Organ Solo Mass* (Novello No. 8) was written about 1770, whereas Pohl contended that it belonged to the year 1778. This short and concise work (autograph preserved by the Society of Friends of Music in Vienna) is written for four voices only, two violins, and organ solo. One of the few more broadly treated numbers of the score is the Benedictus in which a solo soprano competes with an organ solo. At the dramatic climax of the text, the beginning of *et resurrexit* after the end of the Crucifixus, the music of the Gloria is quoted by Haydn. Better than a date on the manuscript the expression mark *perdendosi* used at the end of the "Dona nobis pacem" indicates the period in which this work was written. This pianissimo at the end of the prayer for peace certainly conforms to the idea of the text, although it contradicts the traditional musical construction. It is interesting to see that in Haydn's original manuscript of this mass the notes of the bass and the organ parts were written about twice as large as those of the rest. Apparently the organist—probably Haydn himself—intended to play from the full score.

The *Missa St. Nicolai* of 1772 (Novello No. 7, autograph in the State Library, Berlin), while still a *missa brevis,* is on a larger scale than the preceding work. Two oboes and two horns are added to the orchestra, and the share of the soloists is also more important than in the *Missa St. Joannis.* It stands as one of the most lyrical and tender of Haydn's church compositions. The Kyrie has the character of a pastorale in six-quarter time, the Gratias is a soprano solo, the Benedictus a solo quartet of winning gracefulness. The "Dona nobis pacem" takes up the music of the Kyrie, thus musically uniting the beginning and the end of the work. The modern critic finds it somewhat disconcerting that in the Credo different sections of the text are sung simultaneously; however, similar devices to save time were used not only by Haydn but by other composers of the period also. The sensibility of the Storm and Stress period is expressed perhaps not so strongly in this mass as in other compositions of the year 1772. But the frequent *sforzandi* in the Kyrie, the mournful repetition of the words *et homo factus est* after the menacing Crucifixus, and the moving accents in the Agnus Dei show that Haydn was well aware of the supreme drama unfolding in the text of the mass.

Chapter 15

MATURITY

The Fourth Period: 1780 — 1789

WITH the beginning of the seventeen-eighties Haydn entered upon his classical period of composition. Both the frills of the rococo period and the exaggerated emotionalism of the Storm and Stress period were overcome, although they left their imprint on the master's work. Out of the combination of Haydn's second and third periods of composition there grew his fourth period, the classical style of his full maturity.

The term "classical" can hardly be better explained than by the words: well balanced. In classical music one finds a perfect blend of the work of the mind and the work of the heart; inspiration is as important as is the action of the intellect. Cheerfulness and seriousness, the tragic and the comic spirit are all called upon to make their respective contributions. Classical works seem to be born out of the fundamental qualities of the instruments or voices for which they were written. All technical problems are completely solved and the compositions are neither too long nor too short. The musical ideas fit the musical form to perfection. Those works that deserve to be termed "classical" exhibit a beauty and composure comparable only to the best products of the architecture and sculpture of ancient Greece.

Although Haydn had undergone an artistic development, which seemed to lead him inevitably toward classicism, his work would hardly have reached the full height of perfection had he not been associated artistically with Mozart. It has been shown in the first section of this book that the friendship between the two masters resulted in an amazing musical relationship. Not only did Haydn influence Mozart (this is not particularly surprising, as he was twenty-four years older and by far the more successful of the two), but he allowed himself also to be influenced by the young genius. It was a perfect example of mutual give and take, equally as beneficial to Mozart as to Haydn, for in helping one another each of the two masters reached in the eighties the consummation of his classical style and with it his full artistic maturity.

It is evident that even before the first meeting of the two composers Haydn had already studied Mozart's work, since some of his sonatas for the pianoforte, published before the date of that meeting, show clear signs of Mozart's influence. For instance, the melodic invention in the second movement of sonata No. 35 and the striking separation of the subsidiary subject from the main subject in the first movement of sonata No. 37 (both sonatas having been published in 1780) show a certain similarity to the works of the Salzburg master, as does the connection of the end of the exposition with the beginning of the development in the first movements of Nos. 41 and 49, two sonatas composed after the musicians had first met. In the adagio of No. 49 also the melodic character appears to be to some extent inspired by Mozart.

However this may be, pianoforte sonatas are certainly not among the most representative works of Haydn's classical period. In 1784 three sonatas (Nos. 40–42) were published and dedicated to Princess Marie Elisabeth Eszterházy, the wife of Prince Nicholas. It seems as if the conservative taste of the lady, who at that time was sixty-six years old, restrained Haydn's creative power somewhat. Each sonata has only two movements and the influence of the *divertimento* seems to be particularly strong (especially so in No. 40). A comparison of the brilliant finale of No. 39 with the tame *allegretto innocente* at the beginning of No. 40 reveals a striking difference of character. Obviously, the princess was not in favor of bold innovations and the finales of Nos. 41 and 42 show that a display of strict counterpoint was more to her taste.

Sonatas Nos. 43–48, published during the second half of the eighties, make it equally clear that during his period of maturity Haydn's greatest interest was not in the piano sonata. Only very few movements, like the imposing adagio in No. 46, show the hand of the genius while the first movement of No. 47, possibly influenced by

Clementi, offers a rather shallow display of technical brilliance. The uninspired runs and the passages in thirds and octaves of this movement seem to belong to an *étude* rather than to a work of the mature Haydn.

The big sonata No. 49 in E♭ major, written in 1789–90 for Marianne von Genzinger, is probably Haydn's best pianoforte work of this period. For once the composer completely forgot the educational purpose of his piano music and followed only his inspiration. In the exposition of the first movement the subsidiary and the concluding subjects, although derived from the main idea, show an independent character of their own; the retransition to the recapitulation is full of dramatic tension, and the important coda seems to be a sort of second development. The solemn adagio with its dramatic episode in B♭ minor is reminiscent of Mozart. Haydn himself considered this movement the climax of the whole work, as his letter to Marianne von Genzinger shows (cf. p. 85). The finale is quite different from this middle movement. In its gay and energetic character it supplies a cheerful solution of the conflict; thus Haydn's interest in the piano sonata got a fresh impetus from his devotion to Marianne von Genzinger, for everything connected with her had to be perfect. It is significant that the composer could not even bear the thought of his friend playing the sonata on her old, inferior piano. He was not satisfied until he had persuaded his prince to present Frau von Genzinger with a new instrument, he, himself giving elaborate advice as to the final choice.[1]

Two smaller piano compositions of Haydn, the Capriccio in G major and the Fantasia in C major were published in 1789. We know from Griesinger that Haydn loved to lose himself in his improvisations on the piano. Such extemporizations when committed to writing are probably to be found in these two compositions. While Mozart's big fantasias show frequent changes of mood, it is characteristic of Haydn that he preserved throughout each of these two pieces the same spirit of gay and lighthearted badinage. Although these pieces present the general style of improvisations their musical form is by no means disregarded. The capriccio is written as a sort of rondo, the fantasia approaches sonata form. Haydn had a high opinion of this capriccio, which he offered to Artaria with the following words: "In a humorous mood I have composed an entirely new capriccio for the

[1] *See* letters of Haydn to Frau von Genzinger dated June 20 and 27, and July 4, 1790, in Lady G. M. Wallace, *Letters of Distinguished Musicians* (London: 1857–59).

piano; its good taste, singularity, and elaborate finish are sure to please both experts and amateurs. It is in a single movement, rather long, but not particularly difficult." This work is based on the melody of the north-German folk song. "Ich wünscht' es wäre Nacht." Mozart used the same tune in one of his early compositions, the Galimathias Musicum, which he wrote at the age of ten. The fantasia shows, better even than the sonatas, the colorful character of Haydn's piano playing. We seem to hear in this piece the tone of violins and double basses, of horns and flutes; moreover the rapid crossing of the hands, the arpeggios, and the distribution of passages between the two hands exhibit the composer's concern for purely pianistic devices. The effect that Haydn achieved by holding notes in the bass until they die away (*tenuto intanto finchè non si sente più il sono*) is rather notable. This fantasia was written by a master who exploited the possibilities of piano technique in transcribing ideas of an essentially orchestral nature.

During the fourth period of composition eleven piano trios were composed (Nos. 7, 10, 11, 14–16, 20, 24, 25, 30, 31 of the Peters Edition). On the whole these compositions resemble the earlier trios although the influence of Mozart is occasionally obvious. The piano parts still contain runs and passages given to both hands and also occasional cadenzas. The violin is limited to the first three positions and is entirely subordinate to the keyboard instrument, while the violoncello as a rule merely duplicates the bass of the piano part. The first movement of No. 15, of 1785, in which violin and violoncello are used in conjunction and opposed to the piano, is certainly an exception.

In 1784 Haydn sent to England his six *divertimenti* for first violin or flute, second violin, and violoncello. They were published by William Forster in London as Op. 38; the manuscripts, probably written by Elssler, are preserved in the British Museum. According to Haydn's receipt of the honorarium accompanying the manuscripts these trios may also be performed by two flutes and violoncello. They are pleasant pieces of no great consequence.

Haydn's string quartets, Op. 33, of 1781 (Nos. 37–42 of Haydn's list), were dedicated to the Grand Duke Paul of Russia, and are accordingly known as the Russian Quartets. They are also called Gli Scherzi, as in this series the composer gave the name of scherzo to his minuet movements, or the Jungfernquartette, according to the title page of an old edition. Since the composition of the preceding series of string quartets, Op. 20, of 1772, no less than nine years had elapsed, during which Haydn had composed several operas, the oratorio *Il Ritorno di Tobia,* and many symphonies. The string quartet had temporarily been abandoned, probably because Haydn felt that further progress along the lines established in his Op. 20 was impossible. In the fugue movements of the Sun Quartets a strong concentration of both form and content had been attained, but in time this sort of solution seemed too radical to the master and was not in conformity with the spirit of the string quartet. The progressive Haydn was not satisfied to use an antiquated contrapuntal form of the baroque period in the immature string quartet. He wanted unification and concentration but not knowing how to achieve them adequately, he renounced the composition of string quartets for the time being and it was not until nine years later that he found a solution of his problem.

The Russian Quartets which, according to Haydn himself, were written "in an entirely new and particular manner," raised the principle of thematic development to the status of main stylistic feature. Haydn used thematic development—a method of dissecting the subjects of the exposition and then developing and reassembling the resulting fragments in an unexpected manner—in his earlier works, but never with such logic and doggedness. Henceforth this device, combined with modulations, ruled the development sections of the sonata form. Each of the six Russian Quartets provides examples of this new technique. The quartets, Op. 20 with their fugues had already done away with the predominance of the first violin. In the Russian Quartets all instruments as a matter of course were given equal shares in the melodic work. Even the accompanying and purely filling parts were based on motives taken from the main subjects.

Haydn exercised wise economy in using the sonata form only in the first movement of the Russian Quartets. The slow movements are mainly in three-part (romanza) form with a contrasting middle part instead of a development, while in the finales there is a return to the rondo form. Only in his last period was Haydn to give to the rondo the characteristic features of the sonata form, thus creating at the end of the cycle a counterpart to its beginning. The most apparent innovation of the Russian Quartets, the use of a scherzo instead of the traditional minuet, should not be taken too seriously. An analysis of these pieces shows that the change is limited to the name of the movement and does not affect its character. Only the scherzo of No. 5 foreshadows the piquant flavor and fire of Beethoven's movements of the same name.

The contents of these quartets display grace and liveliness together with depth of feeling; the quiet serenity and simple greatness of the classical style are to be found in them. Still, an experience of the importance of the "romantic crisis" could not but leave its imprint on the master's work. The augmented octaves in the introduction of No. 1, and the last movement of No. 2, with its adagio episode, its grand pauses of increasing length, and its pianissimo ending bear witness to it.

Two quartets of the series are known through nicknames given to them by the players. The finale of No. 2 is called The Joke. It seems to be a pleasant, though not particularly amusing rondo with two episodes. The real fun comes in the coda, for after a solemn adagio episode the eight measures of the main subject are repeated in an odd manner. Each phrase of two bars is followed by a rest of two measures. When the whole subject is played Haydn doubles his rest and starts all over with the first measures of the melody, and before anybody in the audience has a chance of voicing a protest the end has come, leaving the listener puzzled and amused. Perhaps the most charming work of the set is No. 3, The Bird, and no one who is fortunate enough to have heard it interpreted by the Joachim Quartet will ever forget it. The grace notes in the main subject of the first movement, which all four instruments take up in the development, partly explain the name. The real bird movement is, however, the trio of the scherzando, an unusually charming duet between first and second violins.

The following quartet, Op. 42 (No. 43 of Haydn's list) is a sort of foreign body within the whole set of string quartets. The very terse construction of its four movements induced Pohl and Sandberger to classify this composition as one of Haydn's early works. Some details, however, like the dramatic development of the first movement, the pianissimo endings of the first and last movements, and the use of contrapuntal devices in the finale prove Op. 42 to be the product of a later period. Additional evidence is provided by the autograph in the

State Library, Berlin, which bears the date 1785. This work must certainly be considered as a composition of Haydn's maturity and for unknown reasons was partly conceived in the simpler and unassuming manner of his earlier style.

Between 1784 and 1787 Haydn wrote six quartets that were published as Op. 50 (Nos. 44–49 of Haydn's list) and dedicated to the king of Prussia. In these the thematic development employed in Op. 33 is continued. The four stringed instruments are again treated individually but co-operate on a single task: to discuss each subject thoroughly so as to cast full light upon all its potentialities. It is most significant that Haydn, who increasingly exploited the possibilities of the transformation of themes, often rejected the use of a contrasting subsidiary subject. He was anxious to concentrate his compositions not only by using thematic development, but also by letting a whole movement unfold out of a single germ cell. The complete expression of the straightforward and undivided personality of the master is to be found in movements that seem to be hewn out of a single block. Thus the finale of No. 1 shows a monothematic construction. The main subject stated in the first two measures is treated either as a whole or in halves all through the movement. In No. 2 the second section of the minuet (the name scherzo vanishes again in this set of quartets, although the character of Beethoven's scherzo is occasionally intimated) is a development of the first section, not a new idea, thus again emphasizing the idea of unity. Similar tendencies prevail in the first movement of No. 4 in F♯ minor, which is probably the most interesting of the entire set. Although the main subject is in the minor and the subsidiary subject in the major mode, this subsidiary subject is obviously derived from the first idea. The impassioned and subjective character of this movement together with the fugue of the finale seem to indicate that No. 4 originated during the early seventies, but a very important detail shows that the quartet can belong only to a later period. Both the transition to the subsidiary subject and the subject itself display the spirit of Mozart. In the andante of this quartet the main theme in the major mode is followed by a contrasting melody in the minor and there is one variation each on the major and minor sections, followed by a second variation of the main theme which brings the movement to an end. Similar combinations of the variation form with that of the rondo were of the greatest importance in Haydn's later compositions. In

No. 5 the slow movement, which has some elaborate solo passages for the violin, is known as A Dream. In the third movement both the minuet and its trio are governed by the same grace note motive, showing that the idea of unity seemed to Haydn more important than the traditional contrast between minuet and trio. In this rather serious and thoughtful series there is one quartet imbued with Haydn's particular sense of humor. It is No. 6, The Frog, and its finale is filled with gay croaking sounds produced by playing the same notes alternately on two neighboring strings. In some of his chamber music Brahms has made a good use of this same effect.

Between the quartets, Op. 50 and those of Op. 54 the arrangement of Haydn's *Seven Last Words* for a string quartet is inserted in some editions, as Op. 51 (Nos. 50–56 of Haydn's list). This work is discussed on p. 270.

In 1789 the quartets, Op. 54 Nos. 1–3 and Op. 55 Nos. 1–3 (Nos. 57–62 of Haydn's list) were published and in the following year the quartets, Op. 64 Nos. 1–6 (Nos. 63–68 of Haydn's list). All twelve compositions were dedicated to Johann Tost.[2] The boldness and variety of invention in these works and their well-balanced musical form show Haydn at the summit of his quartet production. The twelve quartets are so closely interrelated that they will be discussed together, although technically the second half-dozen belong to the master's last period of composition.

A characteristic of these quartets is again the use of a single subject upon which a whole movement is based. The adagio in Op. 55 No. 1 grows out of one idea only; so do the finale of Op. 64 No. 2 and the first movement of Op. 64 No. 1, which are both in sonata form. In each of these two compositions the subsidiary subject is developed out of the first subject and the composer revealed his desire for unity by using in the recapitulation the main subject itself rather than its transformation. Occasionally Haydn employed contrasting ideas, but

[2] There seems to be some doubt about the personality of this man. Pohl (II, 373) mentions a violinist of this name who was a member of the Eszterházy orchestra from 1783 to 1789. In 1789 he went to Paris and there he carried out dubious transactions with some of Haydn's symphonies and string quartets. About the later fate of this man nothing is known; however, in 1790 a second Johann Tost, who was also a violinist, made his appearance in Haydn's biography (Pohl, II, 228). In 1790 Johann Tost (II) married a rich girl and became a respected cloth merchant. He was the man to whom Haydn dedicated his twelve quartets. The author feels inclined to share Larsen's assumption that Tost (I) and Tost (II) were the same person. It is certainly surprising that we know nothing about the life of Johann Tost (I) after 1790, and nothing about the life of Johann Tost (II) before 1790.

postponed their entrance as long as possible so that they became epilogues rather than subsidiary subjects (cf. the first movements of Op. 54 No. 1 and Op. 64 No. 1). Mozart's type of construction, in which the subsidiary idea is entrusted with a countermelody of sweet and tender character, is not often to be found in these works (the finale of Op. 64 No. 1 provides one of the infrequent examples), and it is significant of the difference in character in the two masters that the older composer stressed unity and the younger contrast in their respective creations.

The Tost Quartets are full of attractive little surprises. Haydn liked to introduce into his rondos and the developments of his sonata forms interesting *fugato* sections, as in the finales of Op. 55 No. 1, Op. 64 No. 2, and Op. 64 No. 5 and the second movement of Op. 55 No. 2. Harmony and modulation sometimes seem to foreshadow the romantic period. The delicately veiled episode of the second subject in the allegretto of Op. 54 No. 1 introduces tender modulations of a hazy and elusive character. With the help of hardly noticeable chromatic progressions and enharmonic changes Haydn modulates from G major over C, B♭ and E♭ to D♭, and back to the initial key. We seem to be lifted by some magic in a fantastic flight through the air, eventually to be deposited at the spot from which we started. The harsh dissonances in the trio of the minuet of Op. 54 No. 2 remind us of modern harmonies built on the interval of the fourth instead of the traditional third, all sentimental conceptions of good old "Papa Haydn" being contradicted by such boldness. The same quartet has a rather striking adagio finale, which in all likelihood was originally meant merely as the slow introduction to a presto. It assumed such proportions, however, that it developed into the main section of the movement, while the short presto in the middle was reduced to a mere episode. The arrangement of the voices in this movement is also most unusual; the first violin carries the melody while the violoncello keeps crossing the middle parts, passing again and again into the treble register. The quartet in F minor, Op. 55 No. 2 is known as the Razor Quartet. In this work the first two movements change places. It begins with a set of variations in slow time, alternately in minor and major but the second movement is an allegro in sonata form of peculiar charm with its sudden half-tone progressions. A forte cadence in F minor is followed, after a grand pause, by a delicate piano passage beginning in G♭ major; later in the same way a cadence in A♭ is succeeded by a passage beginning in A major. Similar devices were used by Philipp Emanuel Bach, for instance, in the big "Heilig" published by Breitkopf & Härtel in 1779. Op. 64 No. 1 exhibits in the development section of its finale an excellent example of Haydn's strong sense of humor. The drumming main subject is used here for a little *fugato*, the constant note repetitions of which make an irresistibly droll impression. Op. 64 No. 2 in B minor is filled with passionate energy. While the exposition of the first movement has a subsidiary subject in the relative major, the recapitulation reintroduces it, surprisingly enough, in the tonic minor and only the following simple and sweet *adagio ma non troppo* in B major brings a harmonious solution. The trio of the minuet, taking the first violin up to the highest positions, shows what great demands Haydn made at that time on the technical abilities of his players. It should not be assumed, however, that the master's reason for inserting this trio was to give the player of the first violin a chance to show off his technical ability. Haydn's motives were purely artistic for after the ponderous heaviness of the minuet the silvery lightness of the high registers was needed to achieve a perfect balance. The finale brings yet another example of Haydn's sense of humor in the entertaining interplay of piano passages as the seeming bearers of timid and faltering questions, and the replies to them in the form of brusque and loudly declaimed unisons. Here again the technique of the comic opera is employed in a work of chamber music. The slow movement of Op. 64 No. 4 has in its parts for the second violin and viola an accompaniment that is surprisingly pianistic in its whole conception. Since Haydn, like other eighteenth-century composers, sometimes wrote pianoforte parts that showed the influence of stringed instruments, so he occasionally inverted this relationship. The lovely first movement of Op. 64 No. 5 is responsible for the name, The Lark, given to the quartet. From the earth-bound accompaniment of the lower parts, the first violin soars up to heavenly heights. The finale of this quartet with its unrelenting motion in sixteenths forms a sort of *perpetuum mobile*. The trio of the minuet in Op. 64 No. 6, a counterpart of the same movement in Op. 55 No. 1, again presents technical difficulties that almost equal those of a violin concerto. The second violin carries the subject while the first violin accompanies like a tenuous chime, with notes ascending to more than four octaves above middle C.

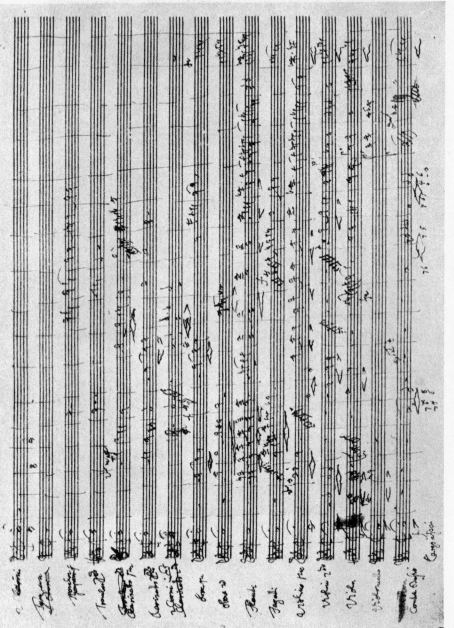

Sketch to the Overture of "The Creation"

Haydn, bust, by A. Grassi, 1799

To this period belong Haydn's six *Feldpartiten* written in the eighties for the military band of Prince Eszterházy, and revised during the nineties. They are octets, some of which are scored for two oboes, two clarinets, two horns, and two bassoons, the others being written for two oboes, two horns, three bassoons, and a "serpent," an obsolete bass cornet in the form of a snake. Some of the slow movements have titles, like *la Vierge Marie,* reminiscent of similar tendencies in the French suites of the seventeenth and eighteenth centuries. The most important of these *partitas* is the one in B♭ major. In 1870 Haydn's biographer Pohl showed a copy of it to his friend, Johannes Brahms, who immediately copied the second movement in his notebook. Fascinated by the "Chorale St. Antonii," the old Austrian pilgrims' song upon which this movement was based, Brahms used it as the theme for his Variations on a Theme by Joseph Haydn, Op. 56, which he wrote during the summer of 1873, almost a hundred years after Haydn's composition.[3] This *partita* (edited by the author of this book in 1932) is in four movements and all exhibit a close melodic relationship; in fact, it may be said that the first movement, the minuet, and the finale are in a way variations of the "Chorale St. Antonii," introduced in the second movement. The old German variation suite of the seventeenth century, in which the different dances of a suite are made up of variations of a main dance,[4] is here revived, and the cyclical form so dear to the composers of the nineteenth century is foreshadowed.

Like the *partita* in B♭ major, the other pieces of this set are in four movements. The simple construction of each *partita,* the use of the same key for all movements of the short suites, the insertion of marches and little character pieces, all show that Haydn had no intention of discouraging the members of Prince Eszterházy's military band by setting complicated music before them.

In 1788 Haydn's Toy Symphony for different toy instruments and strings was written. The charming little piece shows the deep understanding that the childless master had of the world of little ones. It is another example of the composer's amiable sense of fun.

Haydn's two most famous solo concertos were written during the eighties. The authenticity of the violoncello concerto in D major has

[3] *See* Karl Geiringer, *Brahms, His Life and Work* (Boston: 1936).
[4] *See* Karl Geiringer, "Paul Peuerl" in *Studien zur Musikwissenschaft* (1929).

recently been doubted;[5] it has been suggested that Anton Kraft, a cellist of the Eszterházy orchestra and pupil of the master, not Haydn, was its author. But there is nothing among Kraft's known, and incidentally rather mediocre, compositions to justify the attribution of a masterpiece like the D major concerto to him, while this work certainly finds a place among the compositions of the mature Haydn. The part of the solo instrument is not only brilliant but has been made the center of the composition and all other instruments look to it for leadership. The following notice appeared on the first edition of the concerto published after Haydn's death by Johann André in Offenbach on Main: *"Edition d'après le manuscrit original de l'auteur."* Köchel, the great Mozart scholar, saw this manuscript carrying Haydn's signature and the date 1783 in the collection of Julius Rietz in Dresden, and although it seems to have been lost now, there is no reason to doubt Haydn's authorship, particularly since the work is listed in the master's own catalogue. The concerto is usually performed with an enlarged orchestral accompaniment that was provided by François Auguste Gevaert in 1890. The original version using only two oboes and two horns is now also available and is certainly preferable because of its more intimate character.

In 1784 another D major concerto, written for piano and orchestra, was published. This work has not only an attractive solo part, but also a very effective accompaniment for the orchestra. The middle movement grows out of the thematic material of the first eight measures of the *tutti* and a simple motive in which the same note is repeated six times is expanded into an important dialogue between solo instrument and orchestra. The most interesting movement of the concerto is the final *rondo all'Ongarese.* It contains two episodes in the minor, the second's impassioned strength reminding us of nineteenth-century romantic music.

In 1786 Haydn wrote no less than five concertos for two *lire organizzate.* This instrument was a sort of hurdy-gurdy and looked like a big viola. In the interior there was a wooden wheel turned by a crank. This wheel pressed on the strings from below and set them vibrating. The strings were not shortened with the bare fingers but rather with the aid of wooden bridges or tangents, which in turn operated by a system of keys. A little organ attachment was built into the instrument and the keys not only shortened the strings but simultaneously

[5] H. Volkmann, "Ist Haydn's Cellokonzert echt?" in *Die Musik* (March, 1932).

admitted air to the tiny pipes, while the wheel acted as a bow and served to work the bellows.[6] It seems rather surprising that Haydn, who was not particularly interested in the concerto form, should have written so large a number of pieces for this strange instrument. It has been mentioned before that they were composed at the order of the king of Naples, who delighted in playing the *lira organizzata* himself. Furthermore, a close examination of the works will show that they contain very little of the true concerto spirit. The technical possibilities of the clumsy *lira* were more than modest, for its range hardly reached two octaves and fast passages on it were next to impossible. Accordingly, Haydn wrote these concertos as a sort of ensemble music for nine instruments (two violins, two violas, violoncello, two horns, two *lire*) in which the predominance of the solo instruments (the *lire*) is hardly noticeable and their part is not more important than those of the violins and violas. These are pieces for small orchestra in which Haydn, as were the general tendencies of his period of maturity, allotted an equal share in the thematic development to each of the instruments. Accordingly the composer was in a position to use two movements of the first *lira* concerto for his symphony No. 89 written in 1787. The allegrettos of the symphony No. 85 (La Reine) and No. 100 (Military Symphony) also show a certain relationship to the allegretto of the second concerto.

Haydn's symphonies use the same guiding principles of construction as his string quartets and they also show the increasing influence of Mozart's compositions. The master renounced the contrapuntal constructions so important during the seventies and replaced them by the free and unconventional polyphony evolved from the principle of thematic development, using motives taken from the main melodies to weave a rich thematic texture of accompanying voices.

The first traces of the thematic development are to be found in symphonies of the seventies. In comparison with these, No. 73, La Chasse, does not impress us as a very progressive work. The finale of this work, the famous hunting movement making extensive use of horns and oboes, was written in 1780 as a prelude to the third act of Haydn's opera *La Fedeltà premiata*. The preceding movements, according to the testimony of the autograph (in the State Library,

---

[6] *See* Karl Geiringer, *Musical Instruments—Their History in Western Culture from the Stone Age to the Present* (New York: 1945).

Berlin), were added in the following year, 1781. It is probably due
to the fact that Haydn considered the first three movements as a
sort of introduction to the lovely finale that the first allegro does not
show the maturity and accomplishment to be found in the contemporary Russian Quartets.

No. 74, composed before 1782, is one of the earliest symphonic
works to show the influence of the Salzburg master. The first movement has a subsidiary subject in clear contrast to the first one, while
the main idea of the second movement has all the ingratiating qualities of Mozart's melodies.

The symphonies Nos. 75–78 were likewise written before 1782.
No. 75 affords a delightful contrast between a melancholy set of
variations and an extremely gay minuet and finale. The work was
performed by Haydn in England and the composer noted in his diary
that an English clergyman thought he heard the prediction of his
imminent death in the slow movement, and actually died shortly
afterwards.

The thematic development in the two following symphonies is
very interesting. The middle section in the first movement of No. 77
has a kind of *stretto maestrale* (a short-range imitation) of the first
bar of the main subject, in which all the string and wood-wind instruments join. While this movement introduces a contrasting second
subject, in the finale both subsidiary subject and epilogue are derived
from the main idea.

The contrapuntal aspects of the thematic development are also
clearly demonstrated in No. 78. In the middle section of its first
movement a *stretto* of the main idea is accompanied by a "sigh
motive" (a sort of appoggiatura) taken from the subsidiary subject.
A few years later Mozart was to employ a similar device in the last
movement of his Jupiter Symphony. The final rondo of No. 78 approaches the sonata form by using in its last episode a full-sized
development of the main theme instead of a contrasting idea.

Similar tendencies may be noticed in No. 79, written about 1783,
whose first movement resumes the work of development even in the
recapitulation. This symphony, and Nos. 80 and 81 written about
1784, again show an approach to Mozart. The broad cantilena of
flute and first violin in the adagio of No. 80, accompanied by the
Alberti bass of the second violin, and the subsidiary subject in the first

movement of No. 81 are important evidence of the artistic friendship between the two great masters.

The symphonies Nos. 82–92 were composed in or after 1785, mainly for performances and publishers in Paris. In 1784 the board of directors of the Concerts de la Loge Olympique asked Haydn to compose six symphonies for them, which he did during the two following years. Although these works (Nos. 82–87) are not the only symphonies written for the French capital, they are usually referred to as the Paris Symphonies.

No. 82, the so-called First Paris Symphony, was, according to the testimonial of the autograph (in the Bibliothèque du Conservatoire, Paris), written in 1786, one year after the Paris Symphonies No. 2 and No. 6. Its name, L'Ours, is derived from the last movement, the famous bear, or rather bagpipe dance. This piece in its transparent and richly colored setting is certainly one of Haydn's most attractive compositions for orchestra. But the first movement where the thematic development is so abundant that even the transition from the first to the second subject is imbued with it and the charming allegretto with a theme in the major mode, separated from each of its two repetitions by a rather threatening passage in the minor, are worthy of this finale.

No. 83, the second of the Paris Symphonies, got its name La Poule from the subsidiary subject of the first movement, in which the oboe peevishly repeats the same note while the first violin offers a piquant melody adorned with many grace notes. On the whole this movement in G minor shows a surprisingly serious character and the dramatic quality of the following andante is equally unusual. A stubborn minuet and a charming finale in the style of an Italian Siciliano contribute to give this work a peculiar charm.

No. 84, the third of the Paris Symphonies, has a first movement that grows out of the main idea almost completely. Haydn postpones the entrance of the contrasting subject so long that it assumes the role of an epilogue instead of a subsidiary subject. The second movement, an andante with variations, separates the theme in the major from its first variation by a rather dramatic passage in the minor. The finale is gay and carefree; its sudden changes from the pianissimo of a few instruments to the forte of the whole orchestra anticipate the famous "Surprise" of symphony No. 94.

No. 85, La Reine, was most likely a favorite of Queen Marie An-
toinette. The slow movement of the symphony provides a set of
variations on the French romance *La gentille et jeune Lisette,* which
Haydn had also used for one of his *lira organizzata* concertos. These
variations are full of effects of tone color, while the melody and
harmony of the theme undergo but little change. The spirited way in
which the main subject is ushered in during the retransition is a
detail that Haydn may have learned from Mozart.

While the formal construction becomes more and more artistic,
Haydn does not fail to counterbalance it occasionally with movements of a looser structure. The slow movement of No. 86, the fifth
of the Paris Symphonies, shows an affinity with both the sonata and
the rondo forms but without adopting either. Haydn called this interesting and surprisingly serious movement, capriccio. The *allegro
spiritoso* of the first movement and the final *allegro con spirito* certainly deserve the designation "spirited," as they are full of life and
wit. They contribute to make this work one of the greatest of the
Paris Symphonies.

It is characteristic of the lighter and more charming character of
No. 87, the sixth of the series, that among its most valuable sections
is the minuet and especially the lovely flute solo of its trio. It is one of
the least serious of Haydn's mature symphonies.

The four symphonies Nos. 88–91 written in the years 1786 and
1787 are not inferior in value to the previous set. No. 88 in G major
is one of the best works of this period; it is a symphony in which each
of the four movements is of equal importance. The main subject of
the first movement is accompanied by a counterpoint in its first forte
entrance and this counterpoint also appears in the transition to the
second subject. The subsidiary subject is so completely embedded in
material taken from the main subject that the listener hardly notices
the break in the homogenous texture of the movement. The solemn
largo introduces a theme with variations and its beautiful tune has
since been used for the hymn "Praise God from Whom All Blessings
Flow." A characteristic of Haydn's newly acquired unconventional
treatment of instruments is the use of horns and timpani in the minuet. In the composer's early works such instruments were employed
as the typical reinforcements of the *tutti;* now, however, Haydn
employs them in mysterious piano and pianissimo passages as an accompaniment of the main subject. The *allegro con spirito* of the last

movement is a rondo of unusual charm, good humor, and brilliance.

In No. 89 Haydn used for the second and fourth movements material from the first concerto for the *lira organizzata*. The newly composed first and third movements are treated in a somewhat perfunctory manner. Apparently the composer for some reason had to provide a symphony quickly and did so without taking much interest in the task.

No. 90 is again worthy of Haydn's maturity. Its andante uses in turn variations on a theme in the major and one in the minor mode, a form that became increasingly interesting to Haydn at that time. In the last movement the fortissimo ending in C major is remarkable for it is followed, after a grand pause, by a timid pianissimo of the strings and a single bassoon in Db major. (Haydn used a similar device in the second movement of his Razor Quartet.)

Sudden upward progressions are also to be found in the first movement of No. 91, with an unusual chromatic main subject. Here Haydn rises in an almost modern way from Db major over Eb minor to F minor. The second movement of this symphony has an andante with variations, with a contrasting minor passage between the first and second variations (cf. symphony No. 84). Near the end the finale introduces a *stretto* of the main subject in the second violins and basses accompanied in eighth notes by the first violin. Haydn seems to have thought very highly of this symphony, for in his letters to Frau von Genzinger he asked his friend again and again to send him the score from Vienna to London.

The Oxford Symphony, No. 92, will be discussed in the next chapter together with the London Symphonies, for it is related to them in both style and content.

For the classicists the song does not have the importance that was attributed to it in the romantic period. To Haydn, Mozart, and even Beethoven it was a form of little consequence, a form too unimportant to be given much attention. It is well known that in spite of this attitude a few real masterworks were created; but the courage of a Schubert, who printed a single song ("The Erlking") as his Op. 1 in 1816, was inconceivable in the eighteenth century. Only in his maturity did Haydn become interested in the song. The first collection of twelve lieder was published in 1781, a second set in 1784, both through Artaria & Company in Vienna. These lieder clearly show their derivation from the rhythmically and harmonically simple songs of the German Singspiel (a type of opera using simple melodies of folk song character and spoken dialogue). Italian influences may be found in the graceful melodic lines while the master of instrumental composition is revealed in important preludes, interludes, and postludes. In the selection of texts Haydn was helped by his friend, Hofrat Greiner. Nevertheless, or perhaps because of such help, their poetical value is sometimes doubtful.

In a letter to Artaria dated July 20, 1781 Haydn pointed out that three of his songs had previously been set to music by the Viennese Capellmeister, Leopold Hofmann, and added: "Just because this braggart thinks himself on an equal with Mount Parnassus and at every opportunity tries to belittle me in the eyes of certain circles of society, I have composed these same three songs to show these circles the difference—*sed hoc inter nos.*" In the same letter Haydn says: "I particularly request you not to allow anyone to copy or sing these songs at present, or spoil them in any way whatever, for when they are finished I intend to sing them myself to critical audiences. A composer must maintain his rights by his presence, to ensure the proper execution of his works. They are indeed merely songs but not 'street songs' like those of Hofmann, devoid of ideas, of expression, and above all, of melody."

The twenty-four songs are printed in two staves only. A separate line for the voice is not necessary as its melody is identical with that of the top line of the piano part. Haydn frequently used the form of the strophic song (stanza form). The influence of music for the stage is shown in the employment of chromatic progressions, little coloratura phrases, and melodies of a more cantabile character. In the serious or sentimental songs Haydn approached the character of the aria. "Die Verlassene" ("The Deserted Woman"), for instance, is filled with the pathos of dramatic grief. If the *opera seria* is godmother here the charmingly humorous "Lob der Faulheit" ("Praise of Laziness") certainly owes much to the *opera buffa*.

During the eighties Haydn wrote more than a dozen different arias and duets, some of them intended to be inserted, according to the custom of the period, into the works of other composers. In 1786, for instance, the following three arias were written: "Ah tu'n senti amico" for Traetta's *Ifigenia in Tauride* and "Dica pure" and "Signor voi sapete" for Martin's *Una cosa rara*. As a rule they are pieces that

Haydn dashed off quickly to oblige a singer and in spite of pleasant melodic episodes they hardly deserve further discussion.

Of the solo cantata *Deutschlands Klage über den Tod Friedrich des Grossen* for voice and baryton which Haydn wrote for the baryton player Karl Franz, a former member of the Eszterházy orchestra, only the voice part is left. Another solo cantata *Ah cuome il cor mi palpita nel seno,* published in 1782, is preserved, however, and shows a strong relationship to Haydn's contemporary opera arias. It begins with a recitative intoned by horns and flutes that expresses a longing for the beloved person who passed away, and its melody is used again in the slow part of the succeeding aria, thus giving greater unity to the composition.

Haydn was particularly successful with the Italian cantata *Arianna a Naxos* for mezzo-soprano with piano accompaniment, which he composed in 1789. The aria, in which Haydn challenges comparison with no less a composer than Claudio Monteverdi, was a favorite of the master. He called it his "dear Arianna" and accompanied it personally at a most successful London performance (one of the two recitals in which he appeared as pianist in the English capital). Although the work has only a piano accompaniment this part seems like the reduction of an orchestral score, and the various instrumentations that have been made of the cantata are certainly defensible. The relation to the opera is also quite obvious here. As in a dramatic *scena* of Gluck, it is not the aria but the recitative that forms the main part of the piece and this recitative not only precedes, but also interrupts the aria. The music is completely dependent on the dramatic spirit of the text, not a mere indulgence in the beauties of melody. *Arianna a Naxos* is enriched by many striking passages, such as the interlude before the denouement, with its chromatic progressions that describe Ariadne's climbing up the rock and her utter despair at the same time.

Haydn's *dramma giocoso, La Fedeltà premiata (Faithfulness Rewarded)* was first performed in October, 1780, after the opera house at Eszterháza, destroyed by fire in the previous year, had been rebuilt. Haydn's music was written to a weak and confusing libretto and it is therefore not surprising that the best number of the score is a purely instrumental piece, the above-mentioned overture to the third act, later used by Haydn as the finale for his symphony No. 73, La Chasse. Some of the vocal pieces of this opera were preserved by

Haydn's pupil, Fritz von Weber, the stepbrother of Carl Maria von Weber. In 1789 Fritz performed a German *pasticcio, Der Freibrief von Josef Haydn,* at Meiningen and used the music of four numbers from *La Fedeltà premiata.* Music by Mozart was adapted for most of the remaining pieces and Carl Maria von Weber also contributed an aria and a duet. Haydn does not seem to have objected to this arrangement for apparently he felt that the uninspired original work was unworthy of preservation. It is obvious to the student of Haydn's operas that the master had begun to lose interest in a mixed type of opera with serious and comical elements balancing each other.

After *La Fedeltà premiata* the composer wrote but one work of a similar character; namely, the *dramma eroicomico, Orlando Paladino,* based on a libretto by Nunziato Porta and performed in 1782. In this work, however, stress is laid on the heroic element, with the result that there are six serious characters and only two comic parts; the contrast with *Lo Speziale* in which one sentimental hero is balanced by three comic characters is remarkable. The ferocious Orlando and his opponent Rodomonte, the lovers Angelica and Medoro, the sorceress Alcina, and Charon the ferryman of the river Styx are *parte serie* and only the cowardly and vain braggart Pasquale and his friend Eurilla are *parte buffe.* Among the serious portions of the score there are to be found episodes full of dramatic fire which are strikingly described, as in the long finale of the first act, the entrance of Orlando, and the race for life of the people persecuted by him. The simple and lofty song of Charon at the beginning of the third act also exhibits a majesty of expression. The comic element, although much less conspicuous, is treated with particular success. The character of the boastful swaggerer Pasquale is a masterpiece, rivaling his seventeenth-century brother Sancho Panza of Cervantes. The charming aria demonstrating the performance practice and musical ornaments of the period, or the cavatina in which Pasquale, on horseback and having been heralded by trumpets and horns boasts of his feats of valor, rank among the best numbers that the comic opera of the eighteenth century produced.

In 1784 the *dramma eroico, Armida,* based on Tasso's *Jerusalem Liberated* was performed in Eszterháza. This work does away with comic elements entirely. It is an *opera seria* of a completely homogeneous character, for the mature Haydn was increasingly anxious to unify his instrumental music and could no longer endure the mixed genre of the earlier operas. *The Seven Last Words of Our Saviour on the Cross* was forthcoming; Haydn first repressed the comical elements in *Orlando Paladino* and then completely eliminated them in *Armida*. This latter opera is an imposing work full of dramatic power but it lacks some of the greatest assets of Haydn's art: charm, naturalness, simplicity, and humor. The libretto is based on a subject familiar to students of Gluck's works and here again Haydn adopts the principles and methods of the older composer. Gluck said of his overture to *Alceste:* "My idea was that the overture ought to indicate the subject and prepare the spectators for the character of the piece they are about to see." The same might have been said of the prelude to Haydn's *Armida*. While in the older Italian operas the overture was independent of the work to follow, in this case Haydn has produced a sort of tone poem covering the whole plot of the crusader's (Rinaldo) sinful passion for the lovely sorceress Armida, and his eventual return to duty. In its first four bars the opening theme of the overture [7] depicts Rinaldo's carefree life of knighthood and in its second half his youthful longing for love. The energetic second subject portrays the hero's attachment to his military duties but the development of the movement introduces a serious conflict. Abruptly a yearning allegretto is heard, and this corresponds to that part of the opera in which the hero arrives at Armida's paradise. At last Rinaldo breaks away from the arms of the sorceress. The return of the first part of the prelude then reveals the victory of duty over love and the overture closes with the Rinaldo theme, but without the love motive of its second half. This interesting prelude resembles in its form Mozart's overture to *Il Seraglio*, performed two years before Haydn's *Armida*.

In the opera itself, Haydn unfortunately does not follow Gluck's method to the same extent. The old *recitativo secco* of the Italian opera takes up whole scenes but the number of ensemble pieces is very small (one duet in the first act, one trio in the second, and a sextet at the end of the opera). The lovely finales of the earlier operas are completely absent. The best numbers of the score are the big solo scenes. For instance, the aria describing Rinaldo's attempts to escape the bondage of Armida is a real masterpiece. The accompanied

---

[7] The overture is available in a new edition revised by Hans Gál (London: 1939).

recitative, in which the orchestra follows each fluctuation of Rinaldo's expression, the aria growing organically out of this recitative, and the final presto bringing the tragic episode to its climax: all these display such strong dramatic vigor that they counterbalance the formal coloratura arias in other parts of the score. Of almost equal importance is the big monologue of despair by the deserted Armida; and particularly attractive, in spite of the use of conventional means of expression, is a scene in the third act when Armida displays her witchcraft.

With *Armida* Haydn's operatic output reached a crisis. Apparently the master felt unable to give of his best in a purely serious work; yet the mixed genre likewise failed to satisfy him. At the same time he could not help but admire the immortal masterpieces that Mozart wrote for the stage during the following years. The result was that Haydn stopped work on practically all operatic compositions and composed only one opera after *Armida,* the ill-fated *L'Anima del Filosofo* of 1791, which was never to be seen on the stage. More will be said in the following chapter about this work.

During his fourth period Haydn composed two masses that are completely unalike. The *Mass of St. Cecilia* (Novello No. 5) written at the beginning of the eighties is the longest work of its kind composed by Haydn, and also the one most nearly approaching the style of the Neapolitan cantata. The Gloria of the work, for instance, consists of seven parts: several choruses interrupted by solo episodes, a coloratura aria for soprano, and a trio for alto, tenor, and bass. Like Johann Sebastian Bach's *Mass in B minor*, this work is not really meant for liturgical use. The connection between words and music is fairly loose. The printed edition of the mass, published by Breitkopf & Härtel, omits whole movements of the composition and the surplus text is used as well as is possible for the remaining music. Thus, for example, in the shortened edition the words *Domine Deus, Rex Coelestis, Pater omnipotens* are set to music that was originally composed to the words *et in terra pax hominibus bonae voluntatis,* but the change of text does not seem too bad, as the music happens to be quite uncharacteristic. Only occasionally does Haydn show real understanding of the dramatic possibilities of the text of the Mass, one instance being in the striking contrast used for *iudicare vivos—et mortuos.* Also the repetition of the word *credo* after each section of the profession of faith and the use of the orchestral recitative in "Et incarnatus est," anticipating Beethoven, show that Haydn was not satisfied merely to copy the Neapolitan cantata.

Before long the master abandoned this type of mass composition as unsuitable for use in church. His next mass, the *Missa Celensis* (*Mass of Mariazell* in Styria, Novello No. 15) of 1782, shows a greater concentration and a decrease in the number of solo arias. In their place a new means of expression was employed: the quartet of solo voices, which was to become extremely important in the masses of Haydn's last period. The quartet offers the same possibilities for drama and color as do the voices in separate solos, without their excessive display of virtuosity.

In the *Missa Celensis* both elements of the old and the new style are to be found. The Gratias is a real coloratura aria for soprano, while the expressive Miserere Nobis in F minor is given to the quartet of solo voices. The Resurrexit, as in a *missa brevis,* brings simultaneously in each separate voice a different section of the text, so that while the soprano sings *et resurrexit,* the alto has the words *et in spiritum sanctum,* the tenor *et iterum venturus,* and the bass *qui cum patre.* Nor does it inspire great confidence in Haydn's liturgical technique to discover that the Benedictus uses an aria that was originally written for the comic opera *Il Mondo della Luna.* Yet there are passages in this score that show a deep understanding of the true meaning of the text. An excellent example is provided by the aria for tenor "Et incarnatus est." Beginning in A minor it modulates to C major at the words *homo factus est* and reaches the melancholy C minor when the catastrophe of the Crucifixus approaches. This Crucifixus, sung by the chorus and gradually rising from the low bass register is most impressive.

The style of the *Missa Celensis* as a whole is far from homogeneous. As in the opera, Haydn had also reached a sort of crisis in this field. The master may not have resented it when, in 1783, the Emperor Joseph II passed a decree that practically banned the more complicated forms of instrumental music from the church. Haydn accordingly stopped composing masses and when he resumed fourteen years later, after Emperor Leopold II (1790–92) had revoked the order of his predecessor, his style had changed greatly.

Hardly any other of Haydn's works has so interesting a history as *The Seven Last Words of Our Saviour on the Cross*. In 1785 Haydn received the invitation to write an instrumental composition based on the *Seven Last Words,* to be performed in Cádiz during Lent. The master accordingly wrote an introduction, seven "sonatas," and as a finale a description of the earthquake. His orchestra consisted of two flutes, two oboes, two bassoons, two horns, two trumpets, two timpani, and strings. The "sonatas," which are really written in loose sonata form, were preceded by accompanied recitatives in which the individual exclamations of the Saviour were sung by a baritone voice. These lovely recitatives are imbued with deep feeling and prepare the audience most effectively for the following adagios; unfortunately, however, they were omitted in the printed edition in order to avoid the employment of a singer in an otherwise purely instrumental composition. As a substitute the part of the first violin in the printed edition mentions the respective "word" of the Saviour in Latin at the beginning of each piece.

Haydn himself said of his work: "It was no easy matter to compose seven adagios lasting ten minutes each and following one after the other without fatiguing the listener." The warm reception given everywhere to the *Seven Last Words* proved that he had succeeded completely in this task. The composition became extremely popular not only in its orchestral version but still more so in the arrangements for string quartet and piano. The collected editions of Haydn's string quartets usually contain as Op. 51 (Nos. 50–56) the arrangement of the *Seven Last Words*.

The style of this composition is extremely simple. The composer wished to keep his composition readily understandable in order to be sure of the effect "from the heart to the heart" which he was most anxious to achieve. It was just this economy of style that enabled Haydn to rouse the listener's emotions. The second "sonata" for instance, based on the words "Verily I say unto thee, today shalt thou be with me in paradise," is developed entirely out of a single idea. It appears timidly at first in the key of C minor, as if the poor malefactor did not dare to believe in his own good fortune. Gradually, however, the knowledge of God's mercy enters the heart of the tormented man; the main idea is now transposed into Eb major as a noble cantilena full of sweet happiness. In the development section the shadows of death seem to obscure the mind of the dying man but the return of the cantilena, this time in C major, again conjures all the wonders of paradise. The art of developing, as it were, out of a single germ cell ideas of wholly different emotional substance shows that this work is a product of Haydn's maturity. The third "sonata" is based on the words "Woman, behold thy son" and "Behold thy mother!" Jesus brings his beloved disciple and his mother together. Accordingly the beginning of the piece is imbued with beauty and love but at the same time the drama of Golgotha is not forgotten, and the subsidiary theme which grows out of the main idea leads us to its anguish and suffering. The original motive which is played here by the basses now seems like a nightmare. It is of interest that No. 5, "I thirst," is also based on the same motive as No. 3. Here Haydn resumed the idea that was originally used to describe the love of a mother for her son. In his agony the Saviour becomes a child again, asking his mother for help. This can also explain the idyllic character of No. 5. Later, however, when vinegar mingled with gall is given to Jesus, the distress of extreme misery breaks through with elemental force.

In his *Seven Last Words* Haydn successfully avoids the danger of monotony presented by the text. From the powerful introduction to the slightly conventional earthquake new musical pictures are presented again and again, illustrating not only the drama of the Passion but also of the miracle of salvation which grows out of the sacrifice on the cross.

Another version of the *Seven Last Words* made by Haydn in the seventeen-nineties will be discussed in the next chapter.

Chapter 16

CONSUMMATE MASTERY

The Fifth Period: 1790 — 1803

WITH his fifth period of composition Haydn reached the summit of his artistic achievements. As Capellmeister for Prince Eszterházy he had done outstanding work and attracted the attention of the whole musical world; but after thirty years of life in a remote castle, toiling mostly with the same artists and for the same narrowly restricted audience, he found that Eszterháza was becoming less and less a challenge to his genius. Some of the very best works of the eighties, like the Paris Symphonies and the *Seven Last Words* were not written for Haydn's prince. It is therefore not surprising that the composer accepted Salomon's invitation to go to London without a moment's hesitation.

The trip to the English capital provided a complete change of atmosphere for the master: a new landscape, new people with a new culture, a strange language, and the experience of living in the largest city of the world. Of still greater importance was the change in the social standing combined with a change in working conditions. All the honor and esteem accorded to Haydn in Eszterháza never allowed him to forget that he was living there as a servant, dependent on every whim of his employer. In England he was free to do what he liked, free to go where he pleased, and responsible to no one but himself. He felt like a man who had escaped from a golden cage. Furthermore Haydn was now in a position to conduct an excellently trained large orchestra and his compositions were to be played to a most exacting and fastidious audience of a size he had seldom encountered.

Letter from Haydn to Salomon, 1799

The effect of these favorable conditions on the creative output of the master was amazing. Even though he was nearly sixty years old Haydn started to write compositions surpassing both in accomplishment and daring enterprise anything he had attempted previously. The beautiful balance of the classical style was noticeable in these works, their quality being far superior to those written during the eighties. Practically every work of this latest period was a masterpiece, belonging to those compositions for which Haydn is still admired today.

Even after Haydn had returned from London to settle down in Vienna the influence of the English journeys remained alive. He composed more slowly than in any of the earlier periods and the quality of his creative products was permanently on the highest possible level.

The most remarkable feature of these compositions written in the nineties is that they occasionally present a certain problematical and experimental character. There is a definite tendency toward trying out new devices, even at the sacrifice of the poise of former years. Fundamentally Haydn remained a classical composer during this period, but again and again episodes are to be found in his music whose expressiveness and passionate feeling break through the classical composure. Under the influence of the new experience of freedom Haydn's musical style lost some of its former restraint. The master seemed to revive certain characteristic features of his Storm and Stress period. But we shall be nearer the truth if we consider the little irregularities in his later music as the first indications of a movement that was shortly to exercise a profound influence over the whole artistic world: romanticism.

It is significant that at the age of sixty-five Haydn, in his love for experiments, abandoned the instrumental music that had brought him such overwhelming successes in order to devote all his powers to vocal composition. And it is of symbolic importance that the first great achievement in this line, *The Creation,* begins with a piece that in its whole conception unmistakably heralds the great romantic revolution of the future.

Only three sonatas for the pianoforte, Nos. 50–52 of the Collected Edition, were written during the master's fifth period of composition. Oliver Strunk assumes that all three were composed in 1794 for the pianist, Theresa Jansen, who married the engraver, Gaetano Bartolozzi the following year (Haydn was one of the witnesses at the wedding). According to Strunk the sonata in E♭ major (No. 52) is the first of the set, No. 51 in D major the second, and No. 50 in C major the third, the very last composition written by Haydn for the piano alone. While No. 49, the sonata composed for Marianne von Genzinger, displays the full maturity of the classical style, these last works aim at employing a more personal and expressive musical language. No. 52, the autograph of which is preserved in the Library of Congress, Washington, uses in its first movement all the devices of Philipp Emanuel Bach's style. At the same time the second movement, an adagio in the unexpected key of E major, introduces ornaments that may almost be compared to those of Chopin. The relationship between Haydn's third and fifth periods of composition is here once more emphasized. The loose construction in the first movement of No. 51 and its charming second subject presage Schubert, while the powerful energy and mysterious character disclosed in the first movement of No. 50 occasionally foreshadow Beethoven.

Among the smaller compositions for piano the Variations in F minor, composed in 1793 and published in 1799, are of special importance. They belong to the type of variations with two themes in which Haydn proved particularly successful. The main theme is in the style of a funeral march and is followed by a trio in D major. Each of the two ideas is varied twice and a most imaginative coda ends the composition. In the aspects of harmony and color this important work anticipates the first beginnings of the romantic style.

Haydn's compositions for musical clocks are related to his works for the piano. Of the three musical clocks mentioned on p. 226 two were constructed during Haydn's last period of composition. The clock of 1792 was built for Prince Liechtenstein. This tiny instrument with its sweet, weak tone plays twelve pieces, one every hour. Twelve numbers also form the repertory of the clock of 1793 which Haydn gave to Prince Eszterházy before leaving on his second trip to England. Of the twenty-four numbers performed by the two instruments, ten (Nos. 2, 6, 8, 11, and 19–24 of Schmid's edition) were already played by the clock of 1772. This proves the early date of their composition. The remaining fourteen numbers belong partly to the eighties and partly to the nineties. No. 4 is an altered version of Haydn's song "Warnung an ein Mädchen" and No. 5 shows a certain relationship to the trio of the minuet from symphony No. 85, La Reine. No. 25, a march in D major, is also in the repertory of a musical clock constructed in the beginning of the nineteenth century. This instrument plays it together with a grenadier march by Beethoven, a fact responsible for the erroneous attribution of the D major march to the younger composer. No. 28 is a simplified version of the finale of the string quartet, Op. 71 No. 1 (composed in 1793). No. 29 is a minuet which was used in the following year in symphony No. 101 (The Clock) and No. 30 is a sort of piano arrangement of the *perpetuum mobile* from the quartet, Op. 64 No. 5 (published in 1790). Two pieces (Nos. 31 and 32) are preserved in Haydn's original manuscripts but none of the clocks known so far plays them. No. 32 is a sketch for the finale of symphony No. 99 of 1793–94. All together these tiny pieces, in spite of their unpretentious garb, are not entirely lacking in importance. They point to Beethoven's Bagatelles, Schubert's Moments Musicaux, and all those short pianoforte pieces that were instrumental in building up nineteenth-century keyboard music.

Haydn's violin sonatas are not really duets for a bowed and a keyboard instrument, as are the contemporary sonatas of Mozart; they are written as pieces for piano solo accompanied by an optional violin part. The string instrument moves in unison or in thirds with the upper part of the piano score; it accompanies or performs little imitations but even when short melodic fragments are entrusted to it, they may be omitted without really endangering the effect of the composition. No true co-operation between the two instruments is attempted, as the violin part is always considered ad libitum. Out of Haydn's eight violin sonatas, four (Nos. 2–5 of the Peters Edition) were also published as ordinary piano sonatas, by elimination of the violin part (Nos. 24–26 and No. 43 of the Collected Edition). Three others are only simple arrangements of successful ensemble compositions. No. 6 is the transcription of the allegro, minuet, and theme with variations from the *divertimento* for two violins, flute, oboe, violoncello, and bass (No. 11 of Haydn's catalogue), a work probably written in the sixties.[1] The original was much longer than the arrangement; however the abbreviation was not due to musical scruples. It is characteristic of the ideas that Haydn eventually developed toward matrimony that the later version eliminates the andante *Mann und Weib* which was supposed to describe the harmonious co-operation of husband and wife. The violin sonatas Nos. 7 and 8 are arrangements of the string quartets, Op. 77 Nos. 1 and 2, eliminating in each case the minuet and trio of the original composition, since it was a rule of the eighteenth century to limit music for from one to three players to a maximum number of three movements. The only original composition among the violin sonatas is therefore No. 1 of the Peters Edition which was first published as Op. 70 in 1794. In spite of attractive episodes which are to be found in almost any of these compositions Haydn's type of violin sonata in which the bowed instrument always serves and accompanies the keyboard instrument is only of historical interest today. The violin sonata of the seventeenth and early eighteenth centuries concentrated all melodic life in the violin part and used the clavier only as a support. Haydn, like many of his contemporaries, took the opposite attitude, giving pref-

[1] It exists also in a version for piano solo as No. 15 of the Collected Edition of the piano sonatas.

erence to the keyboard instrument and neglecting the violin. As long as only weak and fragile pianos were built, with tones hardly equaling those of violins, this arrangement was well designed but with the arrival of heavier and stronger pianofortes violin sonatas were developed that gave full equality to the two instruments. It is noteworthy that Mozart's sonatas for violin and piano already displayed such a progressive attitude.

Unlike the violin sonata (this form never really interested Haydn) the piano trio changed during his last creative period from an inferior type of composition treated in an offhand manner to a carefully elaborated form. Fifteen trios (Nos. 1–6, 8, 9, 13, 17, 18, 21–23, and 29 of the Peters Edition) belong to the nineties. They are larger compositions than the earlier trios and their contents are of greater importance. The wealth of modulations in these last trios is remarkable. In the first movement of No. 2 in F♯ minor the development, with the help of enharmonic changes, reaches the key of E♭ minor. Gently sliding passages of the kind used by Mozart lead back to the tonic. In a similar way the first movement of No. 4 in E major introduces in the development a section in A♭ major and No. 11 has a first movement in A♭ major followed by an adagio in E major. This adagio ends in D♯ major, which is enharmonically identical with E♭ major, the dominant of the main key. Such well-planned modulations are symptomatic of the new importance that the piano trio now assumes for Haydn. Characteristic pieces, like the lovely theme and variations in the first movement of No. 1 in G major, the simple and fervent prayer of its second movement, and the high-spirited *rondo all'Ongarese* of the finale would never have been written by the earlier Haydn in the form of a piano trio. Remarkable also is the middle movement of No. 4. Its unrelenting ground bass in eighth notes, on which the whole piece is based, makes it appear as a sort of *passacaglia,* reminding us of Johann Sebastian Bach, whose works Haydn heard in Baron van Swieten's home. The finale of Haydn's last trio, No. 8 of 1798, a presto again with some traits common to Beethoven's scherzos, abandons completely the old idea of the piano sonata accompanied by violin and violoncello. The parts of the two bowed instruments are here organically linked together while the accompanying clavier supports their melody. A new type of piano trio in which all three members share the responsibility is breaking through, a type that was to gain increasing importance in the future.

The three little trios and the single movement in G major for two flutes and violoncello [2] which Haydn wrote in London in 1794 (autographs in the State Library, Berlin) are short pieces void of any claim to importance. It is obvious that Haydn did not spend much time on these compositions but even so the middle movement of the first trio exists in two versions, which is characteristic of the greater care he was bestowing in this period on compositions of lesser consequence. The second version is certainly more concise and pithy than the first; the somewhat perfunctory sonata form of the original draft is converted into the romanza form and the theme moving along in equal eighth notes is made more piquant by the introduction of a dotted rhythm.

Fifteen string quartets were produced during Haydn's last period of composition; among them are some of the greatest works the master has given to this form. According to the autographs (preserved in the State Library, Berlin) Haydn composed six string quartets in 1793. They were printed as Op. 71 Nos. 1–3 and Op. 74 Nos. 1–3 (Nos. 69–74 of Haydn's list) and dedicated to Count Apponyi. The master wrote them at a time when he was strongly interested in orchestral composition and accordingly they display a certain symphonic character. An innovation in these quartets is the use of introductions to the first movements, a feature that played so important a part in Haydn's symphonies. In Op. 71 Nos. 1 and 3 and Op. 74 No. 1 this introduction consists only of chords of the full ensemble; in Op. 71 No. 2, however, it consists of a real adagio of four bars. Op. 74 Nos. 2 and 3 have as the preliminary section a unison passage of eight measures which is of great significance in the following movement. Particularly in Op. 74 No. 3 the connection between introduction and exposition is so intimate that the listener is surprised when he finds the main idea at the beginning of the recapitulation and not the unison of the introduction which he had been led to expect. In the first movement of Op. 71 No. 2 the defiant downward octave leaps given out by all four instruments are completely alien to the intimacy of chamber music and approach the realm of symphonic composition. The first violin introduces whirling passages in sixteenths and gradually the other instruments come in so as to carry the melody to a climax. When at the end the violoncello joins the general uproar, the feeling is produced that the contrabass should ac-

[2] New edition by Leo Balet (Hannover: 1931).

company in the lower octave in order to give the necessary foundation to this imposing structure. In the first movement of Op. 71 No. 3 the viola part goes below the violoncello part (bars 21–23 of the development), thus causing undesired six-four chords. While writing this passage Haydn may have been under the illusion that contrabasses doubling the violoncello part in the lower octave would take care of the situation.

The dawn of romanticism is noticeable in the string quartets, Op. 74. Haydn resumes his experiments with the sonata form and the first and last movements of No. 1 contain development work in the recapitulation. The A major trio of its minuet in C major introduces a softly rocking melody which has its roots in Austrian folk song and contains passages that make us think of Schubert. The lovely quartet No. 2 goes even further in the key relations between its minuet and trio. Here the former is in F major and the latter stands a major third lower, in D♭ major. This daring combination would certainly not have been attempted by the younger Haydn. In the first movement of the Reiterquartett, No. 3, the main subject following the powerful introduction is of less significance than the subsidiary idea, accompanied by the triplets of the transitional section. Innumerable romantic compositions of the nineteenth century show this phenomenon, assigning to the second subject more importance than to the first (cf. the two movements of Schubert's Unfinished Symphony). The simple largo in F major (the first movement of this quartet was in G minor!) has a short middle section in E minor. A climax is reached in the brilliant finale with its first and second themes in the Hungarian and Austrian folk vein, introducing some charmingly gay passages in the development.

In the years 1797–98 six string quartets (Nos. 75–80 of Haydn's list) were written and published as Op. 76 with a dedication to Count Erdödy. If an appropriate motto were sought for this series, the word Excelsior should have the first choice. Everything here is condensed and intensified, the expression more personal and more direct. It is characteristic of Haydn that he now repeatedly increases the tempo in the course of a movement, as in Nos. 5 and 6 where the initial allegretto is transformed into allegro while the concluding *allegro ma non troppo* of No. 4 twice increases its speed. The minuet in these quartets has completely lost the character of a graceful allegretto. In Nos. 1 and 6 Haydn's tempo marks are presto and an approach to

Beethoven's scherzo is also evident in the spirit of the compositions. The same quartet No. 1 in G major has a finale beginning in G minor. It would seem as if Haydn wanted to change the mood of his composition but just the opposite is true. The master desired merely to introduce a retardation before the definite solution and the finale, in its second half, passes quite regularly from minor to major so that the beginning and end of the quartet conform with each other. A similar situation may also be found in No. 3.[3] As the quartets of Op. 76 are contemporary with Haydn's *Creation,* it is not surprising that the last movements of two of them should be based on the idea expressed in the immortal passage from minor to major at the words "Let there be light."

No. 2 of this set is known as Quintenquartett because of the use of fifths in its main subject. A strange piece is its *Hexen-Menuett* ("witches" minuet), a canon in which the two violins play the melody in octaves while viola and violoncello (also in octaves) perform the imitation. No. 3 in C major is a surprisingly uninspired quartet and would hardly deserve its place among Haydn's last works of this type were it not for its *poco adagio cantabile*. Like Schubert in his quartet, Death and the Maiden and in his Trout Quintet, Haydn presents in this slow movement variations on one of his own songs, the Austrian national anthem "Gott erhalte Franz den Kaiser." There are only four variations and in each a different member of the quartet is entrusted with the melody. It is a work of great simplicity and dignity, fully deserving the great popularity that it enjoys. No. 4 is known as The Sunrise; its main subject beautifully expresses the feeling of growth and expansion that we experience on an early summer morning. No. 5, based on a single melody, uses in its first movement a greatly simplified sonata form. As the master liked to use two movements of the same form within a single work, the succeeding famous largo in F♯ major (the first movement being in D major!) is similarly constructed. It is a piece full of luxuriant beauty, just as romantic in its whole conception as the variations on the Austrian hymn in the preceding quartet were classical. The first movement of No. 6 introduces a set of variations on an allegretto theme. The last of these variations is faster in tempo and displays traces of serious polyphonic

[3] Donald Tovey points out that Brahms's Third Symphony shows quite similar tendencies. This is by no means the only point that the two composers have in common and as Brahms was a most diligent student of Haydn's scores, the resemblance does not seem to be accidental.

construction. Like so many nineteenth-century composers Haydn concludes his set of variations with a display of counterpoint. The following fantasia moves from B major, through the keys of E, G, B♭, A♭, and finally back to the tonic. This unconventional piece, rich in enharmonic changes, at first has no key signature at all. As in works of Philipp Emanuel Bach and even of some twentieth-century composers, the accidentals are written separately for each note. The trio of the minuet of this quartet uses as a theme the scale of E♭. It runs through all parts, sometimes ascending and sometimes descending, while Haydn constantly invents new counterpoints to it. Beethoven may have remembered this humorous piece when composing his canon on the words: "I beg you, write down the E♭ scale for me."

In 1799 the composer wrote two string quartets (Nos. 81–82 of Haydn's list), the autographs of which are preserved by Prince Eszterházy. They were printed as Op. 77 with a dedication to Prince Lobkowitz.

More than ever Haydn delighted at this time in little experiments in form. For instance, in the recapitulation of the first movement of No. 1, the subsidiary subject has been omitted because Haydn thought that it had been sufficiently used in the development section. In the second quartet the minuet is in F major, the trio in D♭ major. The coda also starts in D♭ major, but as it is thematically related to the minuet it unites the two contrasting sections of the movement. Both this piece and the minuet of the preceding quartet again exhibit features characteristic of Beethoven's scherzos. Striking is the beginning of the andante of No. 2. It is limited to two parts only, thus recalling the distinctive "thinness" of Philipp Emanuel Bach's piano compositions. In this period, when true expression seemed more important to Haydn than a perfect balance between form and content, the composer was getting closer to the style of Johann Sebastian Bach's second son, and at the same time to his own Storm and Stress period.

In 1803 Haydn began his last string quartet, Op. 103 (No. 83 of Haydn's list) in B♭ major. He wrote only two movements, an *andante grazioso* and a minuet. These movements show complete technical mastery but at the same time there is a certain lack of inventive power. Haydn was unable to add the initial movement and the finale to these two middle pieces. The quartet remained unfinished and was eventually published in 1806 as the master's swan song. As a humorous explanation and apology it brings at the end of the minuet a reproduction of the visiting card, which Haydn used during the last years of his life. On it was printed a quotation from the master's favorite four-part song "Der Greis" ("The Old Man"): *"Hin ist alle meine Kraft, alt und schwach bin ich."* (Gone forever is my strength, old and weak am I.)

Of the smaller works for orchestra the eight *notturni* [4] for two horns, two *lire organizzate,* two clarinets, two violas, and bass are the most important ones. Haydn wrote them in 1790 for the king of Naples for whom he had also composed the *lira* concertos. As with these, the composer later changed the instrumentation of the *notturni* by replacing the *lire* with flute and oboe, and the clarinets with violins. It is interesting that in making these alterations Haydn did not modify a single note in his scores. In their changed form some of the *notturni* were performed by Haydn in England.

The *notturni* are graceful pieces but in them Haydn's fantasy is somewhat restrained on account of the soft tone and technical limitations of the two principal instruments. It is characteristic of the master's fine feeling for orchestral coloration that he divided the parts of the violas so as to balance the delicate tone of the two *lire* better. For the most part the works display the traditional three movements and are in either C, F, or G major. A movement like the fugue in the last movement of No. 5 in C major is an exception. Although meant for a small group of players only, they are frequently imbued with the symphonic spirit.

The Symphonie Concertante, Op. 84 for violin, oboe, violoncello, and bassoon, accompanied by full orchestra (autograph in State Library, Berlin) was written in 1792 in London. In this work Haydn revived traditions of the preclassic era. He was mainly interested in the problem of contrasting a group of *concertante* instruments consisting of high and deep-pitched strings and wood wind with the ripieno instruments used to accompany it. During most of the time the four soloists, who vary so greatly in technical possibilities, are used together, or at least in the same way, so as to render imprac-

---

[4] To the seven *notturni* listed by Pohl (II, Appendix, p. 4, Nos. 15–21) an eighth in C major may be added which is preserved in a manuscript score corrected by Haydn and owned by Mr. W. W. Manning, London. It was recently edited by Ernst Fritz Schmid, also responsible for the publication of *notturno* No. 7 in C major (No. 21 in Pohl's list). The *notturno* No. 5 in C major (No. 19, Pohl) was edited by the author of this book and *notturno* No. 6 in G major (No. 20, Pohl) by Edward Fendler.

ticable the development of a style that takes into consideration the technical accomplishments of each individual instrument. Remarkable in the last movement are the little recitative episodes of the violin which are reminiscent of Haydn's earliest symphonies, but also of certain nineteenth-century romantic compositions. It is to be regretted that this attractive work, like other *concertantes* of the late eighteenth and nineteenth centuries (Mozart's Sinfonie Concertante, Beethoven's Triple Concerto, Brahms's Double Concerto) is so seldom heard in public.

In 1796 Haydn wrote a concerto for the keyed trumpet. This is a trumpet with holes in the wall of the tube that are closed by keys. As a rule there are five such keys, which raise the pitch by successive semitones. They are so arranged that the performer can play them with his left hand while holding the trumpet in his right. The invention of the keyed trumpet has been ascribed by experts to the Viennese Anton Weidinger, who is said to have constructed it in 1801, but the instrument is older than this, as Haydn's concerto was written five years earlier. The master's composition reveals the characteristics of the new invention; one looks in vain for the usual triad melodies. The concerto is predominantly diatonic, although there are chromatic passages even in the deeper register of the instrument. Great demands are made on the nimbleness of the trumpet and in the allegro runs of sixteenth notes are not unusual.

Despite Haydn's efforts the keyed trumpet had no real success. The explanation may be sought in the fact that the holes detracted greatly from the brilliant tone of the instrument. The keyed trumpet never succeeded in obtaining admittance to the symphonic orchestra. However, Haydn's work (the original manuscript has been preserved by the Society of Friends of Music in Vienna) was edited in various arrangements for valve trumpet and piano, and the second, as well as the spirited third, movement was recently recorded.

If one reviews Haydn's whole output in the field of the concerto, it must be admitted that the master did not show particular interest in this form of composition. The few masterworks among the concertos hardly make up for the number of uninspired works, composed for a single performance and never meant for wider circulation. This will not surprise anyone familiar with Haydn's personality. Unlike Mozart, the master of Rohrau was no virtuoso. Neither on the piano nor even on the violin was his technique particularly brilliant and above all, his natural disposition was alien to that of a virtuoso. The rather dramatic gifts of the professional performer, which great virtuosos like Liszt, Paganini, and even Mozart possessed in abundance, were completely lacking in Haydn. His shyness made it impossible for him to become a success as a soloist and while he progressed as a composer, his interest in the concerto form gradually faded. The greatest number of concertos were written by Haydn during the seventeen-fifties and sixties, the smallest during the eighties and nineties.

At different periods of his lifetime Haydn composed a large number of marches and dances, even though he himself does not seem to have attributed any great importance to them. His own catalogue mentions only two marches and omits the dances altogether. During his stay in London the composer wrote three marches whose original manuscripts are preserved. One was composed for the Prince of Wales, one for the Royal Society of Musicians, and one for an English officer who had commissioned it. Three other Haydn marches are preserved in his autograph;[5] one of them bearing the date 1802 and entitled *Hungarischer Nationalmarsch*. These are short, strongly rhythmical pieces of a vigorous and virile character and are usually scored for wind instruments only; however, they contain very little of the spirit of the mature Haydn.

A great number of minuets and *allemandes* were written by Haydn for balls and dances. The earliest of them go back to the master's first two periods of composition, while the last and best works were written in the nineties. A few of these collections will be enumerated here.

> Twelve minuets (the original manuscript in the library of Prince Eszterházy); according to the handwriting they were composed in the early sixties or maybe even fifties.
> Six minuets of 1776 (original manuscripts in the State Library, Berlin).
> *Raccolta di Menuetti Ballabili* (fourteen numbers printed by Artaria, 1784).
> Twelve minuets for the harpsichord (printed by Artaria, 1785).

[5] The six original manuscripts of these marches are preserved as follows: two in the Eszterházy library, two in the State Library in Berlin, one in the library of the Conservatory in Paris, and one in the Royal Society of Musicians in London.

Six *allemandes* for orchestra (printed by Artaria, 1785–6).

Twelve *Deutsche Tänze* (printed by Artaria, 1792; the original manuscripts in the library of Prince Eszterházy).[6]

Twelve minuets (printed by Artaria, 1792).

These dances are usually shorter and simpler than the minuets that Haydn used in his orchestral compositions. While many of the little pieces are attractive, very few are of more than mediocre merit. The time for the great Austrian dance music was to come only after Haydn's death.

The twelve London Symphonies (Nos. 93–104 of the Collected Edition) composed between 1791 and 1795, plus an additional one, the thirteenth or Oxford Symphony (No. 92 of 1788) represent the climax of Haydn's symphonic output. Never before did the composer write orchestral works of equal value and no other musician composed in quick succession so large a number of great symphonic masterpieces. Although each of these thirteen works has its own outstanding merits, a gradual improvement in the over-all quality may be noticed. The symphonies Nos. 99–104 written for the second sojourn in London surpass, if possible, the Nos. 93–98 composed for the first visit. No others of Haydn's scores show such virtuosity of instrumentation or such delightful unorthodox treatment of musical forms and contrapuntal devices in the development sections. Remarkable is the imagination displayed by Haydn at such a comparatively unimportant place as the recapitulation in the sonata form. Some composers of the nineteenth century introduce an almost mechanical repetition of the exposition as soon as the development is finished. Haydn, on the other hand, presents the material of the first section in a new way, writing a recapitulation as rich in inspiration as the exposition itself. A last climax is often reached in the coda. This coda, far from being a mere "tail end," develops into a final dramatic concentration of the thematic material. The whole nineteenth century, beginning with Beethoven and ending with Brahms, was able to draw rich inspiration from Haydn's last thirteen symphonies.

[6] *See* the prefaces to O. E. Deutsch's edition of *12 Deutsche Tänze für Orchester* and his various editions of Haydn's dances in piano arrangements (1930–31). Nine dances of the Artaria edition of 1785 were edited by Nana Krieger in *Kleine Tänze für die Jugend* (1935).

The mosaic style of the thematic development has become a matter of course; filling and accompanying voices enjoy the same privileges as the parts carrying the melody, since the same motives are used by all. The baroque division into leading instruments, whose parts are florid and ornamental, and subordinate instruments, whose function is that of giving a foundation to the evolutions of the others, reflects the social cleavage of the period into a ruling and a subservient class, a division which has now been entirely abandoned.

Hermann Kretzschmar called the Oxford Symphony (No. 92 in G major) Haydn's Eroica, as it is the first work to display the full perfection of Haydn's fifth period of composition. In its whole architecture it belongs to the works of the nineties rather than to the Paris Symphonies, though it was actually composed in 1788. Tovey [7] is mistaken when he points out that the Oxford Symphony "was written for the occasion of Haydn's receiving the Doctorate of Music at Oxford." The fact is that symphony No. 92 had to be substituted for the work composed for the solemn occasion (it is not known which symphony this was) as there was not enough time to rehearse a composition unknown to the orchestra.

The Oxford Symphony displays the thematic development in every measure and all the devices of counterpoint are introduced to reveal again and again new sides of the subjects. The work is gay and carefree but at the same time filled with dramatic excitement. The climax is reached in the brilliant finale, which shows so many different forms of its main theme that it seems hard to determine which is the original and which a variation. The score laid out at first for an orchestra of only medium size was later enlarged by the addition of trumpets and timpani.

As in symphony No. 92, so in symphony No. 93 in D major (composed in 1791, autograph formerly in the possession of the court bookstore Leibrock, Braunschweig) the finale, notwithstanding the striking beauty of the first movement with its great coda, is the most impressive piece. It shows the combination of rondo and sonata form which Haydn liked so much in his last period of composition. Such a combination is also used in the symphonies Nos. 94, 95, 100, 101, and 102 and it is characteristic of the consummate mastery of the composer that no two of these movements solve the problem in the same way.

[7] *Essays in Musical Analysis* (London: 1935–1944), I, 143.

Symphony No. 94 in G major, known as The Surprise and composed in 1791 (incomplete autograph in the State Library, Berlin), owes its name to an episode in the andante of its second movement, which has a folk song character. Haydn introduced eight bars of his theme at first piano, played by strings only, and then a second time pianissimo. At the end of this repetition, when the tone may be expected to fade out, quite suddenly a fortissimo of the full orchestra, including the drums sets in. This sort of surprise had been used by Haydn before and the movement owes its popularity more to graceful and simple melodic invention than to the little joke. The andante displays a mixture between variation and three-part-song form, as the freely constructed second variation in C minor takes the place of the middle part. Haydn had the good taste not to repeat in the individual variations the little prank he introduced in the theme. In the coda the childlike and naïve melody of the main subject suddenly assumes an enigmatic character through the romantic harmonies of the stringed instruments used as an accompaniment (bars 145–152). Here we reach the threshold of Beethoven's art.

Much more amusing than the "surprise" of the andante is a detail in the minuet. At the end of the second part (bars 39–40) a ridiculous snort and groan in the violoncellos and bassoons leads us back to the beginning of the main melody. This movement bears no relation to the graceful French minuet of the rococo period. It is a typical Austrian *Ländler*, foreshadowing the waltz of the nineteenth century.

In the final rondo, too, the retransitions to the main theme show unusual humor and fantasy and a brilliant coda concludes this great movement.

The dramatic beginning in unison of symphony No. 95 in C minor, composed in 1791 (autograph in British Museum, London), reminds us of the master's Storm and Stress period. The lack of a slow introduction to the first movement, the frequent doubling by the strings of the parts of the wood-wind instruments, and the baroque use of polyphonic devices in the finale are equally characteristic of an earlier phase in Haydn's creative output. The variations of the andante, however, displaying in their whole construction a great resemblance to the "surprise" movement of the preceding symphony and the rather difficult violoncello solo in the trio of the minuet show that in Haydn's latest period of composition old and new elements are blended together with perfect success.

Symphony No. 96 in D major, composed in 1791 (autograph in the British Museum, London), belongs to the less popular of the London Symphonies. Haydn himself was not quite satisfied with it and wrote in a letter dated March 2, 1792, to Frau von Genzinger: "I wish to alter and embellish the last movement, which is too feeble when compared with the first." According to August Reissmann, this symphony had the name The Miracle because of an incident that happened at the first performance. "Part of the audience pressed forward to look at the popular musician at close range, leaving a vacant space in the concert room. Hardly had they moved when a chandelier crashed down upon this empty spot. There were cries of 'A miracle, a miracle,' because no one was killed or hurt by the accident." In the first movement we find a characteristic detail, also displayed in some of the string quartets. Haydn ends one of the sections of the development with an F♯ major chord in fortissimo, to begin after a general pause with the chord of G. The two chords thus separated by a half tone follow each other without any transitional passage. Very lovely is the use of two solo violins near the end of the andante, and in the waltzlike trio of the minuet solo instruments of the woodwind family are employed effectively. The rondo finale has the character of a *perpetuum mobile*.

In symphony No. 97 in C major, composed 1791–92, the introduction to the first movement is intimately connected with the main part. The characteristic motive of its second measure returns all through the movement, the last time in the coda. Near the beginning of the development section the strings toss backwards and forwards a little motive derived from the main subject. The "Jacob's ladder" effect in the finale of Beethoven's Eighth Symphony (measures 458–469) is foreshadowed in this little episode. In the minuet the traditional repetitions are completely written out, introducing attractive little variations instead of the mechanical reiteration. The same is true of the trio, incidentally one of the most typically Austrian pieces the master ever wrote. The finale of this symphony displays an obvious mirthfulness; near the end, however, in a dramatic move the composer introduces a passage imbued with the spirit of tragedy, which takes the listener completely by surprise. Immediately afterwards the old cheerfulness is restored; the dark shades were used only to give a more effective background to the prevailing bright colors.

In symphony No. 98 in B♭ major, composed in 1792 (autograph

in the State Library, Berlin), the slow introduction in B♭ minor anticipates the main subject of the following allegro (B♭ major) in a way
that was to become customary in romantic music. The adagio cantabile of the second movement, according to Tovey, might almost be
called Haydn's "requiem for Mozart, the news of whose death had
so deeply shocked him during his London visit." It certainly is an
unusually serious piece and assumes a hymnlike character. The first
two movements of this symphony show in their mood and construction certain analogies to the work of the Salzburg master; whereas
the last two movements, and especially the finale, are sparkling with
Haydn's typical love of fun.

Symphony No. 99 in E♭ major, composed in 1793–94 between the
two trips to England (autograph in the State Library, Berlin), is the
first symphony in which Haydn used the clarinets, although these
instruments had been prescribed by him in his *lira* concertos and *notturni.* How well the master understood the possibilities of this wind
instrument is shown in the very first bars of the score. The sonorous
chalumeau register of the clarinet provides an effective bass for the
stringed instruments. Daring modulations give this introduction a
decidedly modern character. In the main section of the movement
the second subject is of greater significance than the first, and a similar romantic preponderance of the subsidiary idea may be noted in
the following adagio, which is one of the deepest and most stirring
pieces written by Haydn. As in the preceding symphony, the mood
changes completely with the beginning of the minuet. This scherzo-
like movement and still more the finale employ all the devices of instrumentation and counterpoint to create pictures of uncontrollable
gaiety.

In the first movement of the symphony No. 100 in G major, composed in 1794 (autograph in the Eszterházy library), known as the
Military Symphony, a trio consisting of a flute and two oboes introduces the main subject; no other instruments are added for support.
So revolutionary a treatment of the high wood-wind instruments,
which in the earlier symphonies are almost never used independently,
shows that the aged Haydn did not cease experimenting and trying
out new effects. The subsidiary subject bears a certain resemblance
to both the main idea of the first movement in Mozart's great G minor
symphony and to one of the most popular Austrian tunes of the nineteenth century, the *Radetzky March* by the elder Johann Strauss.

Even the use of the first three notes of both Mozart's and Haydn's subjects in the respective development sections displays a striking similarity. The work owes its name to the allegretto of the second movement. The piece increases Haydn's ordinary symphonic orchestra by military instruments: triangle, cymbals, bass drum, and the penetrating C clarinet. The master used in this composition the allegretto from his second *lira* concerto, changing only the orchestration and the end of the movement. Even the division of the violas used in the original composition is preserved in the adaptation for the Military Symphony. The composer frequently prescribed the percussion instruments in piano and pianissimo, thus producing charming effects of color. Rather strange is the unaccompanied trumpet signal near the end of the movement, followed by a roll of the kettledrums, increasing from pianissimo to fortissimo. It can hardly be doubted that Haydn, in a purely romantic way, meant to express with this dramatic episode a certain poetical program. From here the way leads directly to the trumpet signals in Beethoven's Leonora Overtures. The brisk final presto uses the same percussion instruments as the andante. It contains several little replicas of the famous "surprise" from symphony No. 94, which are hardly less effective than the original itself. Particularly amusing are bars 118 to 123. Two chords are played by violins and viola, first piano, then after a general pause, diminuendo, and finally after a second general pause, pianissimo. Before this charming effect can be fully grasped the kettledrum crashes in with six powerful fortissimo beats. By omitting the third general pause, which the listener anticipated, and introducing an entirely unexpected fortissimo Haydn set a sort of trap to his audience, the humorous effect of which nobody can escape.

The symphony No. 101 in D major, commonly known as The Clock, was written in 1794 (autograph in the State Library, Berlin). The presto of the first movement and its six-eight time are what one would expect in the finale of a symphony rather than in its initial movement. The andante introduces an accompaniment of bassoons and plucked strings that sounds like the tick-tock of a big clock and is responsible for the name of the symphony. This movement displays Haydn's favorite mixture of variation and rondo form which so strongly impressed Beethoven that one finds traces of it even in the slow movement of his Choral Symphony. In Haydn's andante

continual changes of the orchestration are performed. Particularly
attractive is the entrance of the charming main theme after the dramatic episode in G minor. The tick-tock is here taken over by a flute
so that a tiny clock seems to replace the big timepiece heard at the
beginning. The trio of the following minuet belongs to the type now
frequently used by Haydn, which does not contrast with the preceding dance but rather supplements it. Both sections are also in the
same key, a fact that has induced some conductors to omit the repetition of the minuet after the trio. It is hardly necessary to point out
that such a procedure completely destroys the architecture of the
movement. The finale shows a construction greatly resembling that
of the andante. In spite of its prevailing light and gay character, the
entrance of the main theme after the minor episode assumes the form
in miniature of a double fugue. How solidly this finale is constructed
may be gathered from the fact that the first three notes of the main
subject are used all through the movement, giving the greatest
amount of unity to the composition. The use of the "germ cell" motives in Brahms's symphonies is not very different.

The symphony No. 102 in B♭ major was composed in 1794–95
(autograph in the State Library, Berlin). In the first movement the
subsidiary theme with its fortissimo outcry, separated from the rest
of the melody by a general pause, exhibits one of the most revolutionary ideas Haydn ever had. The adagio displays an orchestration
of unusual subtlety, introducing muted trumpets and muffled kettledrums. It is a simple piece imbued with serene faith and it is not
surprising that at a later date it was arranged as an anthem. Haydn
himself used it a second time; transposing the adagio from the original key of F major to F♯ major, he included it as the middle movement into his piano trio in F♯ minor (No. 2 of Peters Edition). The
hearty and robust minuet has a romantic trio whose chromatic progressions express an ardor and yearning that one would expect in a
composition by Mozart rather than in a piece by Haydn. The brilliant
finale is mainly responsible for the great popularity which this
symphony enjoys. It has in its second half an episode of keen wit,
when the instruments develop a motive, as Haydn likes them to do,
out of the first three notes of the main theme. Near the end the stut-
tering first violin tries to present the main theme for the last time but
never succeeds in uttering more than the first few notes. These grow

more and more confused, whereupon the chorus of the attending instruments rudely breaks in and with loud laughter carries the movement to an exuberant conclusion.

Among the many romantic and highly dramatic introductions that head the first movements of Haydn's London Symphonies, the one written in 1795 for the symphony No. 103 in E♭ major, with the Drum Roll (autograph in the British Museum, London) is particularly interesting. It starts with a completely unaccompanied long roll of the kettledrum. This mysterious first bar is followed by an impressive unison of bassoons, violoncellos, and double basses. Here Haydn wrote the basses an octave higher than the violoncellos, so that the two groups of instruments sound at the same pitch. In this way only can the lonely majesty of the passage be fully expressed. This is another example of the special care that Haydn then bestowed on the problems of orchestration. In the succeeding *allegro con spirito* the composer uses a real waltz tune as a subsidiary subject. Quite unusual, however, is the recurrence of the adagio introduction in the coda, providing a mysterious end to the movement. The following andante is in variation form using two themes that show a certain relationship to each other. The first theme is in C minor, the second in C major and Haydn wrote variations on each of them alternately. The minuet introduces in its second section an effective *stretto* of the main subject, showing that the use of polyphonic devices need not be restricted to the first and last movements of a symphony. The beginning of the finale is just as daring as that of the first movement. Two horns play an unaccompanied signal of the type later used by Schubert and Schumann. This horn theme is nothing but a counterpoint to the main idea, which is presently introduced by the first violin. (Incidentally, these two ideas have a striking resemblance to the beginning of the finale in Mozart's Jupiter Symphony.) The whole movement is based on the one main melody only. Its first five notes—a variation of the old "sigh motive"—lend themselves particularly well to the contrapuntal work that Haydn uses extensively all through the movement. This is certainly one of the master's more meditative compositions but this fact does not deter in the least from its vigorous and inspired character.

Haydn's last symphony, No. 104 in D major, composed in 1795 (autograph in the State Library, Berlin), is sometimes known as his London Symphony, although this name may be applied to any of the last twelve symphonies. It starts with a majestic adagio in D minor, whose impressive fifths seem to be an inversion of the beginning of the Quintenquartett, Op. 76 No. 2 in the same key. It is typical of Haydn's art that a slightly modified repetition of the main idea is used instead of the subsidiary subject. There is also a contrasting melody coming near the end of the exposition and this seems altogether insignificant. But like Beethoven, Haydn employs here the "and-the-last-shall-be-first" technique, choosing as a foundation for his developing work the very theme that appeared least likely to attract his attention. The andante of the second movement is in three-part form; however, Haydn gives it a greater amount of coherence by using for the contrasting *minore* of the middle part material from the first section. In the minuet in D (with a trio in Bb!) the accents on the last beat and the general pause near the end followed by a trill of the wood wind and strings anticipate the scherzos of Beethoven. The main subject of the finale sounds like a rustic dance tune played by a bagpipe. The deep drone of horns and violoncellos, holding the tonic note D as a pedal point through more than twenty bars, accompanies this gay melody and the second subject displays a similar character. Many a great nineteenth-century symphony is indebted to this movement, the last of Haydn's symphonic movements, for its peculiar employment of contrapuntal devices, especially in the development section.

The vocal output of Haydn's fifth period of composition is on an equal level with his creations in the field of instrumental music. The English imprint is on most of these works, even on those written in Austria after the master left England. Haydn gave a surprisingly large amount of his time to the writing of songs. Nevertheless, the creation of songs never became for him—or for that matter for Mozart or Beethoven either—a matter of great importance. He wrote them when he had nothing better to do; they are accordingly pleasant and attractive, but only in exceptional cases do they display noteworthy quality.

The first set of Haydn's "Six Original Canzonettas," written in England to English words, was printed by Corri, Dussek & Company in London in 1792–93; a second set of six English canzonettas followed in 1798. In these songs the inclusion of the vocal part in the right hand part of the piano accompaniment, as exemplified in Haydn's first twenty-four German songs, is given up. The composer now uses a separate line for the voice part; his instrumental introductions become larger and more important, and the whole piano accompaniment is of greater significance. Occasionally it is obvious that Haydn was thinking in terms of the orchestra, even when he was composing for the piano only. The influence of the aria in these songs is just as conspicuous as it is in Beethoven's cantata *Adelaide* for soprano with piano, which was written at about the same time. Haydn's use of coloratura and chromatic progressions, the wide range of the voice part, and the occasional influx of the dramatic spirit show that an opera composer was their author. However, it is not always the Italian opera but occasionally, as in the "Sailor's Song," the simpler German Singspiel that influenced the master. At the same time Haydn still preferred the strophic arrangement, which he had also used in the first twenty-four German songs. "A Pastoral Song" and "She Never Told Her Love" belong to the more attractive pieces of the two English sets; for the latter Haydn used a text from Shakespeare's *Twelfth Night*.

Two more songs which are not included in the twelve canzonettas are settings of English words. "O Tuneful Voice" is based on a poem given to Haydn by Mrs. Hunter before his departure from England (cf. p. 136). It is to be wondered whether this almost tragic composition in the style of the *opera seria* does not take the simple text a little too seriously. To Haydn's best pieces for voice and piano belongs "The Spirit's Song." The master thought Shakespeare was the author of the text and although he was mistaken in this assumption, the idea inspired him to write music worthy of the English poet. For once this expressive composition is void of operatic influence; in its mysterious atmosphere and deep feeling it anticipates Schubert's lied.

Among Haydn's best-known songs are the charming and unpretentious "Un tetto umile" ("A Humble Roof"), printed with Italian and German words in 1803 and especially his "Gott erhalte Franz den Kaiser" composed in 1797 as the Austrian national anthem. For more than a century this immortal melody was used with at least a dozen different texts as the anthem of the Austro-Hungarian monarchy. In Germany Haydn's tune has been employed for the patriotic song "Deutschland, Deutschland, über alles," and in the English-speaking countries as a church hymn.

Folk song and art music in this work came to a classical union. Hardly ever did a composer create with such simple means a work imbued with equal fervor and solemnity. Like every tune of a simple folk song character, the "Gott erhalte" resembles in certain details other melodies. Dr. Kuhač found analogies between Haydn's hymn and the Croatian folk song "Vjutro runo," and came to the conclusion that the master's melody must be of Croatian origin. Even if the Croatian folk song were older than Haydn's anthem the melodic relationship would not prove anything, as similar slight resemblances may be discovered in a great number of other pieces which Haydn most certainly never saw. Tappert,[8] Friedländer,[9] and Botstiber made lists of such "relations" and proved that some of the melodic successions of Haydn's song are also to be found in a minuet from Sperontes' *Singende Muse an der Pleisse;* Hasse's *Pilgrime von Golgatha;* a rondeau for piano by Georg Philipp Telemann; a hymn-book from 1786; Mozart's violin sonata in C (K. 296) and in his *Exultate jubilate* of 1773; in a composition by Christoph Gottlieb Breit-kopf; and in Haydn's own setting of the *Seven Last Words.* (Even long after Haydn's death Brahms used in his piano sonata in F minor a tune with a certain similarity.) This does not mean that Haydn studied all these works; it only shows that even though the recipient of a musical tradition, the master also succeeded in creating some of those basic melodies, elements of which are to be found in works of the most different composers. This fundamental quality, which was reached only after long and arduous work (Haydn made many sketches to this short and uncomplicated song and they are preserved in the Vienna National Library) also accounts for its unparalleled success.

Inspired by Nelson's victory at Aboukir Bay in 1798 Haydn wrote his aria for soprano or tenor and piano "Lines from the Battle of the Nile" (autograph in the Eszterházy library). As in *Arianna a Naxos,* the piano part here bears the character of an orchestral arrangement; thus Ludwig Landshoff's skillful instrumentation of this piece is entirely justified. The gay principal subject of the aria, characterizing the victorious hero, makes its appearance in the introductory recitative. Haydn again subordinates the music to his text and consequently, the recitative is almost more important than the aria itself. "Lines from the Battle of the Nile" is written in the character of one of Gluck's operatic scenes. Far less attractive is the aria "Non partir

[8] *Musikalische Studien* (1868).
[9] Introduction to the volume of songs in the Collected Edition (19).

bell'idol mio" which Haydn wrote in England for the famous Italian singer, Brigida Banti. It displays the traditional coloratura of the Neapolitan operatic area. The introduction and allegretto "Solo e pensoso" composed 1798 for a Russian grand duke is also an "occasional" composition and did not mean much to the master.

Haydn's arrangements of Scottish and Welsh folk songs belong to a special group. Starting on this work in London in 1792, Haydn continued it in Vienna, carrying on with it even after his failing health made really creative work impossible. Haydn worked for three different English and Scottish publishers; at first for William Napier, then for George Thomson, and simultaneously for William Whyte. Robert Burns wrote new texts for the songs published by Thomson. Among the artists who worked at that time or afterwards on similar lines were Pleyel, Koželuch, and Beethoven.

Haydn's catalogue of 1805 lists three hundred and sixty-five of these arrangements but unfortunately only very few are available in modern editions. The melodies were sent to Haydn and it was his duty to furnish the accompaniments for violin, violoncello, and piano. The master accomplished this task with great skill; his accompaniments are charming, without being too ornate, but the fact cannot be overlooked that Haydn showed little consideration for the principles of folk music. The finished pieces resemble compositions by Haydn rather than Scottish or Welsh folk songs. According to the preface in Thomson's edition, the composer wrote to the publisher: "I am proud of this work and flatter myself that I shall live through it in Scotland for many years after my death." But what Griesinger wrote about these songs to Breitkopf & Härtel seems more to the point: "Haydn attaches great value to them; he contends that although the melodies are harsh, often repellent, his added accompaniments and some retouching have made these relics of old national songs most palatable." It must be emphasized that the accompaniments have to be played with violin, violoncello, and piano; this is expressly indicated on the title pages of the attractive old editions. The omission of either or both of the bowed instruments, suggested by the abbreviated notation in the old piano scores, deprives the songs of their characteristic color and much of their charm.

The two chamber duets for soprano and tenor, "Saper vorrei" and "Guarda qui" (the autograph of the latter, dated 1796 and preserved in the British Museum, has a different text) were sent by Haydn in

1800 to Breitkopf & Härtel for publication. They are conventional pieces resembling in their style the Italian aria. Of far greater importance are the thirteen songs for three and four voices begun in 1796, according to the testimony of the autograph in the Paris Conservatory. Griesinger contends that in 1801 Haydn told him that he wanted to write twenty-five of these pieces, but apparently old age made this impossible. With these vocal trios and most of all with the quartets Haydn carried on the traditions of madrigal composition. The master probably received the impulse to create these works in England, where madrigal singing had always been popular. As a true instrumental composer Haydn added piano accompaniments to his compositions. The simple, naturally flowing melodies, avoiding all virtuosity and closely following the intentions of the poet, and the complete lack of theatrical pathos, give these pieces a unique position among Haydn's vocal output. Full of humor are the trio "An den Vetter" ("To the Cousin") with its quaint coloratura, the quartet "Die Beredsamkeit" ("Eloquence") and the quartet "Harmonie in der Ehe" ("Harmony in Marriage") in which Haydn once more delights in mocking a harmonious marriage. The other extreme is marked by the powerful religious songs "Danklied zu Gott" ("Song of Thanks to God") and "Abendlied zu Gott" ("Evensong to God"), pieces that, in spite of their more chamber music character, can well stand comparison with the great choruses of *The Creation* and *The Seasons*. Haydn himself suggested in a letter to Friedrich Zelter that he, Zelter, should make an arrangement of the "Abendlied" for chorus, solo quartet, and pianoforte.

Haydn's rounds and canons are all products of his last period of composition. The famous "Ten Commandments" were written in England to German words between 1791 and 1795. According to the *Allgemeine Musikalische Zeitung*,[10] the master composed them for the Saxon minister in London, Count Brühl. Haydn sent the first of these rounds, using the words "Thy voice, oh Harmony" (instead of the original *Du sollst an einen Gott glauben*), to the University of Oxford in 1792 as a sign of appreciation of the Doctorate of Music conferred upon him. The "Ten Commandments" were repeatedly printed with both English and German words.[11] Haydn's own cata-

---

[10] 12, *Jahrgang* No. 63 (1810).

[11] The first English edition was published in 1809 by Clementi & Company; the first German edition in 1810 by Breitkopf & Härtel, Leipzig.

logue does not contain them but it enumerates another forty canons. The master was very fond of these pieces and used fair copies made by himself, glazed and framed, as wall decorations in his study. After Haydn's death these copies were bought by Prince Eszterházy; additional manuscripts from Haydn's own hand are preserved in libraries in Vienna (National Library and Society of Friends of Music), Berlin (State Library), Leipzig (Breitkopf & Härtel), and Paris (Conservatory).

The first printed edition published by Breitkopf & Härtel in 1810 contained not only the forty pieces of Haydn's catalogue, but two more canons. Pohl [12] reproduced the canon "Turk Was a Faithful Dog and Not a Man" which Haydn wrote in 1794, when he saw a memorial to Rauzzini's deceased dog Turk in the singer's garden in Bath. Otto Erich Deutsch has published an additional two canons [13] and so has W. Gillies Whittaker.[14] All together nearly sixty canons by the master are known, all of them written during the seventeen-nineties.

These canons and rounds are usually for three or four parts, but pieces for two, five, six, seven, and eight voices are also to be found. Particularly subtle is the three-part canon "Thy Voice, Oh Harmony," which may also be sung backwards as a canon cancrizans. A further possibility is that of turning the score of this canon upside down; held in this way the canon may again be sung forwards and backwards. The canon "Das höchste Gut" (entitled "The Best" in Whittaker's edition) introduces an imitation at the third and fifth below; "Warnung" ("Warning") is a canon at the second above and fourth below; there are also several canons for two voices at the fifth below. They all show that Haydn's contrapuntal skill was considerable. In the seventh of the "Ten Commandments" Haydn, according to an unproved old story, used a melody that he himself had taken from another composer, as if to poke fun at the seventh commandment, "Thou shalt not steal." The whole thing is just based on an unconfirmed rumor but is very much in keeping with Haydn's delightful sense of humor.

The texts of the rounds and canons are, following the classical tradition, often facetious and not always sensible; some of them are

[12] In *Mozart und Haydn in London* (*See* Bibliography).
[13] In his study *Haydn's Canons* (*See* Bibliography).
[14] Nos. 3 and 4 in *Rounds and Canons by Haydn* (1932).

positively coarse, although in this respect they hardly rival similar compositions of Mozart. As early as 1810 the German edition changed many of Haydn's original texts and this procedure has unfortunately been continued up to the present.[15] In many cases the expurgated versions are definitely inferior to the originals and it would hardly do any harm to drop prudishness and offer Haydn as he really is.

It has been contended that Haydn's four-act opera *L'Anima del Filosofo,* based on a book by Badini and written in 1791 for London, is unfinished. This is not the case, as an examination of the extensive autograph in the State Library in Berlin shows. The error is due to the fact that in 1805 Breitkopf & Härtel published a selection of seven numbers from the unperformed work, together with four new arias not included in the original score. This selection was printed under the name of *Orfeo ed Euridice* and in spite of its pretentious designation *dramma per musica* it was destined merely for the concert hall. Apparently the master objected to seeing in print the complete score of a work that was really his property no longer, as he had sold it to Gallini (cf. p. 102).

L'Anima del Filosofo was the only opera in which Haydn did not have to take into account the small group of singers of Prince Eszterházy's company. He was thus in a position to make ample use of the chorus which, as in Gluck's operas, plays an important part in the dramatic events. For instance, the fourth act (and this is Haydn's only opera in four acts) contains, besides recitatives and a short instrumental piece, six choral numbers but not a single aria. Mixed chorus alternates with women's and men's choruses. Also the tragic final scene of the work, in which the bacchants administer poison to Orpheus and the boat carrying the body of the singer founders in a storm, is treated as a women's chorus, interrupted by a short accompanied recitative. The important part assigned to the choruses, the tragic ending of the opera, the more concise form in which most of the numbers are cast, and the stirring effect of some scenes (especially of the simple and deeply moving death song of Euridice) show that Haydn was aiming at improving the Neapolitan *opera seria* along the lines of Gluck's operatic reform. Yet he must have encountered a serious obstacle in the lack of concentration and the tediousness of Badini's libretto. Besides he was not able to dis-

[15] Even Whittaker's excellent edition submits new texts for about half of the canons.

pense completely with the *recitativo secco* and some of the pieces, such as the conventional coloratura aria of the Spirit, definitely point back into the past. In spite of its many great beauties, *L'Anima del Filosofo* is certainly not on the same level with the composer's other great vocal and instrumental compositions of the same period. The work shows again that Haydn did not feel sufficiently at home in opera composition to free himself completely from the bondage of the prevailing taste and to create a real musical drama.

Haydn's last work for the stage was the incidental music to an English tragedy, *The Patriot King, or Alfred and Elvida* by Alexander Bicknell (1788) which was performed in Vienna in a translation by J. W. Cowmeadow, as *Alfred oder der patriotische König*. In 1796 Haydn composed for this drama a three-part "Chorus of Danes" for soprano, tenor, and bass; a recitative and aria for the Guardian Spirit and a duet for Alred and Odun, Earl of Devon. The autograph of the chorus is preserved in the archives of Prince Eszterházy. It was first published after Haydn's death with changed words and piano accompaniment as "Kriegerischer Chor" or "Siegerchor" ("Martial Chorus" or "Victory Chorus").[16] The autographs of the other two pieces are to be found in the State Library, Berlin. These are insignificant compositions, equal to the arias that Haydn occasionally wrote at a moment's notice for the operas of other composers. The chorus in C major is a simple and terse piece, very popular in character and easy to sing, as Haydn apparently meant to keep it within the range of amateurs.

As this work concludes Haydn's production for the stage, it seems appropriate to review his operatic output as a whole. The memorandum with which Haydn accompanied in the seventeen-sixties his cantata *Applausus* contained the significant words: "If I have failed to guess the taste of the musicians, it must not be taken amiss, as I did not know the performers or the locality. My ignorance of these matters has really made the work hard for me." When Haydn wrote the opera *La Vera Costanza* for Vienna, an attempt was made to choose singers other than those originally provided; whereupon Haydn withdrew his opera with the indignant remark: "I know what and for whom I am writing." In the famous letter of 1787 to Roth in Prague the master gave the following reason for his refusal to have

[16] Supplement to Breitkopf & Härtel's *Allgemeine Musikalische Zeitung* of 1814.

one of his earlier operas performed in Prague: "All my operas are too closely connected with our personal circle (Prince Eszterházy's in Hungary); they could never produce the proper effect, which I have calculated in accordance with the locality." These utterances, made at different periods, reflect the same basic attitude natural to a composer of the eighteenth century, writing in the style of the Italian opera. The personality of the performers and the place of performance always had to be taken into consideration. The virtuosity of the singers, the technical equipment of the stage, the beauty of the costumes and decorations, and the skill of the stage architect were frequently of greater importance for the success of a performance than the quality of the music.

The peculiarities of Neapolitan opera productions account for certain limitations of Haydn's dramatic output, which was by no means on a level with that of his great friend Mozart. Besides, Mozart's nature was so versatile that he could identify himself with the most different personalities and project himself at one and the same time into the minds of Leporello, Ottavio, and Don Giovanni, or Figaro and Cherubino. Haydn's character was far less complex and there were not so many types that he could endow with real life. Nevertheless, the music of his operas is artistically so valuable that whoever takes the trouble to unearth and study the master's voluminous scores will find his full reward. Haydn's comic and seriocomic operas *La Canterina, Lo Speziale, L'Incontro Improvviso,* and *Il Mondo della Luna* can still be successfully performed in our days.

Among Haydn's minor works of church music his offertory *Non nobis Domine* (composed probably 1799, autograph in the State Library, Berlin) should be mentioned. The inspiration to write it may also have come from England where a canon on the same words attributed to William Byrd was popular in the seventeenth and eighteenth centuries. Haydn's chorus was occasionally inserted into his oratorio *Il Ritorno di Tobia.* A far greater work is the *Te Deum* in C major composed around 1800. Although nearly forty years separate this work from the first *Te Deum,* written in the early sixties, the two compositions resemble each other not only in the use of the same key but in many details, such as the characteristic combination of a melody to the words *In te Domine speravi* with a counterpoint to the words *Non confundar in aeternum.* But the second *Te Deum* calls for a choir only and no solo voices. The orchestra is larger and the whole work simpler, clearer and more expressive than the earlier composition.

In the six masses written between 1796 and 1802 by order of Prince Eszterházy the same mastery is displayed that characterizes Haydn's other works of his last period. These works are:

1. The *Mass in C major* (Novello No. 2, autograph in the Eszterházy library), composed in 1796. Haydn wrote at the head of the score *Missa in tempore belli* (*Mass in wartime*), as Napoleon coming from Italy was at that time threatening Vienna. In the Agnus Dei the use of trumpets and kettledrums emphasizes the war atmosphere, as does the fanfare of the wind instruments at the beginning of the "Dona nobis pacem."

2. The second *Mass in B♭ major* (Novello No. 1, autograph in the State Library, Berlin) in Germany called *Heiligmesse* because of the use of the hymn "Heilig, heilig" by the contralto and tenor in the Sanctus. This mass was composed in 1796 and dedicated to the memory of the monk Bernardus von Offida, who had been canonized in the previous year.[17]

3. The *Mass in D minor* (Novello No. 3), the master's only mass in a minor mode. According to the autograph in the National Library, Vienna, it was composed in 1798 at Eisenstadt within fifty-three days (July 10th–August 31st). While Haydn worked on it the news of the Battle of the Nile arrived. The striking use of the trumpets in the Benedictus is usually thought to be associated with the news of Nelson's decisive victory, which made a tremendous impression all over Europe.[18] The composition is known in Germany as the *Nelson Messe,* in England as the *Coronation* or *Imperial Mass.* In its orchestra no wood-wind instruments are used, only brass, percussion, and stringed instruments.

4. The third *Mass in B♭ major* (Novello No. 16, autograph in the National Library, Vienna), composed in 1799. It is known as *Theresien Messe,* probably after the Empress Maria Theresa, the second wife of Emperor Francis II, who belonged to Haydn's patronesses and was also a gifted singer.[19]

[17] The *Heiligmesse* is usually enumerated before the *Missa in tempore belli,* but as Haydn adopts in his catalogue the opposite order and Schnerich also considers that the treatment of the text in the C major mass points to an earlier date of composition, the order has been reversed here.

[18] After Haydn's death a chart of the Battle of the Nile was found among his papers.

[19] Schnerich's conjecture that the mass was named after the singer Therese Rosenbaum-Gassmann does not seem very likely.

5. The fourth *Mass in B♭ Major* (Novello No. 4), composed in 1801. As it introduces in the "Qui tollis" of the Agnus Dei a quotation from *The Creation,* this mass is known as the *Creation Mass.*

6. The fifth *Mass in B♭ major* (Novello No. 6, autograph in the Paris Conservatory), written in 1802. It is known as *Harmonie Messe (Wind-Band Mass)* probably because of its emphatic use of wind instruments.

The component parts of the older masses are still preserved in these latest works, but the use of vocal solos is greatly reduced and their melodic line simplified in the classical sense. Instead of single voices the solo quartet is now employed, the four voices of which are treated in a loose contrapuntal style, thus effectively contrasting with the plain *tutti* of the chorus, which are conceived on purely harmonic lines. The importance of polyphony is increased in these last masses and fugues are frequently introduced. The Credo of the *Nelson Messe* includes a canon at the fifth and the Incarnatus of the *Heiligmesse* a three-part canon. In the earlier masses the instruments of the orchestra were used mainly to reinforce the vocal parts; in the works written after 1796 they are frequently employed independently, carrying melodies of their own. Haydn's main aim during this period was to furnish an adequate musical interpretation of his text; the composition tries to follow the Ordinary of the Mass in every detail and to deepen its expression. The occasions are becoming less and less frequent when Haydn's musicianship makes him oblivious of the dramatic possibilities of his subject. As an example of such a neglect the Incarnatus of the *Theresien Messe* should be mentioned. Its first part in B♭ minor is followed by a second in D♭ major. The mild and tender character of the second section is musically justified but it hardly fits the words of the Crucifixus to which it is used. On the other hand, instances of excellent interpretation of the text in terms of music are far more frequent. The *Heiligmesse* contains a Crucifixus, the tragic expression of which could hardly be surpassed. In the Incarnatus of the *Missa in tempore belli* Haydn, like Beethoven after him, uses the word *et* (and) in order to increase the dramatic suspense. The whole chorus sings it in a long, drawn out forte based on a diminished seventh chord, before the words *incarnatus est* sung in piano describe the miracle of the union of divinity with humanity in Christ. An anticipation of Beethoven may also be discerned in the menacing use of trumpets and timpani in the Agnus Dei of the same mass. In this connection it may be pointed out that the inclusion of trumpet fanfares into the mass is based on an old Austrian tradition. Christoph Strauss, choirmaster of St. Stephen's Cathedral in Vienna, used it as early as 1631 in his *Missa Veni Sponsa Christi*. For the first time since the *Little Organ Solo Mass* of 1770, the *Creation Mass* introduces an organ solo into the Incarnatus. The delicate warbling and twittering which Haydn provided here is intended to produce a pastoral effect. Beethoven uses a somewhat similar idea in his *missa solemnis*. As in his contemporary instrumental works, so in Haydn's masses the influence of Mozart may be detected. A good example is provided by the Gratias of the *Theresien Messe*, which displays much of the grace and fervor of the Salzburg master.

An attempt to summarize the results of the analysis of Haydn's church music shows that the composer at first used elements of style that had originated in various parts of Italy. Then, with the help of simple melodies of his home country he gradually transformed them into a musical language of his own. The type of sacred composition, which was thus created out of different building stones, proved to be a solid foundation for the mass composition of the nineteenth century.

In 1792 Haydn's chorus "The Storm," based on a text by John Wolcot, was performed in London. This work shows the effective contrast between a realistic musical description of a storm (in G minor) and a melodious and flowing andante (in D major) expressing a hope for the return of quietness. The contrast is also expressed in the instrumental coloring, as the trumpets, timpani, and trombones used in the first part are dismissed in the second section and the chorus is replaced by a quartet of soloists. This piece seems like a precursor of the thunderstorm in *The Seasons* but the repetition of both sections, though certainly justified from a musical point of view, weakens its dramatic power.

The British Museum possesses an original manuscript [20] by Haydn written in 1794 and entitled "Nor Can I Think My Suit Is Vain." This work consists of two numbers from an unfinished composition for solo voices, chorus, and orchestra. The words are taken from M. Needham's *Invocation of Neptune* prefixed to John Selden's *Mare*

[20] Add. MSS. 9284.

Clausum, and were set to music at the request of the fourth Earl of Abingdon. But when Haydn found out that three other men before him, among them his former pupil Pleyel, had composed on the same subject he lost interest in the work. Haydn probably felt also that his scanty knowledge of English did not entitle him to compose a full-sized oratorio in that language. Only two numbers, an aria for bass "Nor can I think" and the following chorus "Thy great endeavors" are composed and written down in full orchestral score. They contain pretty, though not very characteristic, music.

The singularly expressive character of Haydn's music to the *Seven Last Words* has always been noticed. In 1788 the *Musikalische Realzeitung* wrote about the work: "We are able to guess in practically every note what the composer meant to convey by it." It was therefore an obvious idea to convert this instrumental composition by the introduction of voices into a vocal Passion piece. The first attempt in this direction was made by Joseph Friebert, a musician in the little city of Passau in south Germany. Haydn heard this arrangement in 1794 on his second visit to England. The master did not approve of the new version, but he was so interested in it that he decided to use it as a basis for a similar work of his own. The revision of the words was made by Gottfried van Swieten who collaborated with Haydn for the first time in this work. The new text, dealing with the sufferings of our Lord and the redemption of mankind is lacking in any action and is in complete conformity with the sentimental German oratorios of the second half of the eighteenth century which were based on the story of the Messiah. Its content is altogether lyrical, and as far as possible dramatic elements are eschewed; apparently Ramler's *Tod Jesu* served van Swieten as a model. The librettist even appropriated episodes from this work, such as the gloomy and portentous text of the earthquake which concludes Haydn's work. The stilted pomposity characteristic of so many German oratorio texts of the early eighteenth century (even the arias of Bach's *St. Matthew Passion* make no exception) is hardly noticeable in the *Seven Last Words.*

The autograph of the oratorio, preserved in the archives of Prince Eszterházy, plainly reveals the technique adopted by Haydn for his arrangement. The master first had the original instrumental version copied by Elssler onto music paper ruled with a great many staves, only part of which were used. Then he himself started to insert into the score the vocal parts and the new instruments, two clarinets and two trombones. At the same time a number of minor changes were made in the original instrumentation. For instance, in order to increase the harsh grandeur of the introduction Haydn here omitted the flutes of the older version. An important addition to the vocal arrangement consists of a new number, inserted between the fourth and fifth sonatas. It is a largo performed by wind instruments only, which, as a counterpart to the introduction, once more expresses the prevailing tragical spirit with the means of instrumental music. At the same time the oratorio adopts a significant feature of the very first version, each of its movements being preceded by the relevant utterance of the Saviour. Instead of the recitative of a soloist, however, the full chorus is employed to pronounce the "word." Apart from these details the original construction of the composition has not been changed at all. A chorus and a quartet of solo voices were added to the instrumental composition without any considerable alteration of the original music. Nevertheless the text is mostly so well adjusted that the listener who is not informed about the genesis of Haydn's *Seven Last Words* is inclined to accept the work as an oratorio conceived in the normal manner. Only occasionally are text and music incompatible. In the choral section of No. 6, for instance, the words "Woe ye wicked, woe ye blind" are accompanied by music imbued with an almost serene spirit. While the composer, inspired by the words "It is finished" expresses the confidence of mankind in the salvation through Jesus' sacrifice, the poet is still concerned with the drama of Golgotha. Either point of view is justified, but their combination is certainly unsatisfactory. Such shortcomings are, however, infrequent and on the whole it is remarkable how admirably the poet follows the musician, although the peculiarities of the instrumental forms, such as the development and recapitulation sections, do not make his task an easy one.

Very different from the *Seven Last Words* is Haydn's cantata *Die Erwählung eines Kapellmeisters* (*The Election of a Conductor*) which was written in the middle of the nineties. It is a caricature of the pompous cantatas in Neapolitan style intended to pay homage to an exalted person, a genre to which Haydn himself had contributed at an earlier period (cf. p. 219). In *The Election of a Conductor* Minerva and Bacchus each present an aspirant for the post. Apollo sets their minds at rest by informing them that their two candidates, a conscientious scholar and a gay tippler, are really one and the same person, who is accordingly selected. The text reminds us of the little bacchanalian jests that the classical composers liked to use as words for their rounds and canons. *Die Erwählung eines Kapellmeisters* is written for three soloists, chorus, and small orchestra and is made up of recitatives and *da capo* arias for the soloists, and two ensemble numbers for the chorus only. The arias are full of coloratura and exhibit an old-fashioned style. The contrast between the pompous composition and the frivolous and rather silly text must have seemed extremely ludicrous to an eighteenth-century audience. All the performers had to do was to emphasize the contradictions between words and music and the assembled hearers, fully familiar with the weak points of the Neapolitan style, would highly enjoy the unpretentious work.

It is of interest that the exponents of the later romanticism, around the year 1900, looked with a very superior air, almost with contempt, at the first evidence of romantic feeling as displayed in Haydn's *The Creation* and *The Seasons*. I. F. Runciman [21] sums up his discussion of *The Creation* with the words: "After considering the songs, the recitatives, and the choruses in detail it really seems to contain very little. Perhaps it may be described as a third-rate oratorio, whose interest is largely historic and literary."

Today it is no longer necessary to apologize for Haydn's last two oratorios. Nevertheless they do not enjoy in the English-speaking countries the position that they deserve. Performances of *The Creation* are still relatively infrequent and *The Seasons* is practically unknown even to a great number of choral conductors. The great popularity that these oratorios enjoy in Austria and Germany is not paralleled in England and America,[22] although in several respects these two works are more English than they are German.

Haydn had been among the audience of the great Handel Festival of 1791. He found a whole nation aroused by compositions offered in monumental performances. Compared with these concerts on a large scale, his own efforts of earlier years to amuse a small group of music lovers at Eszterháza must have seemed to him almost insignificant. Haydn desired intensely to write, as Handel had done,

---

[21] *Old Scores and New Reading* (London: 1899), p. 92.

[22] The reason for this attitude is not clear. Some years ago the author of this book witnessed a performance of *The Seasons* in Utica, N.Y., under the inspired leadership of Berrian R. Shute which created the greatest possible enthusiasm among both audience and singers. There is hardly any doubt that good performances would be just as successful in America and England as they are in Germany and Austria.

works that were meant for a whole nation. Different types of oratorios were used at that time in Austria and Germany but none of them really satisfied the master. There was the Italian oratorio which he had employed in his *Il Ritorno di Tobia*. But Haydn was now reluctant to use a language foreign to the people for whom the composition was written, reluctant to commit himself to the formalism of this genre with its weak arias and its neglect of powerful choruses. There was, on the other hand, the contemplative and sentimental German oratorio, but the master had just finished the arrangement of his *Seven Last Words* and he had no wish to lose himself again in tearful mellowness. Neither did he care for the dramatic type of German oratorio which produced a sort of disguised sacred opera. After having written more than a dozen operas Haydn felt too clearly that he would never give his very best in a work of a predominantly dramatic character. There remained only one type of oratorio to which he felt really attracted and it was again the oratorio of Handel, of the kind used for his *Israel in Egypt* and *L'Allegro, il Pensieroso, ed il Moderato*. The unorthodox construction of these works, the hymnic impetus of their choruses and their strong feeling for nature deeply impressed Haydn and he decided to follow the example of these great English oratorios rather than to use a German model.

It also happened that a wholly suitable subject for his work was offered to Haydn in England. This was an oratorio text that Lidley had compiled from the contents of the first chapter of Genesis and the seventh and eighth books of Milton's *Paradise Lost*. According to tradition this text, entitled "The Creation," had originally been destined for Handel himself. Haydn brought the English libretto to Vienna, entrusting his friend, Baron van Swieten, with the translation. Van Swieten was certainly the right person for the task, as he was a great admirer of Handel and had proved his skill in the arrangement of an oratorio text with his work on Haydn's *Seven Last Words*. Therefore it is not surprising that the German text of "The Creation," when van Swieten had finished with it, was in many respects akin to Handel's oratorio texts. Wherever it was possible the powerful words of the Bible replaced the sentimental paraphrases used at that time in German oratorios. The old narrator was revived in the persons of three singers: the archangels Gabriel (soprano), Uriel (tenor), and Raphael (bass), who take turns in telling the story of the Creation. Most of all, the important share of the chorus reminds us of the oratorios of Handel.

Van Swieten did not restrict himself to the arrangement of the text; the imperious baron also gave Haydn directions as to how to set the words to music. These instructions are contained in a manuscript of the libretto preserved in the library of Prince Eszterházy. Far from resenting such a tutelage, Haydn followed van Swieten's advice in most cases and it cannot be denied that this was beneficial to the composition. What insight is revealed, for instance, by the baron's advice: " 'Let there be light' must be sung once only!"

The first printed edition of *The Creation*, which was published in 1800 by Haydn himself, contained both German and English words and was possibly the first score ever to be printed in such bilingual fashion. Van Swieten himself was responsible for the English version, which is rather poor and not always intelligible. It became the basis of most English editions of the oratorio, until recently A. H. Fox-Strangways and Steuart Wilson edited a new version for the Oxford University Press. Although this translation is certainly clearer and in better English than the original one its modernizations appear occasionally to go too far. For a performance in our days a compromise between the old and the new versions may seem advisable.

Not only van Swieten's text, but also Haydn's music breathes the spirit of Handel. Haydn certainly did not copy the older master but he found in the works of his great model an excuse for his tendency to abandon formulas accepted in his country. In Haydn's oratorio, chorus and soloists are sometimes used together, at other times they quickly alternate; the form of the arias changes from number to number but is always dependent on the text; the recitatives often assume the form of charmingly accompanied ariosos, displaying in their tone paintings the composer's deep love of nature. All this is typical of Haydn's last period of composition but it is doubtful whether he would have dared to follow his instinct so completely, had it not been for the encouragement provided by Handel's oratorios. In his *Applausus* Haydn subordinated the text to the music; in *Il Ritorno di Tobia* both were treated as equals; finally, in *The Creation* and *The Seasons* the musical construction was determined by the substance of the text in the same way as this has been done by all truly great oratorio composers before and after Haydn.

The apparently spontaneous freedom of expression in *The Creation* is really the product of an extraordinary intensity of work. Haydn, who in earlier years had dashed off big works in an incomprehensibly short time, now worked quite slowly and carefully, first making sketches as Beethoven did after him. Of that easy reliance on sure instinct, which his youthful works had revealed, there is not a trace in *The Creation.*

The master used drafts for many works of this period, such as the last mass and various marches, songs, and canons. None of these sketches is so extensive and so important as those of *The Creation,* twenty-three pages of which are preserved in the National Library, Vienna.[23] As they afford a valuable insight into the gradual shaping of Haydn's ideas, it seems appropriate to mention two characteristic instances.

Particularly interesting are the sketches to the chorus "By Thee with Bliss" which in its final form presents only a shadowy basis on which is raised the swelling hymn of the two soloists. Haydn did not arrive at this justly admired color effect in his first inspiration. As originally conceived, this chorus was a lively movement, opening with imitations and set in C minor, not in C major. But Haydn did not let the matter rest there and the passage appears on another page in the sketches in the key of C major. The soprano solo now occurs in its present form and the chorus is handled far more simply. In the margin Haydn appended the words, so indicative of his irrepressible sense of humor: "It is not good to be interesting," the obvious premise to this comment being undoubtedly: This musical example proves that it is not good to be too complicated. In fact, the final form of the chorus is far simpler than either of the sketches.

For the "Representation of Chaos" there also exist two different sketches. The passage for the first violin in the third and fourth measures, describing the boundless loneliness of lifeless Chaos is missing in the first sketch, as is also the impetuous thud of the orchestra in the fifth measure. The second sketch presents the first part of the introduction in practically the final form in which we know it today, but in the contrasting section in D♭ major there is still lacking the significant accompaniment in sixteenth notes in the bassoon, which contributes so substantially to the resolution of the austerity of the beginning. It is characteristic also that in measure

[23] MSS. 16835 and 18987.

forty-nine of the final draft, Haydn has written a single ascending figure for the bassoon, where in the sketch he had put an ornate flourish for the clarinet, which was twice as long. The composer worked steadily toward the simplification of expression, banning from his work all rococo affectation.

One of the greatest numbers in the score of *The Creation* is this very first one, just referred to, describing the Chaos. Zelter, the friend of Goethe, called it "the crown on a God's head." The romantic note in these dark harmonies full of chromatic passing notes and suspensions is unmistakable, and Tovey even goes so far as to compare them to the music of Wagner's *Tristan und Isolde*. The great musicologist also suggests that Haydn, who had personally met the astronomer Herschel, may have heard about the evolution of the cosmos out of chaos and that these ideas inspired him to write his overture. The economy of the composer's thematic work deserves greatest admiration. The first twenty measures of this prelude in C minor describing the sadness of Chaos are based on the stepwise descending "sigh motive." As soon as the idea of cosmic life is introduced the gentle key of Db major sets in and with it in the wood wind an ascending instead of the former descending motive. The following recitative and chorus contain the famous passage " And There Was Light," with its change from C minor to C major, and from piano to forte. A hundred years later Richard Strauss described in his *Also sprach Zarathustra* the mighty appearance of the sun with very much the same means of expression. The third number "Now Vanish" combines an aria of Uriel with the chorus. It is one of the numerous pieces of this score in which Haydn connects soloists with the chorus, displaying in these mixed pieces an unrivaled fantasy and variety of form. Here the chorus sings repeatedly the words "A new created world springs up at God's command." Whenever the words "a new created world" recur, Haydn changes the harmony.[24] The recitative "And God Made the Firmament" contains some of the innumerable descriptions of nature in which *The Creation* excels. Storm, lightning, rain, hail, snow, a whole menagerie of mammals, birds, fishes, and insects—all this Haydn's orchestra describes with a great sense of humor. The master, who clung to nature and all earthly things more fervently

[24] Haydn's intention is not discernible in the translation of the Oxford University Press, which substitutes "The first of days appears and order reigns at God's command" for the original words.

than almost any other composer, fully succeeded in reflecting the youthful purity of the universe on the first day of the Creation. So sure was Haydn of the expressive power of his music, that his descriptions always precede the explaining text. A powerful solo by Gabriel with a choral accompaniment concludes the second day of the Creation. Raphael's aria "Rolling in Foaming Billows" (Oxford Edition, "See How the Rolling Waters") is partly modeled after Italian examples. It is not free from ornamental coloratura and its key sequences are reminiscent of those used in instrumental music. Nevertheless the text also predominates here over the form and an equal number of musical sections correspond to the four pictures of the poem (ocean and mountains, river and brook). The lovely and purely lyrical aria of Gabriel "With Verdure Clad" (Oxford Edition, "The Fields Are Dressed") contrasts very effectively with the majestic chorus "Awake the Harp." The simple and terse first ten measures of the recitative "In Splendor Bright" (Oxford Edition, "The Sun Is Up"), describing the sunrise, belong to Haydn's greatest inspirations. The melody is lifted slowly stepwise through the interval of a tenth. In almost every measure a fresh instrument is added to the orchestra until the delicate pianissimo has been changed into an overwhelming fortissimo. The chorus, with a trio of the soloists, "The Heavens Are Telling," ends the first part of *The Creation*. It is one of the best known pieces of the score but its popularity ought not to induce the conductors of small choruses to perform it as a separate piece with the omission of the solo voices, as this procedure deprives the composition of much of its charm.

The second part of the oratorio begins with the fifth day of the Creation in which the animals come to life. In the coloratura aria of Gabriel "On Mighty Pens" (Oxford Edition, "On Spreading Wings") the cooing sounds of the pigeons are particularly well imitated by the bassoons and violins. A stroke of genius is found in the recitative "Be Fruitful All and Multiply," in which divided violas, violoncellos, and double basses are employed to express a mysterious saturation and abundance. It is imperative that here the double basses should play the lowest notes F_1, E_1, D_1, and C_1 as prescribed by Haydn for the usual transposition of this passage an octave upwards is likely to nullify the majestic effect intended by the composer. The chorus, with a trio of solo voices, "The Lord Is Great and Great His Might" is as impressive and easy to grasp as a chorus by Handel.

Again the combination of solo voices and chorus gives the piece its peculiar mixture of brilliance, charm, and dignity. The recitative "Straight Opening Her Fertile Womb" takes us to the sixth day of the Creation and with it to a further extension of the zoological cabinet. Haydn's resourcefulness in the invention of effects of color is here matched only by his economy in their employment. The aria of Uriel "In Native Worth" deals with the achievement of the seventh day, the creation of the first human couple. It shows that even when the composer followed tradition he was anxious to observe the most exacting demands of the text. In this aria the first melody returns after a contrasting section, thus implying the use of the *da capo* form. Haydn's real intention was not to employ the antiquated structure of the Neapolitan aria but to introduce husband and wife with the same theme so as to show musically that they belong inseparably together. The end of the second part of the oratorio consists of two great choruses in the same key, based partly on identical words ("Achieved is the glorious work") and music but separated by a trio for the soloists, the result being again a sort of three-part form. The second of these choruses contains a double fugue of such dignity and simplicity as can be found only in the choral works of Handel and Haydn.

The third part of *The Creation* is dedicated to the praise of the Creation through the first human beings Adam (bass) and Eve (soprano) who now replace the archangels Gabriel and Raphael. In the E major introduction to this part Haydn uses three flutes accompanied by the pizzicato of the strings. This intensely romantic description of the early morning seems to anticipate the beginning of the prelude to Wagner's *Lohengrin*. The duet and chorus "By Thee With Bliss" (Oxford Edition, "Thy Bounteous Care") has already been mentioned in connection with the sketches to the oratorio. With its approximate four hundred measures, it is one of the longest and at the same time one of the most inspired and powerful numbers of the entire work. In a way it marks the end of the oratorio, as the following love duet between Adam and Eve displays a slightly incongruous and commonplace character. Its ostentatious show in the *style galant* seems better to fit into a rococo Singspiel than into an oratorio based on the Bible and Milton's great epic. The very last number, a somewhat conventional prayer of thanks for solo quartet and chorus presents a certain difficulty for the conductor as it is the only part of the score in which Haydn prescribes four soloists; the rest of the work employs only three. As the analogy between Mozart and Haydn has been stressed so often in this book, it might be pointed out that there is a slight resemblance between the last scene of *Don Giovanni* (after the death of the hero) and the last two numbers of *The Creation*. A certain anticlimax is unmistakable in both cases and if some conductors have tried to remedy this state of affairs through the omission of part or the whole of the unsatisfactory finales, they are not altogether to blame.

Soon after the completion of *The Creation* in 1798, Haydn started on yet another big vocal composition on which he worked up to the year 1801. Again van Swieten adapted the text from an English poem, James Thomson's *The Seasons* printed in four sections in the years 1726, 1727, 1728, and 1730. This work filled with gay optimism, describes with an abundance of detail the beauties of nature, while any kind of dramatic action is completely absent. The poem offers a continuous series of images full of picturesque variety and these provide an excellent foundation for a musical libretto. Van Swieten showed a certain attitude of independence toward the original work. He eliminated philosophical and historical details and emphasized Thomson's tender lyrical observations of nature. The English poet's fundamental attitude, however, that of depicting the seasons with love and deep understanding but without any attempt to establish a relationship with the human emotions, has been preserved by van Swieten. The contents of Thomson's work as well as of the baron's adaptation are not subjective feelings but objective descriptions.

The English poem did not furnish van Swieten with any suggestions for the arrangement of the text into recitatives, arias, choruses; in this regard the baron again displayed a thorough understanding of the possibilities of a musical setting and particularly an appreciation of Haydn's specific talents. Far less successful was the arranger in transforming the unhappy ending of Thomson's "Winter" in which the wanderer perishes in the cold. But the baron had just as little appreciation of the beauties of nature in wintertime as Thomson himself, and accordingly he changed the scene from the open air to a peasant's house, in which soloists and chorus perform two pieces. For this episode van Swieten used texts written by other poets: "The Spinning Song" by Gottfried August Bürger and a little poem by Christian Felix Weisse (based on a French text by Madame Favart) which Johann Adam Hiller had employed thirty years earlier in his Singspiel *Liebe auf dem Land.* But as the playful tone of the Singspiel seemed to the baron unsuitable for the conclusion of an oratorio, he made a sudden about-face and boldly ventured into the realm of symbolism. Comparing the seasons in nature to the seasons of human life, he came to the conclusion that virtue alone can lead to eternal happiness. The vision of paradise assures a dignified ending to the work. However, it cannot be denied that the heterogeneous elements of van Swieten's "Winter" do not blend well together.

Again the baron was not satisfied with merely writing the libretto. Just as he had done when working on *The Creation,* he advised Haydn how to set the words to music. Max Friedländer, the German musicologist, owned the very copy of van Swieten's libretto that Haydn had made the basis of his composition. The pages of the manuscript are folded and in the margin the baron noted hints for the benefit of the composer. For instance, van Swieten remarked near the end of "Spring": "I believe that at the words 'God of Light! Hail Gracious Lord' a key strikingly different from the one used in the preceding 'Song of Joy' would make a good effect and contribute to the solemn and devout character of the utterance." The change from D major to B♭ major in the majestic invocation of the Lord near the end of "Spring" is here intimated. It is well known that Haydn disliked certain sections of the text of *The Seasons* and particularly resented van Swieten's suggestions of inserting little tone paintings and genre scenes into the music. As stated in the first part of this book, the composer remarked: "This Frenchified trash was forced upon me." But the librettist should not be blamed too severely for having done the "forcing." Although van Swieten was no great poet, his text furnished Haydn with an abundance of musical possibilities and even the notorious episode of the croaking frogs in "Summer" by no means disgraces the composition. The composer's complaint about the unpoetical chorus "Joyful, Joyful the Liquor Flows," is equally unjustified. This piece gave Haydn a chance to introduce a typically Austrian note into the work and even if the words are neither dignified nor poetical, the finished number ranks among the jewels of the score. This is a case of the great and naïve musical Haydn versus the reflective aesthete Haydn and we have to be grateful to van Swieten for having encouraged the former instead of the latter.

Haydn used sketches for *The Seasons* in the same way as he had done in the case of *The Creation*. The master emphasized again and again how strenuous the work was and he must be admired all the more in that the finished product displays no signs of the toil and labor involved in its making. The apparently easy flow of the musical language is really the result of a strain of the composer's every nerve.

It cannot surprise us that *The Creation* and *The Seasons*, having been conceived in quick succession, display frequent similarities. Haydn again uses a solo trio consisting of Simon, a farmer (bass), Lucas, a countryman (tenor), and Jane, Simon's daughter (soprano) instead of the traditional solo quartet. The free and unorthodox construction of the different sections is particularly marked in the later work. It seems to be, in effect, a succession of four loosely connected cantatas and many editions of *The Seasons* (among them the very first one) do not carry the designation "oratorio" at all.

As in *The Creation* the introductions to the different parts of the work express a poetical program. The art of description is so highly developed that some of the instrumental pieces tell a story of their own and the ensuing vocal number carries on the account from where the instrumental introduction left off. These instrumental numbers rank among the very best sections of the score.

The first part of *The Seasons*, called "Spring," opens with an overture "expressing the passage from winter to spring." This begins with a menacing unison of the strings describing winter's reign of terror but as soon as the severe cold is broken the instruments toss to each other in high spirits a graceful motive of the young spring (bar 56) and a more transparent instrumentation suggests the melting of the ice.

Before starting on the analysis of the vocal sections of the oratorio, a word should be said about the English translation of the text which is now in general use. Both the Novello and the Schirmer editions present the same revised version of the libretto which is certainly in far better English than the original translation (according to von Hase, van Swieten was again responsible for the older version). In the following pages the quotations are based on the revised version, except in those cases where it deviates from the original to such an extent that it seems advisable to quote the old text as well, in order to make Haydn's own intentions clear.

The overture to *The Seasons* is followed by one of those recitatives with highly expressive orchestral accompaniment in which this composition so excells. The lovely chorus of peasants "Come Gentle Spring" uses in its middle section alternate groups of women and men, making an effective contrast to the full chorus employed at the beginning and end of the number. In other sections of the oratorio Haydn has occasionally also divided his mixed chorus in order to obtain greater variety of color. The following aria of Simon displays the same attractive simplicity as the chorus. According to the text of the original the husbandman gaily whistles while tilling his field. His "wonted lay" is nothing more than the melody of the slow movement of the Surprise Symphony, a tune that at the time of the composition of *The Seasons* enjoyed the popularity of a folk song. Haydn's naïve self-quotation, in which the flute imitates the whistling of the husbandman, has not been adequately reproduced in the revised version of the oratorio, for here the allusion to the whistling peasant is completely omitted. Mighty numbers for soloists and chorus, separated only by a short recitative, mark the end of "Spring." In the old edition the first of them, "Be Propitious," carried the heading "Prayer," and the second, "Spring, Her Lovely Charms Unfolding," was headed "Song of Joy, with alternating chorus of girls and lads." The revised translation omitted these as well as similar titles and contrary to Haydn's original, it also subdivided the "Song of Joy." The chorus "God of Light" (No. 10) should by no means be separated from the preceding number, as this completely annihilates Haydn's sudden and daring change from D major to B♭ major. Conductors should keep in mind that No. 10 must follow No. 9 *immediately*.

In these last numbers Haydn approaches the language of both Mozart and Handel. The instrumental preludes and interludes to "God of Light" conform both in key and mood with the famous calls of the trombones in *The Magic Flute* and Tovey has pointed out that the theme of the fugue "with pow'r productive" in the "Prayer" strongly resembles the "Quam olim Abrahae" in Mozart's *Requiem*. The last fugue "Endless Praise," on the other hand, is imbued with the ingenious majesty of the choruses in the *Messiah*. In this piece Haydn gives special prominence to the first three notes of his subject and they are used in the second half of the fugue in a very effective augmentation. The analogy with some of Haydn's symphonic movements is obvious.

Consummate Mastery

"Summer" starts with an introduction "representing the idea of morning twilight." The anxieties and fears of the night are described at first in order to create a dark background for the light and cheerful atmosphere of the following scenes. It is interesting to note that the master intended this passage in its original form to sound even more mournful. The old manuscript score, which belonged to the Tonkünstlersocietät in Vienna and shows an earlier version of the instrumentation than the one in the first printed edition, did not use any violins at all in this number. The melody of the strings was confined to the violas and basses, an idea that Brahms later used for his *Requiem*. As soon as the "crested harbinger of the day with lively note the shepherd wakes," the amusing oboe solo effectively dispels the gloomy mood of the beginning. The vision of sunrise at the beginning of "Behold on High He Mounts" is equal, if not superior, in value to the parallel description in *The Creation*. Haydn depicts the sunrise with the help of instruments, solo voices, and chorus, and in particular the device of chromatic modulation is most impressively employed. It takes the composer, who begins the movement piano, six measures only to reach his climax, and in these few bars an urging, growing, driving, and expansion is expressed which we would expect in the work of a youth rather than in that of a man of almost seventy. The cavatina "Distressful Nature Fainting Sinks" is extremely terse in construction and tends to display the character of an arioso.[25] With the help of muted strings, flute, and oboe Haydn paints a most realistic picture of languid prostration. Jane's recitative "O Welcome Now" and the following aria "O How Pleasing" are inserted as a retarding element before the cataclysm of the thunderstorm. In the aria Haydn gives his soprano an oboe as a companion, just as Bach liked to do, thus creating an opportunity for a lovely dialogue between the voice and the related instrument. In the following recitative "Behold! Slow Settling" the revised translation, in its desire to improve the diction, again violates the connection between text and music. It is a mistake to introduce the idea "with vivid flash the lightning gleams" if the German original does not mention it, and all that the music has to offer at this particular place are a few dry chords of a keyboard instrument. Of the different storm choruses that Haydn has written the one in "Summer," "Hark! the Deep Tremendous

[25] Walther's *Musicalisches Lexicon* (1732) explains that *cavata*, the root of cavatina, "means an arioso following a recitative and summarizing its substance."

Voice," is not only the last but certainly the greatest. Its first part describes with striking realism the uproar of nature and the second section, in the form of a fugue with a lamenting subject, the distress of frightened mankind. A disaster and its reflection in the human heart are depicted in colors of sublime grandeur. For the second time in the course of "Summer" the composer introduces a dark, almost tragic element in order to produce a change in the predominantly optimistic gaiety of the composition. The last trio and chorus of this section "Now Cease the Conflicts" is an idyll very different from the majestic endings of "Spring" and "Winter." The dramatic episode of the thunderstorm is over and beast and man enjoy the return of peace. Here Haydn presents some of his most charming nature studies: the lowing of cows (sadly misunderstood in the revised translation which converts the cattle into sheep), the chirping of crickets, the croaking of frogs, and the ringing of evening bells. How delightful is all this "Frenchified trash" and how beautifully it fits into the score! Evening has come, the stars shine and the country people go to sleep. In delicate pianissimo the rustic scene reaches its tranquil end.

If this conclusion of "Summer" is reminiscent of the slow movement of a symphony, the following "Autumn" contains many numbers recalling its scherzo. The instrumental introduction "indicating the husbandman's satisfaction at the abundant harvest" was originally much longer. The aforementioned score of the Tonkünstlersocietät contained, after measure 30 of this piece, twenty-four measures which Haydn later cut out. The composer always avoided drawing out a composition unnecessarily if he could achieve the same effect with fewer notes.

The trio and chorus "Thus Nature Ever Kind" is probably the only number of this oratorio in which van Swieten really did an ill turn to Haydn. The baron's ardent praise of "virtuous toil" and "industry" is slightly nauseating and conductors will do well to give a preference to this piece when looking for possible cuts, in order to bring this enormous composition within the range of an evening's performance. The succeeding duet "Ye Gay and Painted Fair" expresses the tender affection between the young peasant Lucas and the farmer's daughter Jane. The words of each lover are sung to the same melody, thus making the close connection of the couple obvious. This piece of more than three hundred measures, with its coloratura passages and two changes of time, recalls to some extent the form of the great

Italian arias. The *style galant* of the rococo period is also in evidence
in this pastoral scene and it would not be surprising if in spite, or
rather because, of its ostentatious show of artless simplicity, Lucas
and Jane were replaced by Damon and Phyllis.

Next come a number of hunting scenes. They start with Simon's
aria "Behold, Along the Dewy Grass" which describes a shooting
expedition. In the following recitative "Ere Yet the Orient Sun" the
English translators certainly did well not to reproduce van Swieten's
highly disputable statement that the hares enjoy being hunted and
killed! The climax is reached with the stag hunt depicted in the chorus "Hark! the Mountains Resound," in which Haydn, the passionate
hunter, created a composition full of life and fantasy. The fact that
this piece using four horns begins in D and ends in E♭ is characteristic
of the composer's daring inspiration. The best is, however, still to
come; it is the final chorus "Joyful, Joyful the Liquor Flows," an Austrian version of the episodes beloved of the old Dutch painters, showing dancing and drinking peasants. The sturdy realism of this scene
painting the effect of the wine on the merry tipplers could only be so
strikingly depicted by a man who himself came from a wine-growing
country.

The instrumental introduction to "Winter," expressing the thick
fogs at the approach of winter, resembles in its whole character the
"Representation of Chaos" in *The Creation,* also written in the same
key of C minor. It is interesting that this stirring piece was originally
longer. In the old manuscript score of the Tonkünstlersocietät a sequence of nineteen measures is found which in the printed version
is replaced by measures 11 and 12 only, so that the introduction as
originally planned had forty-nine instead of today's thirty-one measures. This again is a proof of Haydn's tendency to concentrate his
composition as much as possible. A cavatina allotted to Jane, "Light
and Life Dejected Languish," describes the darkness and sadness of
winter just as in "Summer" the cavatina of Lucas depicts "the rage
of tyrant heat." In the following aria of Lucas "The Traveler Stands
Perplexed" it seems at first as if the solitary wanderer would perish
in the winter's cold. When finally he reaches a hospitable dwelling,
Haydn changes the key from E minor to E major and at the same time
he replaces the presto of the beginning by the indication, allegro.
Ordinarily allegro is considered as a slower tempo than presto, but it
must not be overlooked that the Italian word *allegro* just means gay

or happy and does not necessarily indicate a rate of speed. Without venturing here into the rather problematical field of the tempo indications in classical times, it is permissible to point out that Tovey is probably right in assuming that in this aria the allegro ought to be taken, if anything, faster and not slower than the preceding presto. One of the most popular numbers of the score is the rondo-like spinning chorus "Let the Wheels Move Gaily," sung in turn by the boys and girls with the solo soprano of Jane as leader. The combination of the whirring and humming noise of the wheels in the instrumental accompaniment with the simple and ingratiating melody of the voices has left its traces in the spinning song of Wagner's *Flying Dutchman*, written forty years later. The next number "A Wealthy Lord," which is separated from the spinning song by a recitative of eight measures only, is again for solo soprano and chorus. The droll story of the conceited lord who is taken in by the "honest country lass" is treated like a number in a German Singspiel and is so completely different from the preceding piece that an entire change in the means of expression could not have provided a greater variety of effects.

Once more the mood of the oratorio becomes serious. The author draws a parallel between winter and old age and the thought of the imminence of death leads him to the hope of God's mercy. As this final number marks the climax of the whole work, a second chorus is now introduced. The antiphonal questions and answers exchanged between the trio of soloists and the two choruses remind us of the ideas expressed in *The Magic Flute:* "But who shall dare those gates to pass?"—"The man whose life was incorrupt."—"And who the holy hill ascend?"—"The man whose tongue was void of guile." An "Amen" which in its four measures is more significant than many similar pieces of much greater length, impressively concludes the oratorio.

To summarize the master's general attitude toward cantata and oratorio, it should be remembered that in the beginning Haydn's work of this type adopted the familiar pattern then current. Like other contemporary Viennese composers, the Capellmeister of Eszterháza followed Italian examples. As a mature artist Haydn attempted a new kind of oratorio, which was predominantly of German extraction, and shortly afterward he turned to the English form of oratorio that had originated with Handel.

Always experimenting and trying out new devices, eager to learn and to improve, never clinging to tradition out of love for the easy way: these qualities enabled Haydn at the age of nearly seventy to write the great oratorios that marked the climax of his creative output.

As a true Austrian Haydn was entirely unprejudiced. He was equally receptive to influences coming from great or small sources, from the north, the south, or the west. He could afford to study and follow new models for he was entirely sure of himself. Haydn, in body and mind one of the healthiest of all great composers, knew that whatever he tried the firm, gentle, humorous, eternally young and optimistic core of his personality would remain unchanged.

EPILOGUE

By all the world is Klopstock lauded;
But does the public read him? Nay!
'T were better to be less applauded
And have our works read every day!

Lessing [1]

DURING the last years of his life Haydn's mind dwelt more in the future than in his own time. He was absorbed in thoughts as to what impression his works would make on posterity. The one thing that really mattered was the eternal life of his compositions or, as he himself expressed it with a characteristic understatement, that he "would not wholly die." [2]

It cannot be denied, however, that these fervent hopes have been only partly fulfilled. The peculiar nature of Haydn's work and his position in the history of music seem to be responsible for this fact.

Haydn was almost thirty years old before he began to develop a personal style and it took him another twenty years to reach artistic maturity. By then he had become the undisputed leader in the instrumental music of his period. German and Italian elements were fused in a masterly manner in his compositions and the polyphonic style was organically inserted in a musical texture that was basically homophonic. The result was a completely logical and strongly coherent work of art which displayed a perfect blend of gaiety and humor with hymnic, passionate, and even tragic elements.

Although Haydn and Mozart worked together to reach the perfection of the classical style, their music shows the same fundamental

[1] Translated by Henry S. Drinker.
[2] These words, which were mentioned by Haydn in his letter to the French musicians in thanks for the medal by Gatteaux, are really translated from the ode by Horace, *Non omnis moriar*, which was also used later by Neukomm for the inscription on Haydn's grave.

difference that may be found between the works of Bach and Handel. Haydn, like Bach, was primarily a composer of instrumental music; Mozart, like Handel, a master of vocal inspiration. Haydn and Bach were forever *playing;* they thought in terms of instruments even if they wrote for voices. Handel and Mozart were always *singing;* they imagined voices even if they composed for instruments. This is certainly one of the facts determining the effect of their music on posterity.

The artistic message of the humble Austrian musician was eagerly accepted by some of the greatest composers of the nineteenth and twentieth centuries; in their instrumental compositions they followed his lead. Beethoven, while refusing to be Haydn's pupil in counterpoint, nevertheless found in the older composer's skillful part-writing, his developments full of dramatic tension, his economy and concentration sufficient reasons for imitation. Schubert was influenced in his piano works as well as his chamber music by Haydn and Brahms was one of the most faithful students of the old master's works. Even the chamber music of a contemporary composer like Hindemith is in some respects dependent on the quartets of the composer of Eszterháza.

For all this the fact remains that after Haydn's death his work did not really have the position in musical life that it deserved. Comparatively few of his symphonies and string quartets were performed, while the church music, the piano works, and even the oratorios were all but forgotten.

The reasons for this are not hard to find. To the romantic period Haydn's music seemed too serene, too simple and straightforward; his utter lack of ambivalent or morbid moods made his compositions appear as "too uncomplicated." A natural inclination among the English-speaking people toward vocal music also made for a certain distrust of the instrumentalist Haydn. Added to this are a number of individual reasons: the reluctance of choir directors to enlist the help of orchestras for the performance of choral works and the difficulty of playing Haydn's oratorios and masses with only an organ accompaniment; the lack of a real chamber music tradition particularly in the United States, where the formation of a group of instrumentalists is usually checked by the difficulty of finding viola and violoncello players; the conservative taste of both orchestral conductors and audiences who like to hear again and again the same symphonies without bothering to investigate the many unknown compositions of equal value.

In spite of all these obstacles a renaissance of Haydn's works seems to be under way. The feeling of the twentieth century is no longer primarily romantic and interest in eighteenth-century music is permanently growing. In the last forty years many hitherto unknown compositions of Haydn were made accessible in modern editions and a quantity of good recordings are available. Moreover, an increasing number of young musicians are taking up the study of orchestral instruments and it is to be hoped that before too long the numerous singers will be balanced by an equal number of players. In this case both chamber music groups and orchestras will need music of great artistic value, which at the same time is not too exacting from a technical point of view. The musicians are bound to turn to Haydn and to find out that more than thirty symphonies by the composer of Eszterháza, an equal amount of his string quartets, and a great number of larger chamber music compositions (*notturni, divertimenti,* and others) are well worth being played. Added to this group may be some of the piano sonatas (the beautiful one in C minor, for instance, is known only to very few pianists!), the F minor piano variations, several piano trios, and some of the concertos (apart from the violoncello concerto, those for trumpet, horn, piano, and violin). As soon as adequate orchestral accompaniment is provided, the vocal composer Haydn will also be in greater demand. Then the two great oratorios, especially the badly neglected *The Seasons,* and excerpts from the great masses (which would be effective also in concert performances) might be regularly performed. As a preparation for the larger choral works, the rounds and canons and the three- and four-part choruses could be used, while some of Haydn's comical or partly comical operas would delight both amateurs and professional groups.

Such a development is by no means utopian; it can and will materialize. Then the truth of the words by Paul Henry Lang will be fully realized: "Haydn's works occupy a definite position in our musical life, a position that could not be filled by anyone or anything else. Love of life, wholesomeness, clarity, purity of feeling, noble and profound sentiments, inexhaustible humor, and impeccable craftsmanship are the characteristic traits of his art which should be treasured by us in whose art they appear so seldom." [3]

[3] *Music in Western Civilization* (New York: 1941).

BIBLIOGRAPHY

ABBREVIATIONS USED IN BIBLIOGRAPHY

ActaM *Acta Musicologica*
DTOe *Denkmäler der Tonkunst in Oesterreich*
ML *Music and Letters*
MQ *Musical Quarterly*
PJ *Jahrbuch Peters*
PMA *Proceedings of the Musical Association*

SIMG *Sammelbände der Internationalen Musikgesellschaft*
StzMW *Studien zur Musikwissenschaft*
ZfM *Zeitschrift für Musik*
ZfMW *Zeitschrift für Musikwissenschaft*

Abert, H. "Joseph Haydns Klavierwerke," *ZfMW*, II and III (1920–21).

Abert, H. and Jahn, O. *Mozart.* Leipzig: 1920–21.

Adler, G. "Die Wiener klassische Schule," *Handbuch der Musikgeschichte*, 2nd ed. Leipzig: 1920.

—— "Haydn and the Viennese Classical School," *MQ*, XVIII (1932).

—— "Joseph Haydn," *Festrede.* Vienna: 1909.

Alberti-Radanowicz, E. "Das Wiener Lied von 1789–1815," *StzMW*, X (1923).

Altmann, W. *Handbuch für Streichquartettspieler.* Berlin: 1928.

Arnold, J. F. *Joseph Haydn.* Erfurt: 1810.

Artaria, F. *Verzeichnis der musikalischen Autographe von Joseph Haydn.* Vienna: 1893.

Artaria, F. and Botstiber, H. *Joseph Haydn und das Verlagshaus Artaria.* Vienna: 1909.

Bartha, D. "Zur Abstammung Joseph Haydns," *ActaM*, VII (1935).

Becker, C. F. *Joseph Haydn.* Leipzig: 1832.

Bernhardt, R. "Gottfried van Swieten," *Der Bär.* 1930.

Blume, F. "Haydns Persönlichkeit in seinen Streichquartetten," *PJ*, XXXVII (1931).

Bombet, C. A. L. *Lettres écrites de Vienne en Autriche sur le célèbre compositeur Joseph Haydn.* Paris: 1814.

Botstiber, H. *See* Artaria and Pohl.

Brand, C. M. *Die Messen von Joseph Haydn.* Berlin: 1939.

Brenet, M. *Haydn.* Paris: 1909.

Breton, J. de. *Notice historique sur la vie et les ouvrages de Joseph Haydn.* Paris: 1822.

Bücken, E. *Musik des Rokoko und*

der Klassik, Handbuch der Musikwissenschaft, V. Potsdam: 1927.

Burkat, L. "Haydn's Symphonies; A Collation," *Musik Library Association Notes,* Series I. 1942.

Burney, C. *The Present State of Music in Germany, the Netherlands* . . . London: 1773.

Carpani, G. *Le Haydine.* Milan: 1812.

Cobbett, W. W. *Cyclopedic Survey of Chamber Music.* London: 1929. (Article on Haydn's chamber music by D. F. Tovey.)

Conrat, H. "Joseph Haydn und das Kroatische Volkslied," *Die Musik,* XIV (1904–05).

Dab, K. "Schubert's indebtedness to Haydn," *ML,* XXI (1940).

Daffner, H. *Die Entwicklung des Klavierkonzerts bis Mozart.* Leipzig: 1908.

Dent, E. *Alessandro Scarlatti.* London: 1905.

Deutsch, O. E. "Haydn's Hymn and Burney's Translation," *Musical Review,* IV (1943).

—— "Haydns Kanons," *ZfMW,* XV (1932).

—— Preface to his edition of Haydn's *12 Deutsche Tänze für Orchester.* Leipzig: 1930.

Diemand, A. "Haydns Korrespondenz mit dem Fürsten K. E. zu Oettingen-Wallerstein," *Ztschr. d. histor. Vereins f. Schwaben,* XCV.

Dies, A. C. *Biographische Nachrichten über Joseph Haydn.* Vienna: 1810.

Edgcumbe, R. (second Earl of Mount Edgcumbe). *Musical Reminiscences of an Old Amateur,* 4th ed. London: 1834.

Einstein, A. *Mozart: His Character, His Work.* New York: 1945.

Engel, H. *Die Entwicklung des Deutschen Klavierkonzertes von Mozart bis Liszt.* Leipzig: 1927.

Engl, J. E. *Haydns handschriftliches Tagebuch des 2. Aufenthaltes in London.* Leipzig: 1909.

Fétis, E. *Biographie universelle des musiciens.* Brussels: 1839.

Fischer, W. "Instrumentalmusik," Adler's *Handbuch der Musikgeschichte.* Berlin: 1929.

—— Preface to *DTOe,* XIX/2.

—— "Zur Entwicklungsgeschichte des Wiener klassischen Stils," *StzMW,* III (1915).

Framery, N. *Notice de Joseph Haydn.* Paris: 1810.

Fröhlich, J. *Joseph Haydn,* edited with an introduction by A. Sandberger. Regensburg: 1936.

Gardiner, W. *Music and Friends.* London: 1838–53.

Geiringer, K. "Das Haydn Bild im Wandel der Zeiten," *Die Musik,* XXIV (1932).

—— "Haydn as an Opera Composer," *PMA,* LXVI (1939–40).

—— "Haydn's Sketches for *The Creation,*" *MQ,* XVIII (1932).

—— *Joseph Haydn.* Potsdam: 1932.

—— "Joseph Haydn," Grove's *Dictionary of Music,* 4th ed. London: 1940. (New article in this work.)

—— "Joseph Haydn," Thompson's *International Cyclopedia of Music.* New York: 1939. (An article in this work.)

—— "The Operas of Haydn," *Musical America* (1940).

Gerber, E. K. *Neues Lexikon der*

Tonkunst. Leipzig: 1790–92. (Article on Joseph Haydn.)

Greilsamer, L. "Le Baryton du Prince Eszterházy," *SIMG,* VI (1910).

Griesinger, G. A. *Biographische Notizen über Joseph Haydn.* Leipzig: 1810.

Grove, G. *Dictionary of Music and Musicians,* 4th ed. Edited by H. C. Colles. 1940.

Gyrowetz, A. *Biographie.* 1848. Newly edited by A. Einstein in *Lebensläufe Deutscher Musiker.* Leipzig: 1915.

Haas, R. "Die Musik in der Wiener Deutschen Stegreifkomödie," *StzMW,* XII (1925).

Hadden, J. C. *George Thomson: His Life and Correspondence.* London: 1898.

—— *Haydn,* revised ed. London: 1934.

Hadow, W. H. *A Croatian Composer.* London: 1897.

Hase, H.v. *Joseph Haydn und Breitkopf und Härtel.* Leipzig: 1909.

Haydn, J. *Collected Works.* So far ten volumes with introductions by E. Mandyczewski, K. Päsler, M. Friedländer, H. Schultz. Leipzig: 1908–1933.

—— "Jubiläumsfeier," *Kongressbericht* (Vienna: 1909).

—— *Katalog der Gedächtnisausstellung.* Vienna: 1932.

Heuss, A. "Die Kaiserhymne," *ZfMW,* I (1918).

Hopkinson, C. and Oldman, C. B. Thomson's "Collections of National Songs with special reference to the contribution of Haydn and Beethoven," *Edinburgh Bibliographical Society, Transactions,* II (1940).

Hughes, R. S. M. "Dr. Burney's Championship of Haydn," *MQ,* XXVII (1941).

Karajan, T.v. *Joseph Haydn in London.* Vienna: 1861.

Kelly, M. *Reminiscences.* London: 1826.

Kinker, J. *Ter nagedachtenis von Joseph Haydn.* Amsterdam: 1810.

Kobald, C. *Joseph Haydn. Bild seines Lebens und seiner Zeit.* Vienna: 1932.

Krehbiel, H. E. *Music and Manners in the Classical Period.* New York: 1896.

Kretzschmar, H. *Führer durch den Konzertsaal.* Leipzig: 1887–1921.

—— "Haydns Jugendsymphonien," *PJ,* XV (1908).

Krienitz, W. "78 neue Haydn Symphonien," *Allgemeine Musikzeitung,* LX (1932–33).

Kuhač, F. *Joseph Haydn.* Zagreb: 1880.

Lachmann, R. "Die Haydn Autographen der Staatsbibliothek zu Berlin," *ZfMW,* XIV (1932).

Lang, P. H. "Haydn and the Opera," *MQ,* XVIII (1932).

—— *Music in Western Civilization.* New York: 1941.

Larsen, J. P. *Die Haydn-Ueberlieferung.* Copenhagen: 1938.

—— *Drei Haydn Kataloge in Faksimile.* Copenhagen: 1941.

—— Replies to Sandberger's Articles in ActaM. VIII (1936), IX (1937).

Laurencie, L. de la. "L'apparition des oeuvres d'Haydn à Paris," *Revue de Musicologie,* XVI (1932).

Lorenz, F. *Haydns, Mozarts, und Beethovens Kirchenmusik.* Breslau: 1866.

Major, E. "Ungarische Tanzmelodien in Haydns Bearbeitung," *ZfMW*, II (1920).

Mayer, S. *Brevi notizie di Giuseppe Haydn*. Bergamo: 1809.

Mencik, H. "Einige Beiträge zur Haydn Biographie," *Musikbuch für Oesterreich*, VI (Vienna: 1909).

───── "Haydns Testamente," *Die Kultur* (Vienna: 1909).

Mozart, W. A. *The Letters of Mozart and his Family*, edited and translated by Emily Anderson. London: 1938.

Neukomm, K. "18 mois de la vie de Haydn," *Revue et Gazette musicale de Paris*, XXI (1854).

Neurath, H. "Das Violinkonzert in der Wiener klassischen Schule," *StzMW*, XIV.

Nohl, L. *Haydn*, new edition by A. Schnerich. Leipzig: 1931.

───── *Musikerbriefe*. Leipzig: 1867. (For English translation *See* Wallace.)

Norton, M. D. Herter. "Haydn in America," *MQ*, XVIII (1932).

Oldman, C. B. *See* Hopkinson.

Orel, A. "Katholische Kirchenmusik," Adler's *Handbuch der Musikgeschichte*. Berlin: 1929.

Parke, W. T. *Musical Memoirs, comprising an account of the general state of music in England, 1784–1830*. London: 1830.

Philips, H. *Musical and Personal Recollections*. London: 1864.

Pohl, C. F. *Joseph Haydn*. Berlin: 1875 and 1882. 3rd volume by H. Botstiber. Leipzig: 1927.

───── *Mozart und Haydn in London*. Vienna: 1867.

Reichardt, J. F. *Vertraute Briefe*. Amsterdam: 1810.

Reissmann, A. *Joseph Haydn*. Berlin: 1880.

Riehl, W. H. *Musikalische Charakterköpfe*. Stuttgart: 1862.

Riemann, H. *Handbuch der Musikgeschichte*, II, 3, 2nd ed. Leipzig: 1922.

───── Prefaces to *Denkmäler Deutscher Tonkunst*, 2nd series, III/1, VII/2, VIII/2.

Rochlitz, J. F. *Für Freunde der Tonkunst*, I. Leipzig: 1824, IV, 1832.

Rosenbaum, J. C. *Diary, 1797–1822*. Manuscript in National Library, Vienna. Ser. nov., 194–204.

Saint-Foix, G. de. "Haydn and Clementi," *MQ*, XVIII (1932).

───── "Les manuscrits et les copies d'oeuvres de Joseph Haydn à la Bibliothèque du conservatoire," *Revue de Musicologie*, XV (1931).

Sandberger, A. "Neue Haydniana," *PJ*, XL (1933).

───── "Zur Entwicklungsgeschichte von Haydns 'Sieben Worten,'" *Gesammelte Aufsätze* (Munich: 1921).

───── "Zur Geschichte des Haydnschen Streichquartetts," *Gesammelte Aufsätze* (Munich: 1921).

───── "Zu Haydns Repertoir in Eisenstadt und Esterház," *PJ*, XL (1933). *See also* Sandberger's articles and Larsen's replies in *ActaM* and *ZfMW* (1935–37).

Sandys, W. and Forster, S. A. *The History of the Violin*. London: 1864.

Schering, A. *Geschichte des Oratoriums*. Leipzig: 1911.

Schmid, A. *Joseph Haydn und Ni-colo Zingarelli.* Vienna: 1847.

Schmid, E. F. "Franz Anton Hoff-meister und die 'Göttweiger Sonaten,'" *ZfM,* CIV (1937).

—— *Joseph Haydn. Ein Buch von Vorfahren und Heimat des Meisters.* Kassel: 1934.

—— "Joseph Haydn und die Flötenuhr," *ZfMW,* XIV (1932).

Schnerich, A. *Joseph Haydn und seine Sendung,* 2nd ed. Vienna: 1926.

—— *Messen-Typus von Haydn bis Schubert.* Vienna: 1893.

—— *Messe und Requiem seit Haydn und Mozart.* Vienna: 1909.

—— "Textliche Versehen in Mes-sen Haydns," Kongressbericht. Vienna: 1909.

—— "Zur Geschichte der früh-eren (und späteren) Messen Haydns," *Zeitschr. d. interna-tionalen Musikgesellschaft,* XIV, XV (1912–14).

Scott, M. M. "Haydn, Fresh Facts and Old Fancies," *PMA,* LXVIII (1941–42).

—— "Haydn in England," *MQ,* XVIII (1932).

—— "Haydn Relics and Reminis-cences in England," *ML,* XIII (1932).

—— "Haydn's 83," *ML,* XIII (1931).

—— "Haydn's Op. 2 and 3," *PMA,* LXII (1935–36).

—— "Mi-Jo Haydn," *Monthly Musical Record,* LXIX (1939).

—— "Some English affinities and associations of Haydn's songs," *ML,* XXV (1944).

Seeburg, F.v. *Joseph Haydn.* Re-gensburg: 1912.

Silverstolpe, F. S. *Negra aterblikar.* Stockholm: 1841.

Sondheimer, R. "G. B. Sammartini," *ZfMW,* III (1920–21).

Smith, C. Sprague. "Haydn's Cham-ber Music and the Flute," *MQ,* XIX (1933).

Steglich, R. "Carl Philipp Emanuel Bach und der Kreuzkantor G. A. Homilius," Bach-Jahrbuch, XII (1915).

Stollbrock, L. "K. G. Reutter (jun-ior)," *Vierteljahrsschrift für Musikwissenschaft,* VIII (1892).

Strunk, O. W. "Haydn," *From Bach to Stravinsky.* Edited by D. Ewen. New York: 1933.

—— "Haydn's Divermenti for Baryton, Viola, and Bass," *MQ,* XVIII (1932).

—— "Notes on a Haydn Auto-graph," *MQ,* XX (1934).

Taylor, J. *Records of My Life.* Lon-don: 1832.

Tenschert, R. *Joseph Haydn.* Ber-lin: 1932.

Thayer, A. W. *The Life of Beetho-ven.* Revised by H. E. Krehbiel. New York: 1921.

Therstappen, H. J. *Joseph Haydn's sinfonisches Vermächtnis.* Wolfenbüttel: 1941 (not avail-able to the author).

Torrefranca, F. "Le origini della Sinfonia," *Rivista Musicale Ital-iana,* XX, XXII (1913, 1915).

Tovey, D. F. *Essays in Musical Analysis,* 7 volumes. London: 1935–44.

—— *See* Cobbett.

Townsend, P. D. *Joseph Haydn.* New York: 1884.

Wallace, Lady G. M. *Letters of Dis-tinguished Musicians.* Edited by Peter Cunningham. London: 1857–59.

Wendschuh, L. *Ueber Haydns Opern.* Rostock: 1895.

Willett, T. E. *A Study of Haydn's Piano Sonatas.* Thesis (unprinted). Urbana, Illinois: 1946.

Wirth, H. *Joseph Haydn als Dramatiker.* Wolfenbüttel: 1941 (not available to the author).

Wurzbach, C. *Joseph Haydn und sein Bruder Michael.* Vienna: 1862.

Wyzewa, T. "A propos du centenaire de Haydn," *Revue des deux mondes* (Paris: 1909).

Wyzewa, T. and Saint-Foix, G. de. *Mozart.* Paris: 1912.

INDEX

333

Breitkopf & Härtel, 47, 77, 129, 146, 154, 156, 181-82, 185-86, 193, 195, 200, 210, 212, 232, 256, 268, 296-99
Bremner, music publishers, 194
Brenet, Michel, 16, 326
Breton, Joachim de, 326
Brühl, Count, 297
Buchholz, Anna, 40
Buchholz, Anton, 39
Bücken, Ernst, 326
Bürger, Gottfried A., 314
Burkat, Leonard S., 327
Burkat Shudi & John Broadwood, 192
Burney, Charles. 31, 36, 42-43, 45, 66, 89, 94, 99, 100, 108, 118, 135, 205-6, 327
Burns, Robert, 296
Byrd, William, 301

Caldara, Antonio, 32, 200
Callcott, John, 113
Cambridge, 101
Canova, Antonio, 138
Caroline, Amalia Elisabeth, Princess of Brunswick, 134, 151
Carpani, Giuseppe, 28, 41, 43, 45, 79, 106, 144-45, 159, 166, 327
Casti, Abbate, 81
Cellini, Gertrude, 62
Charles III, King of Spain, 76
Charles VI, Emperor of Germany, 31, 43
Chopin, Frédéric, 274
Cherubini, Luigi, 78, 139, 166, 168-69, 171
Clement, Franz J., 100, 170
Clementi, Muzio, 94, 132, 137, 249
Clementi & Company, 297
Cobbett, Walter W., 327
Conrat, H., 327
Corelli, Arcangelo, 193, 214
Corri, Dussek & Company, 293
Cowmeadow, J. W., 300
Cramer, John B., 94, 155
Cramer, William, 78, 95, 132
Crosdill, John, 92, 93
Czech, C., 160

Dab, K., 327
Daffner, Hugo, 327
Davide, Giacomo, 97, 98
Dedaelus, 16
Dent, Edward J., 193, 327
Deutsch, Otto E., 285, 298, 327
Dichtler, Barbara, 62
Dichtler, Leopold, 62, 65
Diemand, A., 327

Dies, Albert C., 24, 26, 28, 30, 40, 44, 80, 100, 108, 124, 167, 169, 201, 327
Dillin, Anna and Josepha, 160
Dittersdorf, Carl von, 37, 68, 81, 93, 182
Draghi, Antonio, 138
Dragonetti, Domenico, 127, 155
Dresden State Library, 212
Drinker, Henry S., 323
Dumarest, 161
Duprez, Gilbert, 103
Dupuis, Dr. Thomas J., 134
Dussek, Jan L., 94, 126

Eberl, Anton, 37
Einstein, Alfred, 199, 327
Eisenstadt, 50-58
Elssler, Fanny, 124
Elssler, Johann, 123, 124, 129, 151-52, 160, 166, 172, 185-86, 201, 250, 305
Elssler, Joseph, 123, 183, 184, 186
Engel, Hans, 197, 327
Engl, Johann E., 327
England, 78, 79, 91-116, 124-37
Erdödy, Count Ladislas, 73, 279
Eszterháza, 59-69, 77, 82-83
Eszterházy, Prince Anton, 87, 104, 115, 117, 123, 136
Eszterházy, Princess Hermengild, 141, 169, 170, 171
Eszterházy, Princess Maria Elisabeth, 83, 248
Eszterházy, Prince Nicholas (The Magnificent), 57-68, 70, 81, 83, 87, 97, 205-6, 216, 219, 228
Eszterházy, Prince Paul, 51
Eszterházy, Prince Paul Anton, 46, 50-57
Eszterházy Collection, 183-84, 201, 211, 233, 284-85, 289, 295, 298, 305, 309
Eybler, Joseph, 155

Favart, Madame, 314
Federici, Vincenzo, 132
Ferdinand IV, King of Naples, 79, 87
Ferlendis, Giuseppe, 133
Fétis, Edward L., 327
Firmian, Count, 44
Fischer, Johann von Erlach, 36
Fischer, Ludwig, 124
Fischer, Wilhelm, 190, 327
Forkel, Johann N., 155
Forster, William, 77-78, 181, 185, 250
Fox-Strangways, Arthur H., 309
Framery, Nicolas E., 327
Francis II, Emperor of Germany, 115, 117, 147, 151, 302
Franck, Johann M., 22, 24-28

The Songstress. See *La Canterina*

Oratorios:

Il Ritorno di Tobia, 39, 65, 66, 242-44, 308

The Creation, 142, 144-46, 148-51, 157, 162, 169, 186, 188, 280, 297, 307-18

The Seasons, 149, 156-58, 161, 188, 297, 314-21

The Seven Last Words of Our Saviour on the Cross, 77, 148, 157, 165, 267, 270, 271, 295, 305-8

Overtures. *See* under the respective operas and oratorios

Partitas for wind instruments. See *Feldpartiten*

Pianoforte sonatas. *See* Sonatas for the Pianoforte

Puppet opera, *Philemon und Baucis,* 242

Quartets:

for flute, violin, viola and cello, 211

for strings. *See* String quartets

for voices, 297

Quintet for strings, 197

Requiem (spurious), 180

Rounds. *See* Canons

Salve Regina, G major, 200

Salve Regina, G minor, 244, 245

Scherzandi, 197

Scottish and Welsh folksongs, arrangements. *See* under Songs

Sextet for flute, oboe and strings, 210

Sextet for 2 horns and strings (based on quartet of Op. 2, No. 3), 210

Sextet for wind instruments, 210

Solo cantatas:

Ah, cuome il cor mi palpita, 265

Arianna a Naxos, 79, 83, 84, 155, 265

Deutschlands Klage, 265

"Lines from the Battle of the Nile," 295

Sonatas for pianoforte:

Coll. ed. nos. 1, 2, 4—191, 192

Coll. ed. nos. 3, 5-19—203

Coll. ed. nos. 20-39—224, 226

Coll. ed. nos. 40-49—248-49

Sonata 49 (dedicated to Marianne von Genzinger), 85, 248, 249

Coll. ed. nos. 50-52—169, 274-75

Songs:

Abschiedslied. See "Farewell Song"

"The Deserted Woman," 264

12 English Canzonettas, 293-94

"Farewell Song," 90

German songs (24), 263, 264, 275

"Gott erhalte . . . ," 147, 280, 294, 295

"Lob der Faulheit," 264

"O Tuneful Voice," 294

"Praise of Laziness," 264

Scottish and Welsh folksongs, arrangements, 113, 164, 296

"The Spirit's Song," 294

"Un tetto umile," 294

"Die Verlassene," 264

Stabat mater, 75, 245

String quartets:

"No. 0," 194-97, 207, 208

Op. 1—194-97, 207, 208

Op. 2—194-97, 207, 208

Op. 3—194-97, 207, 208

Op. 9—208, 209

Op. 17—228, 229

Op. 20—229, 230, 251

Op. 33—250-52

Op. 42—252

Op. 54—254-56

Op. 50—253-54

Op. 55—254-56

Op. 64—254-56, 275

Op. 71—275, 278-79

Op. 74—278-79

Op. 76—279, 280

Op. 77—156, 164, 281

Op. 103—281

A Dream, op. 50, no. 5—254

Apponyi quartets, op. 71, 74—278, 279

Emperor quartet, op. 76, no. 3—280

Erdödy quartets, op. 76—279, 280

Gli Scherzi. *See* Russian Quartets

Hexen-Menuett, op. 76, no. 2—280

Lobkowitz quartets, op. 77—156, 164, 281

Quintenquartett, op. 76, no. 2—280

Russian Quartets, op. 33—250-52

Sun Quartets, op. 20—229, 230

Swan song, op. 103—281

The Bird, op. 33, no. 3—252

The Frog, op. 50, no. 6—254

The Joke, op. 33, no. 2—252

The Lark, op. 64, no. 5—256

The Razor, op. 55, no. 2—78, 255, 256, 263

The Sunrise, op. 76, no. 4—280

Tost quartets, op. 54, 55, 64—254-56

String quintet, 197

Symphonie Concertante. *See* Concertos

Symphonies:

Coll. ed. no. 1—199

Coll. ed. nos. 2-40, 49—212-16